To Mary

TOTAL PRODUCTIVITY

Shigehiro NAKAMURA
中村茂弘
中村

Thank you for your good jobs
Nov. 27th '95

Thank you for all your help.
[illegible]

Many thanks, Mary –
especially for Mitsuba!
John Loftus

TOTAL PRODUCTIVITY

The New Science of TP Management

Japan Management Association
TP Management Group

Productivity Europe

The material in section 3 originally appeared in Japanese in
TP Management Annual vols. 1-4 (1991-94)
published by The Japan Management Association (JMA)
Other Japanese source material supplied by JMA

First published in English
by Productivity Europe 1995

ISBN 1-874153-01-9

British Library Cataloguing-in-Publication Data.
A catalogue record for this book is available from the British Library

Contents

Foreword

Over the past ten years I have studied and worked with the tools of World Class Manufacturing, learned from the Japanese developers of Total Quality, Lean Production and Total Productive Maintenance. Over that time new tools have been made available to us, but the systems perspective eluded me. Yes, we could drastically reduce leadtimes in the factory; Yes, we could dramatically increase the overall efficiency of equipment; Yes, we could even slowly develop a Kaizen culture, but still something seemed to be missing from all the panoply of tools from Kanban to QFD.

I believe that the developers of TP Management recognised this a dozen years ago when they sought to create a distinctly Japanese style of management to take them into the next decade. Management in Japan is seen as a forward looking process – managers are not concerned with the smooth running of the company, they are concerned to fulfil the company's dream and drive into the future, setting goals and targets which will stretch their resources and capabilities.

TP Management is a distinctly Japanese style of management, developed in a distinctly Japanese way. The first chapter of this book is written by Professor Akiba, the original developer of TP Management theory. Part of TP Management theory is that it is a theory, an approach characterised by general principles, not a fully fledged management system waiting to be implemented. As such it was up to the users of TP to develop the system, and the mechanism to encourage this was the setting up of the TP Prize, which is described, along with a list of winning companies, in the appendix to this book.

TP Management can only be understood through studying its application, which explains the structure of this book. I have often been frustrated by the denseness of much Japanese material, which tend not to be lucid accounts of systems, but rather reports from the arena of practice. It has taken me some time to realise that this mode of learning and communication is intrinsically more rewarding as well as more challenging.

Professor Akiba's elegant theory is compelling in itself, but we are always left with the question "What do I do on Monday morning?" Mr Nakamura and Mr Shimada answer this question in their chapters, written from the point of view of experienced TP consultants and TP Prize examiners. Mr Nakamura outlines the practice of TP Management, and his colleague Mr Shimada gives practical advice on where to start.

The subsequent case studies come from winners of the TP Prize. They are all reports of prize-winning projects written by the project leaders themselves. This is where the work of understanding TP Management really starts. All these projects are different, as every TP project always will be. They pay repeated study, for in the experience of these diverse companies you can see how the theory and principles of TP are applied.

Read them, devour them, digest them. Only then will we in the West be able to say that we understand what our competitors in the East are doing, and develop our own Western form of management for the next century. That is the essential challenge of TP, not to play "catch-up" once more, but to develop robust approaches to fulfil our own individual and corporate dreams.

Those of you familiar with the work of the developers of the Learning Organisation may recognise some of their ideas and vocabulary in the above remarks. That is no accident. TP Management seems to me to embody the practice of the Learning Organisation; it is about personal and group vision, and about making the connections between individual activities and the whole system. Its quest for making these connections explicit is a way of surfacing mental models and involving everyone in a team learning process. If these concepts are new to you, I would encourage you to study them in parallel with TP Management.

Welcome to these pages. I hope you find them helpful in fulfilling your dreams. This book is part of mine, and in placing it before you I would like to thank those who have made it possible: Shigehiro Nakamura of the Japan Management Association, who has visited me every six months over the past three years and shared his experience with us; the Japan Management Association for their encouragement in producing this volume and making material available; Professor Akiba, Mr Shimada and all the other authors for allowing us to use their words; John Loftus, our indefatigable translator, who has worked with us over these last three years, and who was ably assisted with this particular book by Mary Gillender; and Lesley Carter and John Hardaker, who have set the text and reproduced all the diagrams and matrices which are the heart of the book.

Malcolm Jones
Productivity Europe Ltd

Part 1

Theory

1
What is TP Management?

Masao Akiba
TP Prize Examination Committee Chairman
Professor of Business Engineering, Faculty of Engineering,
Tokyo Science University

Introduction

What is TP Management?

The "TP" in TP Management stands for Total Productivity. The meanings of the three key words are:

Total:	Everyone banding together to align all of an organisation's activities in the same direction.
Productivity:	The effective enhancement of an organisation's production capabilities.
Management:	Business administration expertise.

TP Management's two principal purposes are:

1. To bring together, integrate and intensively apply all the various productivity improvement techniques and activities actually used in running a business.
2. To construct a system able to respond accurately and flexibly to today's innovation-oriented, rapidly changing business environment and achieve outstanding planned results through vigorous, forward-looking activities.

The aims of TP Management can be summarised as follows:

1. To establish specific goals and efficiency improvement benchmarks to assist a business in accurately and effectively doing what it has to do in order to increase its productivity in the desired directions.
2. To adopt the top-down, priority-focused approach as the basic management stance.
3. To ensure that all the business's activities are directed towards the efficient attainment of its goals, and clearly show how each activity contributes to this.
4. To efficiently construct a highly motivated, vigorous and dynamic organisation for implementing the strategies selected in order to achieve the objectives.
5. To deliver the desired bottom-line results by involving all of the business's employees in dramatically enhancing and effectively running the entire production operation.

In this way, TP Management imbues all the productivity-boosting activities conducted by an organisation with the following qualities, as illustrated in Figure 1.1:

Clarity: Everything is clearly defined and spelled out.
Certainty: The outcome of any activity is precisely predictable.
Confidence: Everyone trusts each other and is motivated to work together as a team.

Based on this, TP Management aims to make all activities:

Easy: Use the simplest possible methods to achieve the desired results.
Enjoyable: Foster a cheerful and pleasant atmosphere with no hint of compulsion or coercion.
Encouraging: Accentuate the positive; draw on strengths rather than picking on weaknesses.

The attributes of Clarity, Certainty and Confidence will now be explained in a little more detail.

Clarity

1. Formulate overall objectives that clearly indicate the direction and distance the whole organisation is required to move.
2. Clearly spell out the purpose of each activity and systematically and quantitatively demonstrate its degree of importance and its direct connection to the organisation's overall objectives.
3. Make the progress of the entire system of activities visible and reveal the results achieved.

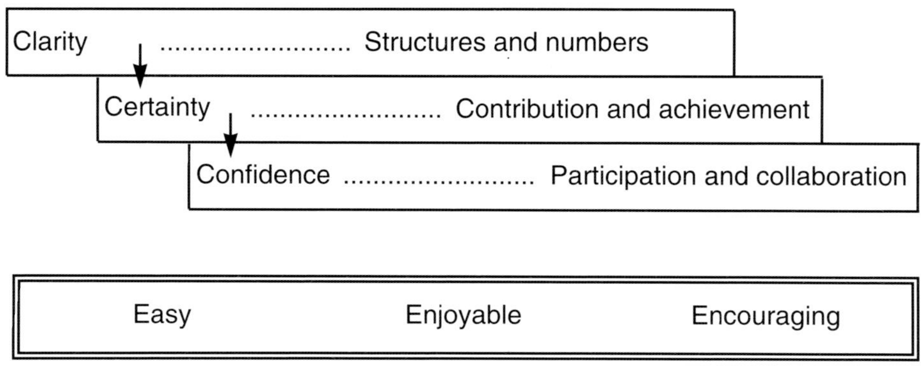

Figure 1.1 Qualities of TP Management

Certainty

1. Develop the well-founded conviction that performance of all the individual activities is bound to lead to the achievement of the overall objectives.
2. Develop the justifiable belief that each section and individual is responsible for an important part of the overall system of activities, that every individual action contributes to the achievement of the overall results, and that no individual's efforts are wasted.

Confidence

1. Create the kind of collective confidence that springs from a sense of solidarity based on the knowledge that everyone is involved in the planning process and is playing his or her part in achieving the results.
2. Build mutual trust by having all sections and individuals work together to generate results.

Environmental Change and TP Management

Today's business climate is changing more rapidly than ever before. Table 1.1 lists some of the internal and external changes taking place. To respond to these, manufacturing departments must build the kind of "constitution" (the entire internal environment of an organisation, including its culture, organisational systems and production setup) described on the next page.

A constitution able to effectively utilise advanced technology to create new products and develop new areas of business.

A constitution able to develop new products with dramatically improved functions through the use of the ultimate in sophisticated, leading-edge technology.

A constitution able to accurately identify the quality of performance expected by the market and comprehensively and consistently manage the product planning, design, production and marketing functions with the aim of delighting customers.

A constitution able to cope instantly and flexibly with today's increasingly diverse product output (ever-expanding product lineups, more frequent model changes, sharper fluctuations in production volumes, etc.).

A constitution able to cut prices and reduce lead times appropriately in order to meet increasing competition on domestic and overseas markets.

A constitution able to create pleasant and cheerful workplaces in which employees are well-motivated and experience satisfaction and a sense of achievement.

A constitution able to use sophisticated systems to paint a clear picture of the organisation's activities (including those previously handled independently) from an overall perspective and manage them comprehensively and responsively.

External Environment	Markets	Diversification of customer needs, shortening of product life-cycles, need for instant response to demands, trend to higher quality and lower prices
	Technology	Innovations in electronics, extreme sophistication of machining techniques, spread of automation, wide-area networking and increasing sophistication of information systems
	Companies	Changes in domestic and world economic conditions, increasingly severe quality and price competition, more intense new-product development competition, increasing entry of companies from other industries
Internal Environment	Production floor	Increasing mechanisation and automation of operations such as machining, transportation, storage and inspection; higher levels of workplace organisation, changes in employees' attitudes, requirement for labour reduction
	Systems	Establishment of sophisticated decision-making and information systems, extension of scope of management systems, advances in data processing and communications equipment, acceleration of cycle of instructions and results

Table 1.1 Changes in the Business Environment

If organisations wish to outstrip their competitors and achieve a high level of profitability, they must urgently establish the kind of constitution able to respond accurately and flexibly to the violent upheavals in the business environment listed in Table 1.1. To achieve this, they must adopt a strategic management posture that will allow them to act as a single entity in moving systematically and efficiently towards the achievement of their stated goals.

TP Management was devised with the aim of meeting these requirements. I hope organisations will use it to create constitutions suitable for today's strategic management era and confidently and dramatically improve their business performance in the desired directions.

Key Features

Like it or not, management from now on faces an ever-present need to innovate. Table 1.2 lists the key points of the reforms now required. The necessity for these renewals has been advocated for some time now, and many companies are already proceeding down this route. In fact, today's business environment makes these changes not only essential but also possible.

Table 1.3 gives a list of questions designed to check your organisation's current state of health. If you answer "Yes" to any of these, your organisation needs TP Management.

Conventional management	Future management
Accumulation of results through bottom-up activities	Top-down objective deployment
Local, one-off initiatives	Comprehensive, systematic approach
Indiscriminate allocation of resources	Selective allocation of resources
Focus on workplace improvement	Focus on overall reform
Laissez-faire management	Management based on certainties

Table 1.2 Management Reform

			Yes	No
1	Existing situation	Is your organisaton the type in which everybody is doing his or her individual best but which has no clear overall direction and offers no certainty of success?		
	Desired situation	Do you wish you could clarify the overall objectives and focus everybody's efforts on achieving them?		
2	Existing situation	Do you feel that your organisation is not doing what is really important and is somehow slightly off aim?		
	Desired situation	Do you want to establish a system for breaking down the overall objectives methodically and pinpointing the important areas?		
3	Existing situation	Are you afraid that things are being left to fate and that nobody can predict the results of their actions?		
	Desired situation	Do you want to link your organisation's strategies and individual objectives with its overall objectives and confidently construct a scenario that will lead to those objectives being achieved?		
4	Existing situation	Do you feel that many of the improvement activities your organisation's employees are engaged in are a waste of time and do not greatly benefit the organisation as a whole?		
	Desired situation	Do you wish that you could increase individual employees' motivation by clearly demonstrating how their activities contribute to achieving the organisation's overall objectives?		
5	Existing situation	Is your organisation doing no more that it has done in the past, even though many people are saying that we face an era of unprecedented change and that management reforms are needed?		
	Desired situation	Do you wish you could create a strategic management system able to respond to changes in the business environment and purposefully obtain stunning results?		

Table 1.3 Productivity Health Check

TP Management Means Productivity Improvement

There are two principal approaches to the issue of productivity: the measurement approach and the improvement approach. TP Management takes the latter.

Productivity Measurement

In the productivity measurement approach, we try to identify the level of a production operation by expressing its productivity in the form of output per unit of input. Expressing productivity as a comparison of output with input in this way allows us to compare different production operations with each other on an equal basis, even though they may take place under very different conditions. This approach plays an extremely useful role in comparing productivity results with business-plan objectives and in comparing productivities achieved over different time periods and with different products, different sites, different companies, different countries and so on.

Productivity in General

A production process can be depicted as shown in Figure 1.2. The following steps take place:

Labour, equipment, and materials are fed in.

Manufacturing activities are carried out.

Products are discharged.

In this approach, productivity is generally defined as output per unit of input, i.e.:

$$\text{Productivity} = \text{output} \div \text{input}$$

Productivity defined in this way can be interpreted in either physical or economic terms.

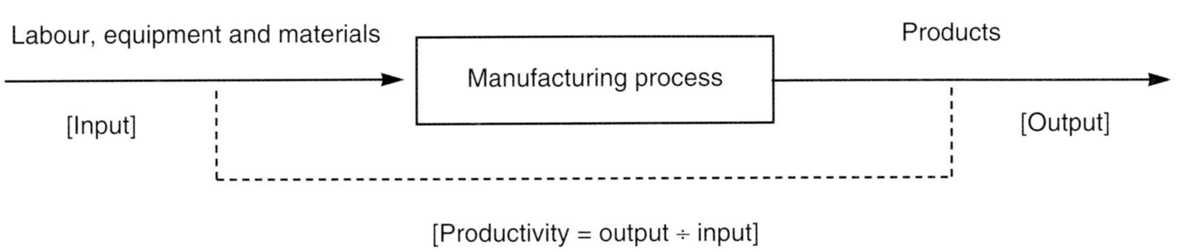

Figure 1.2 The Productivity Measurement Approach

Individual Productivities

Productivity interpreted in physical terms is called "physical productivity". It can take one of the following three forms depending on the particular production input (labour, equipment, or materials) being considered:

Labour productivity
Equipment productivity
Materials productivity

Since the units of measurement are different for labour, equipment and materials, these three types of productivity must be considered separately. Because of this, labour productivity, equipment productivity and materials productivity are called "individual productivities" or "partial productivities". They are defined as follows:

Labour productivity = production output ÷ labour input. This is the amount of output per unit of labour input (e.g. per person or per labour-hour).

Equipment productivity = production output ÷ equipment input. Also known as "machine productivity", this is the amount of production output per unit of equipment input (e.g. per machine or machine-hour, where the machines have a specified or standard capacity).

Materials productivity = production output ÷ materials input. This is the production output per unit of materials input (e.g. per tonne). The inverse of this (the amount of materials input per unit of product output) is called the "necessary amount for a product unit".

Total Productivity

The individual productivities discussed above express the manufacturing capability of an organisation individually in terms of the three separate aspects of labour, equipment and materials. However, these three aspects are not in reality separate but are interrelated. For example, if a new, more up-to-date piece of equipment is introduced, it will probably affect not only the equipment productivity but also the labour productivity. In view of the complex interrelationships that exist within a production system, it is actually not very meaningful to discuss individual productivities in isolation. It would be better to combine them.

However, we need a common unit of measurement if we wish to do this, since labour, equipment and materials are all measured in different units. To create such a unit, the concepts of conversion to an economic value or a labour quantity were incorporated into productivity theory. Since the conversion to labour quantities is rather difficult in today's conditions, the most common conversion is to economic values.

From the standpoint of productivity measurement, the "total productivity" of an operation is its productivity expressed in the form of a single indicator obtained by converting the individual inputs and outputs to a common unit and then combining them. For example one way of calculating this kind of total productivity might be as follows:

Labour input → labour cost
Equipment input → equipment cost
Materials input → materials cost
Output → value of sales

Total productivity = value of sales ÷ (labour cost + equipment cost + materials cost)

Productivity Improvement

Productivity is essentially a measure of the productive capacity of an organisation, and the productivity measurement approach seeks to identify this in the form of a comparison between output and input. This is because it is difficult to measure what is actually going on inside the production operation, for reasons such as the following:

It is technically difficult to express what is actually going on inside a production operation.

It is difficult to build up a single unified picture of a production operation because of the many intricately-related factors involved.

It is difficult to measure production operations in common terms, because no such operation is exactly the same as any other, even within the same industry.

Any production operation constantly changes, sometimes even from day to day, so it is difficult to describe it in fixed terms.

This is why productivity has traditionally been defined in terms of measurable outputs and inputs. The conventional definition of productivity treats the production process as a "black box", making only an overall assessment of it from the outside, rather than providing a picture of its inner workings. Nevertheless, this approach has proved effective in many ways.

TP Management, on the other hand, takes the tack of improving productivity rather than merely measuring it. In TP Management, therefore, we cannot avoid looking at what goes on inside the production process just because it is difficult to do so. We have to examine the production process itself and decide how much we should try to extend each kind of production capability. In the TP Management approach, we:

Make the production system transparent, ...

predict what degree of productivity improvement will result if we improve particular parts of the system by particular amounts, and ...

proceed to extend our production capabilities with confidence.

Productivity Improvement

The activity of production at a manufacturing operation can be depicted in extremely simplified form as shown in Figure 1.3.

In TP Management, productivity improvement activities are not carried out for their own sake. They are done with the aim of addressing specific management issues that can be resolved by increasing productivity, such as securing profits or delighting customers. As part of this process, management must lay down two types of guideline: "overall objectives" and "strategy selection criteria".

Overall objectives

To address management issues effectively, specific numerical objectives must be established for themes such as improving product functions, reducing costs or

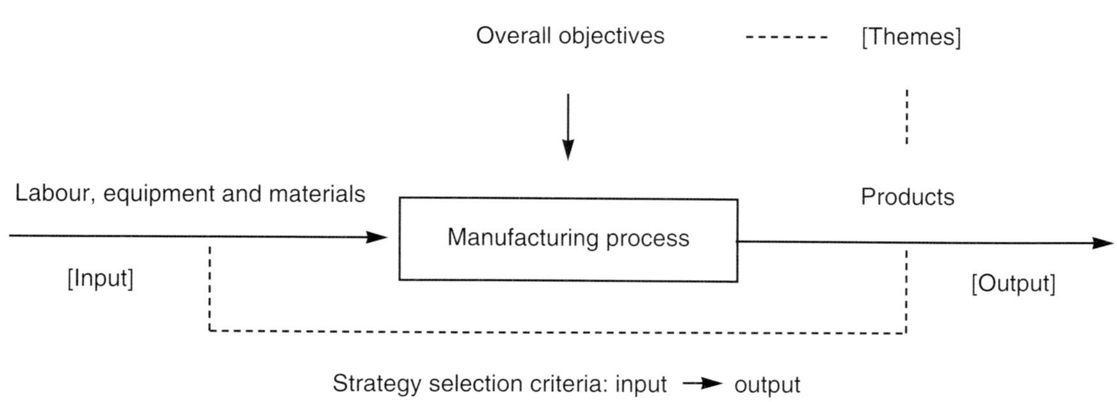

Figure 1.3 The Productivity Improvement Approach

increasing production volumes. The role of production is to produce the kinds of products that are certain to satisfy these objectives, and productivity improvement activities only make sense when these overall objectives are broken down and effective strategies are selected for attaining them. This is because this deployment process links the individual activities directly with the objectives and makes the purpose of the activities abundantly clear.

Strategy selection guidelines

It is of course always sensible to choose the most efficient means of achieving a particular objective. Management therefore establishes guidelines for selecting which of the many possible productivity improvement strategies to implement. For example, the guidelines for a fixed production volume might be:

Minimise losses due to poor quality.
Minimise labour input.
Minimise operating time.

Guidelines like these for maximising the efficiency of the activities from input to output can be regarded as equivalent to the comparison of input with output in the conventional productivity-measurement approach. For example, "minimise labour input" would correspond to "increase labour productivity."

Productivity is therefore evaluated from the following two aspects:

Output side: overall objectives …"necessary" conditions (e.g. was a 20% cost reduction actually achieved, if this was one of the overall objectives?)

Process side (input ⟶ output): strategy selection criteria …"sufficient" conditions (e.g. was the deadline met, and was the time required as short as possible?)

The following differences can thus be seen between the productivity measurement approach and the productivity improvement approach:

Productivity measurement approach: aims to express the state of production by treating the production process as a cause-and-effect system and comparing effects with causes.

Productivity improvement approach: aims to boost an organisation's production capabilities in the required directions by treating the production process as a system of objectives and carrying out activities that satisfy the strategy selection (efficiency) criteria and result in the achievement of the organisation's overall objectives.

The Meaning of "Total" in TP Management

The word "total" in TP Management has two possible interpretations:

- Totalisation of scope
- Totalisation of themes and objectives

Totalisation of Scope

Any drive to increase a company's overall productivity should involve all its departments and all the individuals in them. However, the activities they undertake will only be effective if all those departments and individuals work together. All the departments and individuals included in a TP improvement campaign must assume collective responsibility for the activities and collaborate as a single unit.

In any TP campaign, totalisation of scope could refer to the following:

- Totalisation that seeks to integrate different functions such as engineering, manufacturing, purchasing, and distribution.
- Totalisation that pursues collaboration between front line and support staff.
- Totalisation that aims to establish co-operation between an organisation and its suppliers.

Totalisation of Themes and Objectives

A company does not always have just one theme or objective that it wishes to quest after in improving its overall productivity. Often, it is looking to productivity improvement to fulfil a number of different aims. When such a company follows a particular theme or achieves one of its objectives, this may have a positive or negative effect on the other themes and objectives. This is why it is necessary to consider the relationships among the various themes and objectives very carefully and pursue productivity improvement from the overall standpoint. This is what is meant by the totalisation of themes and objectives.

For example, the following possibilities exist:

Totalisation of themes: simultaneously address several issues relating to productivity improvement, such as customer satisfaction, employee satisfaction and profitability.

Totalisation of objectives: set and simultaneously pursue a number of objectives relating to a particular theme (such as customer satisfaction), e.g.:

Quality: Improve product functions.

Cost: Reduce costs.

Delivery: Improve delivery compliance rate.

In TP Management, it is important to construct and operate a system able to handle this kind of totalisation of scope, themes and objectives.

TP Management Combines "Top-Down" with "Bottom-Up"

There are two main approaches to productivity improvement:

The top-down approach (objective deployment).

The bottom-up approach (upgrading).

TP Management adopts the following approach:

Based on the top-down approach, objectives relating to productivity-improvement themes are broken down and assigned to priority areas.

The upgrading of these areas by means of bottom-up activities is effectively linked to the productivity-improvement themes.

The basic meaning of "top" is the point at which all the organisation's vectors meet. It corresponds to the summit of a mountain or the leader in a race. The top-down approach means first deciding on a desired scenario for the organisation's "top", and then taking action to turn this scenario into reality. Adopting the top-down approach makes it necessary to establish a system that can be relied on to unite every part of the organisation towards the achievement of the organisation's overall productivity improvement objectives.

The "bottom" of an organisation is the part that supports the existence of the whole organisation and all its achievements. The larger the organisation, the bigger the base it requires, so that the whole thing does not tip over. If the "bottom" is not solid, the entire structure will be unstable and incapable of achieving good results. This is what makes it so important to continually upgrade and improve the "bottom" of any organisation. In this sense, the bottom-up approach supports the drive to increase productivity, and effective direction of this upgrading process is the key to achieving excellent results.

If an organisation's bottom-up activities are unfocused and all heading in different directions, no significant results can be expected. In TP Management, we aim to construct a framework that assists us to greatly improve productivity by effectively managing the bottom-up improvement process and linking it accurately to the achievement of our top-down overall objectives.

If we can accomplish this, everyone in the workplace will be able to see that what they are doing is meaningful and that none of their efforts is wasted, and this in turn will imbue all their activities with a burning sense of purpose and energy. I cannot emphasise strongly enough that this really is the secret of giving people a sense of achievement, eliminating their feelings of being subtly pressured into effecting improvements and producing results, and making the workplace far more positive and cheerful.

Top-Down and Bottom-Up

As the following table shows, the important point in the top-down approach is to look closely at what aspect to improve in order to increase overall productivity; in other words, to prioritise.

Top-down	Bottom-up
Set overall objectives	Observe workplace
↓	↓
Deploy objectives (selectively)	Point out deficiencies (comprehensively)
↓	↓
Set individual objectives	Select countermeasures
↓	↓
Select strategies	Predict results
↓	↓
Attain objectives	Upgrade workplace

Table 1.4 Top-Down and Bottom-Up

The Top-Down Approach

Specify a theme that defines the kind of productivity improvement that the organisation as a whole wishes to achieve, and establish overall objectives for it.

Break down the overall objectives systematically and selectively, to show how they should be achieved, and establish specific individual objectives indicating what must be done in order to attain the overall objectives.

Select the most appropriate practical strategies (from the standpoint of the organisation as a whole) for achieving these individual objectives.

Construct a suitable organisational system for implementing these strategies; operate the system and obtain the desired results.

Features of the top-down approach (see Figure 1.4)

The organisation's overall policy and objectives are systematically deployed to its various parts. This has the following benefits:

It enables top management to align the activities of the various parts of the organisation in the direction in which they want the organisation as a whole to move. This enables the organisation to focus its entire effort on pursuing its productivity improvement themes.

Since the overall objectives are broken down systematically and quantitatively into specific individual objectives, it is easy to see the contribution made by each area to the achievement of the overall objectives.

The objective deployment process follows a clearly visible route, starting with the setting of overall objectives and proceeding through the establishment of intermediate and individual objectives to the selection of strategies. Consequently, each part of the organisation knows exactly what is expected of it, and the decision-making process and system are clearly delineated and transparent.

Specific individual objectives are set for each of the organisation's parts. This has the following benefits:

Since specific individual objectives are set indicating in numerical terms exactly what is desired, each part of the organisation knows exactly what it is supposed to do. This inspires a sense of mission and purpose and makes people eager to achieve their objectives by whatever means they can, as well as enabling them to monitor and control their own progress.

Since the individual objectives assigned to each part of the organisation are connected systematically and numerically to the overall objectives, everyone knows the contribution they are making to the overall goal. This strongly motivates them to achieve their objectives.

Since the individual objectives for each part of the organisation are set in specific numerical terms, it is obvious how much progress has been made towards the achievement of those objectives at any time. This enables accurate corrective action to be taken if the required progress is not being made; for example, an objective can be reassigned to a different area.

The entire organisation can be taken into account when selecting strategies. This has the following benefits:

Since the aim is to achieve the productivity improvement objectives for the organisation as a whole, this makes it possible to transcend the organisation's internal barriers when identifying obstacles to productivity improvement or areas that require further upgrading, and avoids the trap of sectionalism.

The full range of strategies that the organisation has for improving productivity can be marshalled when selecting which strategies to implement. This enables the most effective strategies to be chosen.

Taking an overall view of the organisation makes it possible to clarify the relationships among the strategies to be implemented by its various parts. This enables the organisation to identify the effects of each strategy on all the others and ensures that the strategies selected are mutually consistent.

However, the top-down approach carries with it the following risks:

If top management fails to set clear themes and objectives, the subsequent activities will not be firmly linked into the overall system, and may stagnate or decline in efficiency. People's expectations will be disappointed, and they will lose confidence in top management.

If the objective deployment system has not been properly established and the points where decisions must be taken are unclear, the various activities will not proceed purposefully, in a focused manner, and the hoped-for results will not be achieved.

If the objectives are not skilfully co-ordinated across the different departments, the management of the organisation will split down vertical lines. Functional chimneys will be created, and the organisation will not move in the direction of overall optimisation.

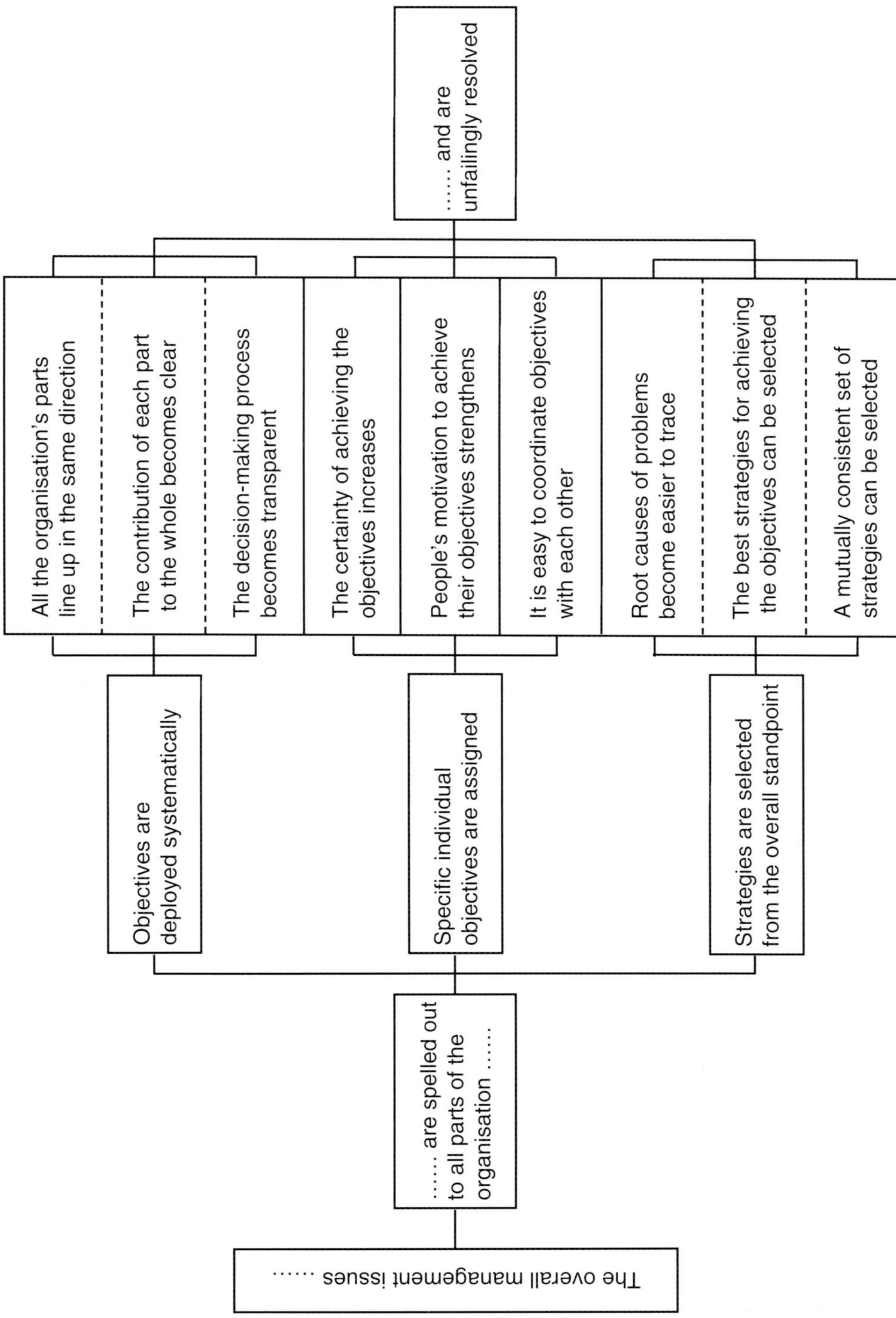

Figure 1.4 Features of the Top-Down Approach

In contrast to the top-down approach, the bottom-up approach proceeds along the lines that follow.

The Bottom-Up Approach

Since productivity originates in the workplace, start by observing the workplace closely.

Identify and point out areas requiring improvement.

Take appropriate steps to improve those areas.

Progressively accumulate individual results.

Raise the general level by continually upgrading individual workplaces in this way.

The bottom-up approach is unselective, and everyone must keep a close watch on their own area to ensure that nothing is left out.

Features of the bottom-up approach

Standardisations and improvements introduced by each department and workplace are progressively accumulated. This has the following benefits:

The people who actually work in a workplace are in the best position to observe its every nook and cranny; they are the ones who know their work best, and they are constantly aware of the problems. Any suggestions they make or strategies they devise will be highly pertinent.

Since TP Management respects the resourcefulness and creativity of groups and individuals, everyone feels a strong sense of active participation in its operation, and excellent results can be expected in terms of keeping the organisation dynamic and vigorous.

Since groups and individuals suggest ways of improving the effectiveness of their own jobs, they take responsibility for their ideas and actively try to turn them into reality.

On the other hand, bottom-up activities are fragmentary and isolated, and people have only a limited range of strategies to choose from. Bottom-up activities therefore entail the following risks:

They may produce little benefit for the organisation as a whole.

They tend to encourage "laissez-faire management", since the overall results usually do not become apparent until the end of a period of activity.

The two styles of management can be characterised in the following way:

Top-down: Externally-focused, offensive, proactive.

Bottom-up: Internally-focused, defensive, reactive.

Nonetheless, this does not mean that we should adopt one to the exclusion of the other. The best results are achieved by skilfully combining the two approaches. Which of the two approaches to emphasise is a question of management balance. At the present time, however, I believe that companies will find it impossible to stay ahead of their competitors unless they actively shift to a more positive, proactive management stance.

TP Management Looks Outwards and Builds on Strengths

If we look only towards the interior of something (be it an organisation or any other entity), we inevitably tend to see only its weaknesses. This leads to a negative, nitpicking climate in which the emphasis is on finding and correcting deficiencies in the status quo. This kind of approach will not enable an organisation to triumph against fierce competition. For example, a soccer team would have little prospect of winning an important match if the players' preparation consisted of nothing more than going into hospital to have their internal organs examined and taking medicine to cure anything found wrong. They have to look outwards, assess their opponents' strengths and weaknesses, and plan their strategy.

Even if their opponents are stronger in attack, this does not mean that the team manager should send all the good players to the back and tell them to spend the whole match standing in their own goalmouth. The team should do the best it can to sharpen up its strikers' skills before the match, and play the game in such a way as to give itself a chance to score.

Likewise, a company must look outside itself if it wants to improve the competitive power of its products. In this context, "outside" can have the following meanings:

Customers: customer satisfaction in the marketplace.

Competitors: other companies making similar products.

Society: the social and physical environment surrounding the company.

The most important of these is customer satisfaction. If a company still cannot delight its customers even after introducing improvements, it cannot be said to have increased its manufacturing power in any real sense, and it is unlikely to increase its sales. It would be surprising if it could even turn a decent profit. This is why TP Management places such importance on the customer-focused approach.

Key Point 1 (Objective Setting) Establish strategic management objectives indicating the overall direction. What are the overall themes that your organisation should pursue? Set overall productivity improvement objectives to this end, indicating in which direction and by how much your organisation as a whole should extend its manufacturing capabilities.
Key Point 2 (Objective Deployment) Cascade the objectives down to priority areas by means of a comprehensive system. Deploy the overall objectives by methodically considering which areas to focus on in order to achieve the objectives and by spelling out specific individual objectives.
Key Point 3 (Strategy Selection) Choose strategies that are effective from the overall perspective. Review the entire organisation to identify the most effective strategies for achieving each of the individual objectives, based on selection criteria designed to maximise efficiency.
Key Point 4 (Organisational System) Construct an organisational system operated with total vitality. Build an implementation system in which everyone is highly motivated to participate as individuals and which enables leadership to be exercised effectively. Base the system on top-down management linked with bottom-up initiatives, and interweave line and staff activities.
Key Point 5 (Overall Results) Achieve excellent overall results through the system as a whole. Reform the system into one which, at the same time as delivering outstanding results, can maintain and improve them in specifically manageable form.

Table 1.5 The Five Key Points for Implementing TP Management

When an organisation turns its attention more to the outside world in this way, it sometimes finds that it is not as expert as it had thought, even in the areas it had prided itself upon. Such uncomfortable discoveries might take the following forms:

Customers want more than it can offer in that area (indicates complacency).

Customers want something else (indicates arrogance).

Competitors are even stronger in that area (indicates conceit).

A company undertaking this exercise soon realises that it needs to develop its capabilities in the direction of increasing customer satisfaction. As this illustrates, it is best to look outwards for hints about which areas of our operations we need to improve.

Looking outwards at customer satisfaction and competitors' strengths leads us on to the idea of corporate citizenship and serving society. Moreover, many real-life examples have demonstrated that following this approach ultimately returns to the pursuit of employee satisfaction.

In this way, TP Management puts top priority on developing and strengthening only those areas that need to be developed and strengthened. The introverted, fault-finding, nitpicking approach is replaced by a culture of building on strengths and accentuating the positive, with everyone's attention focused on delighting the customer. This can also provide the stimulus for major technical advances.

TP Management Implies Total Visibility

TP Management must be transparent. The complete system of objectives, strategies, responsibilities and results covering the entire scope of implementation (plant, company, or corporate group) must be clearly visible to everyone involved. Everyone must be instantly able to see the answers to the following questions:

What are the productivity improvement themes currently being addressed?

What overall objectives have been set in order to address them?

How have these objectives been broken down?

What individual objectives must be achieved as a result of this?

What strategies were considered and selected for achieving these objectives?

Who is responsible for implementing each of these strategies, and what is its timetable?

What results must be achieved through each strategy, and by when?

What results have been achieved so far?

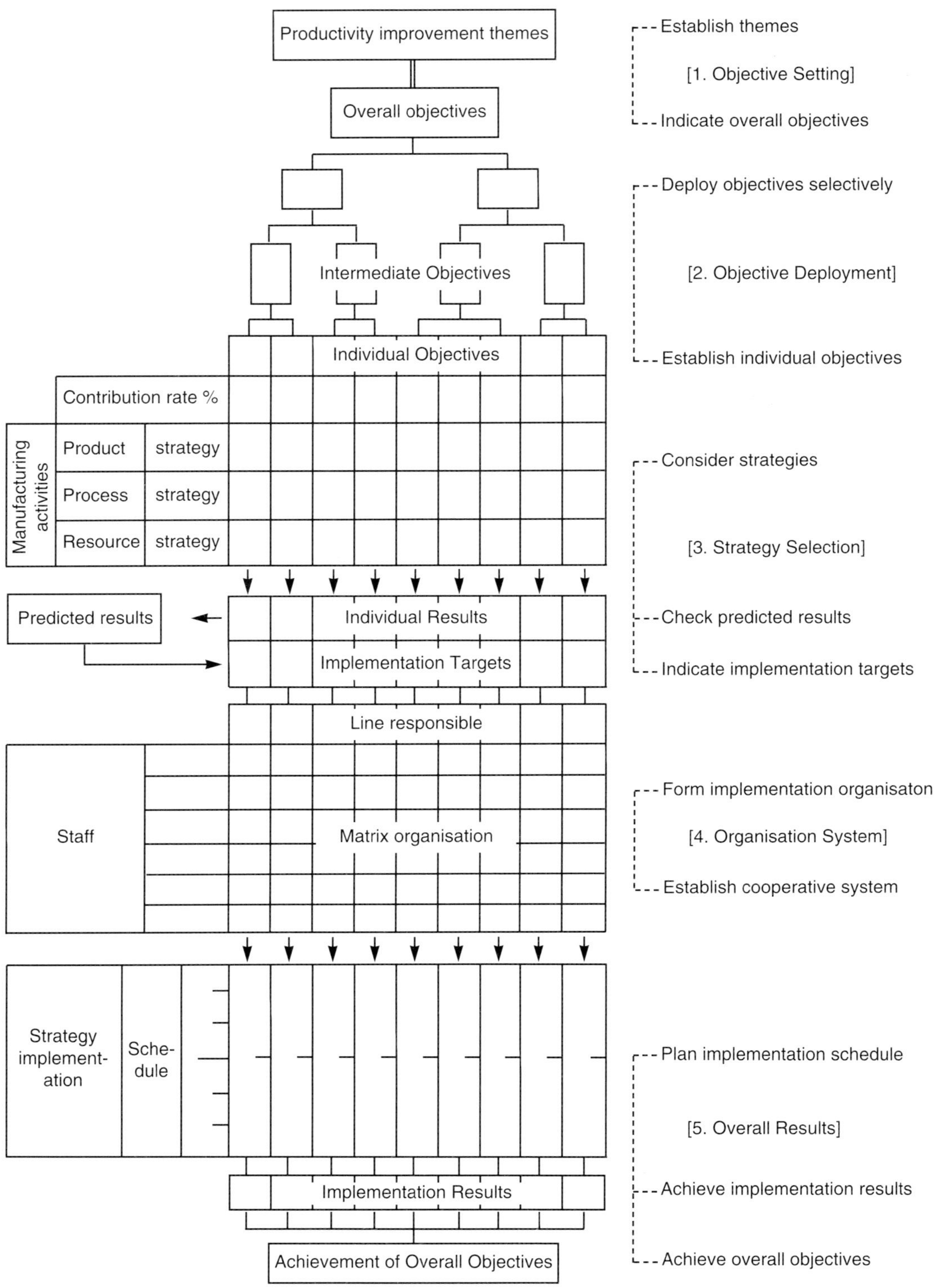

Figure 1.5 The Overall Structure of TP Management

Each organisation must work out its own most appropriate visual display systems for achieving this transparency and for making what has been planned, what is being done and what has been gained through TP Management common knowledge among all its members.

When deciding what to include in any display system, it is useful to take into account the "Five Key Points for Implementing TP Management" shown in Table 1.5. In TP Management, it is extremely important to depict these key steps visually in the form of a TP deployment diagram such as that shown in Figure 1.5.

Part 2

Practice

2
Introducing and Applying TP Management

Shigehiro Nakamura,
JMA TP Management Consultant and TP Prize Examiner

Introduction

The revolutionary new management system known as TP Management was created in Japan approximately ten years ago. Many experts connected with the Japan Management Association (JMA – Japan's premier forum for the development and promotion of management techniques) were convinced that, when the plethora of management techniques such as small-group activities then so popular in Japan eventually peaked in effectiveness and began to produce diminishing returns, it would be necessary for Japan to establish its own new management system. This was the starting point for the creation of TP Management. Extensive discussions were held, fuelled by a sense of urgency and the feeling that the future of Japanese industry looked shaky unless a uniquely Japanese management system with excellent potential for future evolution could be developed.

Many ideas and arguments were proposed over the subsequent three years, but the discussions yielded no definite, generally acceptable outcome. It was therefore decided to start by promoting the main concepts that had emerged from the debate and to award a prize to companies that had achieved excellent results by implementing those concepts and had demonstrated their ability to lead the way for Japanese industrial management in the future. It was hoped that this approach would shed further light on the type of management system that Japanese companies really require.

As a result of these activities, JMA has succeeded in developing a highly visible management system that empowers all the members of an organisation to act in the best interests of the organisation as a whole, free from the restraints imposed by traditional workplace boundaries. This point was reached as a result of a tremendous amount of hard work by Professor Masao Akiba, Chairman of the TP Prize Examination Committee, and the other committee members. The TP Management system that has now evolved is a crystallisation of the experience of people from many Japanese companies who have responded so actively to JMA's initiative. It has attracted considerable interest in Japan and abroad because of its demonstrable results in enabling companies to achieve extremely high profitability even during a recession and equip themselves with the flexibility to diversify into new areas of business.

The call for the re-engineering of corporations being heard in America and elsewhere is further stimulating this interest, because TP Management already includes this concept among its comprehensive armoury of highly practical management techniques and activities. I sincerely hope that as many companies as possible will adopt TP Management in order to ensure their own development and extend their activities to achieve higher levels of customer satisfaction, employee satisfaction and social satisfaction.

The Aims of TP Management – How Can TP Management Benefit Your Company?

As Figure 2.1 shows, one of the major characteristics of TP Management is the way in which it establishes world class ideals and then strives to attain these ideals by accomplishing shared objectives through a combination of the top-down and bottom-up approaches. Rather than adopting the problem-solving approach (selectively exposing and resolving problems currently facing the organisation), TP Management takes the topic-tackling, or project approach (working out what the organisation must achieve, and integrating all its activities towards this end).

The latter approach is the essence of TP Management, and Figure 2.2 illustrates the philosophy behind it. In TP Management, people and organisations strive to attain their hopes and dreams by developing and improving themselves enthusiastically and optimistically. TP Management is a system that makes skilful use of this activity as a means of achieving corporate reform.

The fundamental task of management is to achieve its objectives by following the Plan–Do–Check (PDC) cycle, and TP Management has of course incorporated this concept right from the start. The successive levels of innovation shown in Figure 2.1 are steps on the path to accomplishing the organisation's ultimate objectives. TP Management enables the organisation to focus all its efforts on attaining these.

Figure 2.3 further illustrates the core principles of TP Management. The aim is to eliminate the caste system that exists in many companies and abandon the whole idea of a hierarchy. Instead, all the organisation's employees work together to achieve the successive levels of innovation mentioned earlier.

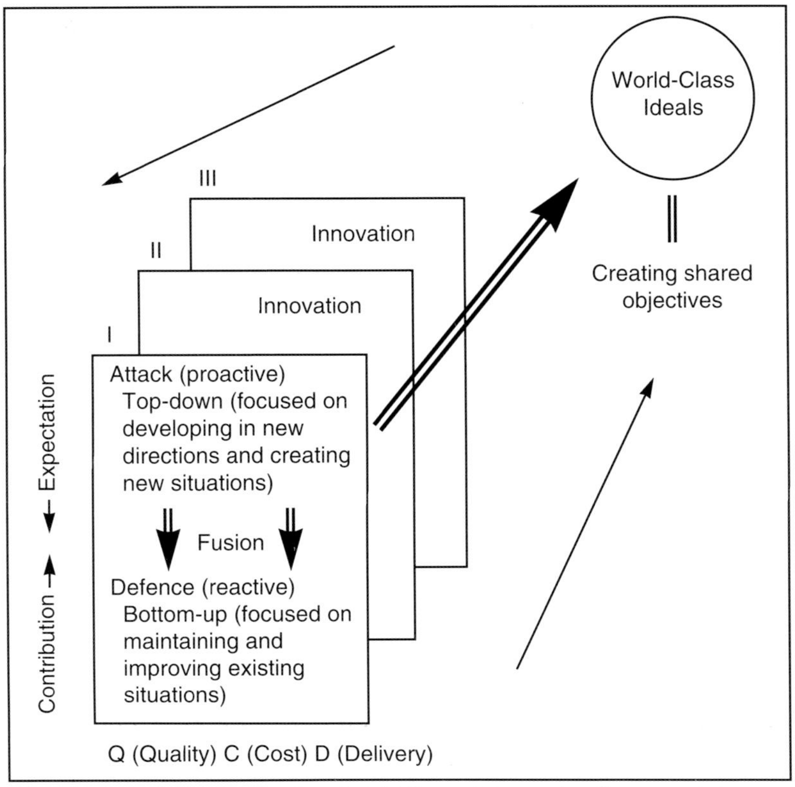

Move from the "It'll probably be all right if we all do our best" approach to a system in which objectives are clearly spelled out, the methods of achieving them are specified, and the priorities are pursued in bottom-up style.

Figure 2.1 Pursuing World-Class Ideals

Because of this, companies that introduce TP Management and try seriously to put it into practice almost invariably find the situation depicted in Figure 2.4 developing. The second major characteristic of TP Management is the smooth progress of activities that cross traditional workplace barriers.

Japanese managers are fond of saying that "A company is its people". Distinctive corporations that constantly strive to build on their employees' existing capabilities and boldly take up the challenge of tackling innovative projects can never stagnate. Such firms will always be growing and will by definition always be at the forefront of their industries. If you approve of the type of management that sets clear, easily understood objectives and empowers everyone to work together in full knowledge of their assigned topics and activities, understanding their roles in the overall effort and accurately aware of the growth being achieved, then it is essential to incorporate this philosophy into your management system. TP Management does exactly that.

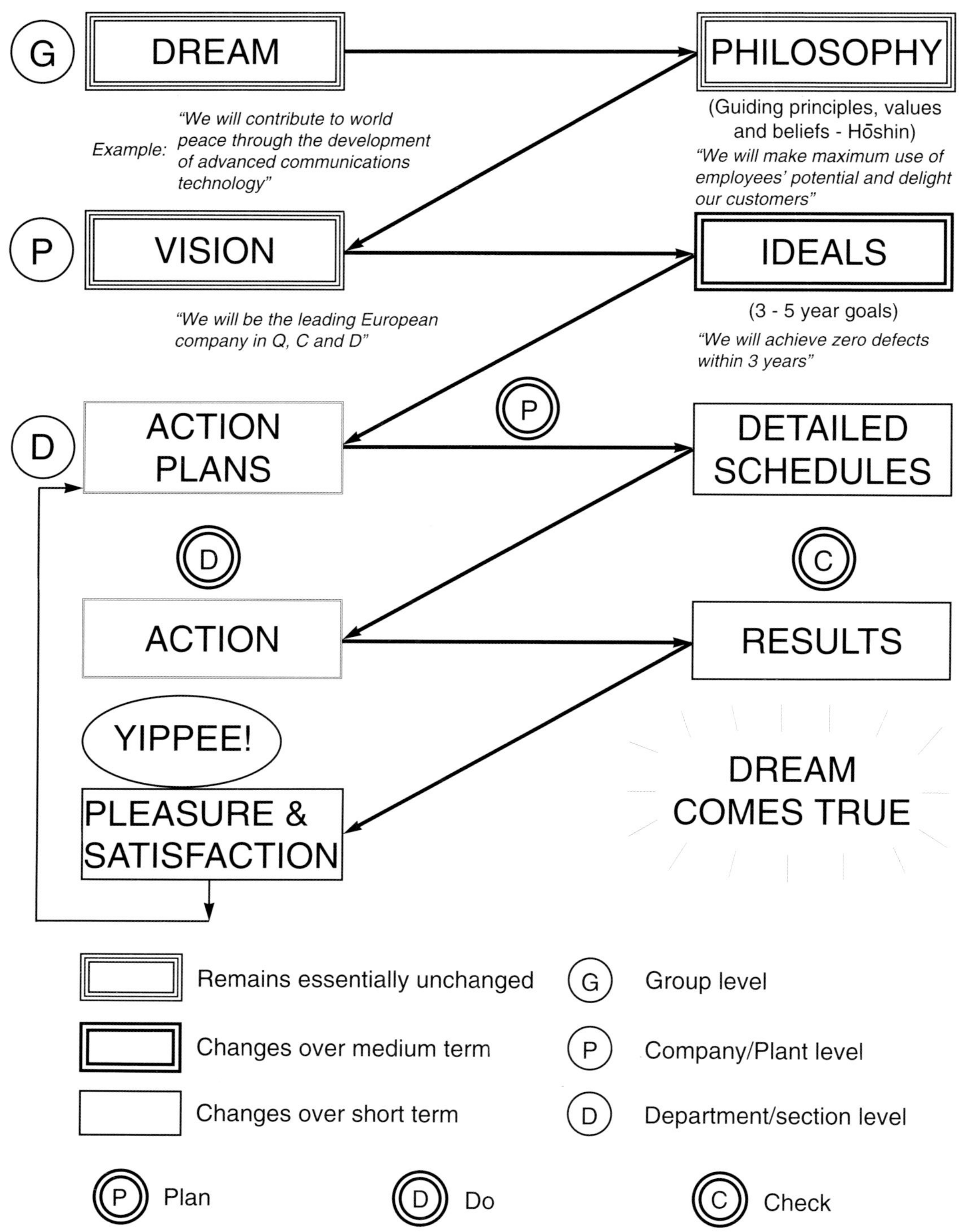

Figure 2.2 Keep on Realising Your Endless Dream

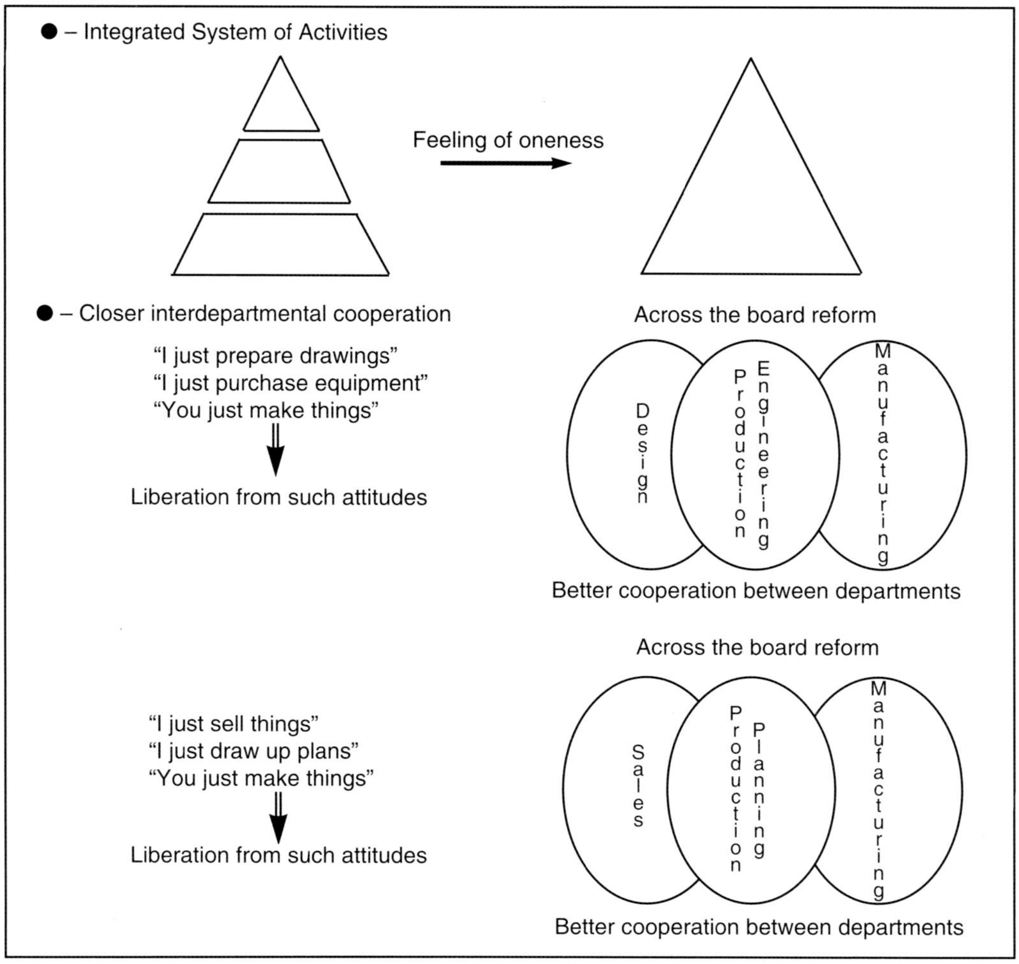

Discussions about how to achieve the objectives and how to implement the priority strategies take place at the planning stage

Figure 2.3 Breaking Down Organisational Barriers

So, what are the aims of TP Management, and how should its activities be evaluated? In this connection, one of TP Management's most distinctive characteristics can be expressed as follows:

"TP Management looks out, not in"

One of the basic insights underpinning TP Management is the understanding that customers decide what to buy on the basis of the quality of the products available, not that of the companies that produce them. TP Management's fundamental philosophy is that *products,* not companies, are what compete in the marketplace. Companies must

Factory Manager

"We've tried a lot of different things before, but TP Management gives us the clearest understanding of the interrelated system of activities taking place in the factory – it's almost as if we're holding it right here in our hands. I'm delighted – the people on the shop floor are really motivated."

Production Engineering Staff

"When we're developing new equipment, TP Management also helps us to incorporate lessons learnt from past shop-floor problems and make improvements related to product design. We're turning out some really effective machines now."

A more positive, optimistic workplace

Production Department

"Our work has become much easier and more enjoyable. It doesn't feel as if we're being bossed around any more."

"Managers and engineers come to the shop floor now and work with us to think up improvements. They take information on design flaws and equipment weaknesses back to their own departments and try to solve the problems at their source."

"Everyone gets together before the start of the financial term to work out TP targets and plan strategies, so we can see exactly what we have to do."

Production Control Department

"We never thought that shop-floor productivity could be increased simply by changing our planning methods, and we now have an overall picture of how to shorten our manufacturing lead times."

"The sales department is increasing the accuracy of its sales forecasts and the factory is reducing its lead times. If we each achieve our objectives, the whole operation is bound to improve."

Figure 2.4 The Benefits of Implementing TP Management

therefore put themselves in their customers' shoes and work out how cheaply and quickly they can provide them with excellent products. All of a company's efforts must be directed towards producing good products and making them as competitive as possible.

For example, let us imagine that a particular company has conducted a successful improvement campaign and won a prize for multiplying its productivity a certain number of times. Will customers really take this as evidence that they are better off buying that company's products? Aren't they more likely to think, "Winning a prize may make the people at that company happy, but it doesn't do much for us."?

When the situation is viewed this way round, it is obvious that the conventional technique-centred management approach requires a major rethink. If we trace the connections between what we do in our companies and the satisfaction of our customers (customer satisfaction, or CS) and review our activities from the management standpoint with the aim of improving our products in ways that our customers desire, we will probably find that the topics we must address and the priorities we must place on them will be very different from what they were before. Successfully addressing the matters uppermost in our customers' minds will naturally make our products more competitive and boost our sales.

In undertaking such activities, we should not tackle Quality (Q), Cost (C) and Delivery (D) problems separately. We must work out the best balance of Q, C and D for satisfying the customer, and set our objectives with this in mind. Doing so will make the activities we undertake extremely relevant. In this context, TP Management establishes a system for assessing the overall situation using the following formula:

$$TP = \frac{Q \nearrow}{C \searrow \times D \searrow}$$

The major features of TP Management are therefore as shown in Figure 2.5. The TP deployment diagram, to be described shortly, embodies all of these.

The Structure of TP Management

One of TP Management's most striking features is the way in which it depicts management objectives, priorities and activities visually. The idea of this is to make the information available to everyone, and the tool used for achieving it is the TP deployment diagram.

Figure 2.6 shows the basic structure of the TP deployment diagram, the key diagram used in promoting TP Management, in simplified, schematic form.

The first step in preparing a TP deployment diagram is to set the company's overall factory innovation objectives from the top and break them down into sub-objectives (Point No.1 on the diagram). The next step is to work out the strategies necessary for achieving those sub-objectives, while checking that the strategies will actually increase customer satisfaction (Point 2). Customer satisfaction is the most important consideration in selecting the strategies by which the objectives will be achieved.

When doing this, we use evaluation formulae such as those shown in Figure 2.7 (which take account of the conditions under which customers will use the product) to establish specific methods of improving product quality and functionality and formulate factory automation plans for improving productivity. As Figure 2.7 shows, this step could cover everything from users' expectations of products to their satisfaction with its performance over the entire period from initial use to final disposal.

● What is "Productivity"?

$$\text{Productivity} = \frac{\text{Output}}{\text{Input}} = \frac{\text{(Product Power)}}{\text{(Resource Utilisation)}}$$

TP Management rethinks the conventional concept of industrial productivity with the aim of raising product power (customer satisfaction) to world-beating levels, while minimising resource utilisation by reducing waste through efficiency improvement.

● What is "Total"?

In TP Management, "total" means enabling companies to mobilise the totality of their resources strategically to improve overall productivity ("total productivity"). It also means making all the company's employees from senior management to the lowest level of the hierarchy fully aware of their roles and responsibilities, across all departments including sales, design, development and administration as well as production.

● What is "Management"?

In TP Management, "management" means setting and deploying strategic objectives, combining the top-down and bottom-up approaches and helping people to select the most effective strategies for achieving the objectives, all on a priority basis. It also means efficiently constructing a vigorous, highly-motivated implementation organisation and establishing a creative management approach that makes full use of the company's particular strengths and individual characteristics.

● The TP Management System

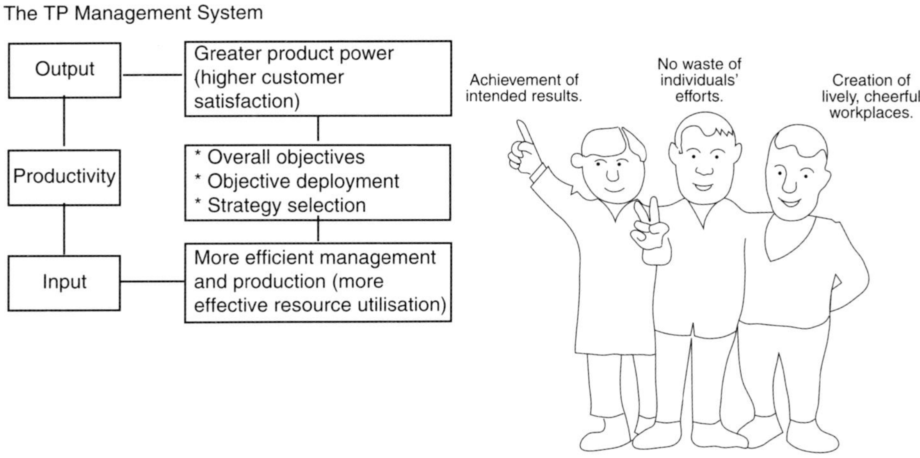

● Creating a Constitution for Change

NOW IS THE TP ERA

Goal	Revolutionise the company's internal environment – create a corporate constitution that is customer-oriented, focused on overall optimisation and always ready to take up fresh challenges –
Application	Product and manufacturing innovation – well-balanced quality, cost and delivery –
Means of Reaching Goal	Fusion of top-down and bottom-up management – priority-based, systematic approach –
Activities	Flexible combination of line and staff activities – project-type implementation system with total employee involvement –
Objective Deployment	Objective deployment for strengthening product power – keep stretching (build on strengths) –

Figure 2.5 The Major Features of TP Management

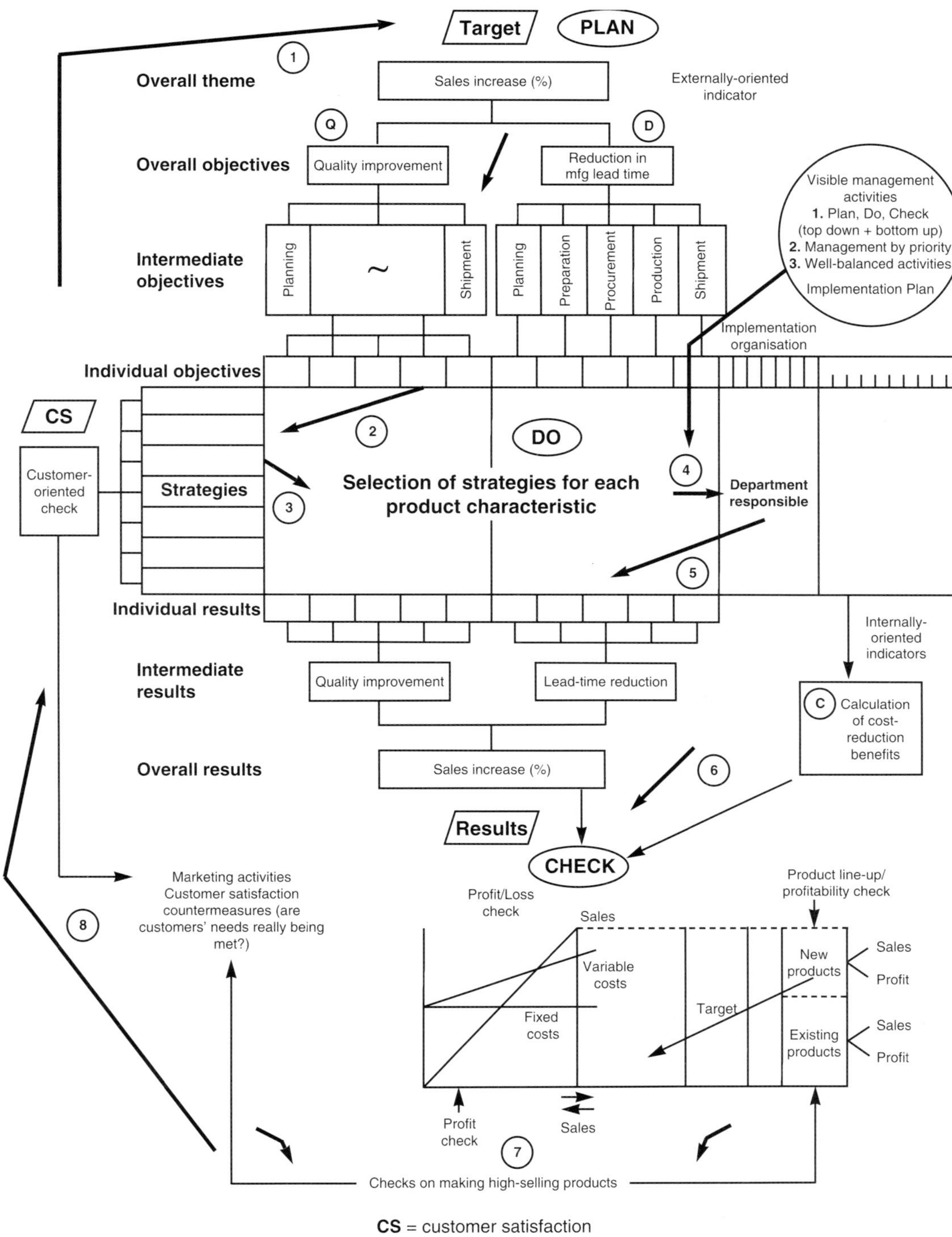

Figure 2.6 TP Deployment Diagram (in Schematic Form)

MQC evaluation index = (expectation of product) + (degree of satisfaction in use)

Expectations towards product:

$$= \frac{\text{selling price}}{\text{price level hoped for by market}} + \frac{\text{actual functions and performances}}{\text{market function and performance levels expected by market}} + \frac{\text{achievable delivery conditions}}{\text{delivery levels and reliability promised to market (including coordination with customer's new product development and marketing plans)}} + \frac{\text{actual product attractiveness index}}{\text{market attractiveness index (colour, shape, size etc.)}}$$

$$+ \frac{\text{actual usability index}}{\text{market usability index (by standard-value assessment; user's policy on installability, operability, applicability/developability, exchangeability, maintainability, remodelability, etc.)}} + \frac{\text{product's image index}}{\text{image index at time of use (technical reputation, reliability, sales figures, safety, etc.)}} + \text{other (e.g. quantity)}$$

Degree of satisfaction in use:

$$+ \frac{\text{new running costs}}{\text{old running costs}} + \frac{\text{new serviceability}}{\text{old serviceability (MTBF, after-sales service, future outlook when model changes are introduced)}} + \frac{\text{new life expectancy}}{\text{old life expectancy and durability}} + \text{other}$$

Note: Ability to supply the required quantities, provision of sales routes, etc. may be included in the 'other' item under expectations towards product.

Figure 2.7 MQC Evaluation Index
MQC = "market-in" (customer-focused) quality control

After this step, we move on to Point 3, where we formulate the strategies to be implemented in the factory by combining the objectives cascaded down from above with the results of our CS analysis. Next (Point 4), we use the 5W1H technique to review these strategies exhaustively and decide which department is responsible for implementing each and the schedule for its implementation, at the same time as checking its cost and profitability. The steps taken up until now constitute the plan phase of the TP deployment diagram. Having assessed the merits of the activities in this way, we proceed to implement them (Point 5). After implementing the strategies (the do phase), we check the results (the check phase – Point 6). This is the basic structure of the TP deployment diagram, used for the routine day-to-day management of all the activities carried on in the factory. Two final steps to take are checking corporate profitability (Point 7) and reviewing the contents of the TP deployment diagram (Point 8).

The Relation Between the TP Deployment Diagram and Social Satisfaction

As described above, one of the principal features of the TP deployment diagram is the way in which it provides an instant visual image of the relationship between each individual strategy and the company's overall business management posture, together with the contribution to be made by each organisational unit towards achieving the overall objectives. Simply by looking at the diagram, managers and workers responsible for controlling and implementing strategies can see the significance, degree of contribution and importance of the specific issues they must address in terms of their relationship to the system as a whole.

This naturally increases the efficiency of the organisation's business management, and the TP deployment diagram has consequently come to be regarded in Japan as an important tool for management innovation. It is presently being used by many companies and has proved extremely successful in ensuring the smooth progress of top-down, customer-oriented initiatives and bottom-up implementation proposals.

The Relation Between the TP Deployment Diagram and Management Activities

We will now use a TP deployment diagram to summarise once more the structure of the diagram and the management benefits that can be expected from it.

Deploying TP objectives

The TP deployment diagram cascades top management objectives down to the section and subsection level (or, in the case of products, to the level of assemblies and components), clearly defining overall and individual objectives. It is possible to agree with a general conclusion while disagreeing with the particular arguments leading up to it. Similarly, it is possible to support a general objective but disagree about the specific means of achieving it. In TP Management, progressively breaking down the superordinate objectives into sub-objectives makes the connections between individual sub-objectives and overall objectives abundantly clear. As a result, this unambiguously defines people's areas of responsibility and identifies the contributions that they will make to the company's bottom line results by achieving their sub objectives. This is in fact the purpose of carrying out the objective deployment exercise in TP Management.

Clarifying improvement policy and countermeasure methods

In preparing the TP deployment diagram, the company's improvement policy is stated and specific strategies for achieving the associated objectives are devised.

The company's improvement slogan is usually posted on one side of the TP deployment diagram. At the same time as indicating the company's improvement policy (and the means for achieving it), it also gives an idea of the improvement know how and technology that the company has accumulated. It shows what kinds of technology improvement techniques are to be used from the management standpoint. A large number of implementation strategies will be selected as means of achieving the various objectives as a result of establishing top-management policy in this way. Since individual workplaces may freely select their methods to suit their own particular circumstances, conditions and levels, this approach means that an overall balance is achieved and problem-solving techniques that make use of the particular characteristics of the plant are skilfully established. One of the notable features of TP Management is the way in which it elicits bottom-up proposals directed towards achieving the company's overall business improvement policy and selects the best methods for individual workplaces from among the vast number available.

Clarifying objectives and the means of achieving them

The system of individual implementation strategies that emerges when a TP deployment diagram is drawn up forms a road map for the implementation of overall management strategy. The TP deployment diagram is a chart that permits unified control of all the proposals for achieving the objectives; it is a tool for managing both the overall situation and its constituent parts.

To permit individual strategies to be adjusted to fit in with the overall objectives, it is important to draw up the TP deployment diagram on a single sheet of paper. Even though a particular department in a company may produce good results by resolving a certain issue, its actions may adversely affect other departments. Again, when one strategy fails and another must be devised, the replacement strategy must also contribute to achieving the overall management objectives. The TP deployment diagram enables this kind of management simulation to be carried out and alternative proposals to be checked. For this purpose, it is also necessary to pool ideas at points where improvement policies intersect with improvement objectives, based on the thinking outlined above. To do this, we create a map by numbering the diagram vertically and horizontally to provide addressed cells in which ideas can be recorded. This is another useful feature of the TP deployment diagram.

Following the PDC cycle using visual controls

In TP management, we strive to achieve our objectives by rotating the PDC wheel.

The TP deployment diagram is managed by prioritising individual strategies using the symbols ◎,○,△ and monitoring the progress of each topic by colouring these priority symbols red, yellow or blue. In this way, visual controls are used to manage priorities and chase progress. The symbols are used as an advance warning system for indicating priorities and checking adverse effects; once a group of strategies has been decided on for each intersection on the diagram (it is usual for at least 100 sub-strategies to be established for each intersection and several thousand strategies to be implemented and managed overall), the three colours are used in the following way:

Red: Problems occurring; immediate plant level countermeasures needed.
Yellow: Project incomplete; investigation required.
Blue: Project proceeding on or ahead of schedule, or already completed.

We use this system to manage priorities and monitor any departures from the normal. The degree of attainment of objectives may also be indicated using a pie chart. Whichever method is adopted, the diagram is constructed with the aim of achieving unified, centralised control of the PDC cycle. The colour blue in particular indicates that the extremely important management activity of delegating authority has been undertaken, and managers (particularly top management) can therefore remove their attention from the blue areas and concentrate their efforts on other important, problematic areas. The use of the TP deployment diagram is extremely effective in achieving the kind of management in which people trust each other and do not try to blame individuals for problems but try to solve them by focusing on them from the standpoint of the company as a whole.

Providing readily appreciated feedback to all employees on the success or failure of their activities

The TP deployment diagram can be used as a progress chart that allows people to experience the joy of achievement.

The secret of improvement is "success breeds success". It is important to praise good efforts right away and make use of the energy and confidence generated by one success in achieving the next objective. For this purpose, we use colours and figures on the TP deployment diagram to show the results of our activities and their contribution to the overall objectives.

I would now like to analyse what I have been discussing so far from the management perspective. Figure 2.8 shows the basic structure of the TP deployment diagram.

The TP deployment diagram shows why each individual strategy should be implemented and what exactly should be done (the management objectives indicating "Why?" are deployed down the vertical axis, while the strategies showing"What?" are indicated across the diagram; the symbols ◎,○,△ at the intersections invite all employees to suggest the "How?"). The activity guidelines showing what should be done are thus indicated on the horizontal axes, and the company's managers should specify these. The means by which the "What?" is to be achieved (the "How?") are left up to the departments directly responsible (and related departments). In this way, measures for achieving objectives or solving problems are submitted and implemented in bottom-up style.

As each topic is completed, the relevant strategy is coloured blue.This means that the various groups will vie with each other to get as much blue on the diagram as possible, since this is a direct indicator of their achievement. As a result, people compete to sharpen their improvement skills. Enabling employees to experience the joy of achievement is an effective management technique for developing their abilities. It entails creating a situation in which people compete with one another as well as sharing their techniques, enjoy the satisfaction of completing each project successfully, and use the enthusiasm generated by this to motivate them for the next project. The TP deployment diagram employs colours and symbols to put these basic elements of human resource development into practice.

- **Business strategies:**
  Strategies for raising profitability; measures for increasing sales and reducing costs.

- **Production strategies:**
  Technical innovation and management reform strategies; innovative strategies for shortening physical distribution times and improving quality.

- **Product strategies:**
  Marketing strategies; strategies for introducing high-value-added new products; pricing and sales strategies.

Checking strategies in terms of the four dimensions of innovation

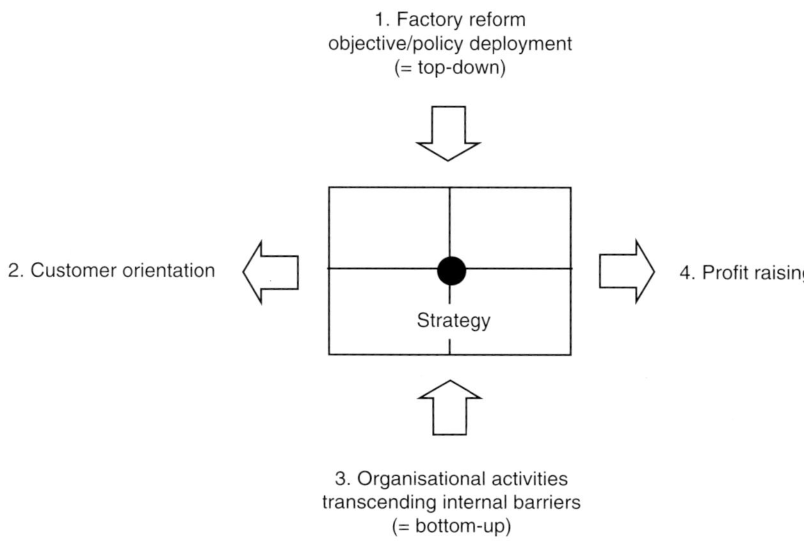

This technique shows people what contributions their actions make to their factory and company (1 and 4), themselves (3) and their customers (2).

Checking strategies in terms of the essential conditions that apply to manufacturing

- Competition in the marketplace is competition among products. It is therefore vital to check the quality, cost and delivery of products, and implement strategies that achieve a good balance among these factors.

Note: If objectives are confused with slogans (e.g. "Quality First!", "Shorten Lead Times!"), the company will suffer from the "flavour of the month" syndrome. It is important to achieve the right balance among quality, cost and delivery.

Good management means deciding *what* to do and *why* to do it, before deciding *how* to do it.

Figure 2.8 Establishing Overall Management Strategies

Acting with a single mind

The TP deployment diagram uses visual controls to achieve concerted action; it encourages everyone to play his or her own part while helping others if they are having trouble.

The previous section indicates that, in TP Management, all the members of the organisation are shown exactly what they must do, and feel obliged to do their best to achieve their own individual objectives. However, some teams may have weaknesses in some areas. The TP deployment diagram makes it clear that the overall objectives must be achieved even if it means that people have to help each other to do so. In this way, TP Management prevents people from considering their work over once they have completed their allotted tasks. If their team has not achieved its objectives, it will be seen to have failed. This naturally engenders the desire to help each other out when necessary.

Once such a climate of competition and cooperation has become established and people voluntarily extend themselves to help others even in different workplaces, teams will form themselves organically and work together well in a relaxed way without managers having to give directions and check on progress at every turn. By looking at the TP deployment diagram, everyone concerned will be able to see this at work. As a result, proposals will emerge from both the bottom-up and the top-down, and excellent teamwork will be achieved. Simply displaying the status of management in visible, easily-understood form in this way leads to easy solutions of management problems previously regarded as intractable. This is one of the great benefits of using a TP deployment diagram.

Practising flexible project management and creating networked organisations

In TP Management, project teams transcending workplace barriers are formed to tackle topics and solve problems.

To resolve issues effectively on a plantwide basis, it is essential to tackle topics in an intensive, focused way with the best possible teams; in other words, it is best to adopt the task-force project system used in value engineering (VE). The matrix-type organisation used to be regarded as the best arrangement for this purpose, and this type of organisation has been investigated extensively by many companies. There have been many reports of the use of this system to set objectives skilfully, operate effectively and achieve excellent results. However, putting such an organisation in place brings with it questions of status, rewards and so on.

TP Management takes a different approach. The TP deployment diagram aims at achieving overall optimisation. This makes it important to ensure that the diagram clearly shows who must do what, and why they must do it in order to improve the overall situation. Since the system needed for addressing particular topics is constantly changing, it is more important to ask the question, "What must I do to achieve overall optimisation?" than to engage in long-winded discussions of organisational or systems theory. With the TP deployment diagram, people do this anyway without having to be asked. The diagram also shows without any need for explanation that the organisational system must respond flexibly to changes in customer satisfaction (CS) requirements. Without it even being talked about, a network-type organisation begins to function. In this way, a flexible, universally-acceptable problem-solving type of organisational management system comes into operation.

Achieving clear understanding of overall and individual activities

As a result of the visual control facilitated by the use of the TP deployment diagram, plantwide communication becomes easier and more active.

In view of what has already been said above, this probably needs little further explanation. The TP deployment diagram is a kind of communication board; it covers everything necessary for integrated, centralised management of the plant's activities and answers questions such as "What must I do for my company, my colleagues and our customers?", "Where must I provide assistance so that we can achieve our overall objectives as quickly as possible?", and "Where are the problems occurring?".

In the above paragraphs, I have tried to explain the connection between the TP deployment diagram and various topical management issues. It is clear that the TP deployment diagram covers almost all of the issues dealt with in conventional management studies. We could say that the main role of the TP deployment diagram is to show people in both overall and particular terms what they must do and why they must do it. One of its most significant features is the way in which it enable a good balance to be maintained between the whole (overall objectives) and the parts (individual strategies). It enables people to see that each time they implement a strategy they are helping to achieve the objectives set by top management, and shows them how they are acting to strengthen their company's customer-focused product competitiveness. Moreover, because people are freely able to select the means by which they implement their allotted strategies (the bottom-up approach), their activities benefit both themselves and their colleagues. The diagram also shows that this will lead directly to higher profits and continued growth for their company in the future, thereby helping to raise everyone's motivation.

These are the benefits of the TP deployment diagram as seen from the four dimensions of innovation illustrated in Figure 2.8; it leads to the type of management that motivates people and stretches their abilities. Not only is TP Management a system for continuously extending and enhancing individuals, topics and ideas; it is a form of improvement activity that leads directly to better business results.

Medium-Term Business Plans and TP Management

Implementing TP Management brings home to the people practising it the importance of management. Top managers should not leave everything up to the people in the workplace; it is their job to know their employee's strengths and their company's equipment and technical capabilities and decide which areas need improving and in which directions they should lead their company.

This has recently been identified as an important issue for many Japanese companies. Have managers established appropriate improvement themes? Have they laid down effective improvement guidelines (when setting objectives taking account of present capabilities and future potentials)? These are some of the most important questions confronting managers today. Imagine you are the captain of a ship. Your vessel is beautiful, well-managed, technically advanced ... everything is perfect. So, where are you to take it? What is it for? Is it doing anything useful for its passengers or the world as a whole? This example clearly illustrates the importance of managers establishing policies and themes and giving direction to their organisations. In short, deciding where to take the ship and why to take it there (the "What?" and the "Why?") is the captain's (top management's) responsibility. It is essential to specify the "What?" and the "Why?" before thinking about the "How?"

In view of this, how are we to put the ideas expressed in Figure 2.2 into action? In other words, how must we proceed step by step in the direction of our long-term objectives, and how are managers to put together medium-term plans, communicate these to the people who are to implement them and steer the organisation? A new TP deployment diagram should be drawn up every year or accounting period; and, whenever this is done, the organisation must be pointed in the right direction. Some firms adopt a copycat management style ("Other companies are achieving good results with this, so let's do it ourselves."), but TP Management rejects this approach. TP Management came into being in answer to the question, "What new management system can lead Japanese industry into the future?" It is a system that respects companies' independence and individuality. This is why a company is allowed to win a TP Prize every three years and can reapply as many times as it wants. This rule also demonstrates that winning a TP Prize is useful and valuable at the time but that the success it represents does not last for ever.

As these remarks indicate, the practice of TP Management demands that companies must set specific management objectives. In other words, management's role is to specify and communicate the three overall management strategy items shown in Figure 2.8. Figure 2.9 illustrates this concept.

In this diagram, TP Management is represented as a growing tree in the process of producing delicious fruit. The tree is a climber, like an espalier apple tree, so unnecessary branches need to be pruned off as shown by the crosses. Healthy shoots should be encouraged to grow up the three supporting poles representing the company's management strategy axes. Management that starts off rather vague and ill-defined must become more detailed, precise and innovative as the tree grows, and individual management strategies must be more clearly connected to the overall care of the tree. If the tree is well managed in this way, it will produce beautiful fruit – the company's products. Naturally, the roots must absorb all kinds of nourishment; likewise, the company must assimilate a wide range of possibilities and techniques and use them appropriately.

The company's top managers must pull their company up by expressing these ideas in the form of medium-term plans and communicating them to all employees. Figure 2.10 represents this schematically.

In TP Management, a company's managers must prepare a TP deployment diagram every year or accounting period detailing what is to be done to move in the direction of their "vision" based on "ideal objectives". As mentioned before, this means that managers must set objectives for their company (an effective method of doing this is to make skilful use of my "mechanism for determining corporate policy" shown in Figure 2.11).

TP Management vs Conventional Management

When drawing up a TP deployment diagram, it is important to avoid the copycat approach to selecting objectives ("Other companies are doing this"; "Other companies are achieving good results through this"); use TP Management and the TP deployment diagram as a management activity that respects your company's unique strengths and establishes its own direction. Figure 2.12 shows the differences between TP Management and conventional management activities. This table, which compares TP Management with conventional "How to"-based management approaches such as TQC and TPM, illustrates this point.

The Meaning of "Total" in TP Management

When applying TP Management, it is essential to have a solid, reasonable objective-setting story covering everything that the company's employees must take as their objectives. Figure 2.13 depicts this based on my experience of various organisations'

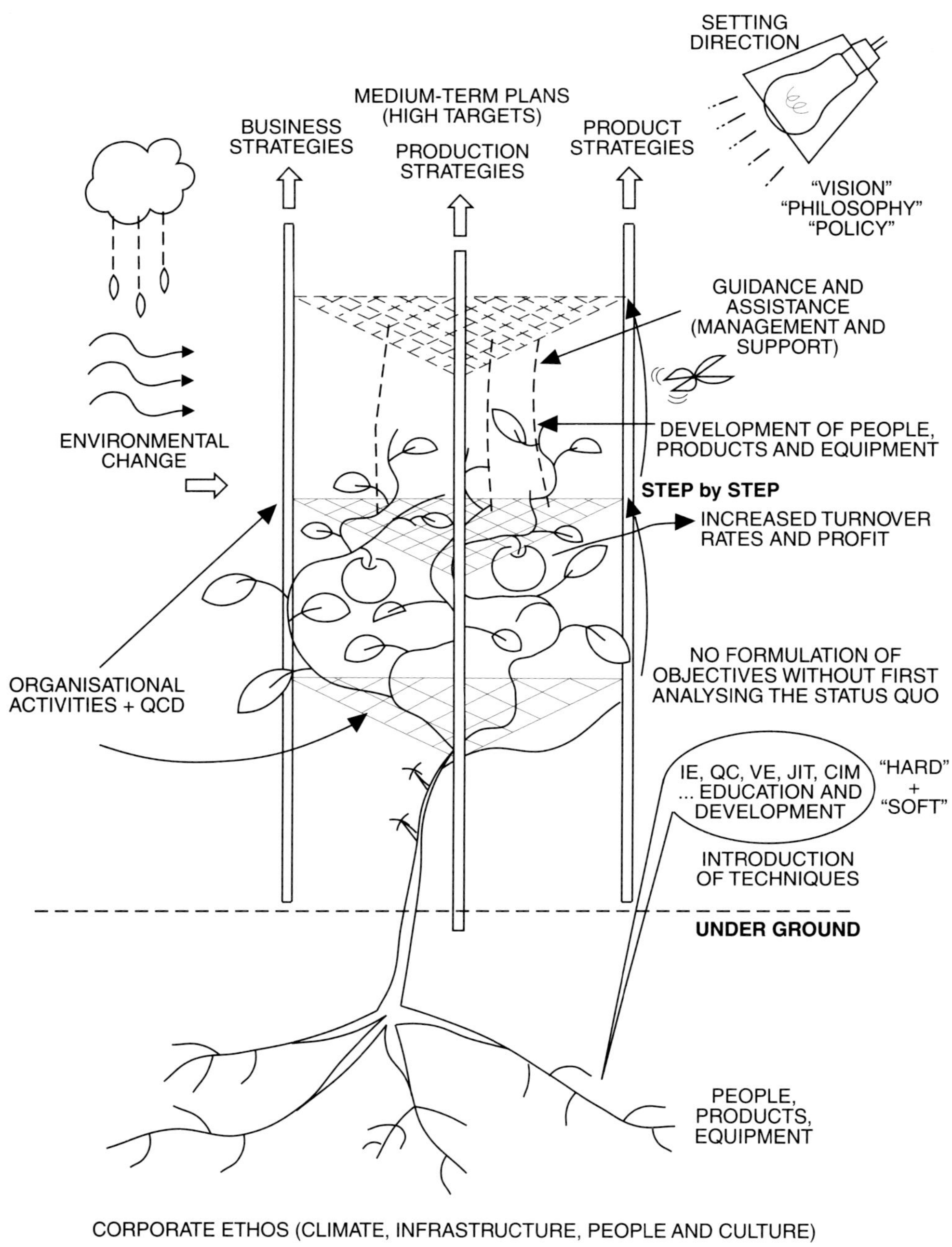

Figure 2.9 A Pictorial Representation of TP Management

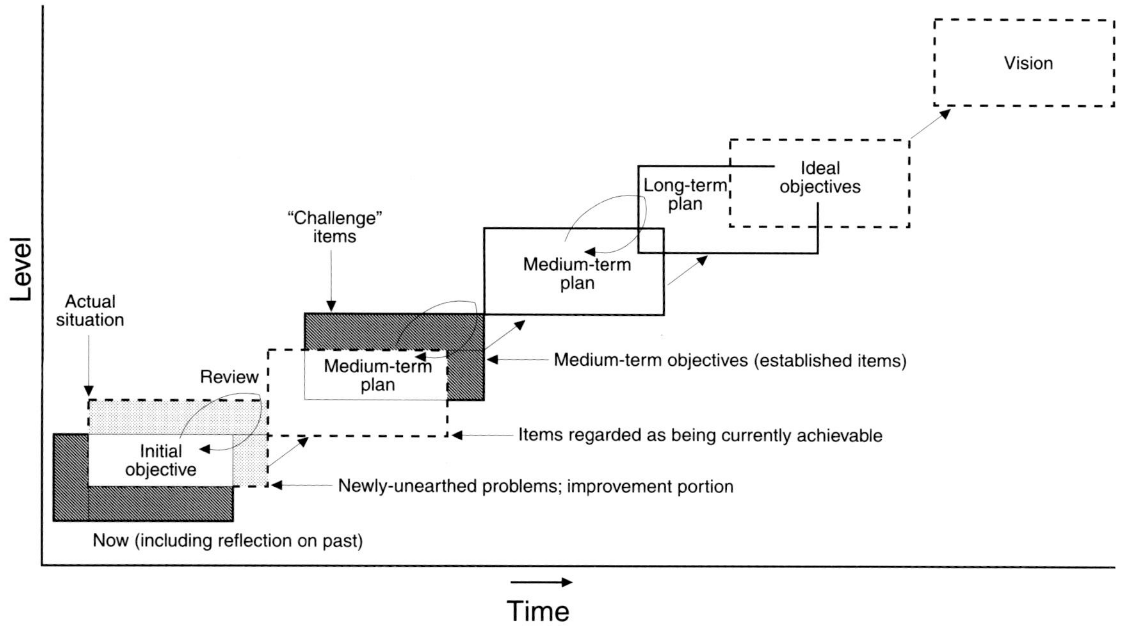

Figure 2.10 The Concept of Rolling Planning

efforts to implement TP Management. I call the use of this diagram MŌLT (Management Theme Organisation Technique through Long Term). The MŌLT system specifies a process and guidelines for setting objectives. In establishing numerical objectives, it is necessary to do the following:

Perform a marketing analysis (including an analysis of competitors' trends).

Collect unquantifiable information such as the problems, desires and opinions of employees.

Accurately check and review the present situation.

An analysis of successful companies usually reveals the following three common points of excellence:

Top management sets firm objectives, gets people to buy into them, and acts vigorously and enthusiastically on a daily basis.

The existing situation is precisely analysed and the problems and the means of solving them are carefully organised.

To achieve the objectives, a series of attainable medium-term objectives is set, and the organisation is operated with total participation by all members with the aim of reaching those objectives.

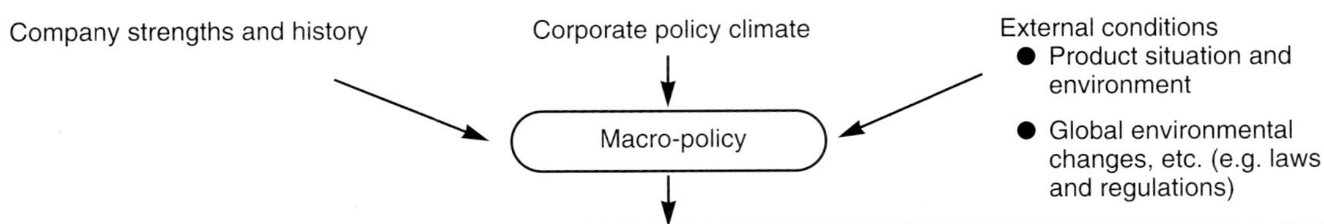

Procedure for determining policy	Stage evaluation
Needs: top-management demands, society demands Issues that must be addressed as a result of the changing times (What?)	Continuous incremental improvement ➝ reform ➝ revolution (Example) ● Technology and costs acceptable to the outside world ● Non-polluting automated factories, etc.
Wants: sort out what must be done for what purpose ● Product strategies ● Technology and management innovation strategies ● Business reform strategies	(Examples) ● Diversify applications and sales of electronics components ● Secure markets by establishing manufacturing facilities overseas ● Run the business without borrowing money ● Achieve customer satisfaction through JIT
Targets: clarify what targets and objectives to aim for when systematising	(Examples) ● Achieve x% market share; be No.1 in industry ● Achieve x% new-product ratio ● Achieve x% per-capita productivity ● Achieve world-class processing value-added
Mission: decide on the means for doing what needs to be done Systematically determine what means should be used for what purpose 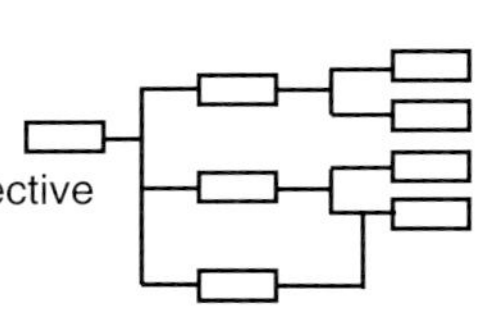 Objective Target | Means Express in story form	(Examples) ● Improve QCD at the CAD/CAM design stage ● Automate and computer-integrate process X ● Set up an integrated production system with a lead time of X days ● Create a flexible production system with daily changeovers using small robots ● Establish technology Y ● Eliminate process Z
Conditions: balance what you want to do with what you can do	(Examples) "Must" items: things that must be done "Want" items: things that you want to do Consider negative effects and constraints
Policies: summaries of targets and priority strategies	Put all the above together in story form and give it a title ("Because X, we must do Y")

Figure 2.11 Mechanism for Determining Corporate Policy

Management approach	Establishing a Firm Foundation: TQC	Establishing a Firm Foundation: TPM	Creation of a Constitution for Change: TP
Objective	Improve the company constitution (improve business results and create energetic and cheerful workplaces)		Reform operational set-up Achieve overall optimisation; create organisation eager to take up fresh challenges
Application (what is being managed?)	Quality (output side; results)	Equipment (input side; causes)	Product and manufacturing reform Quality, delivery and cost
Means of achieving objective	Systematise management (including standardisation); "soft"-oriented	Bring workplaces and equipment into their ideal state; "hard"-oriented	Fuse top-down + bottom-up structure and behaviour
Personnel development	Centred on management techniques (QC tools)	Centred on engineering techniques (equipment and maintenance technologies)	Centred on quick response and "virtuous circles"
Activities	Autonomous circle activities	Integration of standing-organisation activities and small-group activities	Regular and project activities
Targets	ppm-order defect rates	Complete elimination of loss and waste (aiming for zero)	Greater product power

TQC: Total Quality Control

TPM: Total Productive Maintenance

TP: Total Productivity Management

We are now moving from the local (partial) optimisation era to the overall (total) optimisation age.
TP Management is attracting the attention of industry as a management technique for accomplishing this transition.

Figure 2.12 A Comparison of TP Management with Conventional Technique-oriented Approaches

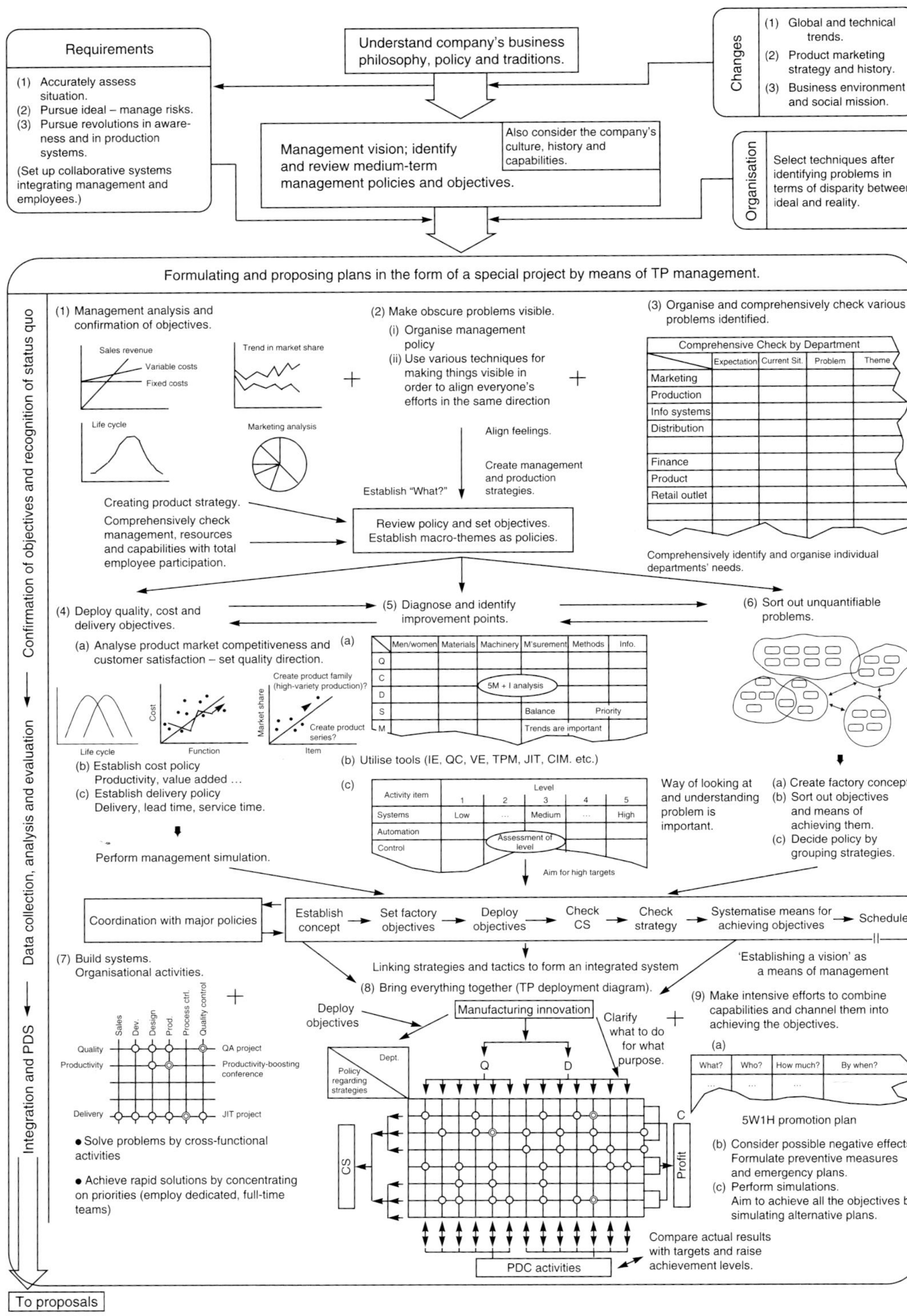

Figure 2.13 Outline of MŌLT

Rome was not built in a day, and neither can this kind of thing be achieved with a single day's activities. Just like making a fine "Malt" whisky, the whole process must be operated skilfully until it matures and starts producing good results. MŌLT also has another connotation – like animals shedding their winter coats, MŌLT is a method by which a company can shed its old skin and be born again. This is why I chose the abbreviation MŌLT for my objective setting procedure, the preparatory stage for implementing TP Management. The actual practice of MŌLT can follow the guidelines illustrated in Figure 2.13.

The next question is how to proceed with implementing TP Management. The meaning of "total" in TP Management is the totalisation or integration of a variety of management issues through the use of a unified system. So far, the following kinds of items have been developed and put into practice:

Q + C + D + ... totalisation of management issues.

5M + I ... totalisation of improvement targets (example: linking standardisation or layout improvement with information management).

IE + QC + VE ... totalisation of techniques, utilising them in combination and linking them to upgrading of levels.

Production + administration + shipping + suppliers + sales and marketing ... expansion and integration of activities of different departments (see Figure 2.14).

Objectives + strategies + action organisation ... personnel development (integration of medium-term objectives and specific activity objectives).

ES + CS + SS ... totalisation of policy.

Production → design → ... totalisation of the manufacturing process

Other ... integration and communisation of top-down + bottom-up activities, information, etc.

Each company will approach the achievement of its overall objectives in its own way, based on the items described, and this requires totally participative activities that lead directly to improved business results. For this purpose, it is important to tackle and solve workplace problems at the same time as promoting reform. It is essential that the people in each workplace feel free to enumerate the difficulties they are facing, so that these can be co-ordinated with top-management requirements and objectives. One practical way of doing this and achieving the objectives is to use the "pocket matrix" tool recently developed by the Japan Management Association (JMA). Figure 2.15 illustrates the procedure for using this tool. This technique, together with four others in the set of improvement tools known as the "Go-Go Tools", is described more fully in a

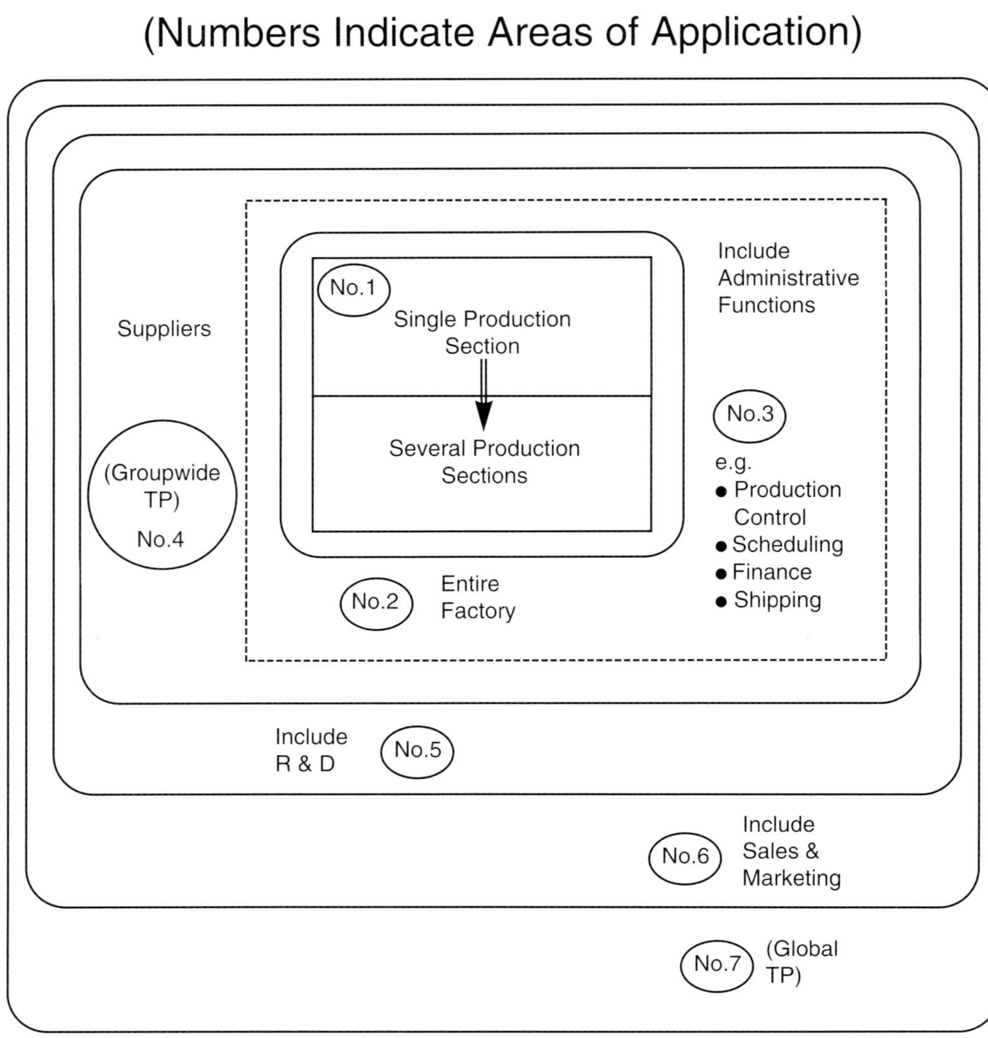

Figure 2.14 Range of Application of TP Management

forthcoming book to be published by Productivity Europe in 1996.

I have described some of the main features of TP Management and have presented the framework and essential elements of what has been developed up to now. I sincerely hope that you will make extensive use of the special qualities of TP Management and apply it successfully for achieving management reform.

- Step 1

  Write the problems (topics) on cards or Post-it ™ notes.

- Examples
  - "This job is too tiring/too difficult/ought to be done differently".
  - "I want us to become able to do this (dreams), I want this to happen (aspirations)."
  - "Inexperienced people find this job too difficult. Nothing gets made unless I am there."
  - "My boss thinks this job should be done one way, but I think it ought to be done differently."
  - "I don't like being complained at. I want to become as skilled as my more experienced colleagues as quickly as possible."

- Step 2

  Draw up a matrix -type chart showing the keys for tackling the problem.

Production Inputs (5M's + I)

	1 Quality/ Claims	2 Cost	3 Time/ Delivery	4 Safety	5 Morale
1 Materials (+ Design)					
2 Machines					
3 Measurement					
4 Methods					
5 Men/ Women					
Information					

- Step 3

  Stick the Post-it ™ notes on the chart (managers and workers do this separately).

  Include among the topics things that other departments are doing better.

- Step 4

  Calculate the potential benefits.

  Do this one by one, starting with the topics regarded as the most important.

- Step 5

  Highlight the topics likely to produce the greatest benefits from the smallest labour input.

Figure 2.15 Organising Topics - The "Pocket Matrix Technique"

3
TP Management Self-Diagnosis

Kazuhiro Shimada
JMA TP Management Consultant and TP Prize Examiner

The Aims of TP Management

Establishing Creative Management

Because of the great diversity of requirements presented by today's markets, manufacturing companies are now required to supply a huge variety of products on a just-in-time basis while at the same time minimising their inventories and reducing their costs. Many companies are now vying with each other to find the best ways of attaining these conflicting objectives.

We have become extremely adept at improving our operations through the extensive use of IE, VE and QC techniques. However, we now urgently need to establish a more creative style of management, i.e. the type of management able to maximise product competitiveness based on the nature of our companies' resources and on trends in markets and business structures.

Pursuing The New Productivity

Productivity can be expressed in terms of a relationship between input and output. Improving (i.e. increasing) input was a fairly easy task in the days when the main concern was to expand production volumes. Today, however, the focus is on improving the quality of both input and output.

Consequently, we must now revise our ideas about productivity and raise it to a higher level than merely that of an internal management indicator. We must examine our existing concept of productivity to determine whether it really measures the status of our products, functions and processes from the customer's standpoint. In short, we must make the concept do an about turn, from being internally-directed to being externally-directed.

We must thus pursue a customer-focused definition of productivity; but this is not a task for the manufacturing department alone. All departments directly and indirectly involved in the manufacturing process must cooperate in the quest.

Creating Dependable Systems

Many companies are now striving to raise their total productivity and thereby win a far higher reputation than their competitors in their customers' eyes for quality, price and delivery. Systems and mechanisms are required for ensuring that such results are unfailingly maintained and continuously improved. TP Management is a reliable and effective system for creating this kind of scenario.

The Importance of Objectives and the Key Points for Activities

Aims and Targets

Skilful integration of the top-down and bottom-up approaches is a vital factor in implementing TP Management. The three key points in achieving this are aims, targets and activities.

An objective should be a strategic aim that anticipates future changes. Like being unable to see the wood for the trees, an organisation will work hard but achieve little if it fails to consider the whole picture when deciding on its aims. A company's managers must thoroughly and comprehensively review their organisation's entire operation and decide where its priorities lie. Resources such as labour, funds and time will be allocated differently depending on the actions to be taken.

Every company tries to set desirable objectives and achieve excellent results through sound management and superior technology. However, when it comes to deciding on their objectives, many organisations tend to fudge the issue. An organisation that sets its objectives based on a precise understanding of what it must do and why it must do it will always achieve far better results than one that sets its objectives without such understanding.

There are three main aspects to an objective; its necessity, its feasibility and its "ownership" (i.e. the degree to which people have participated in the process of creating it). Furthermore, an objective must be set high enough to induce "breakthroughs" - dramatic changes that convert an old situation into a new and better one. The improvements that we make nowadays must be revolutionary. This is why it is necessary to set targets high enough to require a radical change to the existing situation. Revolutions do not take place without a vision of the desired situation and the construction of a detailed scenario describing how to turn that situation into reality. Moreover, the basic philosophy underpinning all the activities of an organisation should be an optimistic, forward-looking one of accentuating the positive and building on strengths.

Getting Activities Going

Why are activities conducted by cross-functional groups such as project teams, task forces and cross-functional committees so popular nowadays? Because the changes taking place in the business environment have created a need for such activities. The task of a project team is not to go on accomplishing the organisation's routine, day-to-day work. It is to achieve a particular, one-off objective, and the project comes to an end once this objective has been reached.

When people work on a project as a member of a team, they experience a dynamic and intense period of activity unfettered by the usual forms and procedures, and they develop in stature and skill as a result. Projects provide opportunities for people to change their ways of thinking and cultivate their abilities. Their desire to acquire the relevant expertise is rekindled, and their motivation to tackle their allotted task enthusiastically and energetically is restimulated.

These days, most companies' personnel management and employment systems emphasise promotion on merit rather than on seniority. From now on, the movers and shakers in companies are likely to be specialists operating in project teams. Companies must constantly devote their utmost efforts to developing new technology and new products and opening up new areas of business. To respond to these management needs, they require a pool of creative and resourceful personnel with a high level of competence in their respective fields.

The Aims of Innovation

Reforming Non-Repetitive Tasks and Upstream Areas

Generally speaking, we are good at improving the quality and productivity of repetitive work such as that done on a factory's production floor. However, we are not so effective when it comes to non-standard tasks such as development, design, and production engineering, and this has now become a major management concern. Innovations are required in upstream departments, where the work originates, using the production floor as a model.

Linking Customer Requirements through Technology to Business Results

In the past, we have energetically tackled and disposed of a whole range of problems as they have cropped up. However, looking back, it is apparent that we have only worked on the parts and have not thought very deeply about optimising the whole. We must now focus on how to improve our business results through technical innovations linked to the needs of our customers (see Figure 3.1) and how to manage our organisations in such a way as to make full use of those organisations' strengths.

Reforming Production Engineering for Greater Total Productivity

Production Engineering's Moving Target

In the high-growth era, the major aims of production engineering were to develop high-speed manufacturing techniques, shorten the transition from sample fabrication to volume production, reduce defect rates, and achieve non-stop operation (see Figure 3.2). This was fine at the time, but economic growth rates have slowed down and stabilised, and the focus is now on product diversification and differentiation rather than on sheer volume. A product's value is now determined by the technologies and methods used in its manufacture, and the commercial viability of many products currently depends on the development of novel production techniques and manufacturing processes. I also believe that developing and supplying genuinely attractive new products is the only way we can extricate ourselves from our present adverse economic circumstances.

What is Required of Production Engineering Managers?

As the people responsible for running their organisations, managers must possess a wide range of attributes. The following is a list of requirements suggested by production engineers who have taken part in my seminars. These are extremely interesting indicators of the new situation we are now facing.

At the same time as possessing sufficient leadership ability to set directions themselves and pull people and organisations along with them, production engineering managers must be capable of creative, hands-on management based on top-down policy.

Production engineering managers must be capable of generating functional innovations that affect upstream departments (planning and development) and downstream departments (manufacturing) and of acting as the driving-force behind the shift to concurrent development and production.

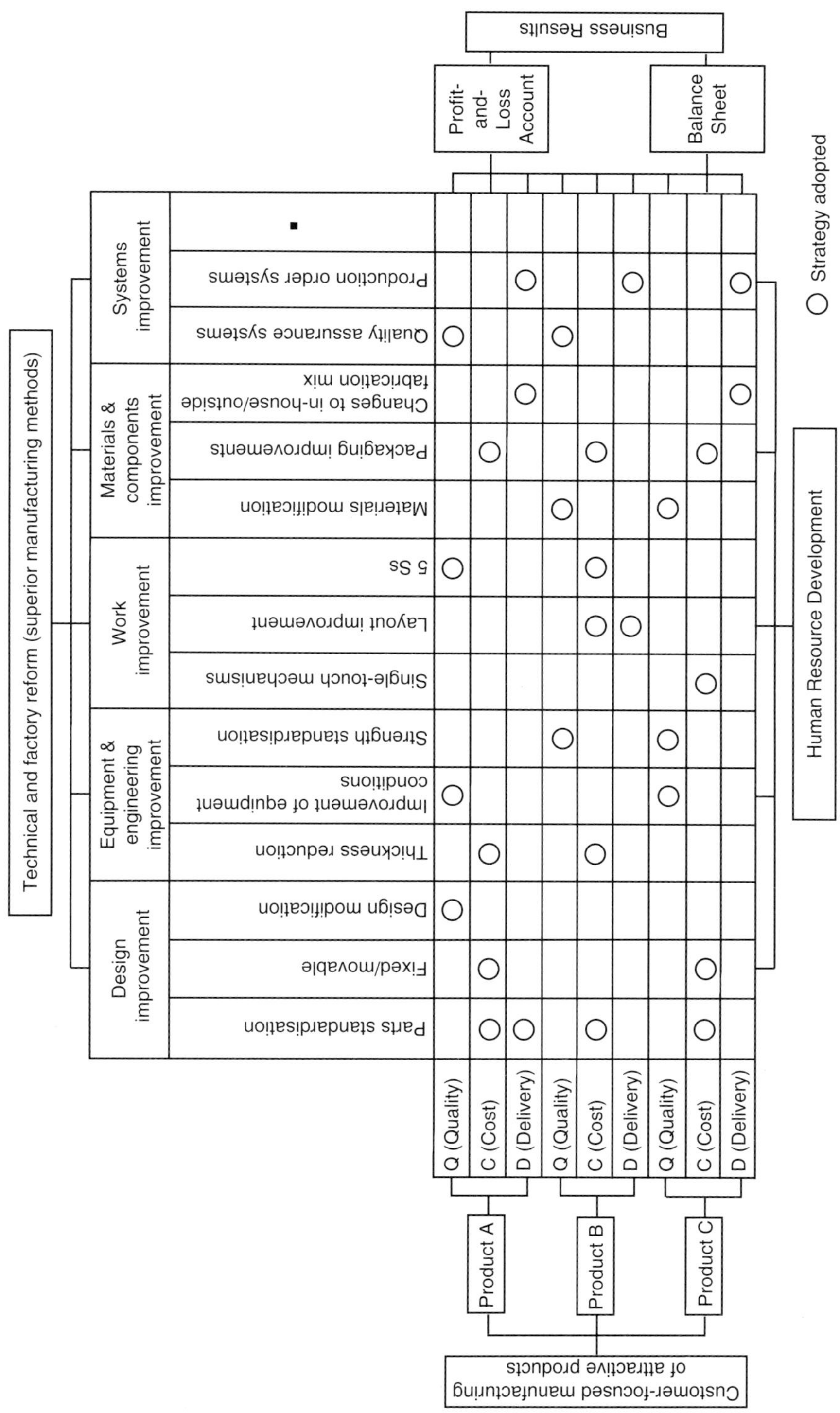

Figure 3.1 Relationships among Customer Needs, Technologies and Business Results

Conventional production engineering viewpoint		Current and future production engineering viewpoint
Cost reduction	→	High-value-added production
High-speed, high-volume production	→	High-variety, low-volume, flexible production
Mechanisation and automation	→	Development of new engineering techniques and processes
Reduction of manufacturing lead times	→	Reduction of overall lead times
Factory productivity	→	Timely productivity (time and quantity)
Reduction of defect rates	→	Zero defects
Fast transition from pilot production to full-scale production	→	Elimination of pilot production
Use of modular technology	→	Development of modular technology
Use of computers for rationalisation	→	Use of computers as a means of developing technology

Figure 3.2 Production Engineering's Moving Target

A production engineering manager's judgement is more important than his or her knowledge. He or she must be able to shake off the influence of long-serving members of the organisation, relinquish past successes and move boldly into new fields.

Production engineering managers must be able to keep their own and others' departments constantly active through job rotation and the operation of project teams, without clinging on to their more able subordinates.

I believe that our only chance of discovering the new kind of management required as we approach the 21st century is to radically alter the present situation from the kinds of novel standpoints indicated above.

Self-Diagnosis in TP Management

The following list of ten checkpoints was compiled with the aim of allowing an organisation to assess its TP Management level. It will help an organisation to upgrade the quality of its activities if its members discuss each of these points in turn, compare them with their organisation's existing management approach and make any changes necessary.

1. Have you drawn up a vision of what your organisation should aim to be like in three to five years' time, and do you base your annual objectives and plans on this?

   Have you identified the social, economic, political, technical and environmental changes now taking place in the external environment, analysed your organisation's strengths and weaknesses, and discussed your organisation's vision of how it should be in the future and what each of its departments must be like in order for this vision to be realised? Or, is your organisation content merely to go on accumulating the same kinds of results that it has in the past?

   Has your organisation identified the steps it needs to take in order to realise its vision? (In other words, has it divided the gap between the existing situation and the required situation into stages, established the tasks it must accomplish in order to move from each stage to the next, ensured that all its members understand and buy into its objectives, and selectively and strategically deployed its human resources?)

2. Has your organisation established a system for enabling the members of each of its departments to discuss issues such as "top-management thinking and expectations", "what other departments expect of our department", "the problems faced by our department", and "workplace problems", and has it sorted out the conclusions systematically and formulated plans and methods for achieving reforms in the areas identified?

   Does your organisation have a system for exchanging opinions within departments, between departments and between different hierarchical levels,organising the conclusions, introducing new technologies, and using these in the next round of tasks and strategies?

   Does your organisation identify and sort out its existing problems and thoroughly analyse their causes, before deciding on its objectives and the means and methods of attaining them?

3. Has your organisation classified its product lineup by customer and field of application, and does it give top priority to activities connected with improving customer satisfaction in order to strengthen product competitiveness?

   Has your organisation identified its customers' needs for each of its product groups and has it set overall quality, cost and delivery objectives based on the findings?

   Is your organisation implementing activities designed to achieve its quality, cost and delivery objectives simultaneously?

4. Are the objectives of each of your organisation's departments tightly linked to the organisation's overall objectives?

   Have each department's objectives been systematically linked to the objectives of the organisation as a whole; are these objectives expressed in numerical terms; are the aims and priorities made clear by means of indicators such as contribution ratios, and is all this done transparently at each stage of the objective deployment process?

   Is each department carrying out activities aimed at increasing product competitiveness in concert with all other departments? Have integrated plans been made for evolving the activities of all departments including sales, engineering, distribution and suppliers?

5. Does your manufacturing department get together with all the other departments to plan the process of deploying objectives and formulating strategies before the beginning of each financial year?

   Before deploying objectives and formulating strategies, do your company's managers and engineers review and improve their understanding of their roles and responsibilities and the basic philosophies and attitudes that they should possess?

   In drawing up objective deployment and strategy tables, do your company's front-line employees play the central role, with staff members acting in a supporting capacity?

6. In formulating strategies for achieving the objectives, does the discussion start with processes upstream of manufacturing?

   Since deficiencies in previous processes such as product design, engineering,equipment design, process design, purchasing, planning, and systems design all eventually show up in the manufacturing process, does your company's arsenal of strategies include ones that affect these previous processes? Do the strategies adopted actually originate in the workplace?

   Are employees' improvement suggestions and ideas collected systematically, and is this pool of ideas used when considering which strategies to adopt?

7. Is the strategy deployment scenario skilfully combined with implementation plans?

   Are the strategy deployment steps (the improvement scenario) properly planned? (In other words, are the details of the strategies selected for achieving the objectives carefully considered and is the sequence for implementing them clearly decided?)

   Are clear objectives set for each of the strategy development and implementation plans?

8. Has the activity system been clearly established and is it operating smoothly? Is participation in the activities helping to bring the whole organisation to life?

   Have appropriate implementation organisations been selected depending on the issues being tackled, their scope, the difficulty of the objectives and the period of activity, and are project teams, committees, regular activities and small-group activities functioning effectively?

   Are interim reporting meetings, results announcements, top diagnoses and other events held at each juncture, are these injecting vitality into the organisation, and are proper follow-up activities conducted when objectives are not achieved?

9. Does your company's education and training programme meet the needs of the workplace?

   Do your company's human resource development plans focus on the abilities needed to implement the strategies required for achieving the objectives?

   Are training programmes for increasing skills and imparting management expertise conducted in the workplaces where they are most needed, and are they useful both for the individuals attending them and for their workplaces?

10. Are the technical methods and improvement expertise acquired through activities designed to increase total productivity organised and systematised so that anyone can utilise them?

    Is there a skilfully-designed system for collecting and organising improvement techniques and expertise?

    Are these techniques and expertise effectively disseminated to other work areas and departments?

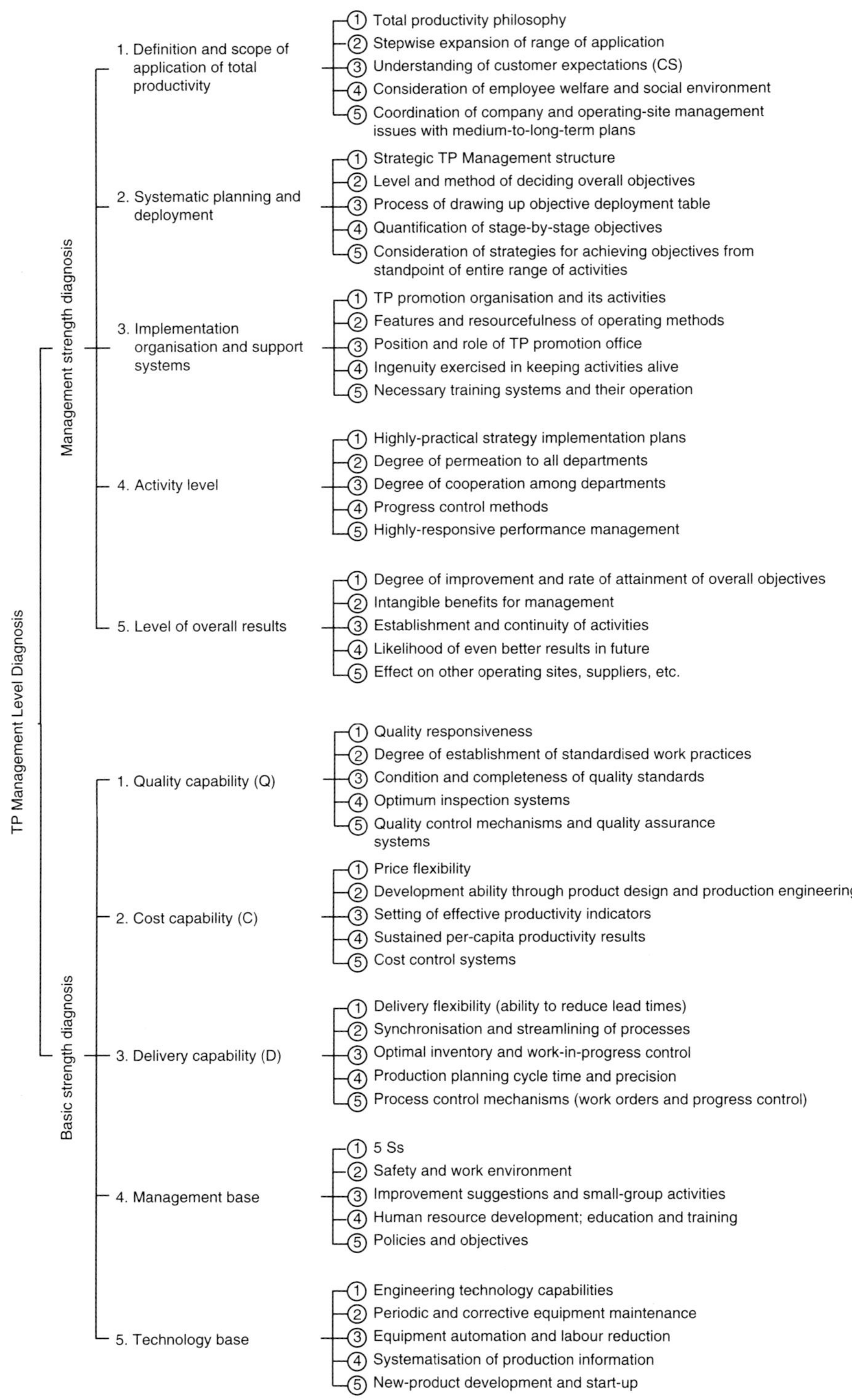

Figure 3.3 TP Management Level Diagnosis Chart

Evaluating the Level of TP Management

The level of a company's TP Management can be evaluated from two main standpoints. The first is simply assessing the existing situation (the "situation-indicator" approach). The second is deciding where priority needs to be placed in improving quality, cost and delivery for each product from the standpoint of customer requirements and technical trends (the "management" approach). I hope that readers will emphasise the latter approach and work out how to raise their organisations from their existing level to their desired level.

The TP Management level diagnosis chart and tables shown in Figures 3.3 and 3.4 (a to f) were compiled in TP seminars, and we use them in our TP consultations. As situation indicators, we use "management strength diagnosis" (raised through improved vertical and horizontal communication within the organisation) and "basic strength diagnosis". Each of these situation indicators is divided into five components, each of which is further divided into five items. Each of these items is assessed on a five-point scale, so that if a company scores the maximum of four points for every item, it will achieve the maximum total score of 100 points for that particular indicator.

If the scores for each component are recorded on the TP Management Diagnosis Radar Chart shown in Figure 3.4 (f), this reveals your company's strengths and weaknesses at a glance and clearly indicates the directions in which its activities should be developed in the future.

Item evaluated	4 Points	2 Points	0 Points
① Total productivity philosophy	Clearly defined	Defined	Poorly-defined
② Stepwise expansion of range of application	Precisely carried out, with future extension of scope clearly defined	Present and future steps defined	Imprecise
③ Understanding of customer expectations (CS)	Customer expectations clearly identified for each product group	Customer-focused thinking included	Internal-management-oriented thinking predominant
④ Consideration of employee welfare and social environment	Policy on employee and social issues clearly defined and implemented	Thinking defined; some action taken	Little action taken
⑤ Coordination of company and operating-site management issues with medium-to-long-term plans	Issues well organised from viewpoint of overall system of activities and clearly reflected in plans	Issues sorted out and directions indicated	Issues sorted out

Figure 3.4 (a) Definition and range of application of total productivity (20 points)

Item evaluated	4 Points	2 Points	0 Points
① Strategic TP Management structure	Connection with medium-to-long-term plans clear; objectives efficiently deployed according to correct procedure; TP deployment diagram drawn up	TP deployment diagram drawn up	System not properly organised
② Level and method of deciding overall objectives	Overall objectives excellent in both extent and direction	Overall objectives set; method of deciding on them comprehensible	Overall objectives set
③ Process of drawing up objective deployment table	Objectives properly deployed through close collaboration between all line and staff members	Objectives deployed by certain management and staff members	Objectives deployed mainly by staff members and TP promotion staff
④ Quantification of stage-by-stage objectives	Objectives quantified in terms of both necessity and feasibility; contribution ratios known	Objectives deployed in accordance with situation workplace; contribution ratios known	Objectives deployed uniformly, not selectively; no stepwise deployment visible
⑤ Consideration of strategies for achieving objectives from standpoint of entire range of activities	System in place and operated for considering strategies from standpoint of organisations's activities as a whole, including everything from most upstream to most downstream processes	Each work area considers its strategies in consultation with other areas	Little consultation with other work areas; strategies not considered sufficiently thoroughly

Figure 3.4 (b) Systematic planning and deployment (20 points)

Item evaluated	4 Points	2 Points	0 Points
① TP promotion organisation and its activities	Mutual relationships and functions within TP promotion organisation clear	TP promotion organisation and nature of activities clear	TP promotion organisation vague and ill-defined
② Features and resourcefulness of operating methods	Unique activities tailored to specific characteristics of company and business unit skilfully carried out and managed	Activities unique to company and business unit carried out	Activities taking place at individual level
③ Position and role of TP promotion office	TP promotion office actively monitors management situation and supports each work area	TP promotion office supports each department and chases schedule delays	TP promotion office plays coordinating role only
④ Ingenuity exercised in keeping activities alive	Top management itself actively promotes in-company presentation meetings and workplace diagnoses; reporting system exists	Creative efforts made to keep activities on boil	No visible efforts made
⑤ Necessary training systems and their operation	Ability maps drawn up; advance training carried out systematically	System of education and training for specific requirements set up	Education and training take place

Figure 3.4 (c) Implementation organisation and support systems (20 points)

Item evaluated	4 Points	2 Points	0 Points
① Highly-practical strategy implementation plans	Deployment process brought to a level at which highly-practical strategies can be implemented without wasting individuals' efforts; everyone highly motivated	Discussions of how to achieve objectives and how to implement priority strategies carried out at planning stage	Implementation plans formulated
② Degree of permeation to all departments	Each topic cascaded down to individual level across all divisions and all employees	Activities permeated to all divisions	Activities implemented in some areas
③ Degree of cooperation among departments	Organisational barriers broken down, and people cooperate well; activites imbued with great mutual trust	Departments work together; activities well integrated with each other	Departmental barriers still exist; general thinking is that all will go well if each part of the organisation does its bit
④ Progress control methods	Progress of all departments and procedure for retrieving slipped schedules clear	Progress of each strategy monitored; follow-up activities to retrieve slipped schedules carried out	Deadlines monitored, but nothing else done
⑤ Highly-responsive performance management	Permanent daily performance management system able to maintain, up-grade and revolutionise performance established	System of daily performance management exists	Performance management inadequate

Figure 3.4 (d) Activity level (20 points)

Item evaluated	4 Points	2 Points	0 Points
① Degree of improvement and rate of attainment of overall objectives	Overwhelmingly superior results obtained, leading whole industry	Planned overall objectives attained	Results unsatisfactory
② Intangible benefits for management	Outstanding qualitative benefits obtained in areas targeted by TP Management	Qualitative benefits visible	Benefits only obtained in certain areas
③ Establishment and continuity of activities	High degree of sustainability achieved through systematic deployment with emphasis on reproducibility	System firmly established with good maintainability thanks to track record of at least two years	System in process of becoming established
④ Likelihood of even better result in future	If it continues its activities, company can be expected to achieve best-in-class results	In view of company's experience of running system and results obtained so far, it can be expected to achieve revolutionary results in future	Good results can be expected
⑤ Effect on other operating sites, suppliers, etc.	Activities have become a model for other operating sites and suppliers and are being extended even further	Activities have had a major impact on other operating sites and suppliers	Some effect has occurred

Figure 3.4 (e) Level of overall results (20 points)

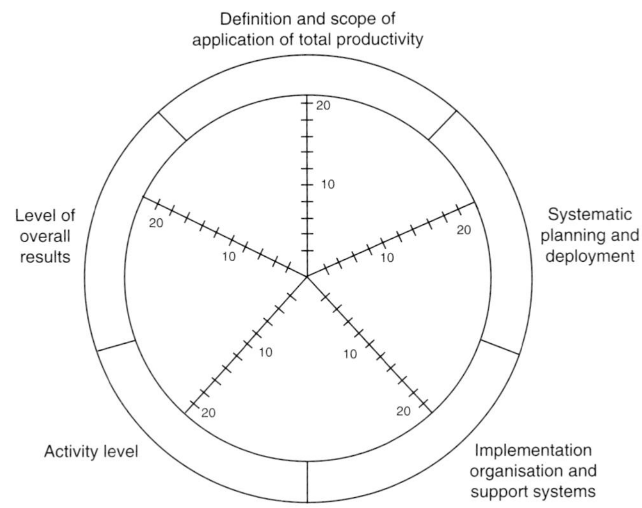

1	Definition and scope of application of total productivity	---- points
2	Systematic planning and deployment	---- points
3	Implementation organisation and support systems	---- points
4	Activity level	---- points
5	Level of overall results	---- points

Company	
Operating Site	

Figure 3.4 (f) TP Management Diagnosis Radar Chart

Constructing the TP Management Deployment Scenario

Figure 3.5 (a and b) shows the various stages of TP Management implementation. TP Management starts at Stage 1 with activities to increase the total productivity of the production floor. This approach is based on the idea that every deficiency in upstream processes such as planning, design, equipment engineering, production scheduling, materials procurement and so on eventually manifests itself on the production floor. This is why it is necessary to include all strategies relating to the entire production system (not just those relating to the actual workplace) in the pool of strategies for increasing the overall productivity (quality, cost and delivery) of the production floor.

The range of application of TP Management is then gradually extended in the twin directions of process innovation and product innovation. The final aim is to strengthen coordination among the development, manufacturing and marketing functions.

Many companies are also focusing on production engineering, using TP Management to strengthen its coordination with the previous process (i.e. design) and the subsequent process (i.e. manufacturing). The sequence by which the application of TP Management is broadened out to cover all areas of the company's operations (the "application scenario") will depend on the company's product characteristics and life-cycles, technical trends and management strategies. Figure 3.5 (a and b) shows a typical development scenario.

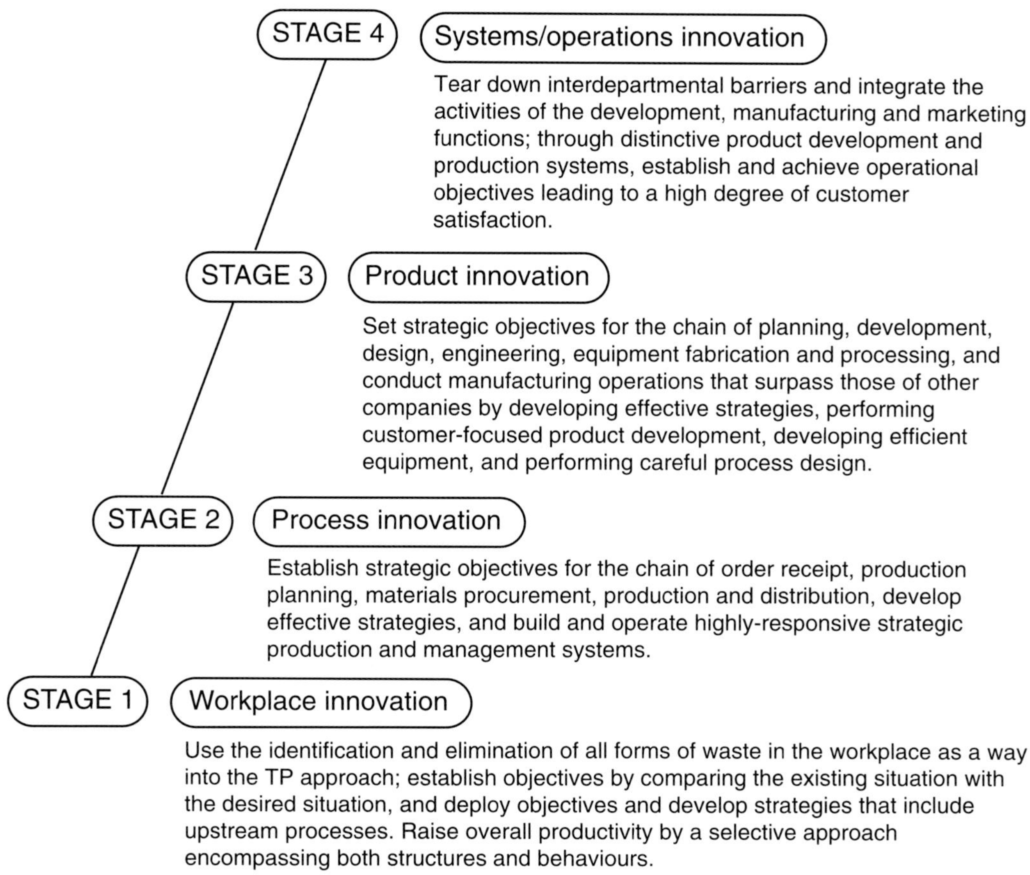

Figure 3.5 (a) Example of TP Management Development Scenario

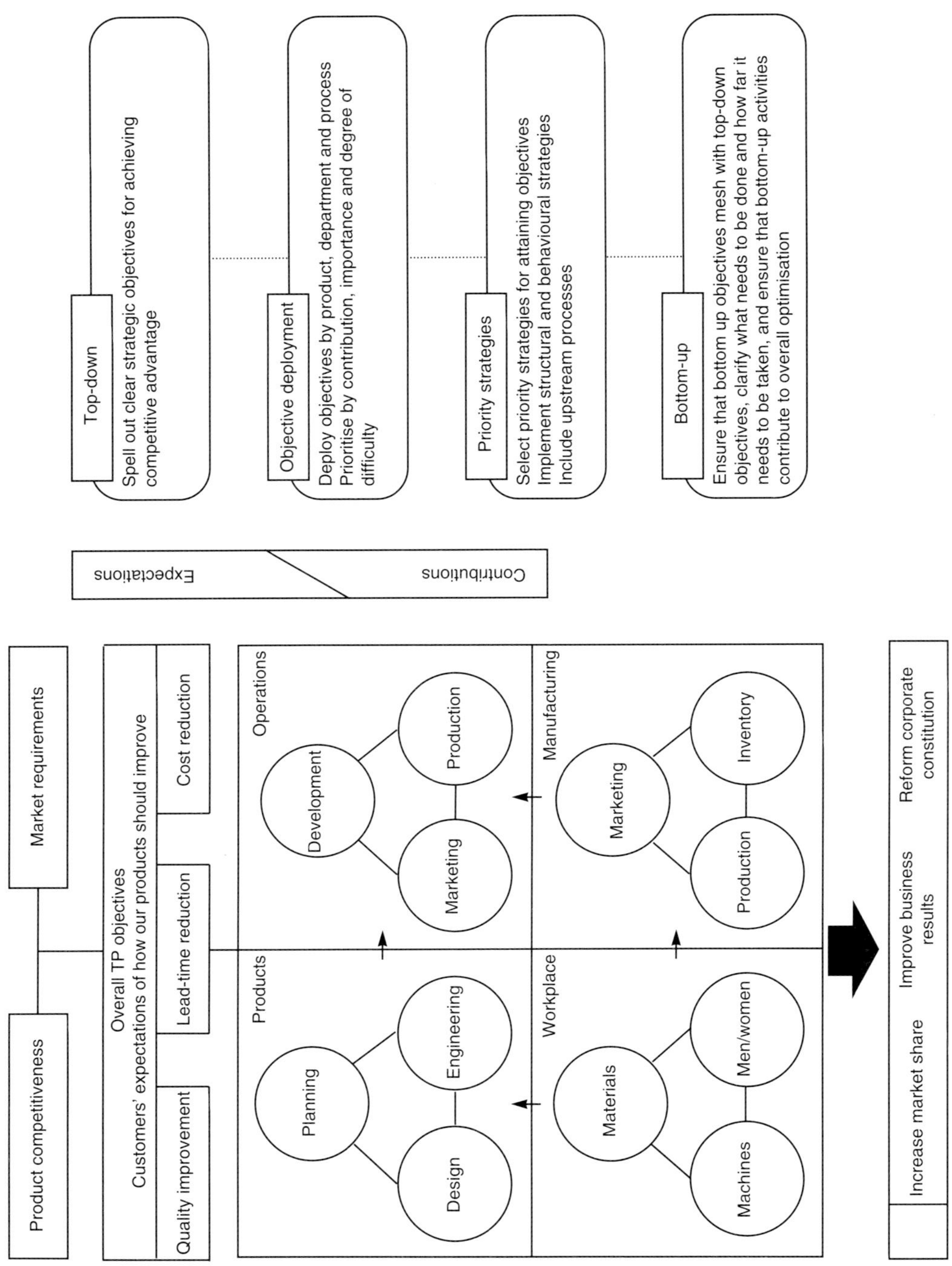

Figure 3.5 (b) Example of TP Management Development Scenario

Part 3

Case Studies

4
Toshiba Corporation, Ōme Works

Slashing Development, Production and Marketing Lead Times Through CIM-Based TP Management

Kin'ichi Takeda, General Manager
Jun'ichi Iwata, Senior Manager, Production Engineering Department
Jun'ichi Matsuura, Manager, Production Engineering Department
Toshiba Corporation

Introduction

Since coming on stream as the nucleus of Toshiba's information processing systems business in 1968, the Ome Works has produced hardware and software for devices equipped with the latest in systems technology, electronics and mechatronics. These devices include information processing systems, OA equipment, peripheral devices and other products designed to meet the needs of our increasingly computerised society. The plant has always handled all the links in the supply chain, from development and design to manufacturing and shipping.

The Ome Works' main products include distributed processing computers, minicomputers, LAN equipment, packet-switching devices, data-exchange devices, office computers, personal computers, word processors, and a variety of workstations, OCR devices, magnetic disk devices and other computer peripherals, as well as a wide range of computer systems and communications systems combining all of the above.

Ōme Works' Position Within Toshiba's Corporate Structure

Toshiba is one of Japan's largest all-round electrical equipment manufacturers. Its three main business areas are heavy electrical machinery, consumer electricals, and data communications systems/electronic devices. The company's data communications operation is at the heart of its "I Strategy", intended to win Toshiba the leading position in these new businesses and new markets.

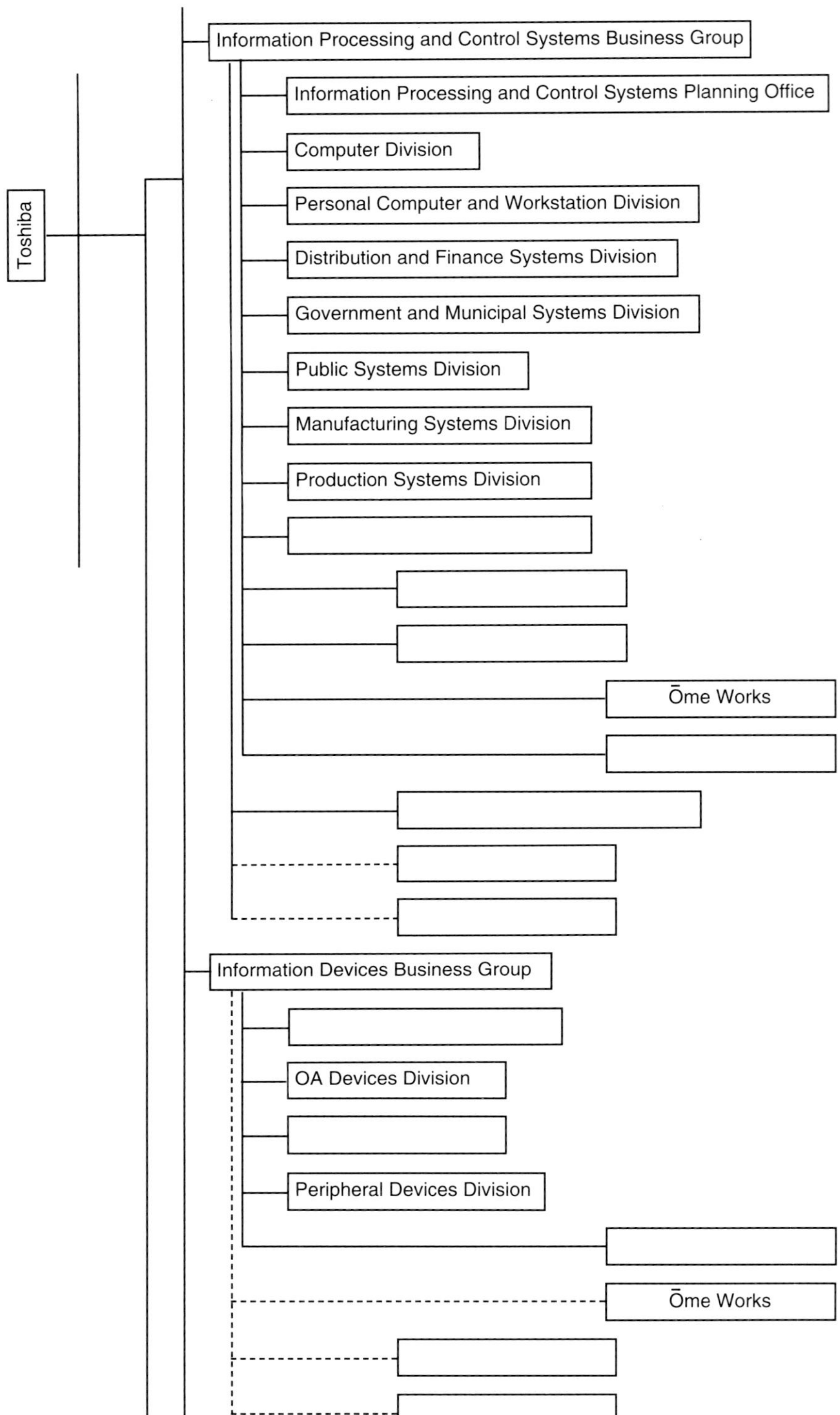

Figure 4.1 Position of Ōme Works within Toshiba's Corporate Structure

Toshiba's "I Strategy" was named after the following three "I's": "Integration" of the information-processing technology and communications technology amassed in the company's years as a general electrical manufacturer; the "Intelligence" needed for the development of a society founded on sophisticated data processing; and "Information", the bedrock of today's knowledge-intensive society.

The Ōme Works, where the "I Strategy" is being implemented, is responsible for the development, design and manufacturing functions of seven of the divisions belonging to the Information Processing & Control Systems Business Group and two of the departments belonging to the Information Devices Business Group (Figure 4.1).

Size of Plant

- Site area: 120,000m^2
- Floor area: 75,000m^2
- Number of employees: approximately 2,500

Adapting to Changes in the Commercial Climate

The "Three Companywide Campaigns"

Confronted with a changing market, major innovations in technology, increasingly internationalised production, and other upheavals in the commercial environment, Toshiba is implementing a number of companywide reforms. Some, like the "I Strategy", take a "vertical" approach, aiming to develop new generations of established products. The Three Companywide Campaigns, however, cut across the company horizontally, their goal being to improve quality in manufacturing, marketing and technology.

Figure 4.2 shows how the Three Companywide Campaigns relate to each other. The first to be launched was the TP Campaign, shown at the bottom left-hand corner of the triangle. The production systems for the mature products that Toshiba had been manufacturing for many years dated from Japan's period of high economic growth, when the company had introduced large, high-speed, dedicated installations designed for mass-production. The warehouses employed by these systems were not centralised, so products had to be carried to and fro. To adapt to leaner times, Toshiba launched its TP Campaign in June 1985. This was a productivity rationalisation campaign revolving around the production control and manufacturing functions. Its aim was to identify and eradicate the basic failings of a system created in the high-growth years, replacing it with a new, flexible system able to react to market demands.

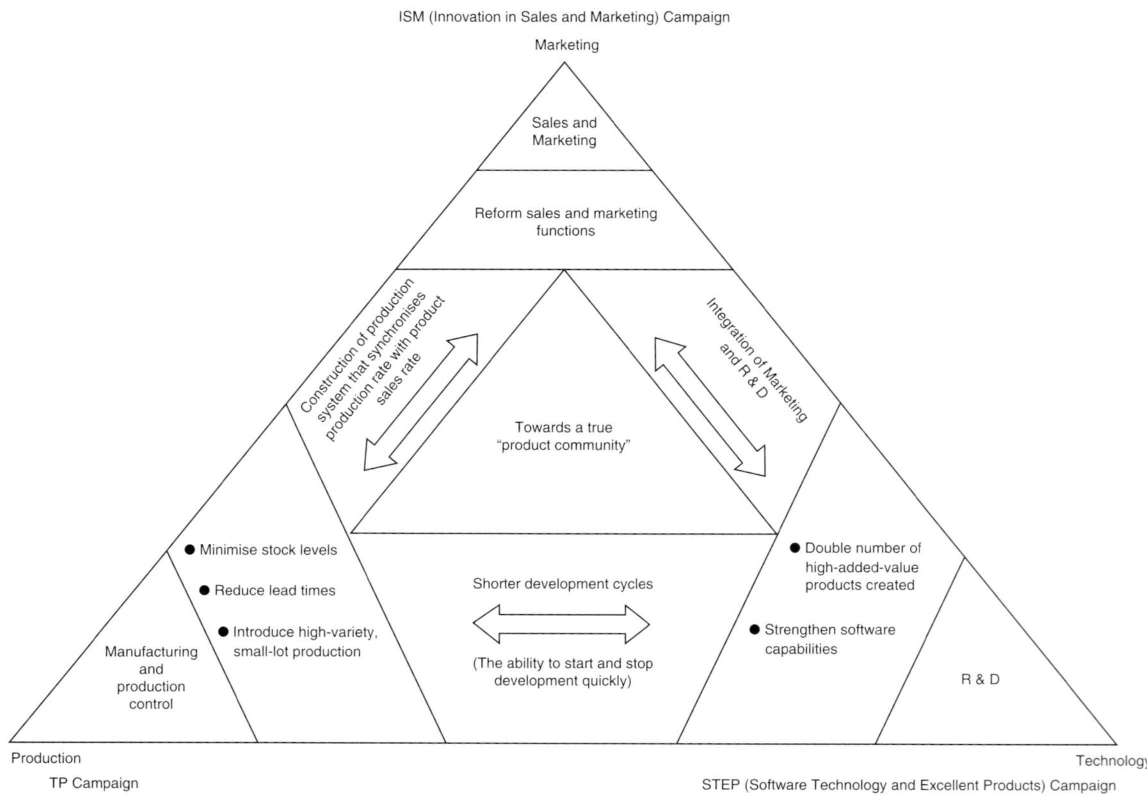

Figure 4.2. The Three Companywide Campaigns

The STEP Campaign, shown at the bottom right-hand corner of the triangle, began in April 1987, focusing on technology. Its aims were to double the number of high-added-value products created over the next three-year period and enhance the company's software production capabilities.

The ISM Campaign, shown at the top of the triangle, targeted the sales function. Its goal was to double the company's sales capacity in three years by raising the quality of its sales operations and creating a system that increased the visibility of the sales effort.

By implementing the Three Companywide Campaigns, Toshiba aimed to create a "fast-reacting, highly-sensitive product community".

TP Management Deployment at Ōme Works

Against the background of the Three Companywide Campaigns described above, the Ōme Works is also deploying TP Management with a new touch – the idea of "tailoring" the system to the specialities of its products. This process is outlined below.

Setting Total Productivity Targets

Why is time-to-market so important?

The commercial constraints on the Ōme Works' products are:

Increasingly diverse user needs
Increasingly fierce market competition
Faster and faster technical advances
Shorter and shorter product life-cycles
Less and less chance to benefit from economies of scale
Increasingly internationalised corporate activities

The main tasks facing Toshiba were to set up a production control system capable of adapting quickly to these changes, and find a way to get top-selling products on to the market at the right time. This could not be done without reducing time-to-market, which in turn meant reducing lead times in both production and marketing on the one hand, and development on the other. We therefore set the reduction of these lead times as our overall theme (Figure 4.3).

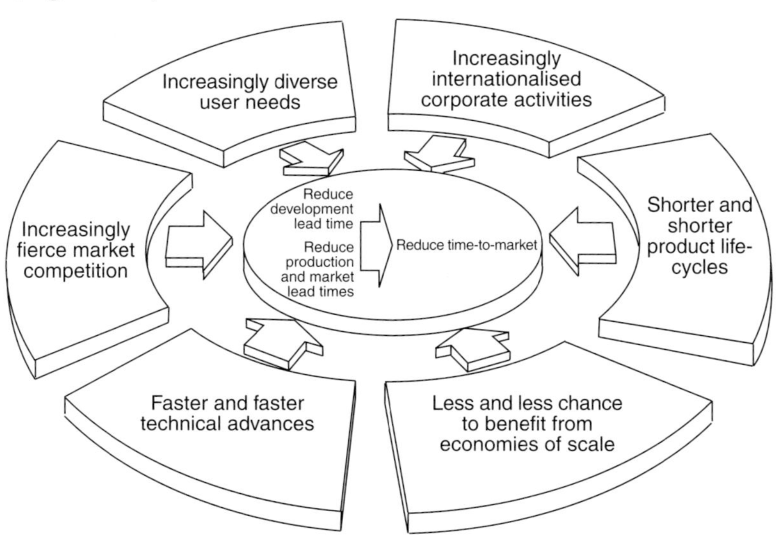

Figure 4.3 Business Environment Surrounding Ōme Works' Products

The Basis of TP Management Deployment

The objectives were deployed top-down, with reducing time-to-market as our overall target. The system created in order to achieve this objective was based on the TP deployment process depicted in Figure 4.4, in which horizontal and vertical "threads" are interwoven to form a matrix. The horizontal thread is the "system capability" of our computer integrated manufacturing(CIM) infrastructure, which uses the plant's resources and technological strength to the full. The vertical thread is the bottom-up implementation of strategies designed to increase the plant's development and production capabilities.

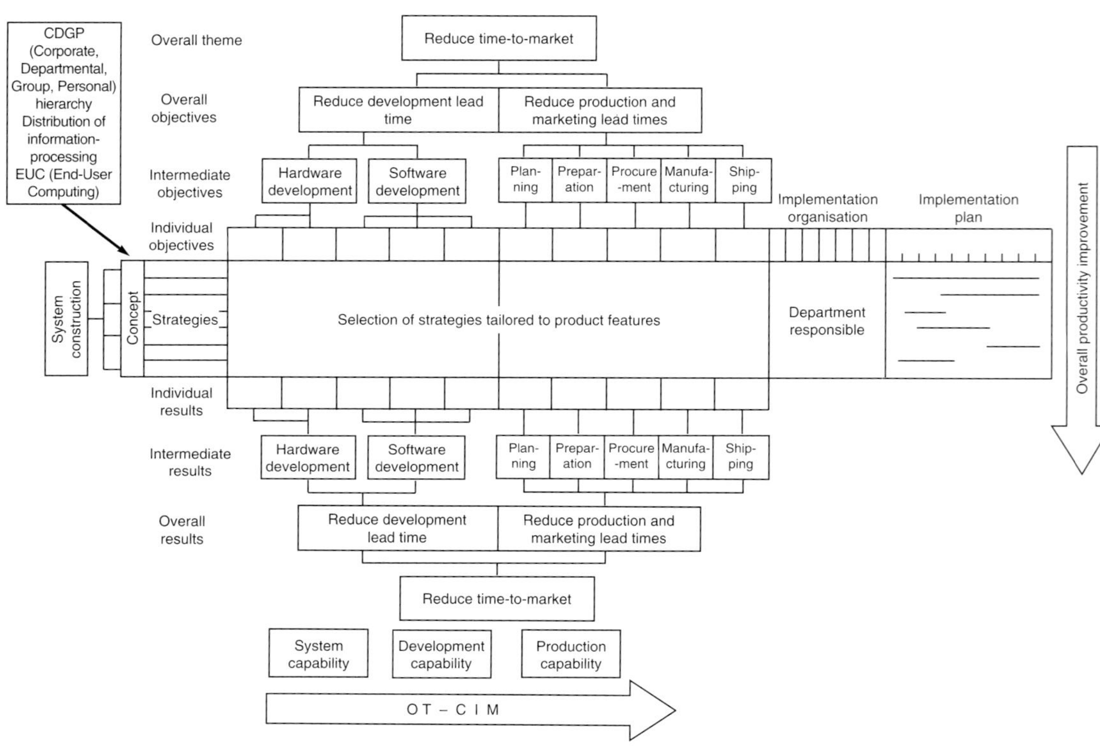

Figure 4.4 Overview of TP Management System for Overall Productivity

The keynote of TP Management at the plant was the way operations were speeded up by radical reductions of work in progress (WIP) and idle time in the handling of both physical objects and information. Instead of a piecemeal approach, this was done comprehensively, from a consistent viewpoint. One of the chief obstacles to improving total productivity is the barriers formed by interdivisional cultural differences, systems and ways of thinking. If we had left these barriers in place, and tried to raise efficiency through local optimisation, the overall waste would probably actually have increased.

To overcome this problem and proceed towards total optimisation, it is essential to expose the hidden waste of management resources caused by partial optimisation. At this plant, interdivisional barriers were broken down by judicious use of techniques such as information-sharing and "increasing visibility". The systems set up for these purposes were tailored to the different characteristics of product categories such as make-to-stock, make-to-order and custom design.

Productivity Improvement Activities Designed to Raise Development and Production Capabilities

Principles and Basic Themes of the TP and STEP Campaigns

The "vertical thread" in this fabric was the productivity improvement drive intended to raise the plant's capacities for development and production. This basically consisted of formulating a "desired scenario", working out effective strategies for achieving it, and then getting everyone involved in implementing these strategies. The launching-pad for this process was our plant's TP and STEP Campaigns, two of the Three Companywide Campaigns alluded to earlier.

As already stated, the basic purpose of these campaigns was to create a "fast-reacting, highly-sensitive product community". To be a market leader, Toshiba has to be highly responsive and highly sensitive to market trends and technical advances. All its employees must know exactly what they are supposed to be doing, and be well versed in the concepts of aiming for improvement and uniting in the pursuit of overall efficiency. Everyone must tune into the basic philosophy of getting the product onto the market.

Working backwards from this idea, we set out our basic themes. One of the basic themes of the TP Campaign was to rethink our approach to manufacturing, creating "a production system that synchronises the production rate with the product sales rate". The other basic idea was to speed up the flow of both physical objects and information by revamping our planning and distribution functions (Figure 4.5).

The basic theme of the STEP Campaign was to create top-selling products by dramatically increasing Toshiba's ability to develop products that satisfy customers' needs, and develop them at the right time (Figure 4.6).

With these basic themes in mind, we proceeded to develop strategies tailored to the special features of various product categories.

Setting Up the CIM Infrastructure

The CIM infrastructure, which forms the "horizontal thread" of the plant's TP matrix, is based on a two-part concept. One part is the distribution of on-line processing using a

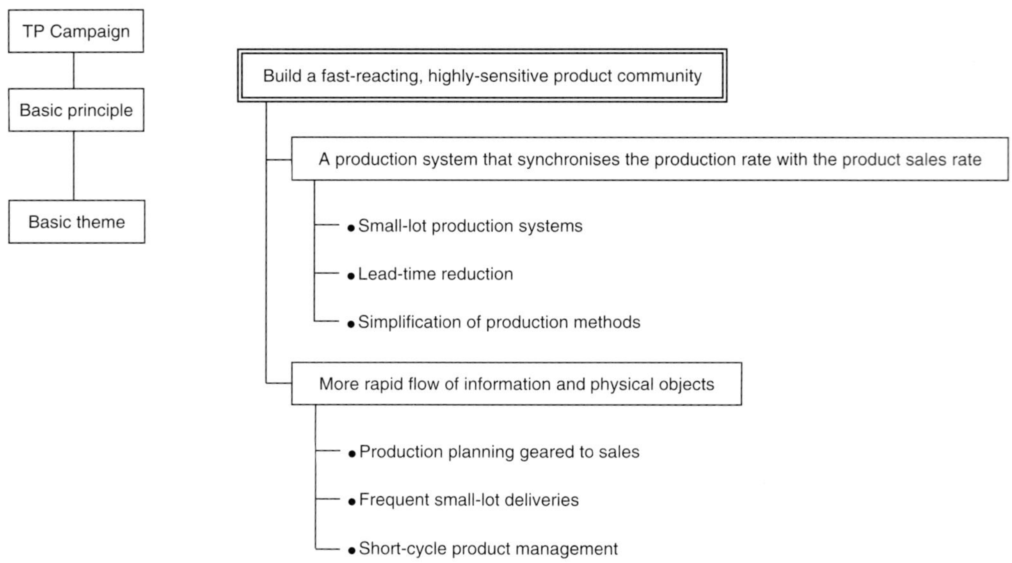

Figure 4.5 Basic Principle of Ōme Works' TP Campaign

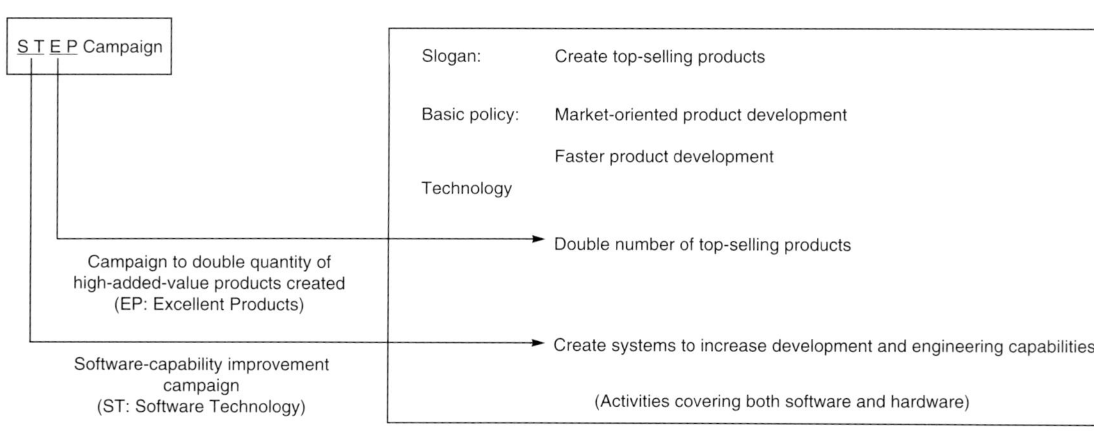

Figure 4.6 Basic Themes of STEP Campaign

CDGP (Corporate, Departmental, Group, Personal) hierarchy instead of a conventional system based on a central host computer and either dedicated terminals or paper documentation. The other is the implementation of EUC (End-User Computing) for on-line, real-time processing, using one or more laptop computers per person.

Implementing EUC (End-User Computing)

EUC was introduced as a tool for speeding up the cycle of acquiring, processing, transmitting and storing information, to help individual employees make appropriate decisions based on up-to-date information in the course of their work (Photographs 4.1 and 4.2). The aim of EUC was to ensure that information could be utilised (acquired, processed, transmitted and stored)

at any time (with 24-hour support)
anywhere (on-line)
with the necessary scope (from selected databases)
quickly (in real time)
simply (with easy operation)
safely (with good security)

Introducing EUC allowed us to improve our work processes by linking every single employee into the computer network.

The CDGP Hierarchy and the Distribution of Information Processing

We wanted to create the kind of office automation (OA), engineering automation (EA) and factory automation (FA) systems that would deliver real results in raising the effectiveness of the work done in each functional area. Our aim in doing this was to achieve overall optimisation through information sharing and "increasing visibility", and we therefore designed our information system around the concepts of a CDGP (Corporate, Departmental, Group, Personal) hierarchy and distributed processing. Figure 4.7 illustrates these concepts, while Figure 4.8 is a schematic diagram of our plant's computer network.

Integrating the CIM Infrastructure with the Productivity Improvement Drive

The goal of TP Management at this plant was not just to speed things up, but to ensure that "total productivity" really was "total", by breaking down barriers between people, divisions and systems. This was done by working top-down from the overall productivity target of reducing time-to-market. The sub-objectives were integrated with the "vertical thread" of improving development and production capabilities and the "horizontal thread" of the CIM infrastructure. Strategies and methodologies tailored to our various product categories were systematised and linked in with practical system development. The integration of production and marketing was tailored to the product category. In the case of make-to-stock products, for example, the "tailoring" consisted of improving the accuracy of sales forecasts by monitoring sales information using a real-time database. In the case of make-to-order products, "tailoring" meant reducing lead times and accommodating earlier delivery dates. This was done by preparing for production on the basis of "unfinalised" information – such as unconfirmed orders

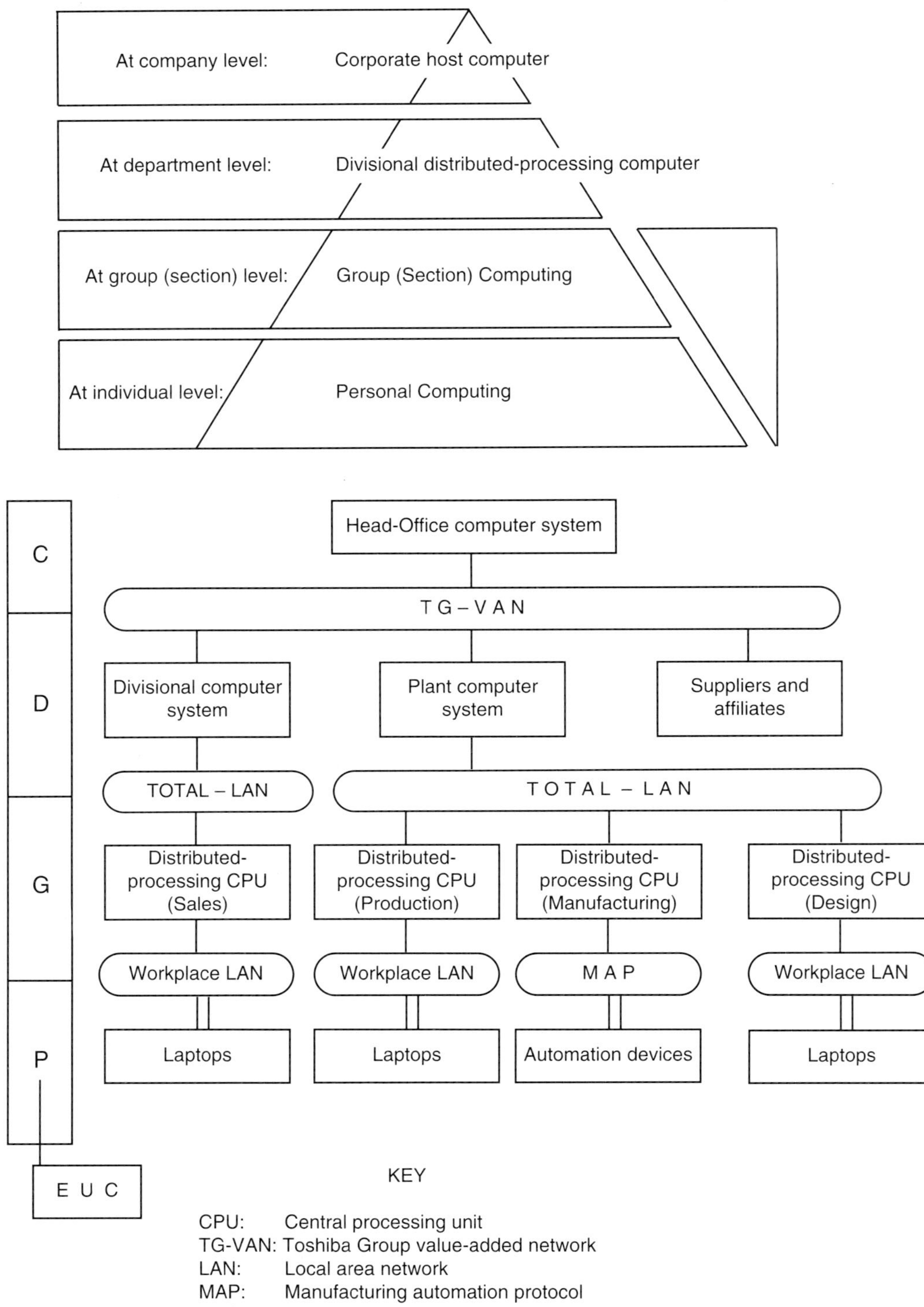

Figure 4.7 CDGP (Corporate, Departmental, Group, Personal)

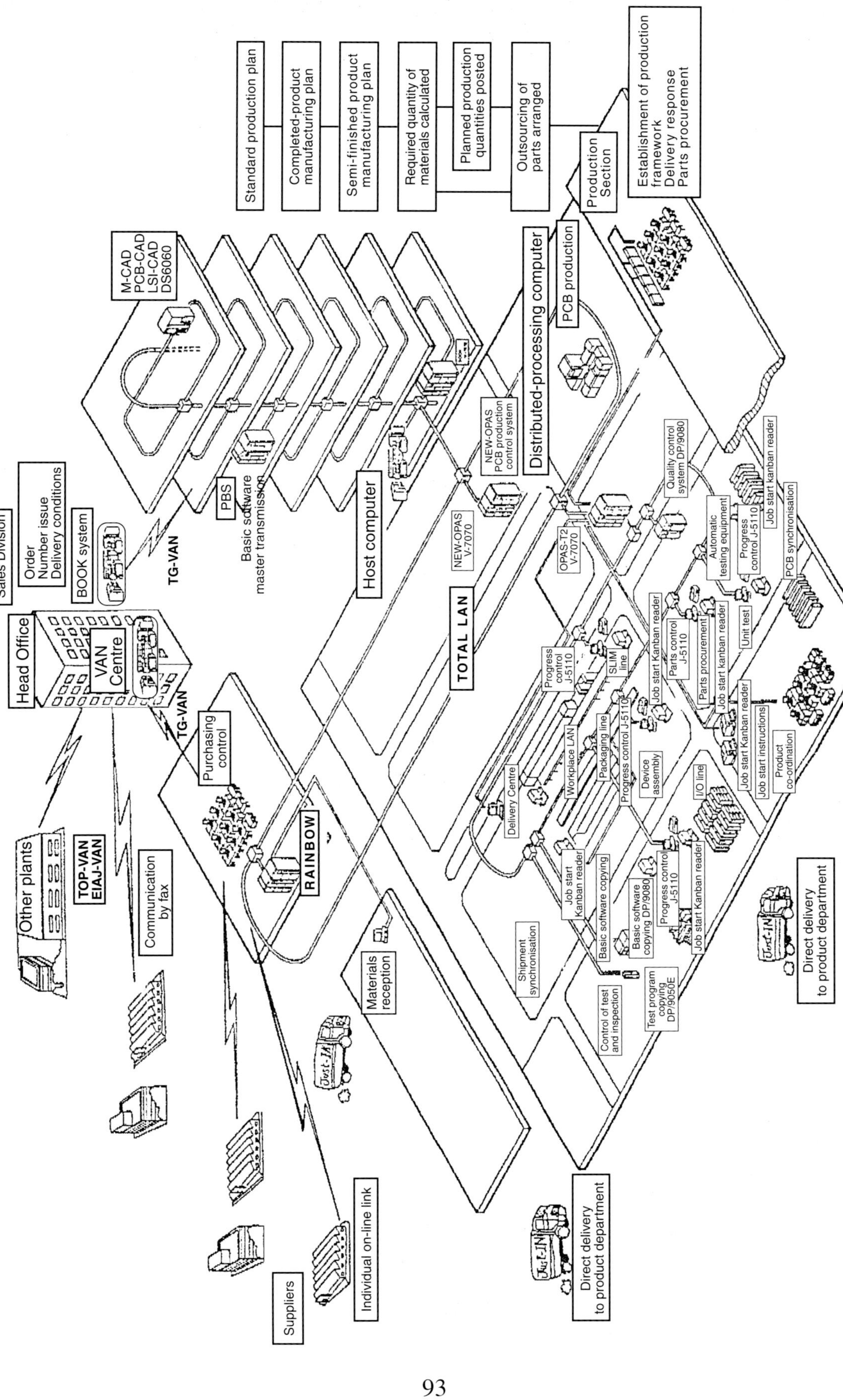

Figure 4.8 Schematic Diagram of Ōme Works' Computer Network

Photograph 4.1 Engineering Centre Office

Photograph 4.2. Manufacturing Support Office

received from the Marketing Department – while continuously monitoring the finalisation process. Conversely, in the case of custom-designed products, "tailoring" meant starting out with finalised information. Figure 4.9 shows the how the "horizontal thread" of our plant's CIM infrastructure was interwoven with the "vertical thread" of the productivity improvement drive. This is a close-up view of the centre left-hand part of the overall TP deployment diagram.

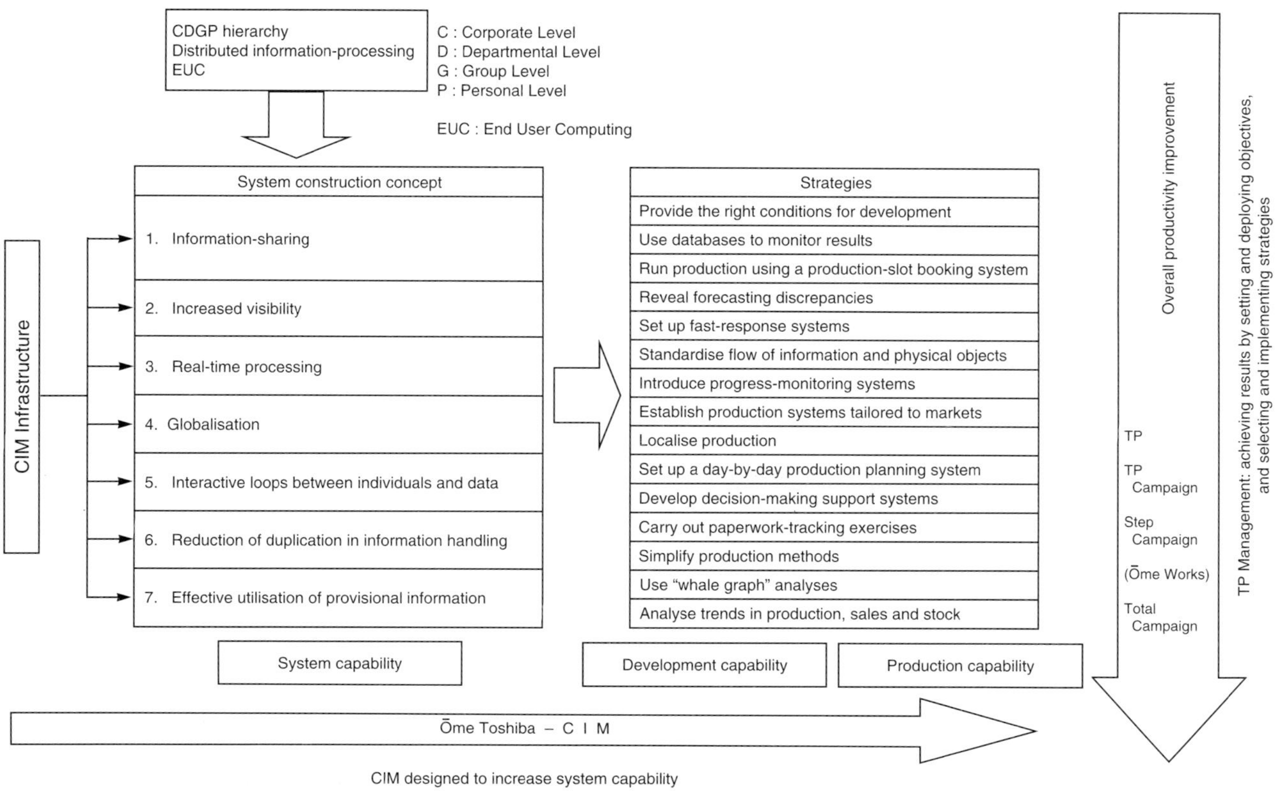

Figure 4.9 Fusing CIM with the Productivity Improvement Drive

So far, we have given a general picture of the main features of TP Management as deployed at the Ōme Works. In the remainder of this report, we shall outline the results of TP Management in the case of a specific product: the word processor, one of Toshiba's main make-to-stock products.

Word Processors: A Case Study in TP Deployment

The Japanese word processor grew out of the computer technology originally developed for processing Japanese script. Toshiba led the way, launching the first such word processor in 1978. At first, Japanese word processors were sold almost exclusively for office use, but with the launch of the JW-R10 personal word processor in May 1985, they began to catch on in earnest with the general populace. In the years that followed, Toshiba used all the latest electronics technology to turn OA devices into mainstream products.

During this period, electronics technology advanced by leaps and bounds, and many other manufacturers entered the field, whipping up savage competition to develop new products for the domestic market. Companies concentrated on high-tech mechatronics technology, so word processors and computers in general became more powerful, smaller, lighter, cheaper, and easier to use. The product trend graph for Toshiba's personal word processors given in Figure 4.10 shows this very clearly. Obviously, in this market climate, the top management priority was to shorten the time-to-market, as mentioned earlier.

Setting Overall Productivity Targets

Table 4.1 shows the overall time-to-market reduction targets for word processors, while Figure 4.11 shows how the overall productivity targets in the TP deployment diagram for word processors were arrived at. TP Management was implemented with the aim of reducing both the development lead time and the production and marketing lead time in steps, by the percentages shown in these diagrams.

Prioritising Objectives

Figure 4.12 shows a specific example of objective deployment and prioritisation in the case of the word processor. Time-to-market (the subject of the overall theme) is split into development lead time and production and marketing lead time, defined below. These are then further broken down in accordance with the flow diagram for each process, and the resulting targets are assigned as individual objectives.

Reducing Development Lead Times

The development lead time subsequent to the product planning stage can be divided into hardware development lead time and software development lead time. Hardware and software development are interrelated, more or less parallel tasks. In trying to reduce the development lead time, the critical path through these tasks must therefore always take priority in the process of working out individual objectives and selecting the strategies for achieving them.

Reducing Production and Marketing Lead Time

Production and marketing lead time was divided into the five categories defined below. At the level of individual objective deployment and strategy selection, the categories were linked together to allow overall optimisation, although each department was assigned clear responsibilities in terms of the improvements it was expected to make at each stage.

Lead-Time Category	Start	Step 1	Step 2	Step 3
Development Lead-Time	—	1	3/4 (25%)	1/2 (50%)
Production and Marketing Lead-Time	1	2/3 (37%)	1/3 (65%)	1/6 (83%)

Figures in brackets show percent reductions

Table 4.1. Overall Objectives for Word Processors

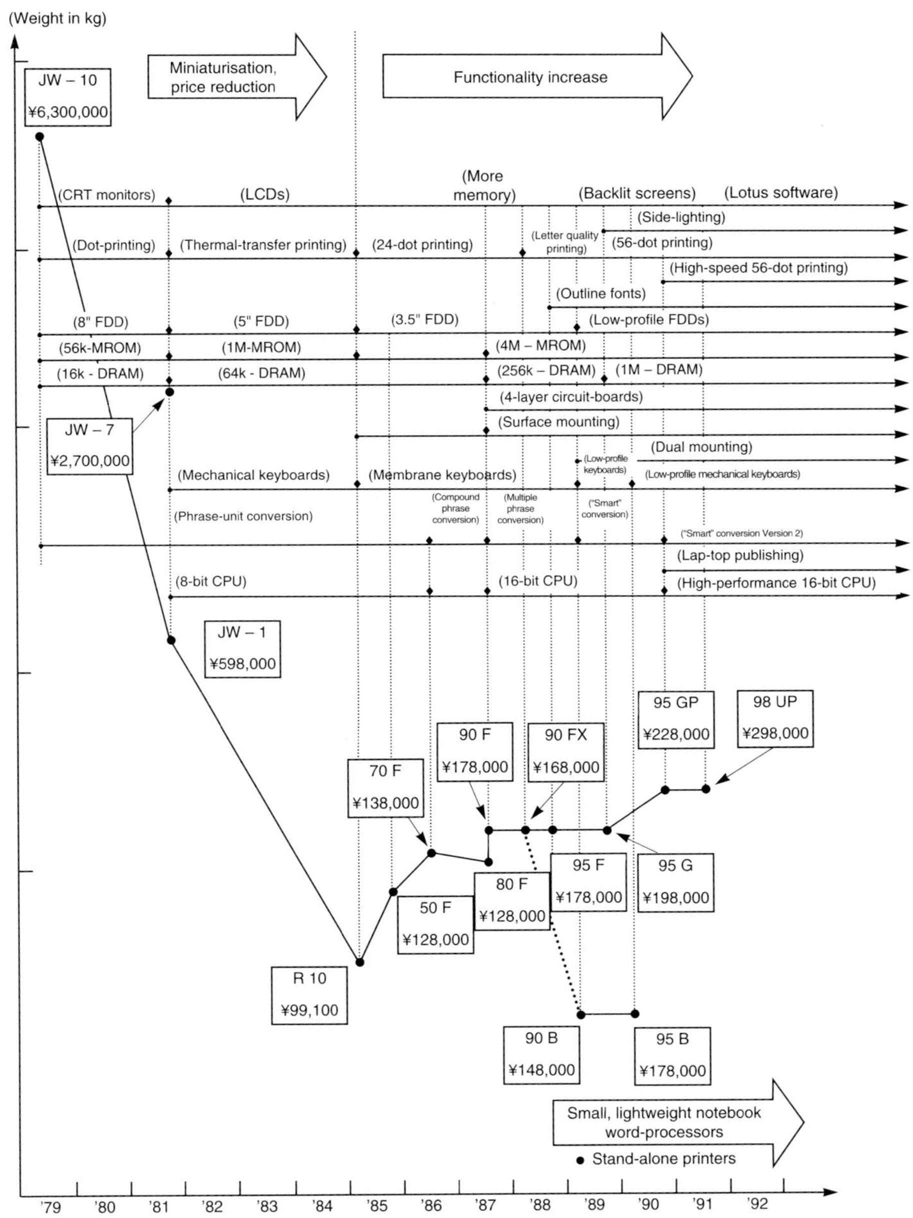

Figure 4.10 Product Trends for Toshiba's Personal Word Processors

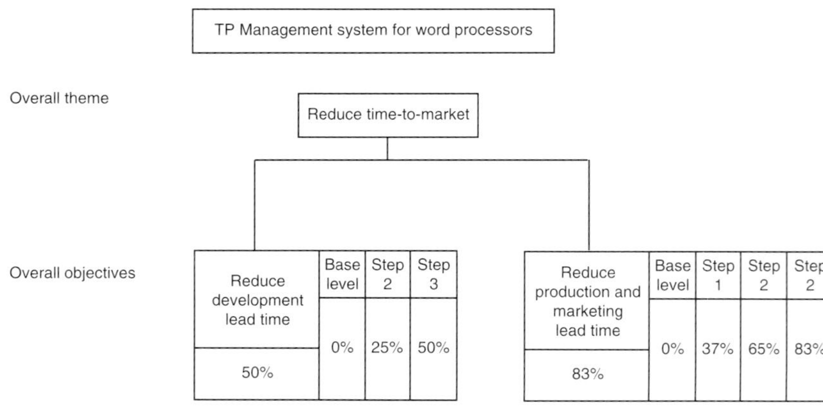

Figure 4.11 Setting Overall Productivity Targets for Word Processors

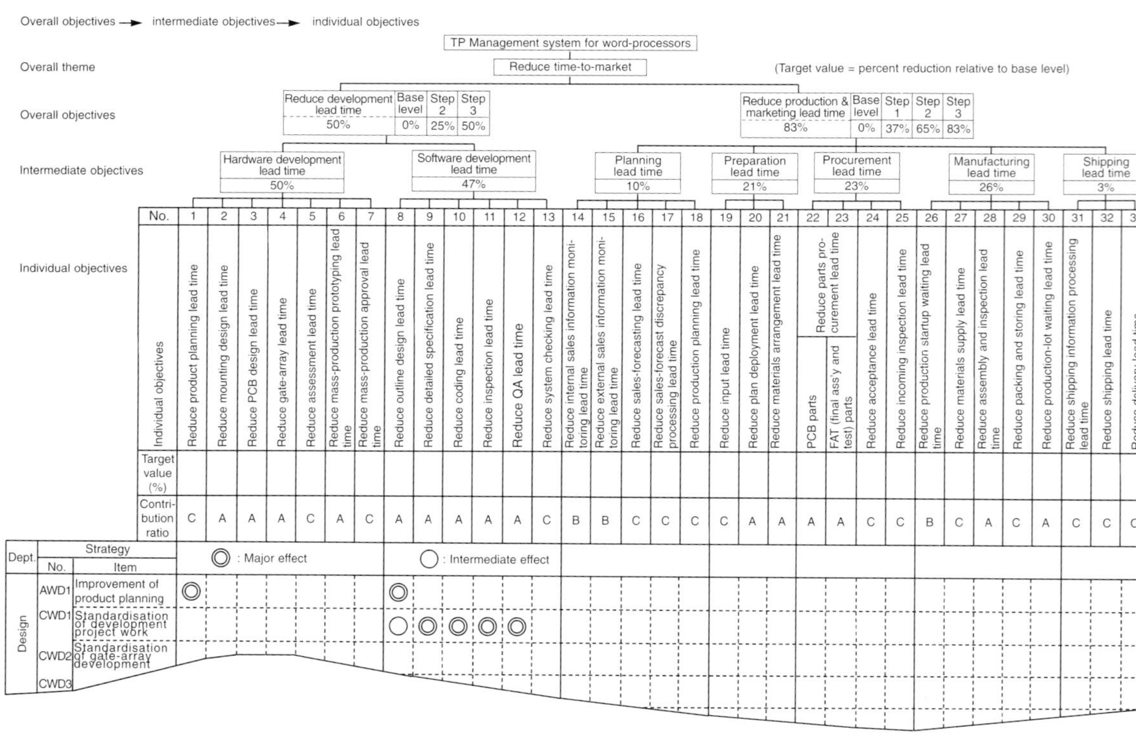

Figure 4.12 Specific Example of Objective Deployment

1. Planning lead time

This is the number of days required to calculate business performance from collated sales data, predict discrepancies in production, sales and stocks estimates, revise the production plan, and notify the appropriate departments.

2. Preparation lead time

Measured from the date on which production instructions are received, this is the number of days required to calculate the quantity of materials required and either place orders with suppliers or notify them of delivery dates for pre-placed orders.

3. Procurement lead time

This is the number of days from the date on which the suppliers receive their instructions (i.e. the date on which the order is placed or the suppliers are notified of the delivery date for pre-placed orders) until the plant takes delivery of the materials and completes the acceptance procedure.

4. Manufacturing lead time

This is the number of days elapsed from acceptance of materials until warehousing of completed products.

5. Shipping lead time

This is the number of days elapsed from the date on which shipping instructions are received until the date on which the goods arrive at their destination.

Strategy Selection: a Practical Example

As explained in the foregoing pages, the creation of a CIM infrastructure was cross-linked with the productivity improvement drive, and the individual objectives for word processors reflect this. Figure 4.13 shows some of the most effective strategies selected for achieving the individual objectives. It is part of a matrix designed to show systematically where the priorities lie in each of the strategies. Its vertical axis shows four top-priority strategies: "improve development efficiency", "set up day-by-day production planning system", "simplify production methods", and "introduce small-lot production", while its horizontal axis shows the three functions responsible for executing one or more of these strategies – Design, Production Control, and Manufacturing. The cells of the matrix contain numbered sub-strategies, some of which we shall now explain.

Priority Department		Design Department	Supply/Demand Planning	Manufacturing
Individual Strategies	Improve development efficiency	1. Speed up gate-array development 2. Eliminate waste in software development processes 3. Speed up development of kana-kanji conversion dictionary 4. Speed up font development		
	Set up day-by-day production planning system		1. Monitor external sales information • PSI (production, sales and inventory) 2. Improve accuracy of sales forecasting • "Match-race" competition • "Whale graphs" 3. Perform production planning more frequently • Total stock (days)	1. Control of ordering and delivery separately 2. Rationalise delivery
	Simplify production methods	1. Implement variety reduction programme 2. Expedite production design	1. Do paperwork-tracking exercises	1. Improve parts synchronisation rate 2. Increase frequency of incoming deliveries 3. Improve packaging of incoming deliveries 4. Streamline production flow
	Introduce small-lot production	3. Standardise mounting design		1. Produce all models every day 2. Improve parts supply 3. Make production lines more compact 4. Improve buffer, flow and intensity values 5. Reduce number of labour-hours 6. Extend error-proofing systems 7. Improve straight-through rate

Figure 4.13 Priority Strategy Selection for Word Processors

Using "Whale Graphs" for More Accurate Sales Forecasting and Better Strategic Production Planning

A "whale graph" (see inset of Figure 4.14) shows the sales figures for a particular model up the vertical axis, versus time along the horizontal axis. The name comes from the shape of the graph, which resembles the back of a surfacing whale, especially in the case of an "instant-hit" product such as a word processor. The graph's sales data is compiled from figures obtained from Toshiba's own information centre as well as from external data survey organisations, trade journals, fixed-point surveys carried out at railway stations, and so on. Several of these "whale graphs" can be plotted against sales price as in Figure 4.14 to permit an at-a-glance comparison of the sales performance of different models. They are also used to analyse market trends and sales trends for individual models, and these analyses are in turn used in adjusting production in line with product planning, sales forecasting, strategic production planning, and changing sales trends.

"More Frequent Production Planning" to Keep Pace with Market Fluctuations

To enable us to adjust production promptly to market fluctuations, we constructed an on-line network linking us to our marketing companies. Thanks to this network, we can continually update the sum totals of our sales, warehouse stocks and other stocks in real time. Simulations based on day-to-day fluctuations in these figures, combined with forward planning, enable us to predict future deviations from standard stock levels and "sound the alarm" so that production plans can be adjusted to restore normal stock levels. This has allowed us to shorten the production planning cycle, adjust production more frequently, and maintain minimal stock levels.

"Paperwork Tracking": an Improvement Strategy for Overall Optimisation

Paperwork tracking is a technique for tearing down the barriers between people, departments and systems, shortening lead times, reducing data-processing work-in-progress (WIP), eliminating waste, and effecting other improvements conducive to overall optimisation. It is used to discover when, by whom, where and how information is processed, how and to whom it is delivered, and how many levels of the organisation it passes through from origination to end use. To perform a paperwork tracking exercise, a number of large sheets of paper are pinned along a wall, side by side. All the paperwork used – forms, slips, chits, vouchers, printed documents, handwritten memos and so on – is attached to these sheets in a sequence representing the complete process flow, starting with marketing, moving through sales, and ending with revenue collection. This renders the entire paperwork process visible to anyone at a glance,

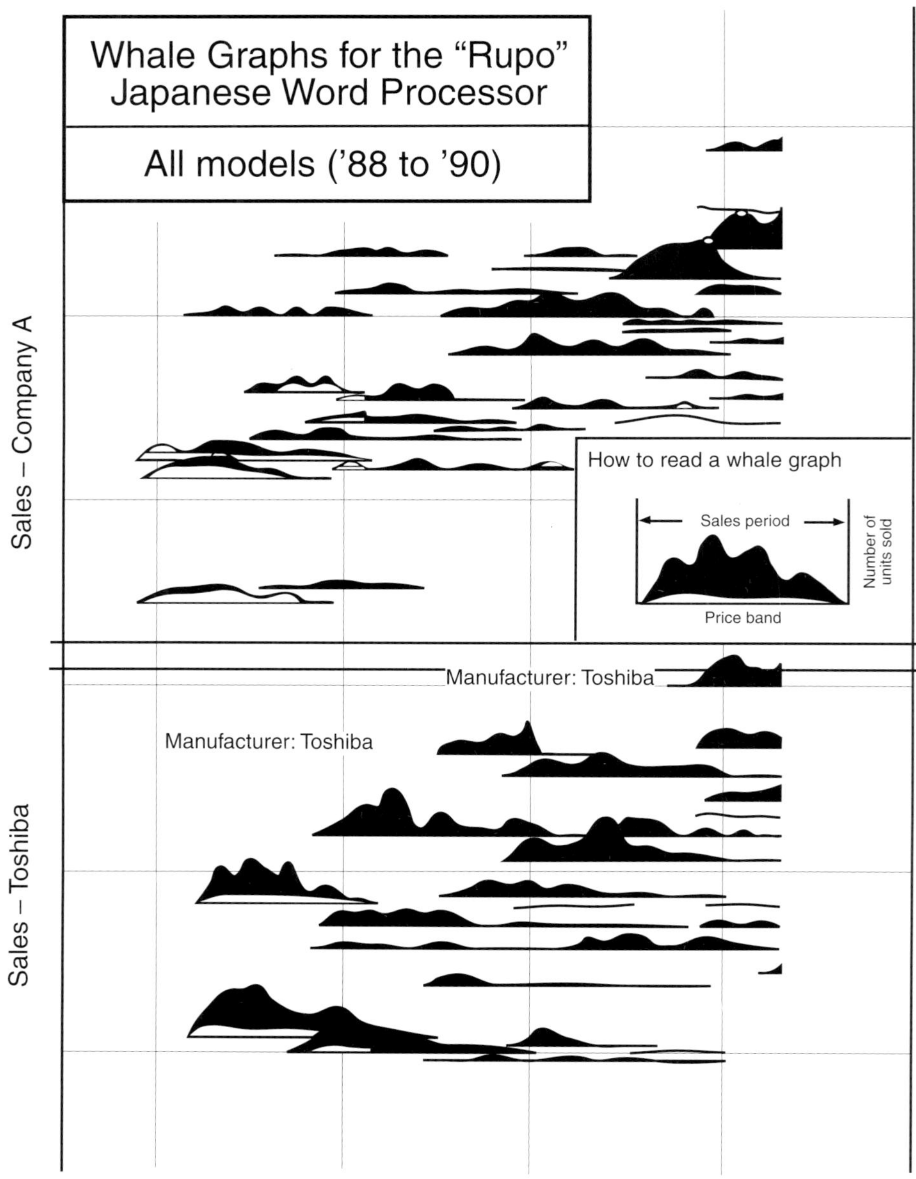

Figure 4.14 Whale Graphs

making it much easier to identify and classify problems and work out strategies to solve them. Photograph 4.3 shows the paperwork-tracking display for word processors, which reached a length of 21 metres. The progress of improvement can be gauged from the number of metres cut off the length of the paperwork-tracking chart, the reduction in the number of stages the paperwork passes through, and the reduction in the number of pieces of paper used.

Quantifying Workplace Improvement Using "B", "F" and "I" Values

As mentioned earlier, we wanted to set up a "production system that synchronises the production rate with the product sales rate". To this end, we designed flexible production systems using speedy, simplified small-lot production methods. To quantify improvement in the production lines at our plant, we used the "B", "F" and "I" values explained below.

1. "B" (buffer) value
The buffer value is the number of pieces of work-in-progress on a particular production line divided by the number of processes performed on that line. The larger the figure, the more wasteful the line. The target value is 1.

2. "F" (flow) value
The flow value is the time scheduled for the work divided by the number of labour hours actually used. The higher the figure, the more wasteful the line. Again, the target value is 1.

3. "I" (intensity) value
The intensity value (a new concept devised at our plant) is an index of the intensity of the work being done on a production line. It is defined as follows:

I value = (work-factor rating) x (line balance ratio) (%)

This index is based on the principle that a line is only working really effectively when

Photograph 4.3 Example of Paperwork-Tracking Display

both the work speed and the line balance are good (Figure 4.15).

All three values are assessed in terms of zones corresponding to ranks. The values are carefully monitored, and our aim is to raise each value by one rank every six months.

Results of Activities

Results for Overall Objectives for word processors

As Figure 4.16 shows, we achieved the following overall results, thereby attaining our objectives:

Development lead time: approximately halved in 3.5 years
Production and marketing lead time: reduced to approximately one-sixth in 5.5 years

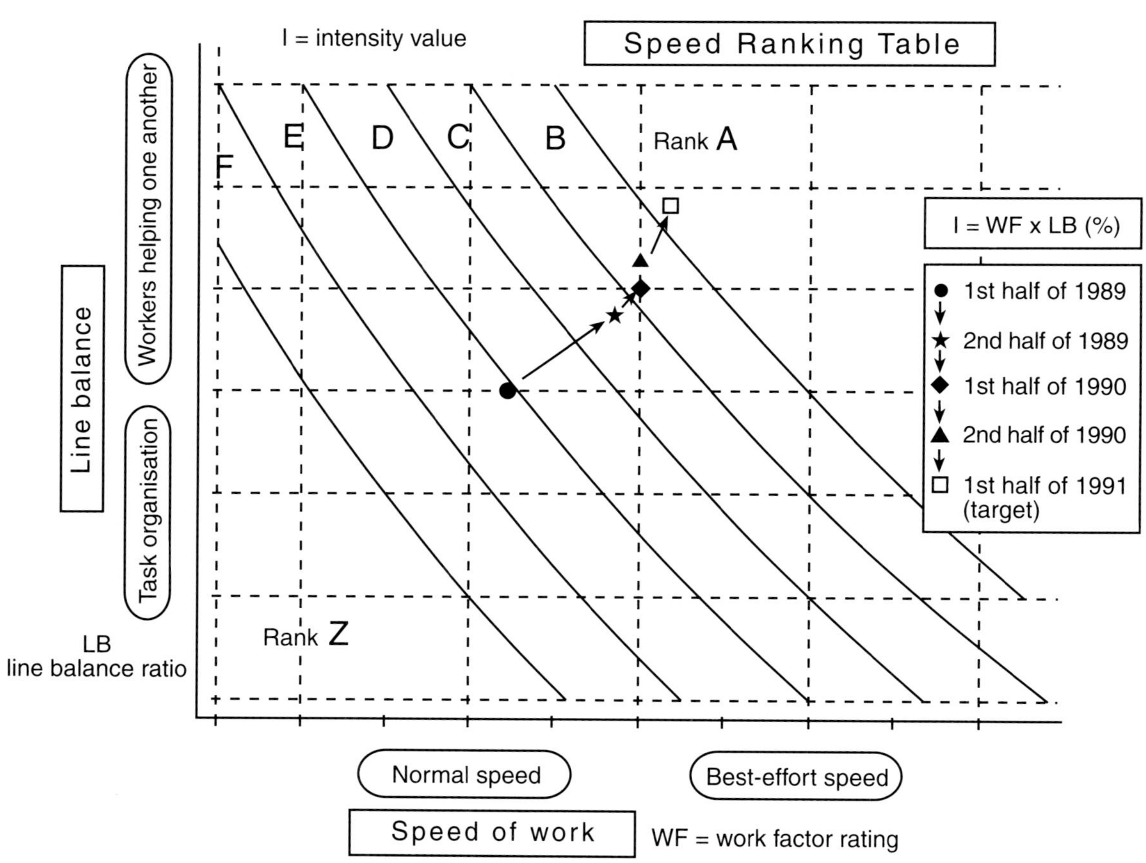

Figure 4.15 Intensity Value

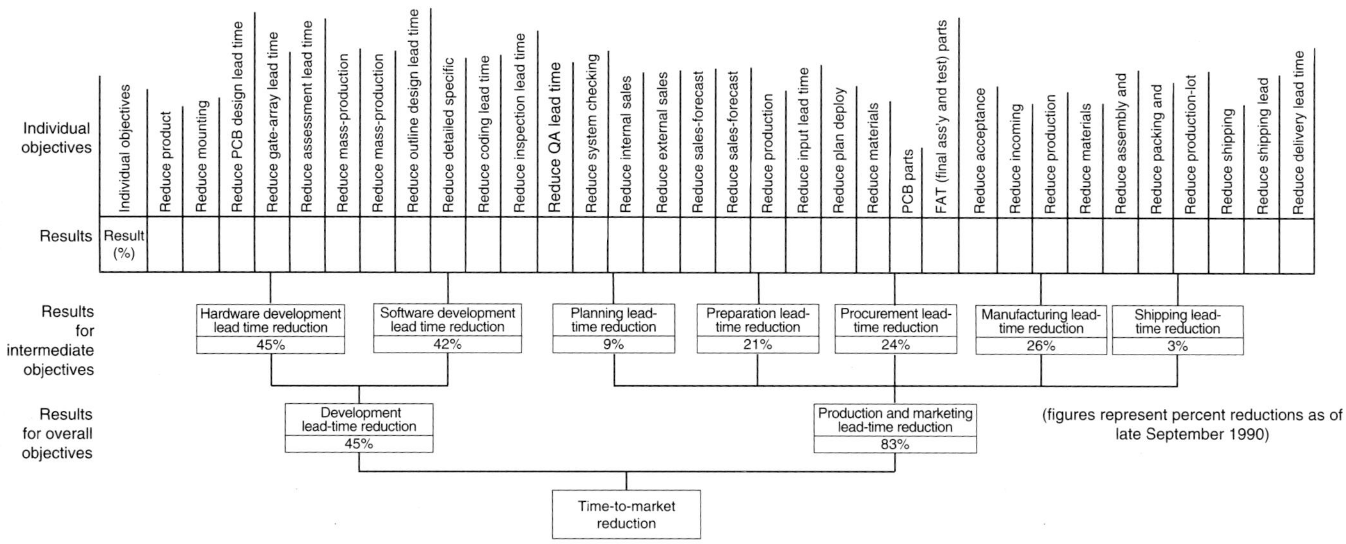

Development lead-time: approximately halved in 3.5 years during period from first half of 1987 to first half of 1990
Production and marketing lead time: reduced to approximately one-sixth in 5.5 years during period from first half of 1985 to first half of 1990

Figure 4.16 Results for Overall Objectives for Word Processors

Results of TP Management and Other Campaigns in the Case of word processors

As well as reducing lead times, we managed to obtain the following results indicative of management efficiency:

Number of days' sales inventory: reduced to approximately one fifth in 5.5 years
Number of days' production inventory: reduced to approximately one seventh in 5.5 years
Labour productivity: approximately tripled in 5.5 years

A variety of sub-objectives were also used as detailed indicators of the effectiveness of the methods we employed. However, there is not sufficient space to describe them all here.

Future Deployment of TP Management

In our view, TP Management at our plant should in future be developed as follows:

1. Use TP Management as a framework for planning any improvements required in terms of quality and cost for the purpose of reducing lead times.

2. Extend the framework of TP Management to include customer-focused product development. The essence of product development is finding out which features and functions the customer wants, and then providing them through quality planning. Lead times are strongly affected by quality issues, such as the need to nip latent problems in the bud even before the pre-production or prototype stages and thereby reduce the amount of rework necessitated by design faults and the like.

3. Strengthen our manufacturing and development capabilities by building systems more closely tailored to our products' characteristics and improving our human resource management systems. We must systematise the relationships between these and establish them as firm guidelines for our CIM development policy, which will form an important means of implementing TP Management in the future.

5
Sekisui Chemical, Kansei Heim Plant

Setting up a TP Management System in a Short Space of Time, Allowing Stocks to be Halved and New-Product Startup to be Accomplished Rapidly Without Sacrificing Quality, While Doubling Scheduled Production Capacity

Eiichi Irino, General Manager, Kansai Heim Plant
Tokurō Tamura, President, Kansai Sekisui Industry
Sekisui Chemical Corporation

Introduction

The plant described in this case study has been in operation since 1971 as part of Sekisui Chemical's Housing Division. This division is the market leader in the production of houses by the unit construction system, in which room modules ("units") are manufactured in the plant and assembled on site. Borrowing the German for "home", Sekisui calls the steel-framed dwellings it builds in this way "Sekisui Heims" (the timber-framed equivalents are called "To-You Homes").

Figure 5.1 shows the Kansai Heim Plant's position within Sekisui Chemical's overall corporate structure, while Figure 5.2 compares the plant's share of the total production of homes with that of the Housing Division's other plants, together with the destinations of the plant's products.

Figure 5.3 contrasts the unit construction system with the conventional construction system and the prefab construction system, while Figure 5.4 shows the production, transportation and installation processes for the unit construction system.

Plant Outline

Site area: 77,300m^2	Number of homes produced per year: 5,714
Factory footprint: 28,600m^2	Number of units produced per year: 73,992
Number of employees: 707	Floor area produced per year: 776,000m^2

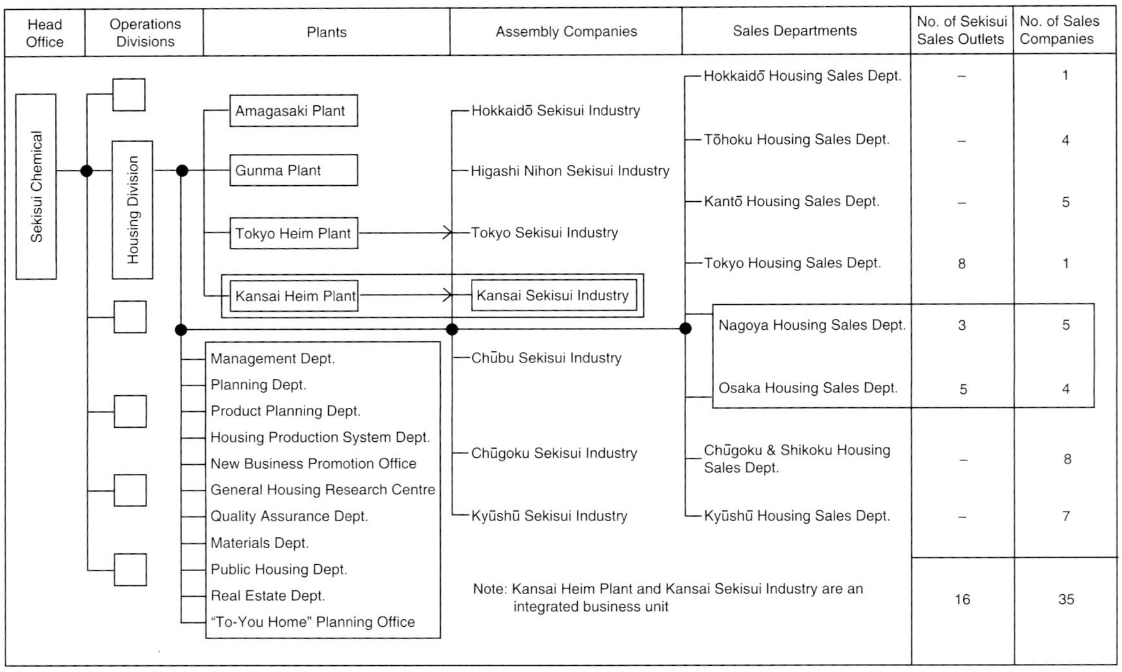

Figure 5.1 Position of Kansai Heim Plant within Sekisui Chemical's Overall Corporate Structure

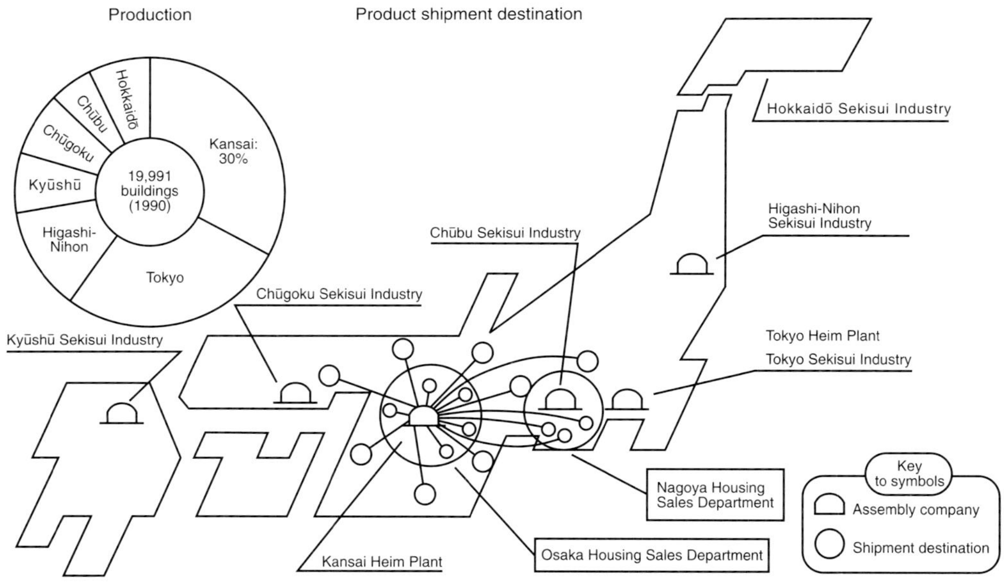

Figure 5.2. Relative Production of Completed Homes by Each Plant; Destinations of Kansai Heim Plant's Products

Organisation

As Figure 5.1 shows, the operation actually consists of the Kansai Heim Plant plus Kansai Sekisui Industry (a member of the Sekisui Group and a company in its own right). The Kansai Heim Plant operates the staff functions, while Kansai Sekisui Industry is responsible for the line functions.

Sekisui Heim Supply System

Figure 5.5 shows the Sekisui Heim supply system. Sekisui Heims are designed by the Housing Division's product planning and product design staff. Based on construction plans finalised by the sales and design functions, materials are then procured and the necessary units are manufactured at the plant. The units are then shipped to the construction site using the company's own transportation system, and the building is handed over to the customer after the construction work has been completed. A Heim Service company then takes over, providing an after-care system that includes free regular checks.

Features and Philosophy of Sekisui Heims

Besides their high quality, Sekisui Heims are best known for their speed of construction, and the standard construction period is now 30 days. This speed has been achieved by fully utilising the advantages of the unit construction system, in which 80% of the production work is carried out at the plant. With this as its basis, our guiding principle has always been to strive for ever higher customer satisfaction.

Background to Introduction of TP Management

Medium-Term Business Plan

One of the factors influencing the operation's medium-term business plan was the Japanese government's policy of expanding domestic consumer demand. As Figure 5.6 shows, the objectives of the medium-term business plan were to double production volume, triple the number of products offered, and quadruple the number of parts used, between 1985 and 1990.

		Production process		Costs	Quality
	Procurement of materials	Manufacturing	Construction		
Conventional System	Materials purchased from builders' merchants	Manufacturing carried out at plant: 0 Construction period	Assembly of components (directed by foreman) 269.0 labour-days/ building	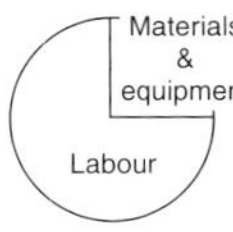	• Highly variable • On-site adjustments needed
Prefab System	Purchased from dealers Some manufactured in-house	Principal components manufactured at plant (Manufacturing carried out at plant: 40%) 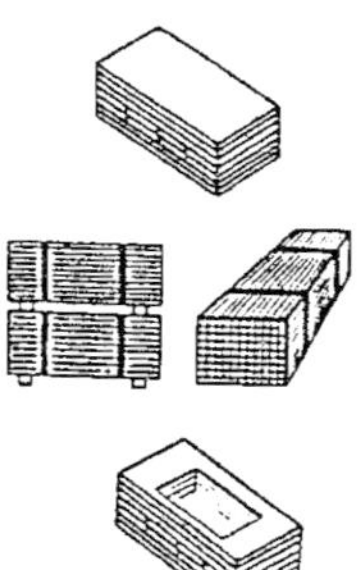 Construction period	Standardised assembly of components 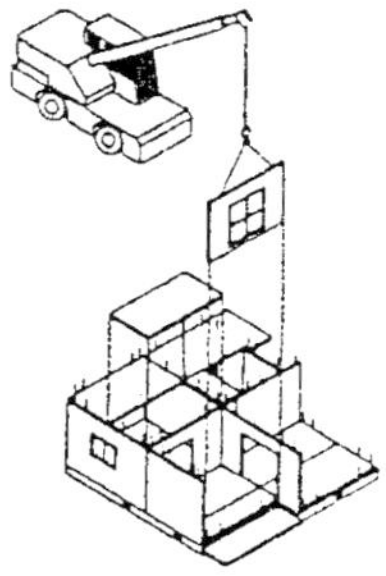 146.6 labour-days/building	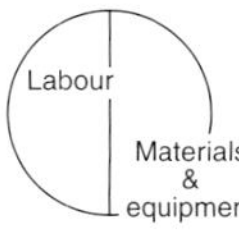	• Highly variable • Experienced, skilled craftsmen needed
Unit System	Only raw materials purchased Principal components manufactured in-house • Standard roofs • Pent roofs • Internal walls • External walls • Bathroom fixtures • Kitchen fixtures • Porches • Stairs • Built-in cupboards	Each living-space is manufactured in-house as a single unit (Manufacturing carried out at plant: 80%) 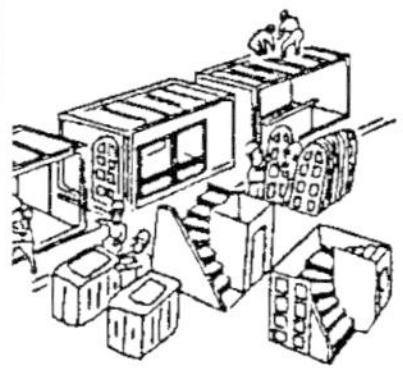 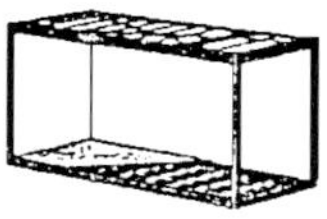 Construction period	Standardised coupling of units 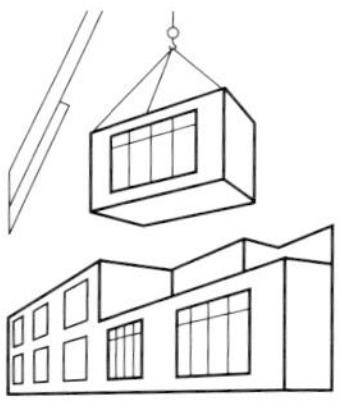 A wide range of needs can be met by combining units of varying sizes and types 64.2 labour-days/building	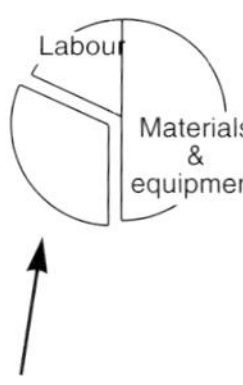 Home functions improved by spending labour cost savings (approx. 50%) on materials and equipment	• Little variation originating in factory production • Very little carpentry required • Skilled craftsmen not required

Figure 5.3 Unit, Conventional and Prefab Construction Systems Compared

Factory production

External wall mounting process

The external walls, which form the building's "face", are preassembled together with the sash windows on sub-assembly lines in the required order. They are mounted on the units in a single operation, using a specially-designed hoist.

Discharge of units

The units are discharged from the assembly line at the rate of one every 1.5 minutes, ready for transportation to the construction site.

Transportation and installation

Units being transported

As the photograph shows, the units are transported to the construction site en masse, using purpose-built trucks. On average, 12 units are used for one building.

Construction site

A Neighbour's Comment

"I'm sure there wasn't a building here when I left for work this morning!"

The living-space units manufactured at the plant are installed by mobile crane in their designated positions. Roofing and weatherproofing are completed in a single day.

Figure 5.4 Production, Transportation and Installation Processes for Unit Construction System

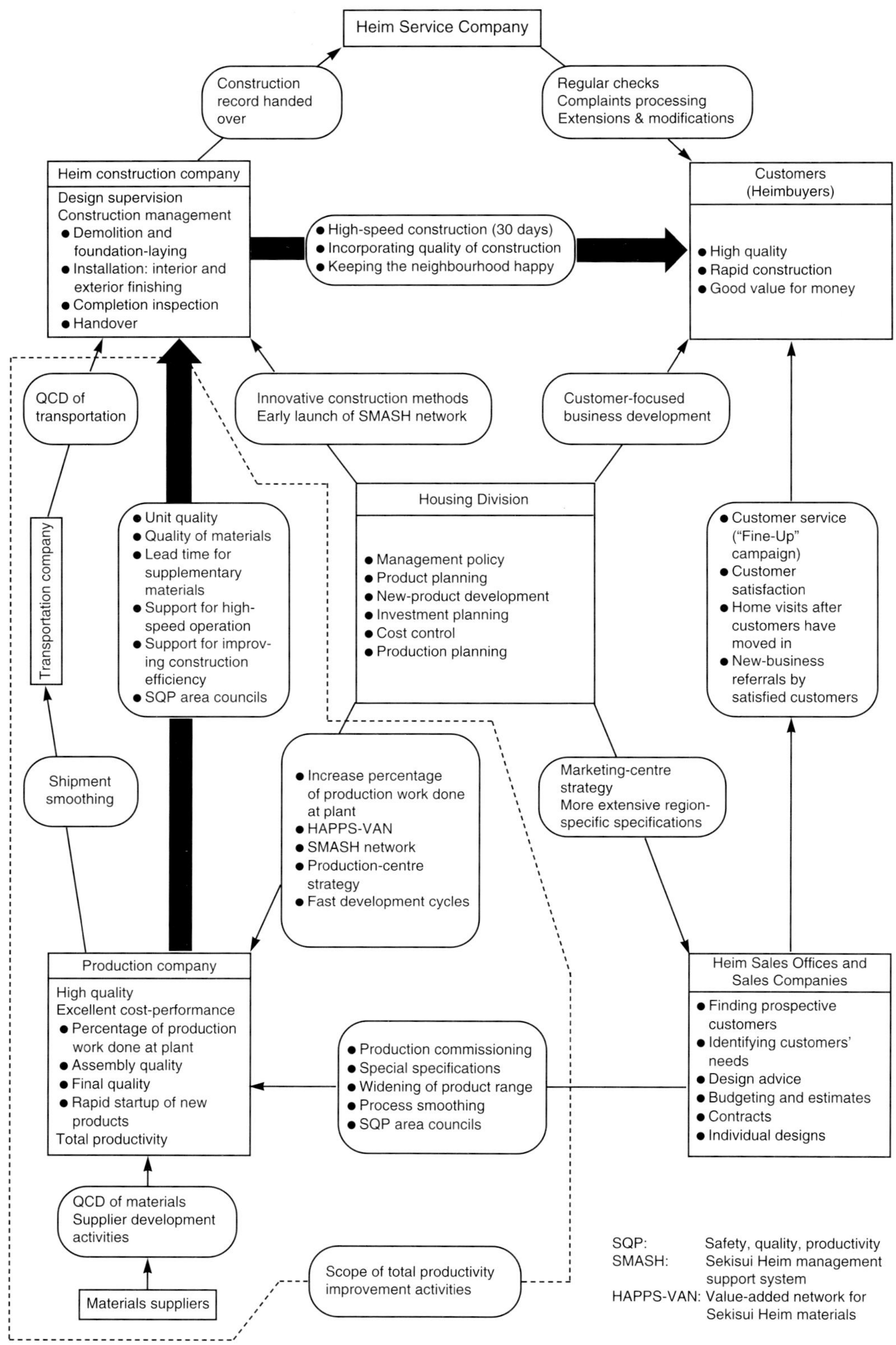

Figure 5.5 Sekisui Heim Supply System

Location Conditions

Figure 5.7 shows the overall layout of the plant. Its principal features are:

1. The plant is spread among five separate sites, some of which are separated by public roads.
2. Three of the sites are leased, making expansion problematical.
3. Expansion is out of the question on the remaining two sites, even though these are owned by the company, because of restrictions on the building-to-land ratio.

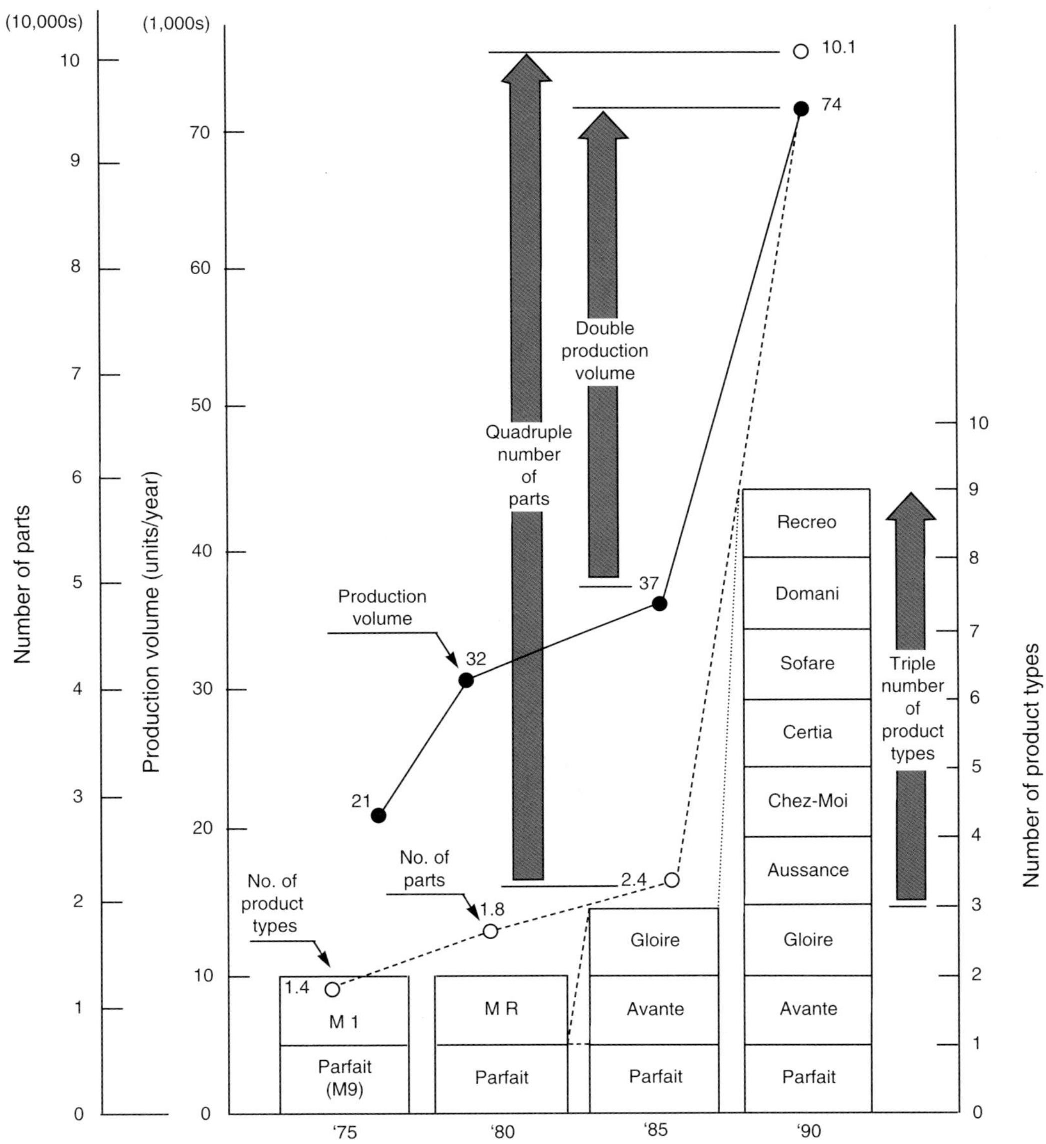

Figure 5.6 Product Range and Volume Targets within Medium-term Business Plan

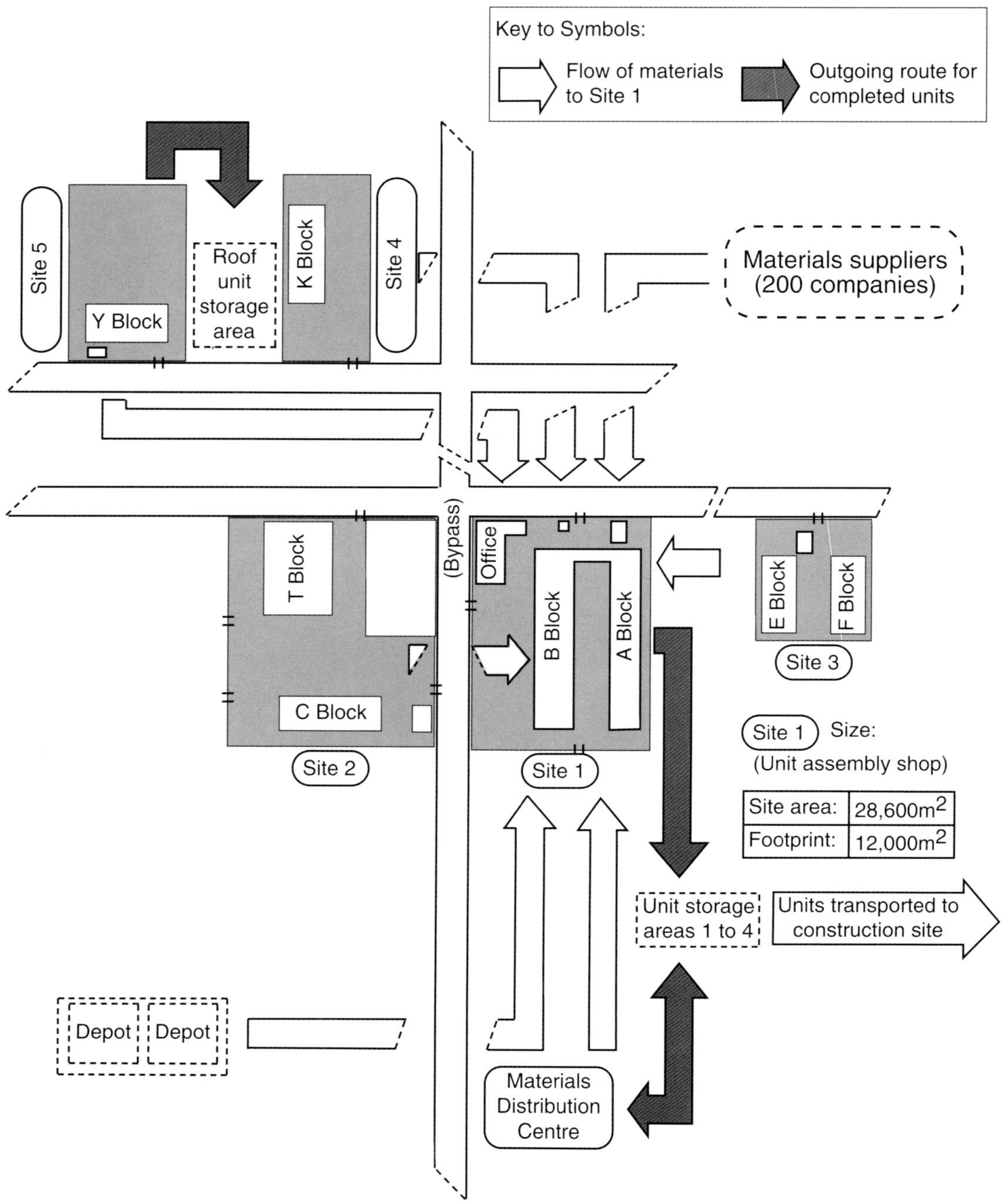

Figure 5.7 Kansai Heim Plant's Layout

4. Materials from suppliers, depots and the plant's materials processing shops (located on Sites 2 to 5) are all carried in to Site 1, where they are assembled into units. The medium-term business plan's objectives had to be accomplished within these constraints.

Introducing TP Management

To accomplish the objectives of the medium-term business plan, the range of reform activities shown in Figure 5.8 was implemented at the plant from 1986 onward. These activities were solidly supported by the organisational strength already cultivated through the plant's TQM campaign. The TP Management programme was launched with the aim of integrating the various reform activities and achieving the plant's objectives for 1990, the final year of the medium-term business plan.

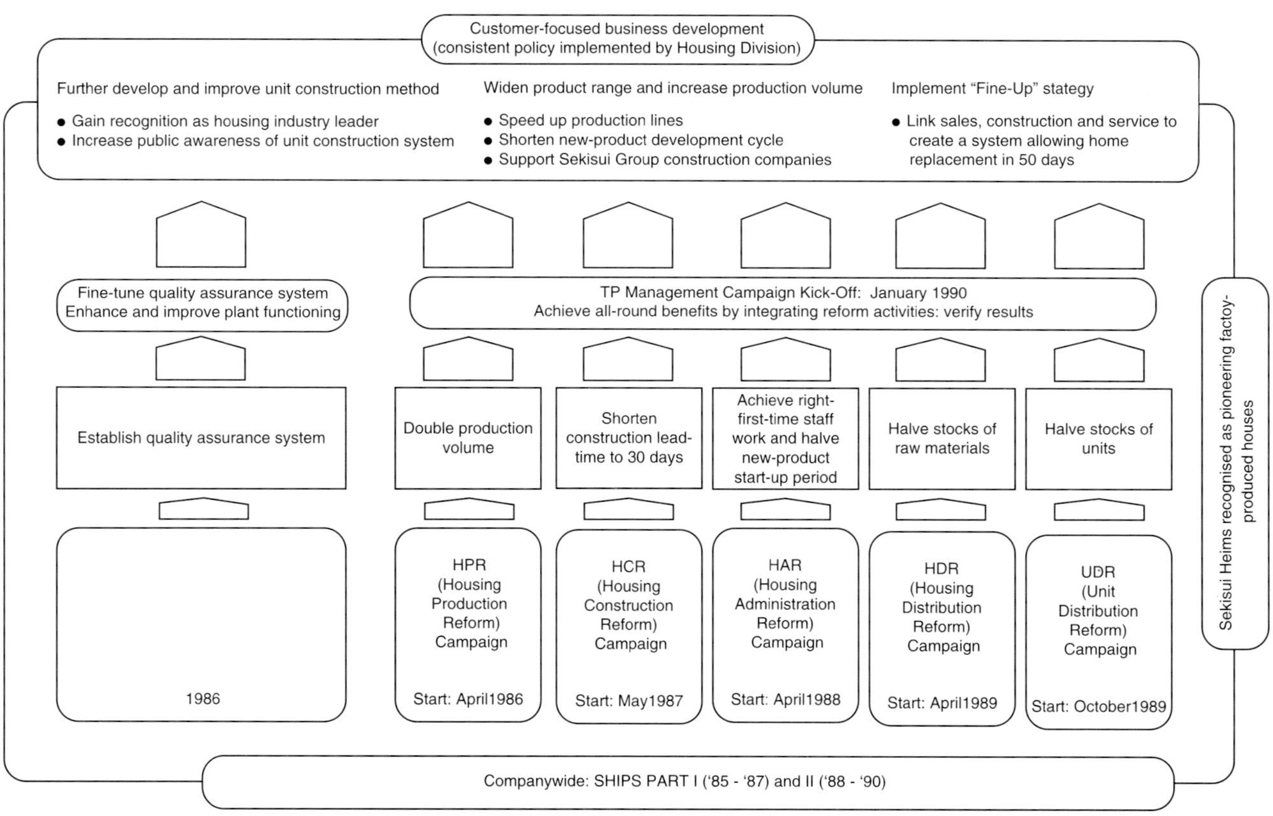

SHIPS : Sekisui High Improvement on Production Systems

Figure 5.8 Customer-focused Business Development and Reform Activities.

Introductory Training

When deciding to introduce TP Management, the decision-making process and the subsequent introductory training are of the utmost importance. We will not evaluate these in detail here: suffice it to say that, when the decision to introduce TP Management had been taken, 84 members of staff from team-leader level upward were given two introductory training sessions within a short period of time. The emphasis was on developing practical ability, particularly in the second training session, when actual topics were used as teaching materials. We think this contributed greatly to the attainment of the results described later.

Defining Overall Productivity and Setting Objectives

The Customer-Oriented Approach

As mentioned before, our basic philosophy in manufacturing Sekisui Heims is to achieve greater and greater customer satisfaction. To make the overall objectives of the business abundantly clear, we first identified five major elements in terms of "meeting our customers' requirements". The conditions relating to each of these five elements that had to be fulfilled in order to "make our products more competitive" were then identified and arranged in a chart entitled "TP and the Customer-Oriented Approach" (Figure 5.9).

Our Definition of Total Productivity

The analysis depicted in Figure 5.9 showed that the plant's overall objectives could be developed along two principal "axes of endeavour" – "maximise quality" and "maximise cost-performance". We therefore used quality and cost-performance as our definition of total productivity.

Setting Overall Objectives

Taking total productivity as being the two "axes of endeavour" described above, we broke down each of these to give five items. "Maximise quality" was broken down into "improve factory quality" and "support high-speed construction", while "maximise cost-performance" was broken down into "increase scheduled production capacity" (the plant's capacity within normal working hours, without overtime), "decrease inventory", and "achieve rapid startup of new products". We took these as our overall objectives for improving total productivity, setting a target value for each. Figure 5.10 shows the overall deployment scheme.

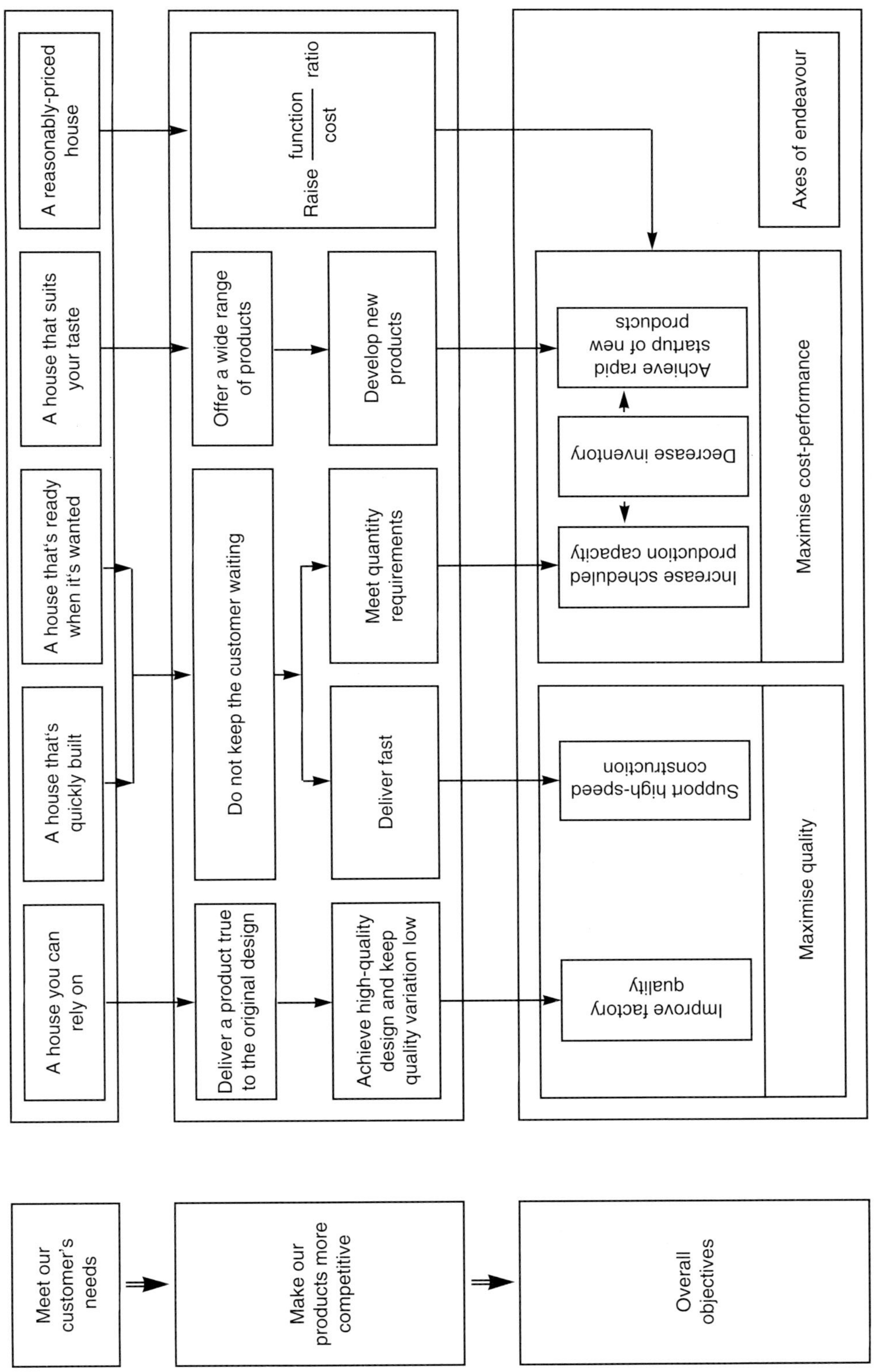

Figure 5.9 The TP Campaign and the Customer-focused Approach

TP Management Promotion Organisation

When promoting TP Management, it is vitally important to make the promotion setup crystal-clear. Therefore, as with our established reform activities, we gave selected line and staff managers overall responsibility for coordinating and promoting TP Management within their respective functions. These managers chaired the various committees and action groups in their own departments and held regular TP promotion meetings with the aim of ensuring smooth coordination between line and staff departments.

A special feature of our approach to TP Management was our incorporation of its implementation steps into the policy management system we had been operating since introducing TQM.

Implementing TP Management

TP Deployment Diagram for "Maximise Quality" Objective

Figure 5.10 shows that the "improve factory quality" first-level sub-objective was broken down into three second-level sub-objectives: "improve acceptance quality", "improve assembly quality" and "improve final quality". It also shows that factory quality was defined as the overall quality loss rate, a measure we had been using previously.

Figure 5.11 shows the deployment of the "maximise quality" overall objective in more detail. "Support high-speed construction" was one of the special items on the "maximise quality" axis of endeavour (see Figure 5.9), and this was taken as a first-level sub-objective. In concrete terms, one of the things this implied was raising the percentage of manufacturing done at the plant, as can be seen in Stage 2 of the objective deployment process. From the plant's viewpoint, this meant increasing the production load. However, from the customer's viewpoint, shorter delivery lead-times are an important quality factor. This was a bold challenge undertaken with the aim of increasing the total productivity of the entire manufacturing and construction operation.

TP Deployment Diagram for "Maximise Cost-performance" Objective

Figure 5.12 shows the section of the TP deployment diagram concerned with maximising cost-performance. "Decrease inventory" was the crucial item in this part of the deployment process, since reducing the amount of materials on the factory floor was essential if we were to improve our productivity within the limited space available while

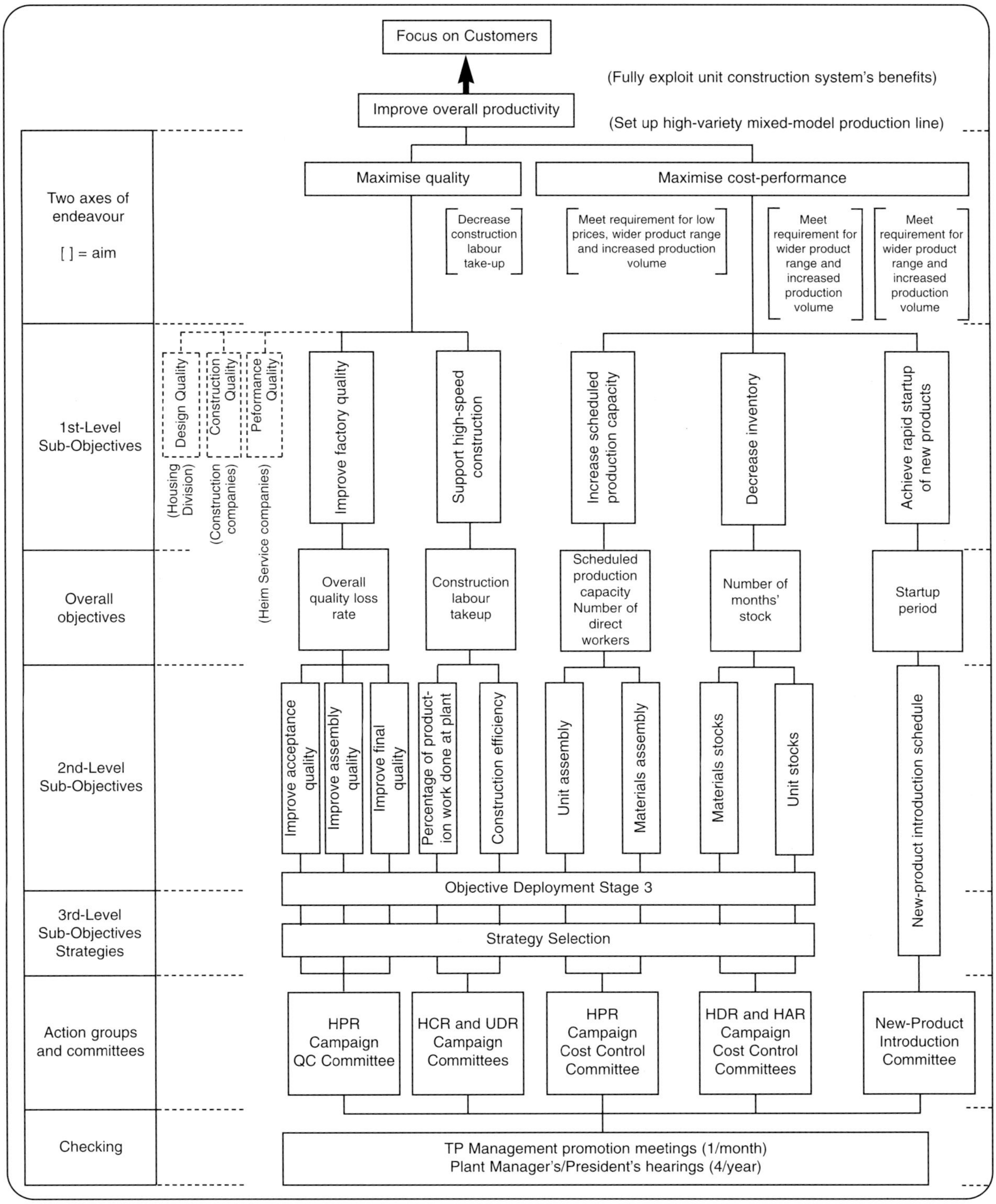

Figure 5.10 Setting and Deploying Overall Objectives

Scope	Control Characteristics	Targets	Assessment Criteria	Constraints
From supplies procurement to construction completion	Monetary value of total quality loss	34.99 → 20.06	Set individually	• By March 1991 • Total investment must come out of HPR budget
	On-site construction labour-hours saved	1,500 labour-minutes/building	Up to 1/5 of factory labour-hours	

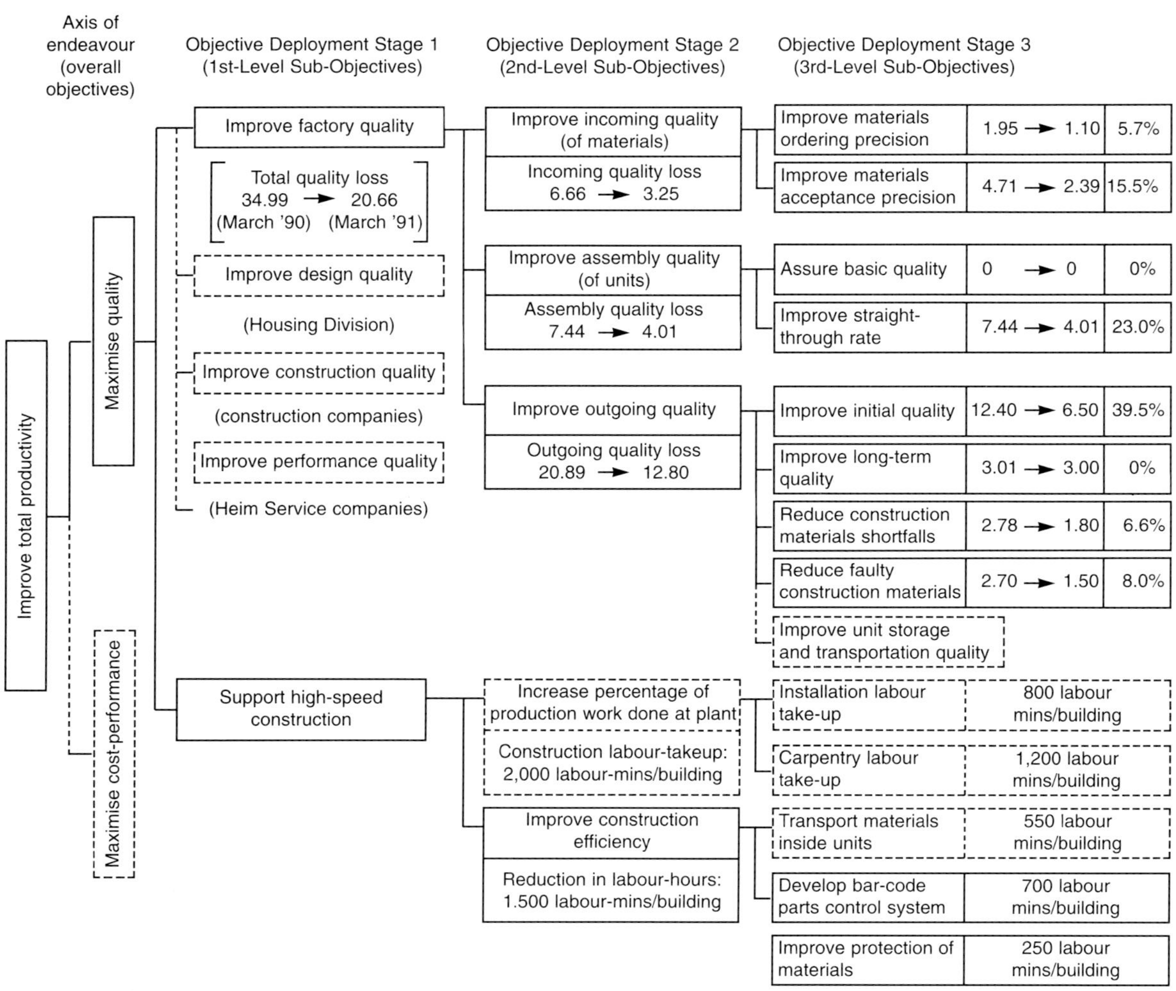

Figure 5.11 TP Deployment in the Drive Toward Higher Quality

expanding our product range and increasing the number of parts. Moreover, the only way of achieving this objective was to set up a new synchronised-production, synchronised-delivery system capable of realising the just-in-time ideal. Inventory reduction also contributed greatly to the "increase scheduled production capacity" and "achieve rapid startup of new products" first-level sub-objectives.

The sub-objective that yielded the best results for this plant was "increase scheduled production capacity". This was achieved by cascading the objectives down to the level of individual processes and carefully selecting the most effective strategies for achieving them. The strategies selected naturally included strengthening liaison between line operators and staff. We placed particular emphasis on establishing a reliable and effective shopfloor management system, and succeeded in doing so. Figure 5.13 shows how the scheduled production capacity increased after TP Management was introduced, together with the principal milestones in the TP campaign.

Results In Terms Of Overall Objectives

As Figure 5.14 shows, the targets for all the overall objectives were achieved. We believe that this was due to our skilful combination of the top-down and bottom-up approaches, an essential principle of TP management.

Ancillary Benefits

Figures 5.15 and 5.16 and Table 5.1 outline the ancillary benefits we secured through TP Management. Achieving our overall TP objectives enabled us to attain the increases in product variety and production volume that were the principal objectives of our medium-term business plan. The increase in the range of building types is a particularly good example of the beneficial side-effects of TP management. This increase in variety led to a marked improvement in our ability to cope with widely varying building sites and utilise space effectively, and enabled us to offer customers a greater variety of external walls, roofs and equipment with improved functions. It also allowed us to perfect what we call our "free planning system", a system that helps us to meet our customers' every need.

The function/cost ratio of our homes also improved. As Figure 5.16 shows, increasing productivity and supporting high-speed construction by raising the percentage of manufacturing done at the plant enabled us to keep prices low and functions high.

Scope	Control Characteristics	Targets	Assessment Criteria	Constraints
From materials input to product output	Scheduled producton capacity	231 → 280 u/DO	Set individually	To be achieved by March 1991
From materials receipt to product shipment	Number of month's stock	0.27 → 0.20	Set individually	
From initial production of new products to completion of startup period	Startup period of new products	42 days (Domani) ↓ 21 days (Recreo)	Not more than 1/2 of that of previous new product (Domani)	

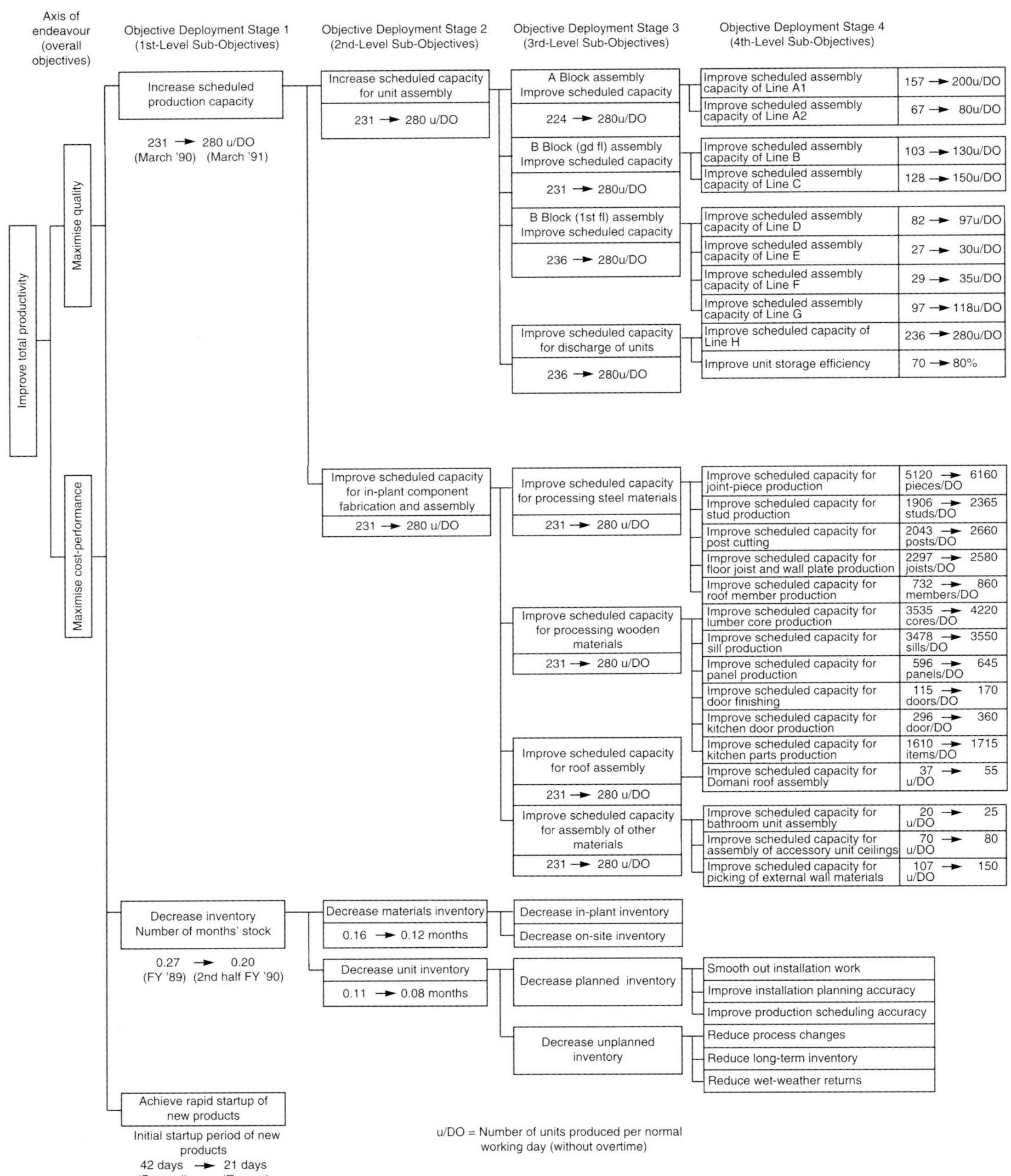

Figure 5.12 TP Deployment Diagram for "Maximise Cost-Performance" Objective

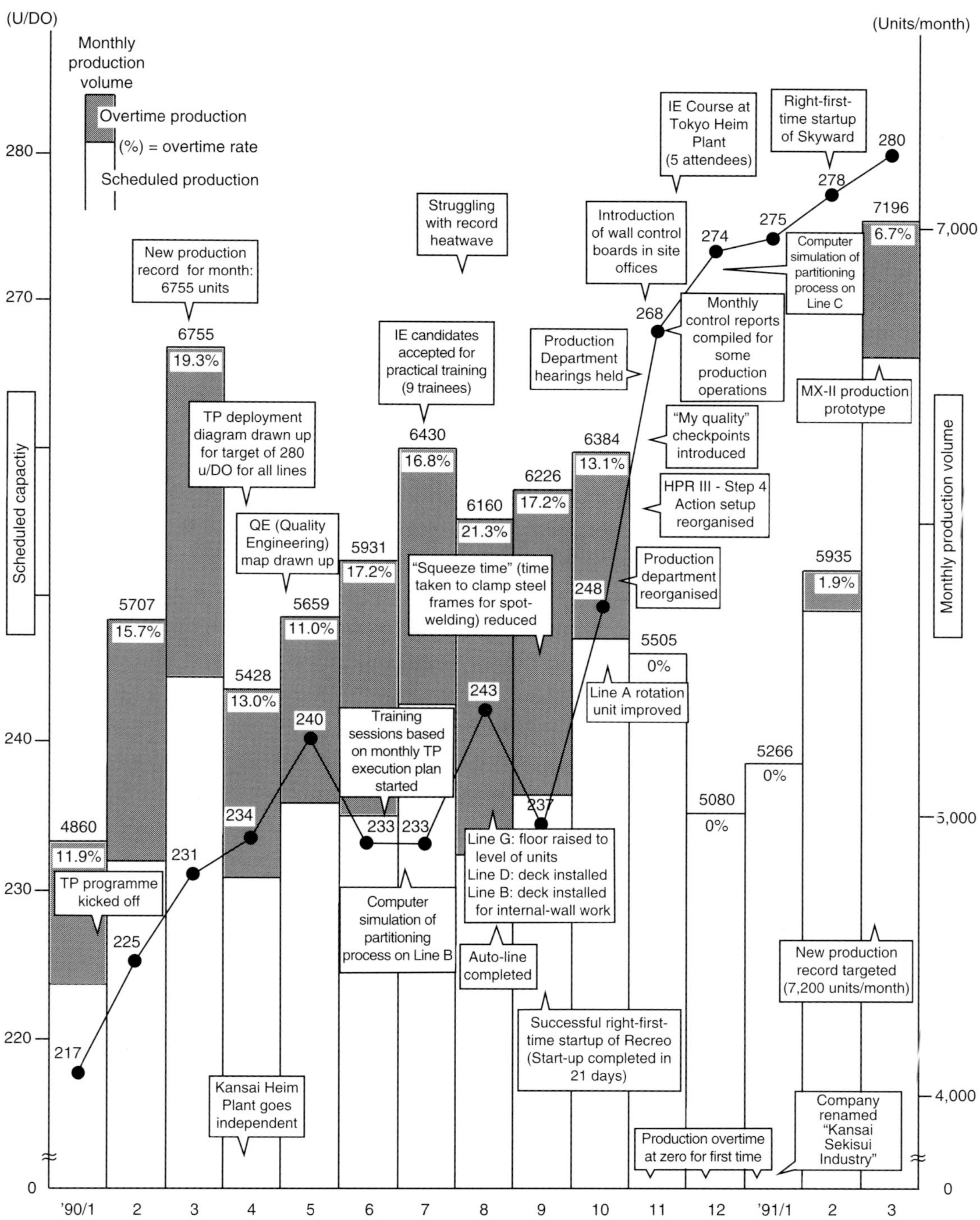

Figure 5.13 Progress Achieved in Increasing Scheduled Production Capacity

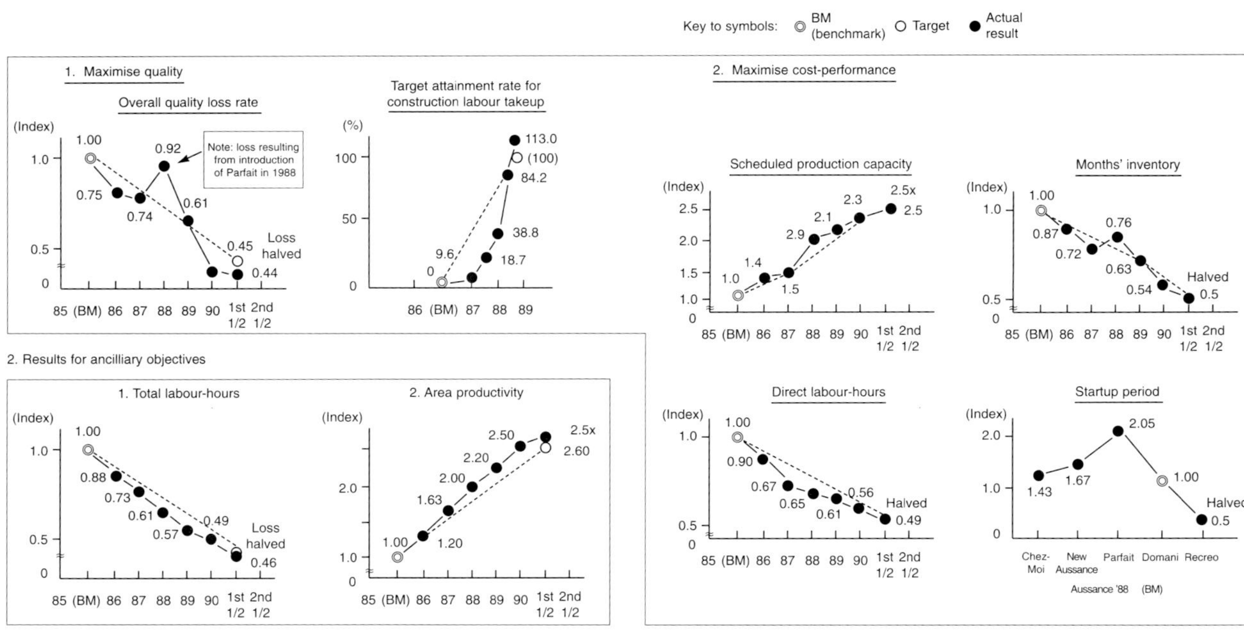

Figure 5.14 Results in Terms of Overall Objectives

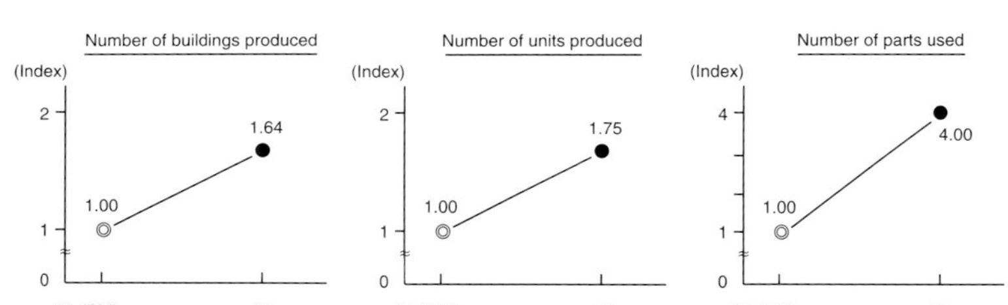

Figure 5.15 Responses to Requirement to Increase Production Volume and Product Range

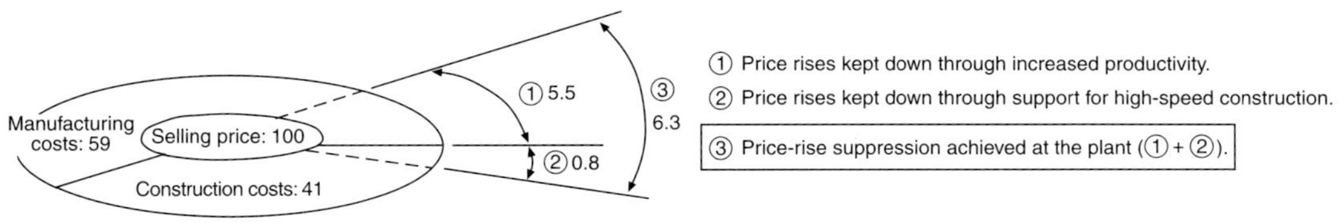

Figure 5.16 Suppression of Price Rises (compared with 1985)

	FY 1985	Now	Principal additions
Main structures	9 types	23 types	• High ceilings • Trapezoid units
External walls	3 types	8 types	• Outer wall finish options: ceramic tiles, aluminium or Synthelite
Roofs	2 types	3 types	• Hipped roofs, special roofing materials
Equipment	80 standard installations provided	Functions upgraded	• Marble finish, dishwashers, washbasins with shampooing fixture, home automation equipment

Table 5.1 Meeting Customers' Increasingly Sophisticated, Diverse and Individual Needs

Future Policy

Desired Scenario

The desired scenario for the plant can be expressed in terms of the following two objectives:

1. Win top share for Sekisui Heims in the housing market by implementing our "Fine-Up" strategy (a system for allowing an existing house to be replaced by a brand-new Sekisui Heim within 50 days).

2. Further pursue and exploit the advantages of the unit construction system.

Future Tasks

In our view, we have the following three main tasks for the future:

1. Widen the area of application of TP Management.
2. Improve the quality of TP Management.
3. Use TP Management to accelerate the improvement cycle.

Future Policy

In view of the desired scenario and future tasks described above, we believe that our future policy should consist of the following:

1. Work towards acquiring the leading market share through product power. Do this by formulating an even clearer customer-focused top-level policy and aligning everyone's efforts, both off-site and on-site, towards delighting the customer.

2. To pass on the benefits of the unit construction system directly to the customer, continue to decrease the amount of work done by craftsmen on site and increase the percentage of manufacturing done at the plant.

3. Broaden our TP Management system to include materials manufacturers, suppliers, construction companies, Heim Service companies, transportation companies and so on.

4. Continue to raise quality by educating the workforce through practical activities, as well as by utilising TP management as the main tool in formulating the plant's medium-term business plans.

5. Set higher targets and increase their speed of attainment by applying TP deployment even more thoroughly, thereby further improving line-staff co-ordination as well as line-line and staff-staff.

6
Data Storage & Retrieval Systems Division, Hitachi Ltd

An Integrated Stratification, Development and Lead-Time Management System for Developing World-Beating Technologies and Products

Katsuhiko Katō, General Manager, Data Storage & Retrieval Systems Division
Shinpei Saba, General Manager, Manufacturing and Engineering Division
Hitachi Ltd.

Introduction

Position of Data Storage & Retrieval Systems Division within Hitachi's Corporate Structure

Hitachi's Data Storage & Retrieval Systems Division has grown steadily ever since it was established in 1966 for the development and production of computer peripherals. As Figure 6.1 shows, the division is the nucleus of Hitachi's Computer Group.

Table 6.1 gives the Division's current vital statistics. We have arrived at this scenario through expanding our production base by establishing a plant in Ibaraki Prefecture, setting up Hitachi Systems Plaza, Odawara, and constructing plants in the USA and France.

Site area:	approx. 106,000 m^2
Total floor area:	approx. 110,000 m^2
Number of employees:	approx. 3,470

Table 6.1. Outline of Division

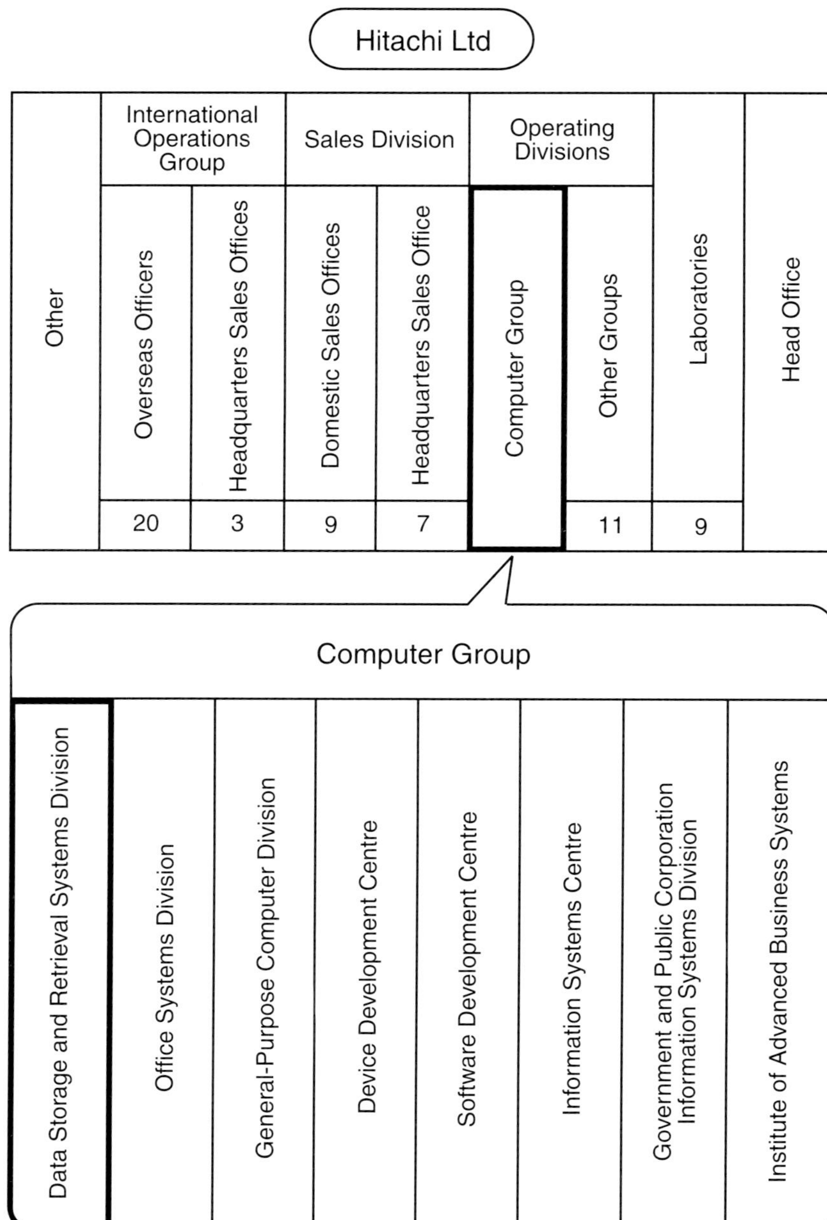

Figure 6.1 Position of Data Storage and Retrieval Systems Division within Hitachi's Corporate Structure

Products Made By Data Storage & Retrieval Systems Division

Our Division, as we said before, develops and produces computer peripherals. As Figure 6.2 shows, our main products are large magnetic disk devices, compact magnetic disk devices, magnetic tape devices, optical disk devices and other external storage devices designed to accommodate today's ever-increasing volumes of data. We also develop and produce most of the other peripheral devices required by modern computer systems, such as optical disk filing systems used as I/O (input/output) devices capable of storing untreated image data.

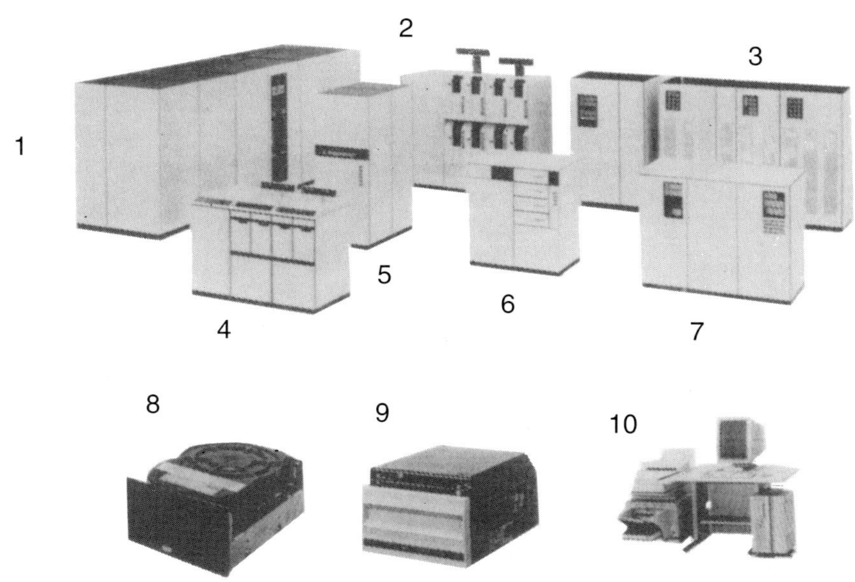

1. Magnetic tape library devices
2. Magnetic tape devices
3. Large magnetic disk devices
4. Magnetic tape devices
5. Optical disk library devices
6. Optical disk devices
7. Semiconductor storage devices
8. Compact magnetic disks
9. Optical disks
10. Optical disk filing systems

Figure 6.2 Product Lineup

Business Climate and Sales Trends for Large Disk Devices

Business Climate for Large Disk Devices

In today's "information age", businesses need to handle ever-increasing amounts of data. As Figure 6.3 indicates, the total number of large disk devices delivered worldwide has increased slowly but steadily over the last decade or so. However, their storage capacity has shown a much steeper jump, to the tune of a 2.5-fold increase over the last five years. Our division has responded to market needs by continually developing high-performance, high-capacity devices (see Figure 6.3).

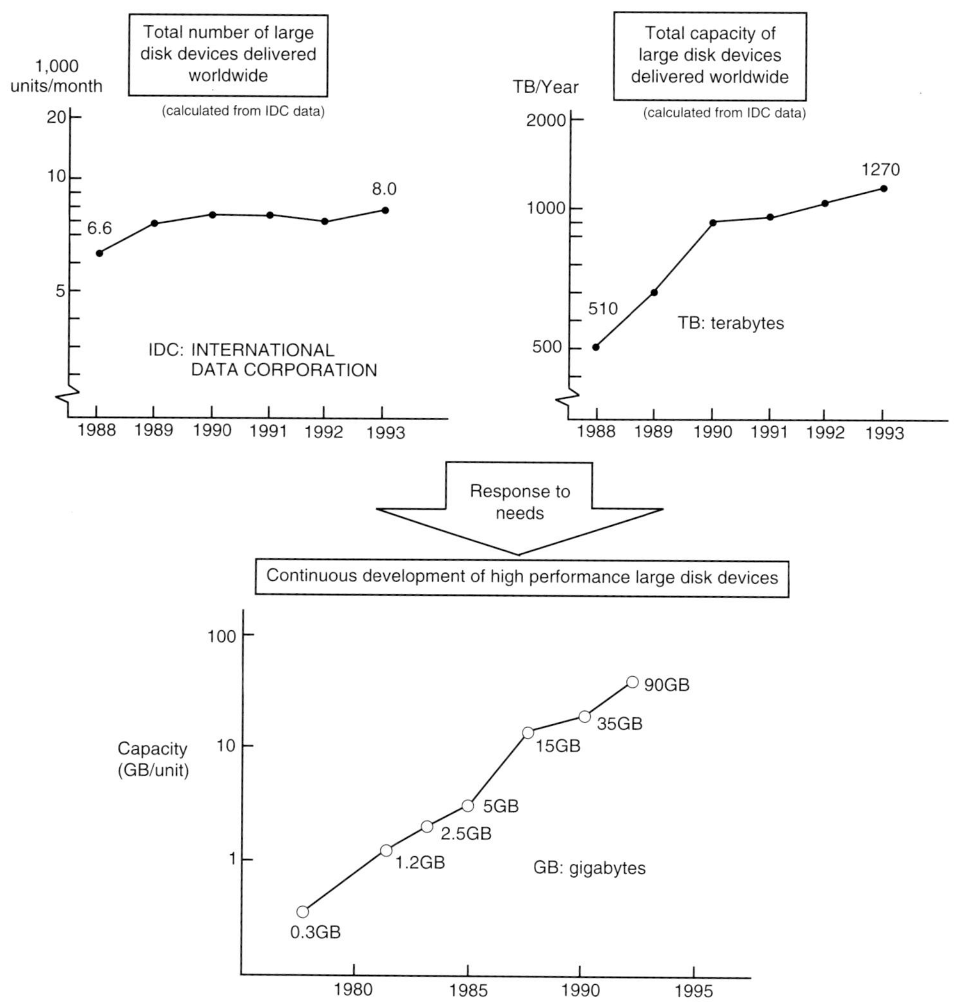

Figure 6.3 Sales and Capacity Trends for Large Disk Devices

Sales Trends for Data Storage & Retrieval Systems Division

Thanks to the market climate described above, our Division's sales figures have continued to improve. As Figure 6.4 shows, large disk devices make up a high proportion (60%) of our sales, and we have maintained our upward results trend by relentlessly developing and marketing new products in this field. This clearly shows that our principal management task is the effective management of the development and production of these devices.

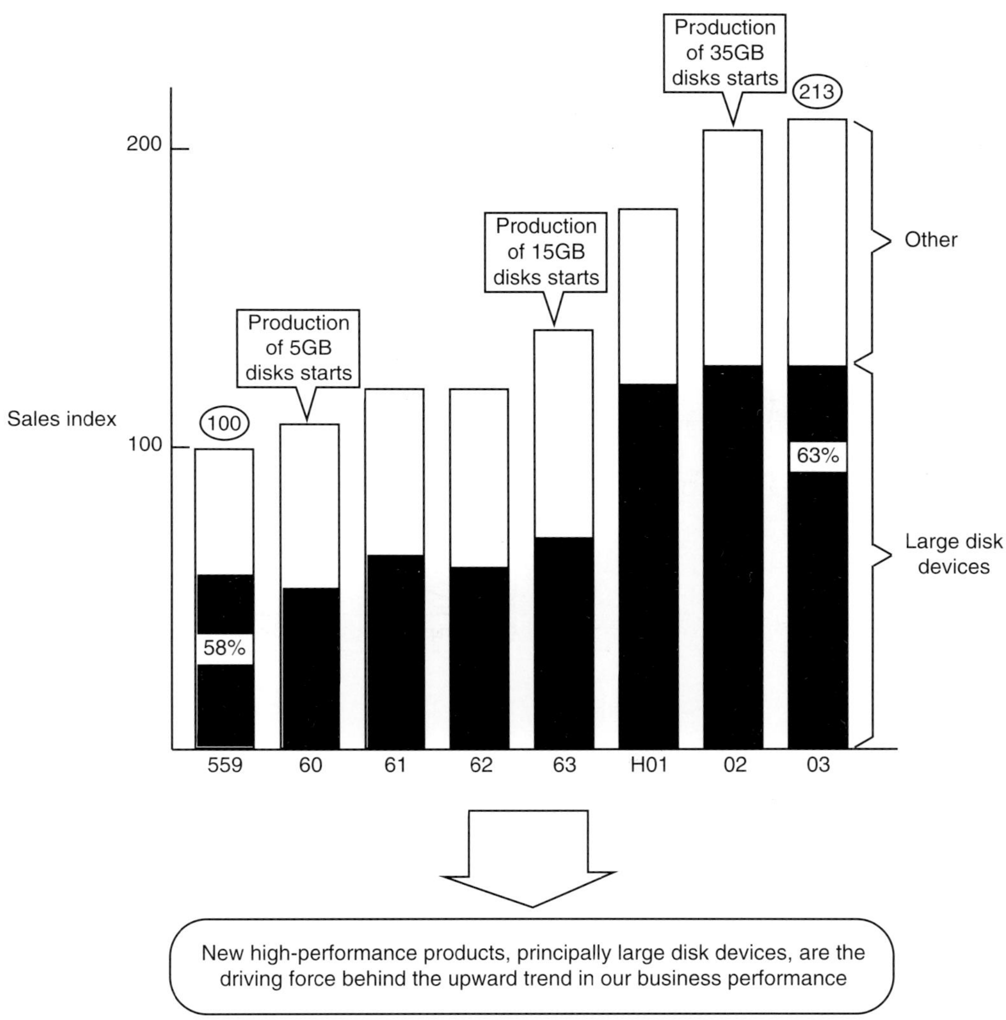

Figure 6.4 Sales Trends for Data Storage and Retrieval Systems Division

Advanced Technology Used in Large Disk Devices

Technology Used in Large Disk Devices

This section outlines the sophisticated technology that has underpinned the rapid advances in the performance of large disk devices.

A large disk device is basically a combination of several magnetic heads and magnetic disks, like the disk-head combination shown in Figure 6.5. The disk stores the data, and the head reads and writes it. As the disk rotates, data is recorded in the circular direction (the recording direction). The head is positioned over the correct track by a mechanism that moves it radially across the disk (the track direction), enabling it to read or write data at a given location.

The main thrust of current magnetic-disk technology is the pursuit of higher recording densities. This is being achieved by compressing the recording length in order to raise the density in the recording direction (BPI, or bits per inch), and by reducing the track width to increase the number of tracks, thus raising the density in the track direction (TPI, or tracks per inch).

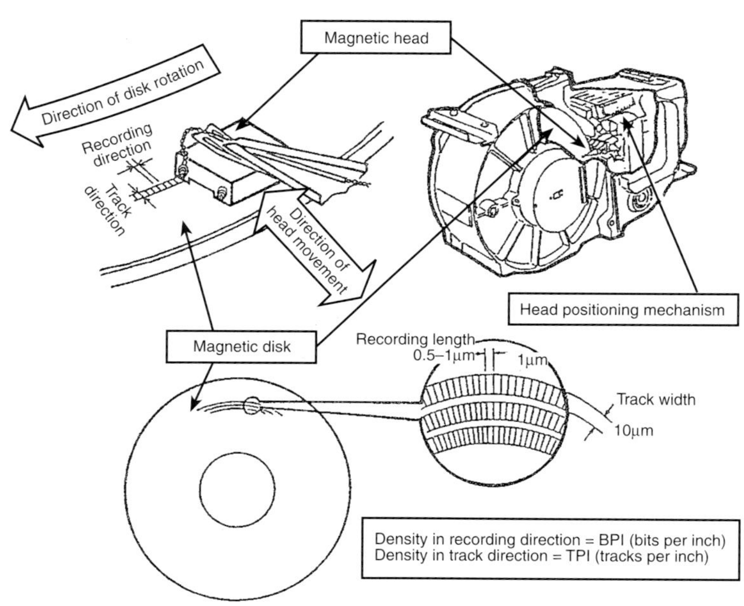

Figure 6.5 Advanced Technologies Used in Large Disk Devices

Trends in Magnetic Disk Recording Density

The development of high-performance large magnetic disk devices requires a combination of advanced electromechanical technologies. Figure 6.6 illustrates the history of their development, focusing on recording density as a basic specification parameter. The figure shows that over the 25-odd years since these devices first came on the market, their storage capacity has increased by a factor of 12,000. The surface recording density of the disks (the product of BPI and TPI) has also increased, by a factor of 1,200. These figures clearly indicate the rapid tempo of development in the technologies involved.

TPI: Tracks per inch
BPI: Bits per inch

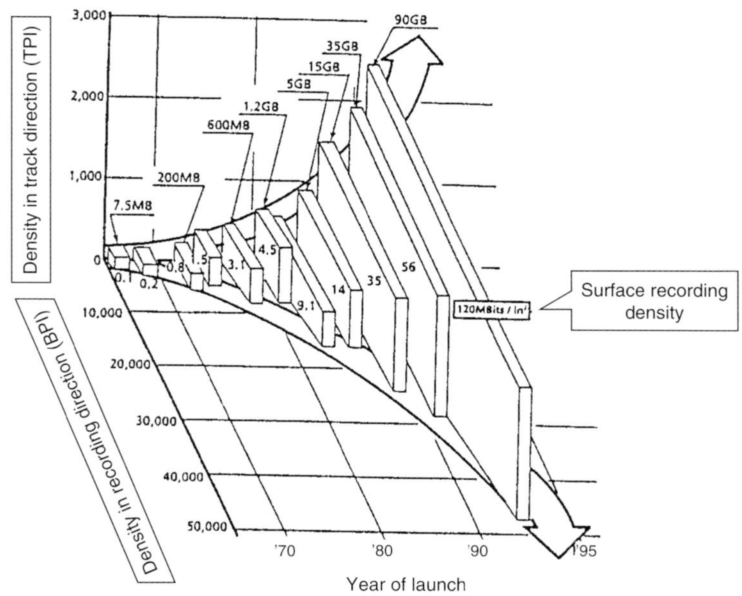

Figure 6.6 Trend in Recording Density in Magnetic Disks

Magnetic Head Floating Height

The principal technologies involved in raising the recording density of magnetic disks are the magnetic head floating height, the magnetic disk surface precision, and the magnetic head positioning precision.

To raise the recording density, it is necessary to reduce the height at which the magnetic head floats above the disk surface. The graph in Figure 6.7 shows how the floating height has become progressively lower. Floating height remains a basic factor in raising the recording density, and the smallest height currently achievable is 0.12 microns, a mere 1/580th of the diameter of a human hair. To picture the relationship between the head and the disk in more vivid terms, imagine a jumbo jet 70.5 m long, flying at a speed of 128 km/h, just 2.6 mm above the ground.

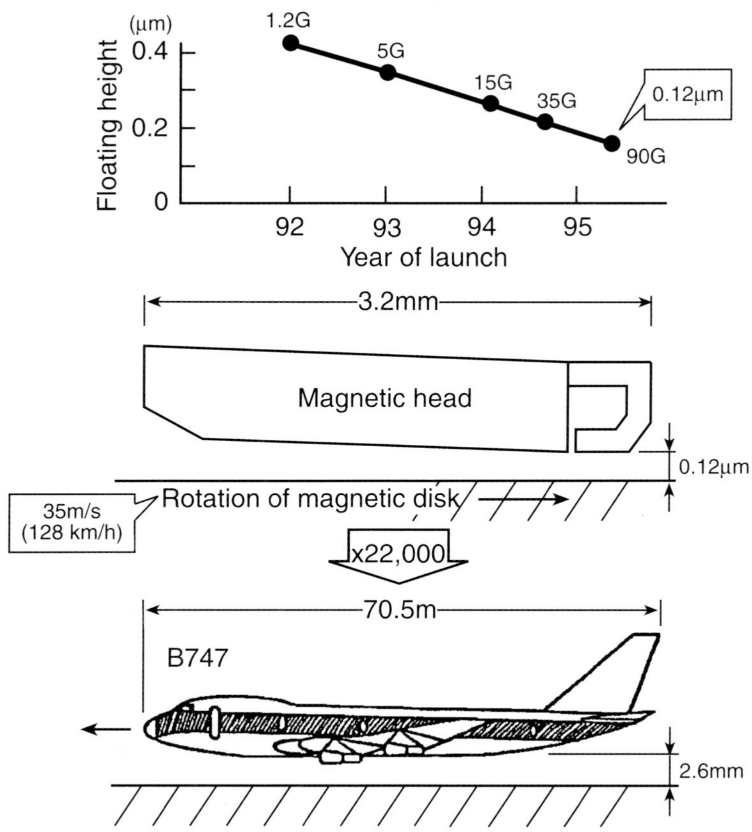

Figure 6.7 Magnetic Head Floating Height

Magnetic Disk Surface Precision

As Figure 6.8 shows, the surface of a magnetic disk is finished to a precision of within 0.07 microns. This is equivalent to ensuring that an area 4,000 km wide (the width of America) is free of any protrusion taller than a person of slightly above average height (180 cm).

Magnetic Head Positioning Precision

As Figure 6.9 shows, magnetic head positioning precision has improved from approximately 10 microns ten years ago to under 1.0 micron in the latest devices. To use a golfing analogy, this is equivalent to the precision needed to score a hole-in-one from 4,200 yards.

These examples show exactly why we need to develop advanced technologies.

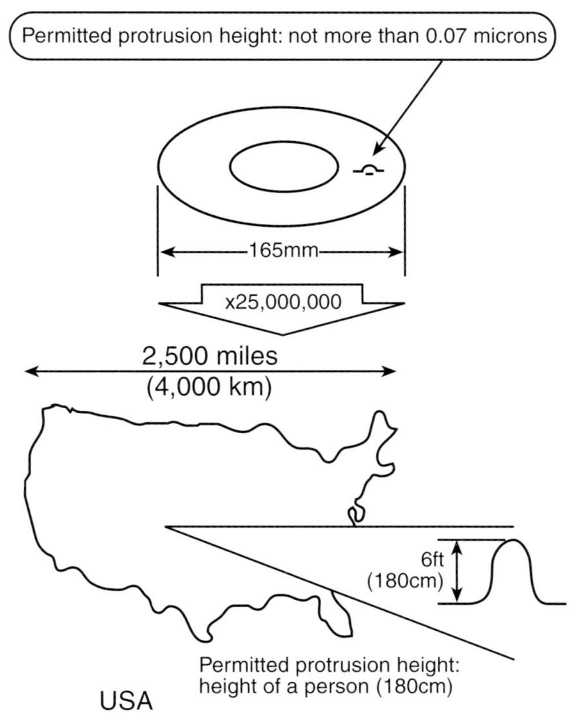

Figure 6.8 Magnetic Head Surface Precision

Management Policy in Data Storage & Retrieval Systems Division

Features of the Division's Management Approach

The previous sections described the position of large disk devices on the storage device market, and the sophisticated technologies involved in their manufacture. Figure 6.10 shows the keynotes of our division's management approach to these issues. Our management activities are based on two firm mainstays: anticipatory investment in leading-edge technologies (looking several product generations ahead), and co-ordinated mobilisation of Hitachi's total technological muscle. This approach enables us to stay at the forefront of global product trends, developing new world-beating products continuously at just the right times and supplying them to the market in large volumes.

To this end, our TP Management of new product development is characterised by "three-dimensional management of the development process" and "co-ordinated mobilisation of Hitachi's total technological muscle". These two concepts are explained below.

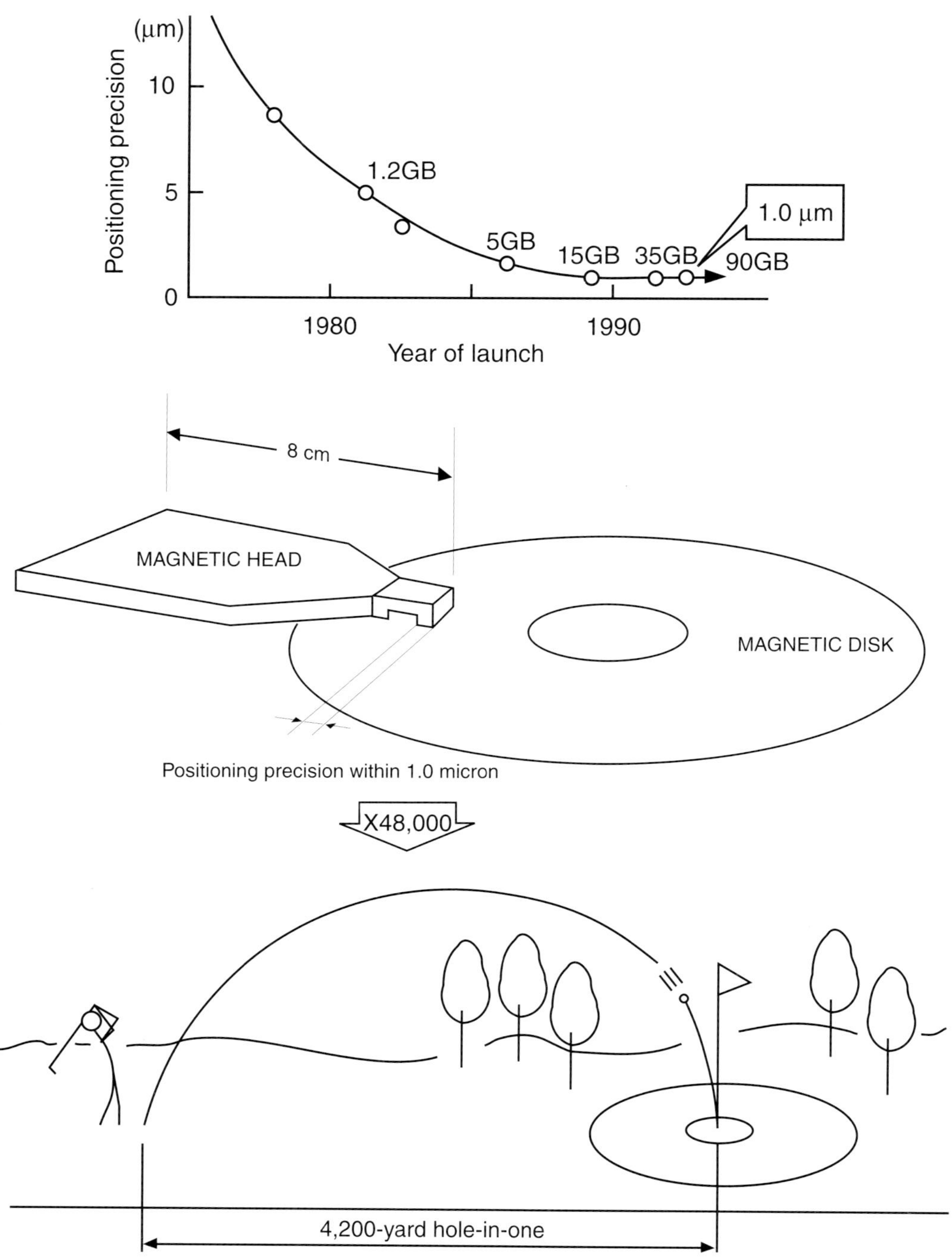

Figure 6.9 Magnetic Head Positioning Precision

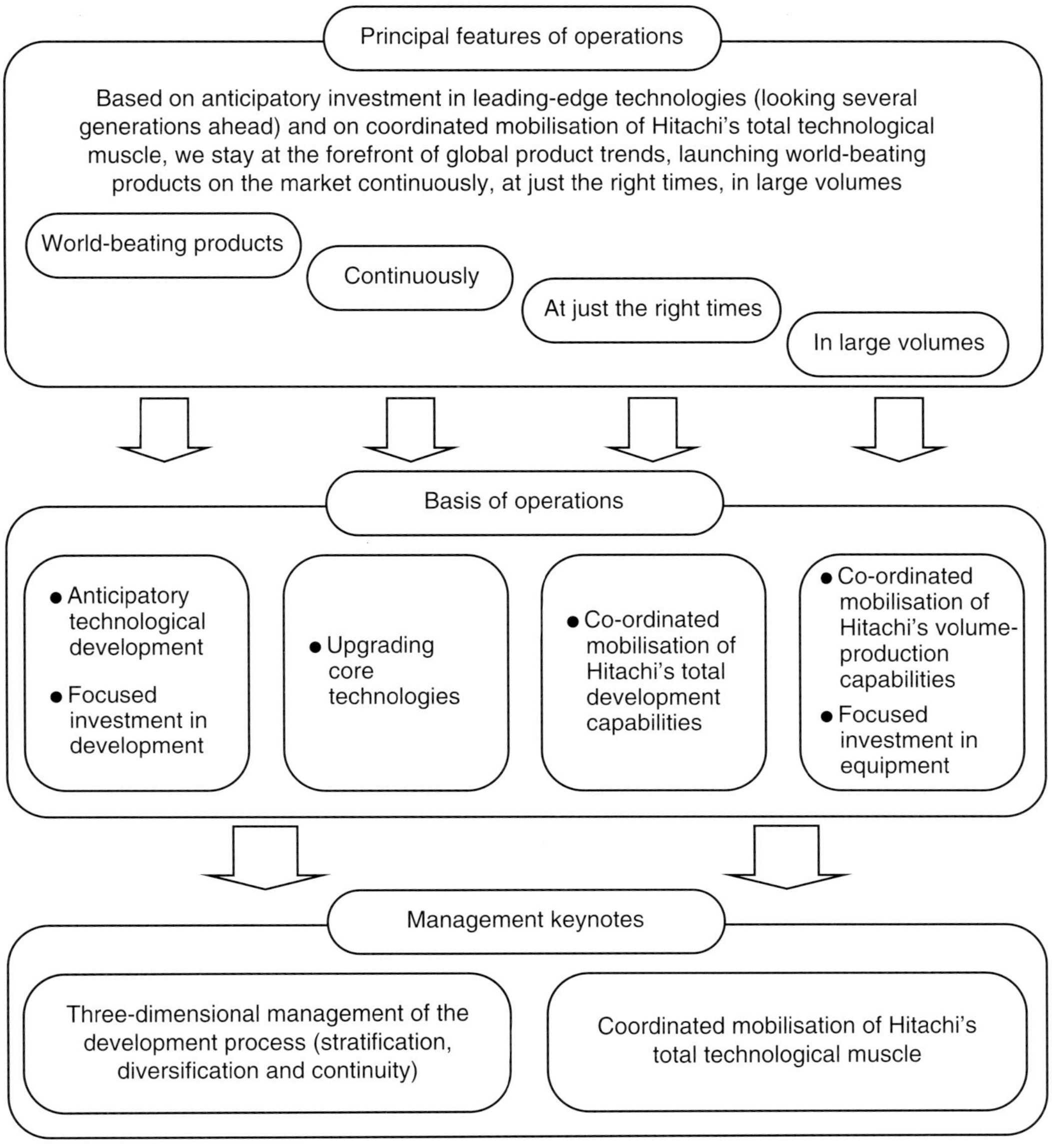

Figure 6.10 Keynotes of Division's Management Approach

Objective Deployment in Terms of Total Productivity

Total Productivity

The TP Management activities described in this report enabled us, with the guidance of the JMA, to create a management system for the development of new products. The system is focused on the development of large disk devices, since these are our flagship products and the mainstay of our business performance.

Our first step was to set our overall TP objectives, in line with our division's management policy of developing new products in response to market needs. To achieve the product differentiation needed to win us top market share, we set high performance as our principal objective, with high reliability and low price as supplementary objectives (see Figure 6.11(a)).

We defined TP Management as the product of three factors: "three-dimensional management of the development process", "co-ordinated mobilisation of Hitachi's total technological muscle", and "lead-time management" (see Figure 6.11(a)).

As Figure 6.11(b) shows, the baseline for these activities was the 5GB disk we brought to the market in 1985. The development of the 15GB disk was Step 1, and the development of the 35GB disk was Step 2. This report covers the activities carried out from setting the development objectives to putting the products into volume production.

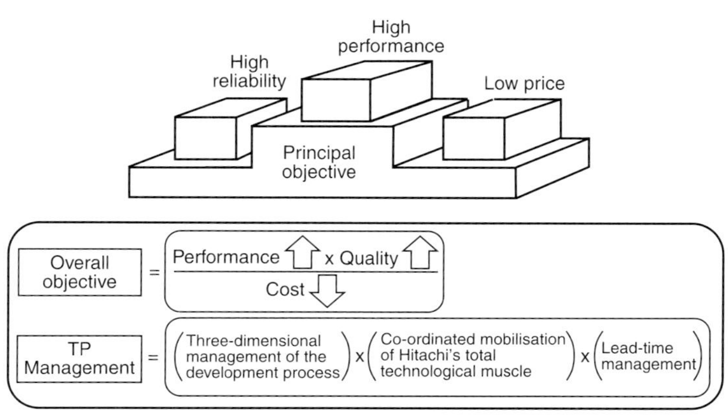

Figure 6.11(a) Total Productivity Objective

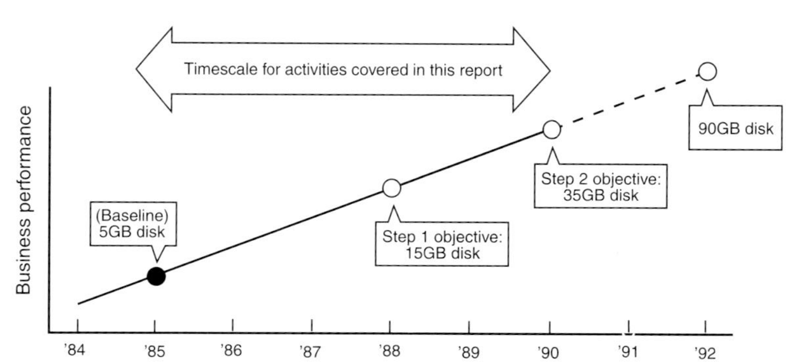

Figure 6.11(b) Target of Activities, with their Timescales

Setting the Overall Objectives

The main factors affecting disk performance are storage capacity and transfer time, so we used a combination of these as our index for high performance (our principal development objective). As Figure 6.12 shows, we aimed to achieve a level of performance that would put us ahead of the competition, based on our assessment of the future market trend, with separate objectives for Step 1 and Step 2.

We then set our "high reliability" objective in terms of number of defects and our "low cost" objective in terms of bit cost. We managed our three interrelated objectives using the methods described below.

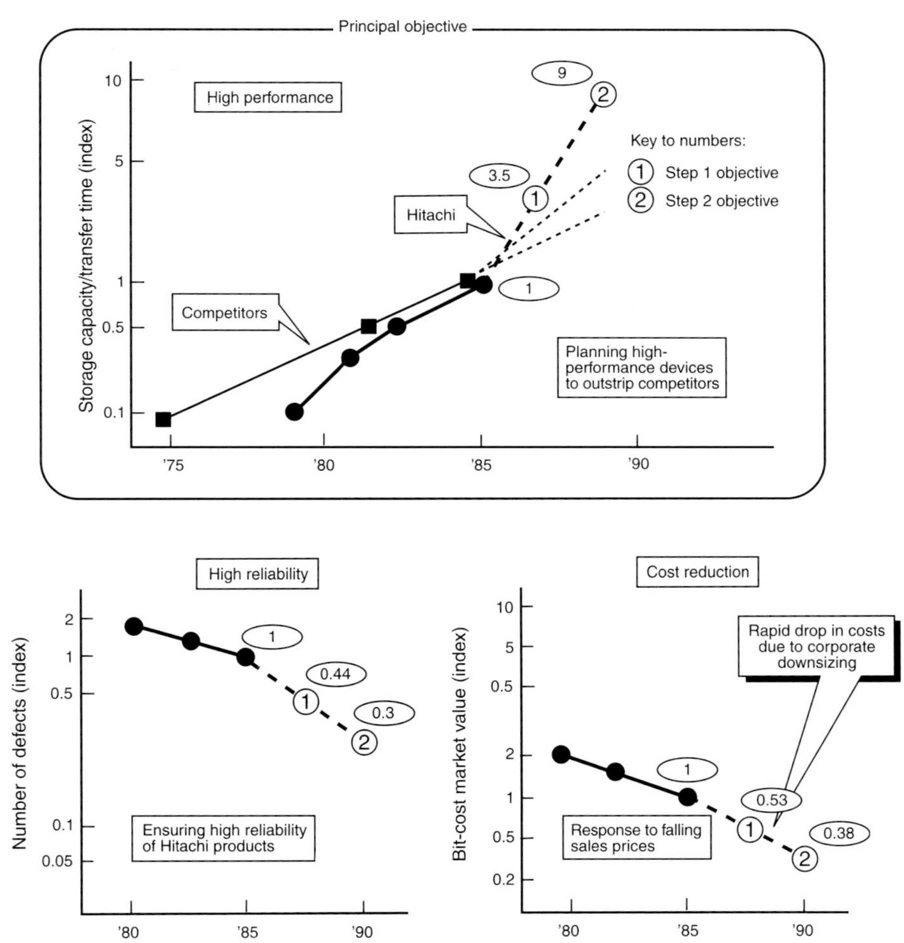

Figure 6.12 Setting Our Overall Objective

Overview of Development Management System

Three-dimensional management of the development process

To achieve our objectives of high performance, high reliability and low cost, we had to implement a range of strategies. Our overall approach to the development of new products can be summed up by the three terms "stratification", "diversification" and "continuity" (see Figure 6.13).

By "stratification", we mean splitting the development process into five distinct phases and creating an R&D system tailored for maximum effectiveness at each phase, with each phase operating independently and producing independent results.

By "diversification", we mean the development of a full range of technologies likely to be needed in the future. When the time comes to put a product on the market, we select the best technologies currently available and relay the results to the next phase for further development. At this stage, we assess the potential of the individual technology elements and their complexity, and decide whether we have sufficient resources to develop them.

By "continuity", we mean the continuous development of established technologies with the aim of upgrading our core technologies and developing new products one after the other, without interruption. This approach allows us to develop the technology for the next generation of products while still working on the technology for the current generation and to manage the development of new products on a continuous basis.

Overview of Development Management System (1)

As described above, we set out to achieve our overall objectives through three-dimensional management of the development process (based on stratification, diversification, and continuity). As Figure 6.14 shows, we also incorporated two other factors into our management setup: co-ordinated mobilisation of Hitachi's total technological muscle, and lead-time management.

Lead-time management consists of overall control of the schedules for each development strategy. The whole infrastructure is underpinned by the "FI (Factory Identity) Drive", a campaign to reform the organisation and culture of the Division's operations departments.

Stratification and Continuity of Development

Figure 15 shows a more detailed picture of the concepts of stratification and continuity described in the previous section. This section outlines each of the development phases, starting with "research of technology elements" (Phase 1 in the

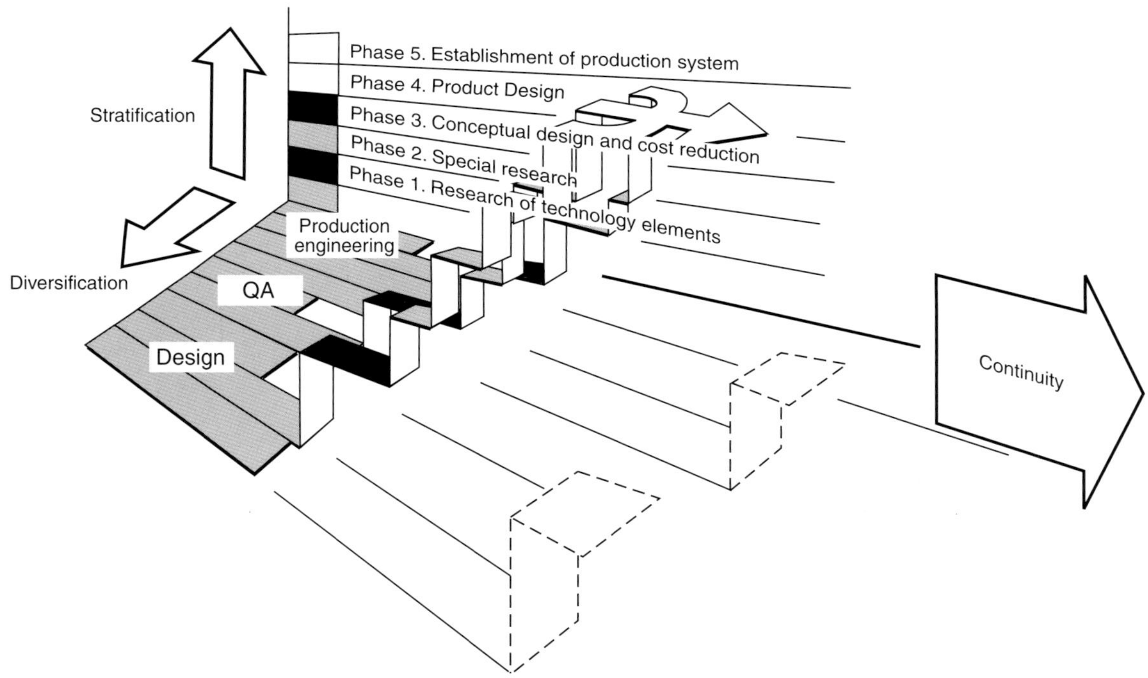

Figure 6.13 Three-dimensional Management of the Development Process

"development of technology elements" stage), and finishing with "establishment of production system" (Phase 5, in the "product development" stage).

Figure 6.15 shows how projects (here represented by "new disk device" and "next disk device") are initiated in succession, overlapping in time as they progress. At any given instant, the new disk device and the next disk device are being developed in parallel in different phases. This system allows continuity of development. Project members see the project through to completion at each phase, allowing technologies to be "inherited" and improved on a long-term basis.

Example of Development Continuity

Our development of the magnetic head is an excellent example of development continuity in practice. Figure 6.16 shows how, as recording densities have become higher, new head technologies have been successively developed and translated into products. The thin-film head project we are currently working on involves technology established over twenty years of anticipatory technology development, starting from the development of the individual technology elements. By working on other projects simultaneously, we have maintained continuity of development in these kinds of anticipatory technologies and have consequently succeeded in establishing dry-process film-forming technology as the leading technology in this area.

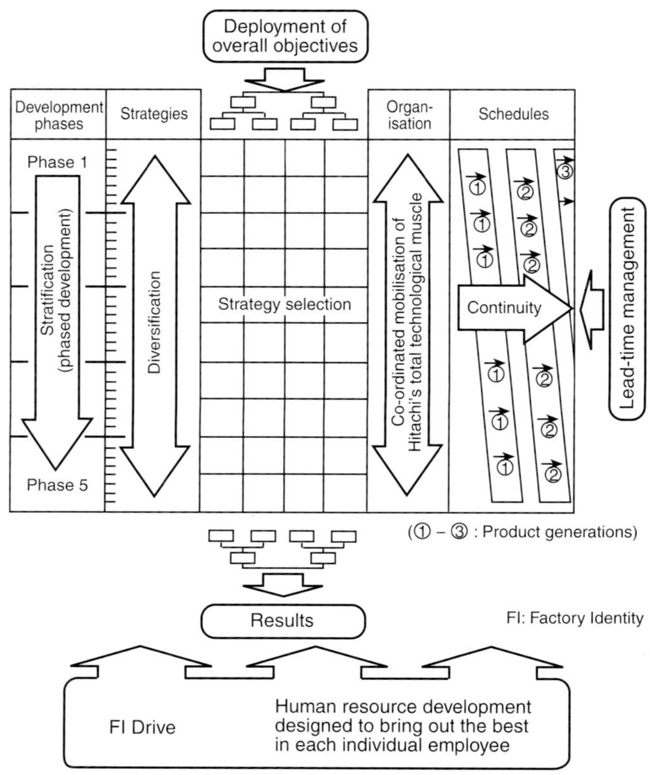

Figure 6.14 Overview of Development Management System (1)

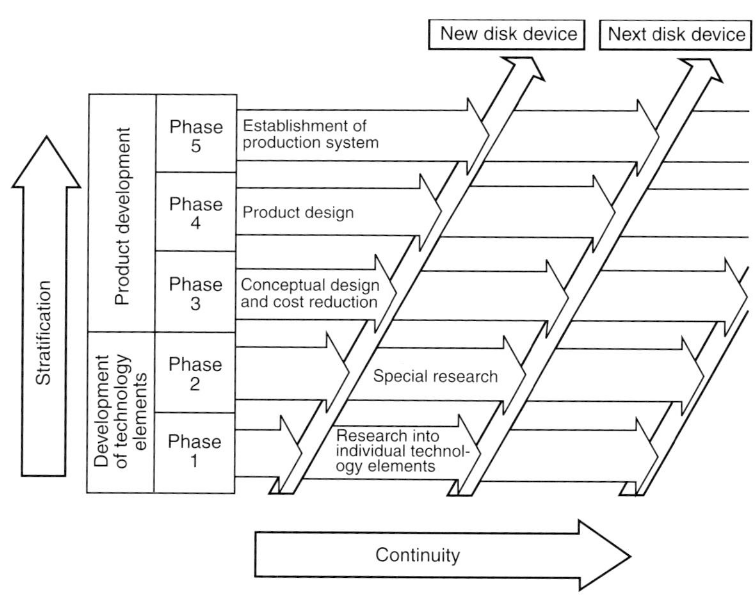

Figure 6.15 Stratification and Continuity of Development

Objective Deployment

Relationship of Development Phases to Overall Objectives

Figure 6.17 shows the five development phases in relation to the overall objectives. In Phases 1 and 2, where the individual technology elements are developed, high performance is the main objective towards which strategies are implemented. The technology elements needed to satisfy product performance requirements are combined at this point, and product development objectives are set for Phases 3 to 5.

As the development proceeds through Phases 3 to 5, the principal objective changes from high performance to low cost (Phase 3) and then to high reliability (of design in Phase 4 and of volume production in Phase 5). Prioritising the objectives in this way with the aim of ultimately attaining the threefold objective of high performance, low cost and high reliability enables us to develop strategies on the basis of a clearly-defined principal objective for each phase.

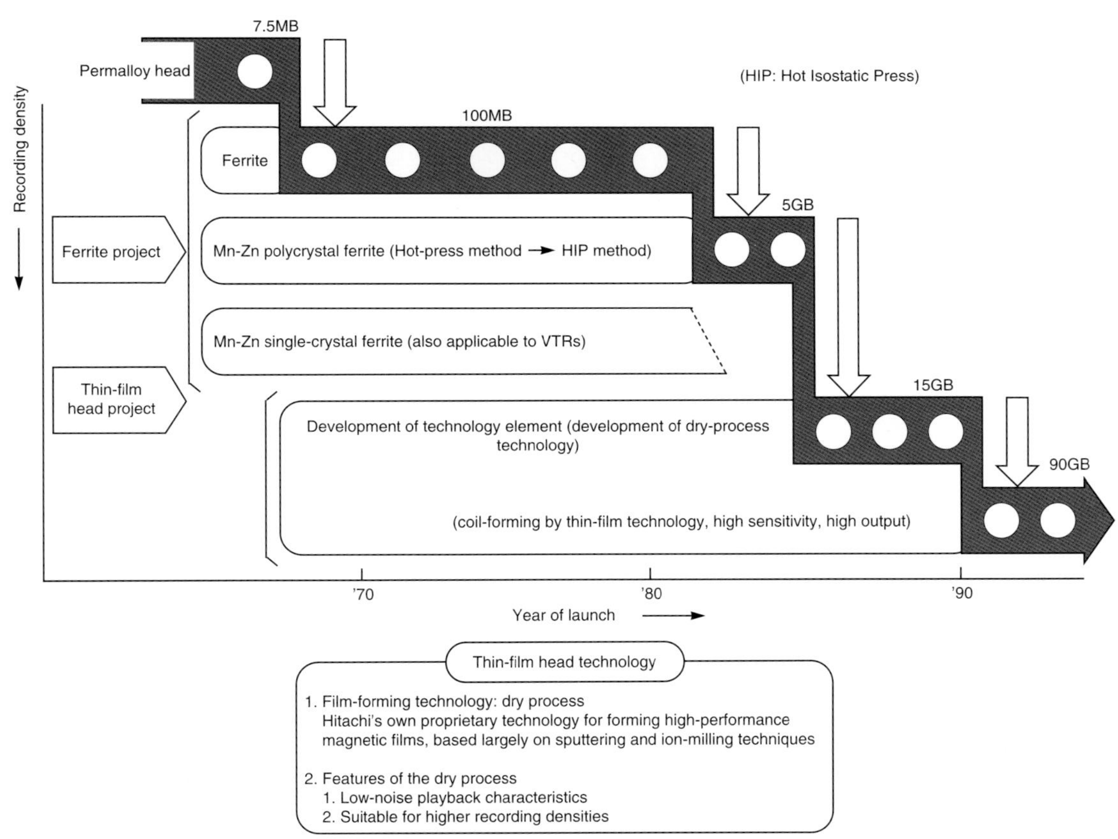

Figure 6.16 Continuity of Development (in Magnetic Heads)

Overview of Development Management System (2)

As noted, the development management system shown in Figure 6.14 is subsequently reorganised under a new set of objectives, and development is finally implemented using the system shown in Figure 6.18.

In Phase 1, the main objective is to research the individual technology elements needed to achieve high product performance. In Phase 2, the individual technology elements are developed towards attaining provisional objectives for the new products. In Phases 3 to 5, the product development objectives are finalised on the basis of the results obtained with respect to the development objectives for the individual technology elements.

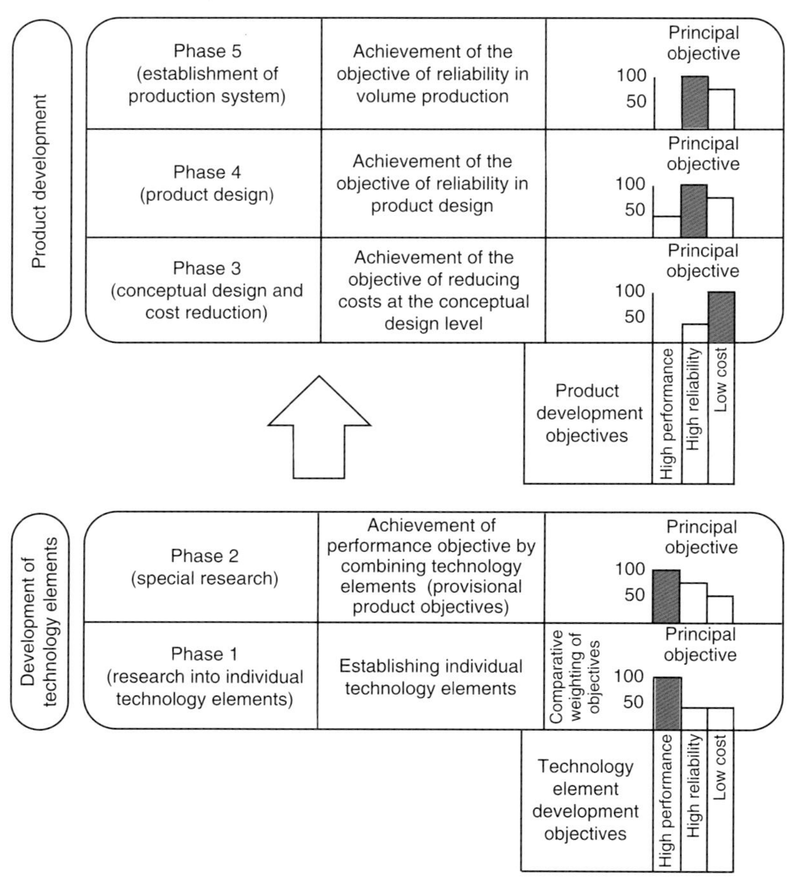

Figure 6.17 Relationship of Development Phases to Overall Objectives

Objective Deployment (for High Performance)

Figure 6.19 shows our objective deployment system, using the product development objective of high performance as an example. The overall objective is first broken down into major objectives, then into intermediate objectives, and finally into individual objectives for each of the product's constituents. The apportioning of these objectives takes account of the development potential of the technologies involved and the relationships between them, and clear-cut objectives are assigned to each department.

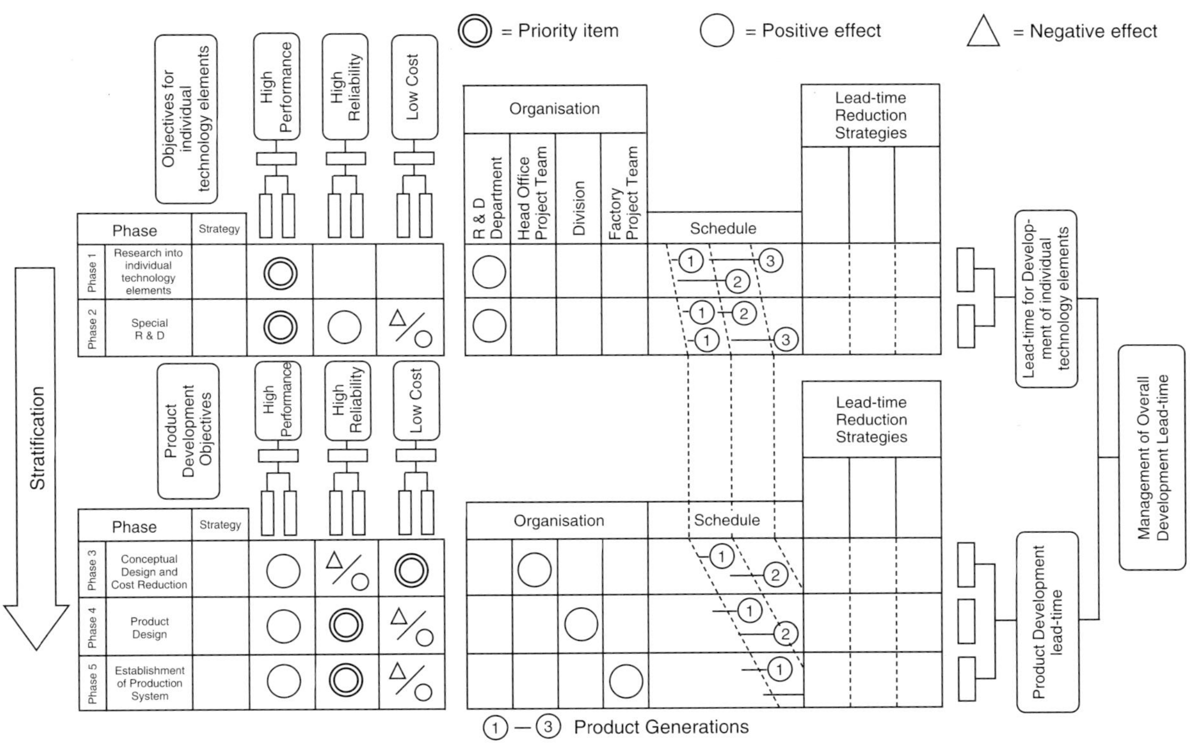

Figure 6.18 Overview of Development Management System (2)

Development System

Development System for Co-ordinated Mobilisation of Hitachi's Total Technological Muscle

This section describes the infrastructure used to promote our strategies. The development of large disk devices by the Data Storage & Retrieval Systems Division is characterised by the in-house manufacture of key components such as heads and disks, requiring a wide range of state-of-the art technologies.

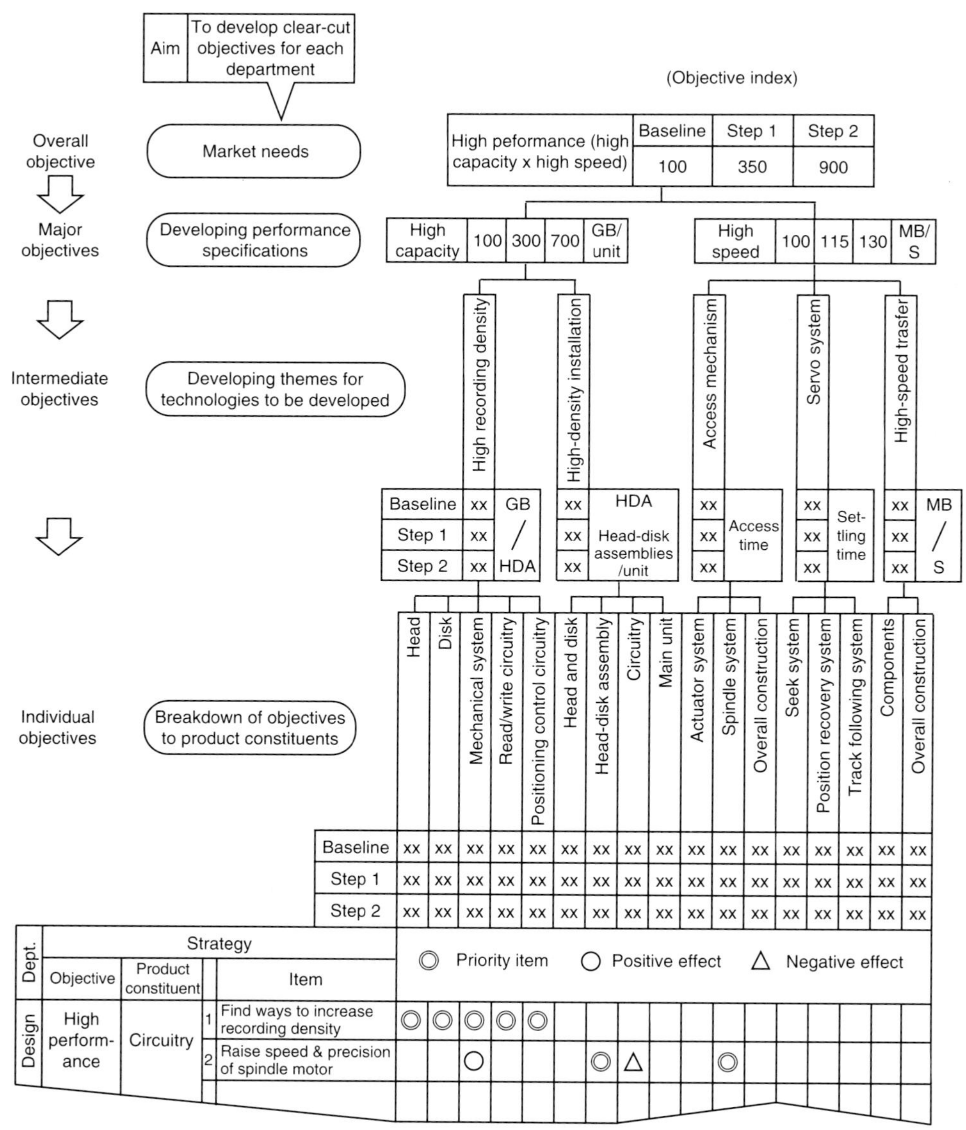

Figure 6.19 Objective Deployment for High Performance

Figure 6.20 shows how the Division acts as the hub of each of its development projects, supported at the appropriate phases by the laboratories within the Hitachi Group, the Head Office, and the various Groups.

In carrying out the special research projects that form Phase 2 of the development process, we aim to focus Hitachi's entire range of technological development resources on the development of strategic products in accordance with the following procedure:

1. Formulate business strategy
2. Establish product strategy
3. Submit special research proposals
4. Receive Head Office go-ahead

The project is run by a system of committees and subcommittees, with the relevant laboratories and divisions united under the leadership of the General Manager of the Advanced Technology Research and Development Division.

In Phase 3, cost-reduction projects are implemented in co-operation with Head Office's VEC (Value Engineering for Customers) Centre. These projects are conducted

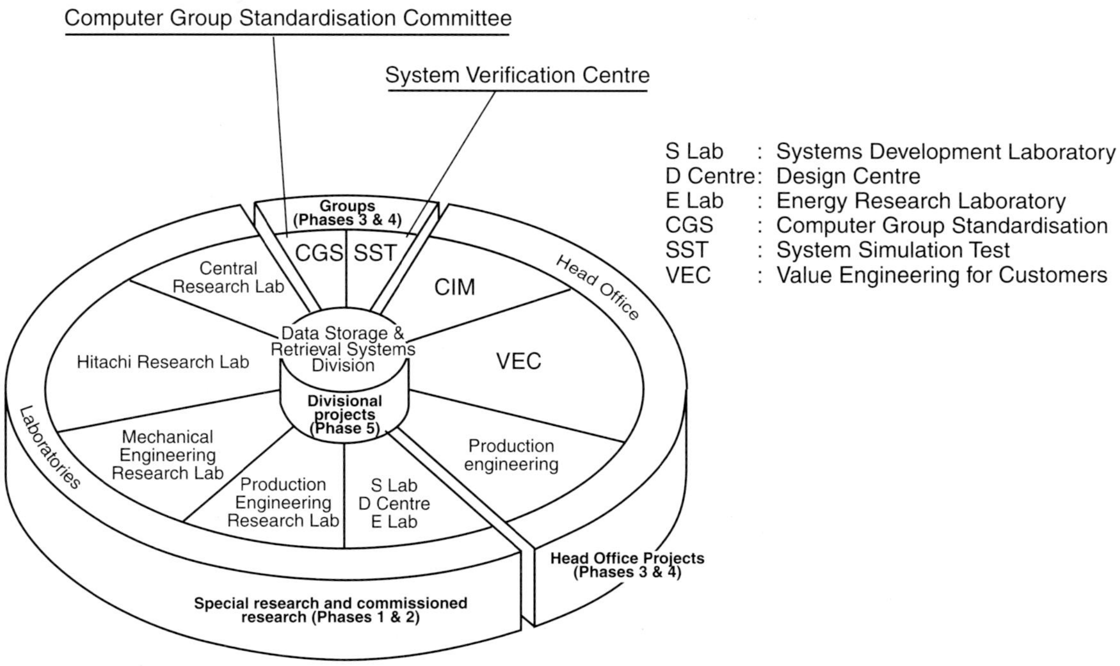

Figure 6.20 Development System for Co-ordinated Mobilisation of Hitachi's Entire Technological Muscle

by the Head Office VEC Centre and the key staff members responsible for cost reduction from the divisions involved.

The design of the volume production lines is also carried out in project style by the Division's Production Engineering Department with the cooperation of Head Office's Production Engineering Department. Our aim in doing this is to ensure that Hitachi's entire technological capability is utilised systematically in the development of production technology as well as in the development of the products themselves.

In this way, we have created a system that allows Hitachi to use every bit of its technological muscle in all the phases of development.

Ensuring High Reliability and Establishing a Production System

Ensuring High Reliability

Strategy management in the area of reliability assurance is characterised by the implementation of DRs (Design Reviews) and a programme of quality assurance. Figure 6.21 shows how the system works. We improve product reliability and cope with technical advances by developing assessment techniques right from the initial phase of product development and by using design reviews (DRs) to provide feedback.

We also improve reliability by applying strategies for evaluating quality and for building quality into the products at the volume production stage. Quality assurance is managed in this way in synchronisation with the five product development phases.

Establishing a Production System (Family Design)

Figure 6.22 shows the steps taken to construct the production line for a new product as part of the process of establishing a production system. These steps, which are also synchronised with the five product development phases, are as follows:

1. Development of equipment technology elements
2. Family design (design for productivity)
3. Line design
4. Line construction

Family design needs a word of explanation at this point. A "family" is a group of products under development; for example, the 15GB device (Step 1) and the 35GB device (Step 2) of the development project illustrated in Figure 6.11 constitute a family. The aim of family design is to increase development efficiency by using the same basic product technologies and structures for successive products, and raise the cost-

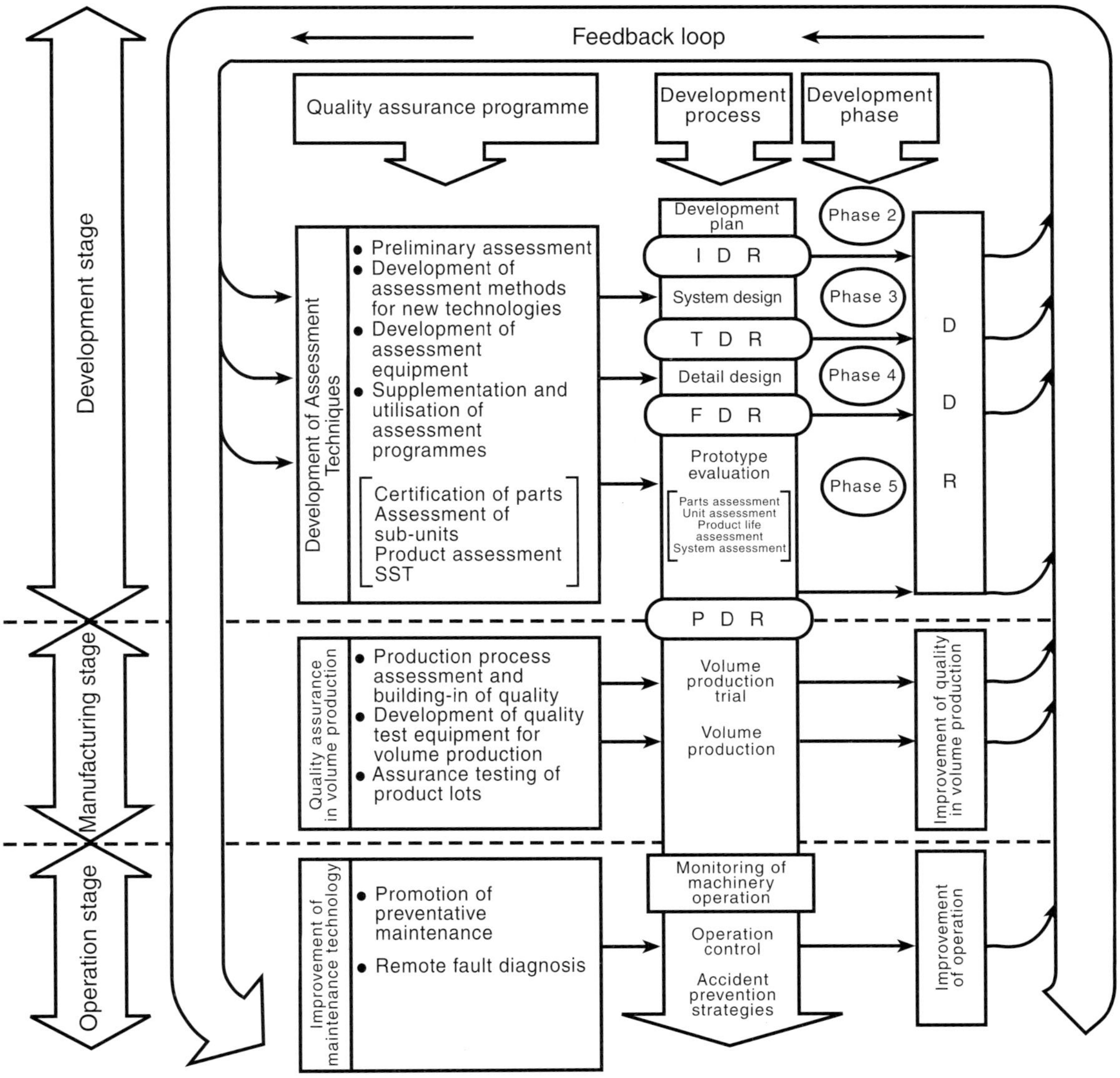

IDR : Individual Design Review
TDR : Total Design Review
FDR : Follow up Design Review
PDR : Production Design Review
DDR : Detail Design Review
SST : System Simulation Test

Figure 6.21 Ensuring High Reliability (Relation between Quality Assurance Programme and Development Process)

effectiveness of equipment investment by enabling the same equipment to be used for each new product generation.

Like our reliability assurance setup, the management of the establishment of our production systems is characterised by advance preparations synchronised with the five product development phases.

Using a "Manufacturing Cost Centre" System to Make Manufacturing Costs Competitive

To make our manufacturing costs competitive with those of other companies, we employ a Manufacturing Cost Centre system, whose principal features are shown in Figure 6.23.

Each manufacturing section is designated as a "Cost Centre". In other words, each is treated as though it were an outside supplier, with its manager as the "company president". The object of this exercise is to foster independence by making the sections submit quotations, bidding against external manufacturers.

Although some of the manufacturing sections in our Division are horizontally-separated, while others are vertically-separated, each section has to compete, as an individual "supplier", against real outside competitors. The costs itemised on the quotations submitted by these internal "suppliers" are compared with those of our competitors on equal terms, and a cost reduction budget is set and followed up for each accounting period.

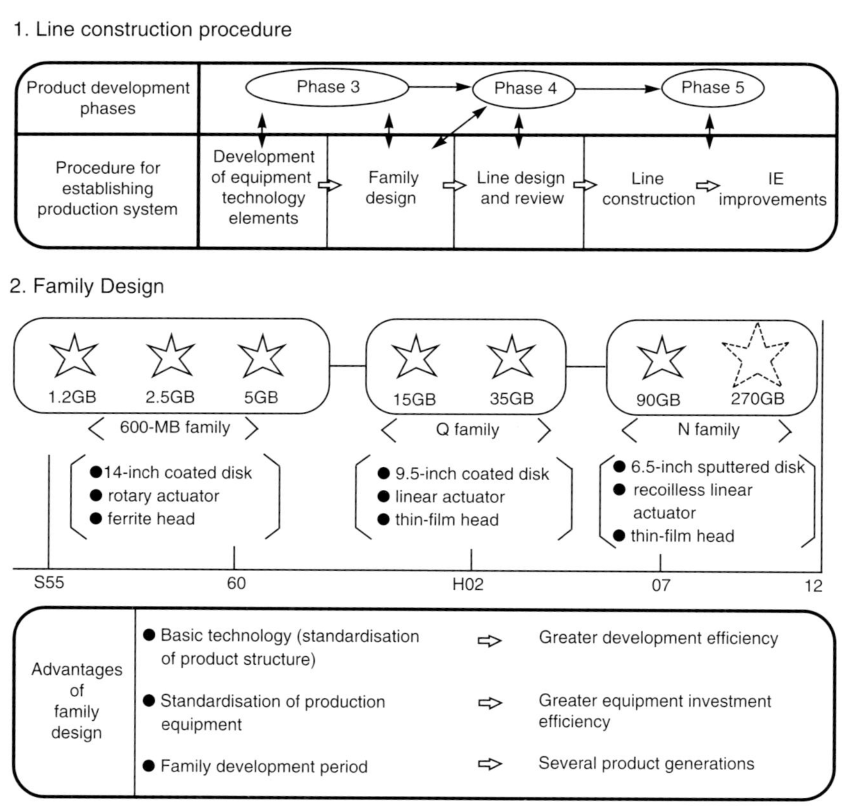

Figure 6.22 Establishment of Production System (Family Design)

1. Aim: To foster independence by treating in-house manufacturing sections as "suppliers"

- Each manufacturing section manager becomes a "company president" (i.e. head of a Manufacturing Cost Centre)
- Each Manufacturing Cost Centre submits quotations in competition with external manufacturers

2. How the system works:

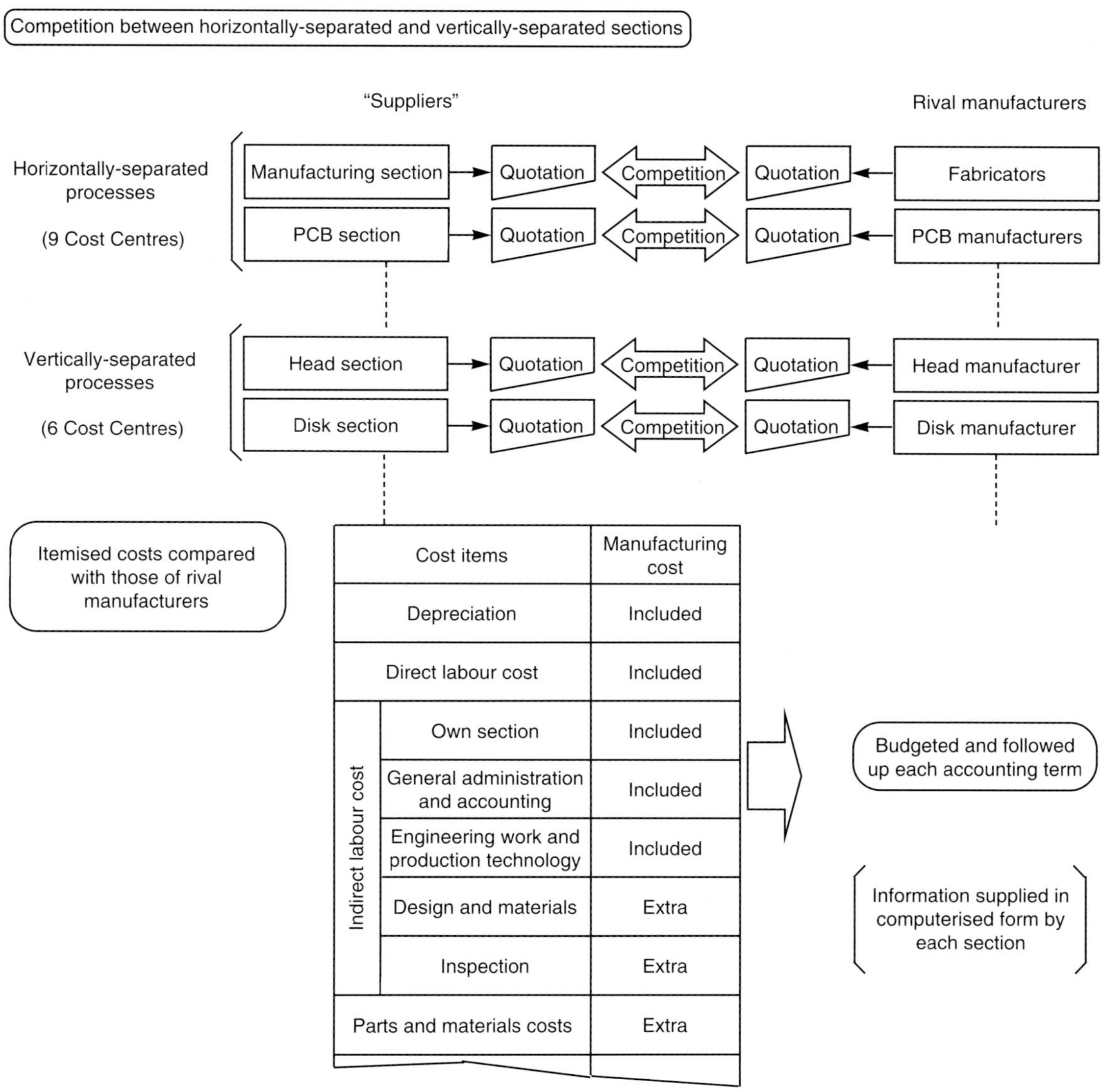

Figure 6.23 Making Manufacturing Costs More Competitive

Results

By implementing product development management strategies directed towards our overall objectives, as described above, we were able to increase sales by 110% and per-capita productivity by 70%, in addition to posting the other results shown in Figure 6.24.

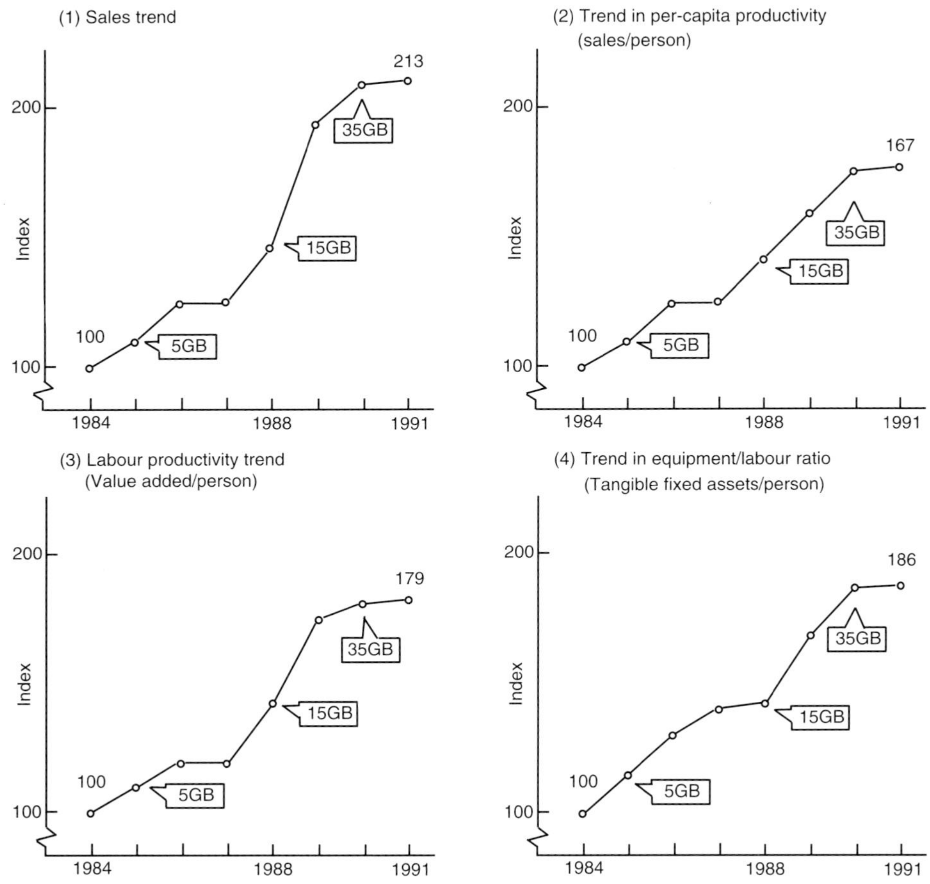

Figure 6.24 Results

7
Kaneka Corporation, Kashima Plant

Totally-Participative TP Management Integrating Technical and Managerial Capabilities Required for Achieving Objectives

Masaaki Sakai, General Manager
Kunishi Nakagawa, Control Section Manager
Kaneka Corporation, Kashima Plant

Overview of Kashima Plant

Kaneka Corporation's Kashima Plant is located in the Kashima Coastal Industrial Zone approximately 60 miles from Tokyo, near Narita Airport, Tsukuba Science City, and the abundant waters of Lake Kasumigaura.

Since starting operation in 1970 as the centre of Kaneka Corporation's production operations in Eastern Japan, the plant has steadily expanded its PVC production capability and added other facilities equipped with the most up-to-date technology. Having developed a comprehensive range of high-quality products answering the needs of the market, it is now the company's top plant in terms of profit and sales per employee.

Over half of the site is still vacant, but plans for utilising this in developing new areas of business have been included in the company's recently-announced long-term business plan. The aim is to turn the plant into a model general chemical production facility tailored to the requirements of the next century.

Site Area:	approx. 570,000 m^2
Factory footprint:	approx. 43,000 m^2
Number of Employees:	approx. 210

Table 7.1 Outline of Kashima Factory

• PVC
• PVC paste
• Expandable polystyrene
• Extruded polystyrene foam boards
• Polypropylene foam by beads method

Table 7.2 Main Products

Features of TP Management at Kashima Plant

TP Management at the Kashima Plant is characterised by the following three main features:

1. The Kashima Plant was the first chemical plant to introduce TP Management

   Process plants in the glass and metals industries have won TP Prizes before, but the Kashima Plant is the first chemical process plant to have done so.

   This shows that product diversification (a topic that the fabrication and assembly industries have been tackling for some time) has also become an issue for chemical plants. They now need to introduce many reforms in response to this challenge, focusing mainly on improvements to the plants themselves and the way they are operated. The Kashima Plant has addressed this issue by introducing a flexible production system that involves all its employees in planning and management as part of the New-KPS (New Kaneka Production System) initiative. Figure 7.1 summarises the reasons why chemical plants now need TP Management.

2. The plant has employed the MAP technique to efficiently integrate the top-down approach (its management capabilities) with the bottom-up approach (its technical expertise).

   When we talk about plant improvement at the Kashima Plant, we do not mean the conventional type of improvement campaign in which problems occurring in the plant are identified and everyone tries to solve them while basically retaining the existing setup; we mean reforming the entire production system with the aim of achieving total product flexibility.

   Success in such a venture requires the type of approach in which top management sets the objectives and gives guidelines for attaining them, while everyone else

Previously	• Little concern with the way things are made • Process industry .....plant design considered most important • Chemical-reaction-centred..... formulation considered most important Technology concentrated on these two aspects • The IE approach focused on equipment and paid little attention to the movement of people and materials • Few people ..... little interest in personnel movements • Low variety, large volumes ..... little interest in materials movements
Recently	• Increasingly severe customer quality requirements and heightened need for product diversity • Labour market changes (resulting from avoidance of manufacturing industry and hard, dirty or dangerous working environments by young people) • Increasing need for more flexible production (IE-type workplace improvement, labour-saving systems, FA and systematisation) • Increasing need for comprehensive innovation, not merely local improvements

Figure 7.1 TP Management in Chemical Plants

concentrates their technical expertise on accomplishing their appointed tasks. To combine the top-down and bottom-up approaches skilfully, we employ the MAP technique, a method that we were already using before introducing TP Management. This enables us to deploy our objectives in the intended way. The use of this technique will be described later.

3. TP Management is promoted through the existing system, and top-management objectives are cascaded down to the level of individual employees.

We did not establish a "TP Promotion Office" or similar centre for promoting TP Management. Rather than setting up new, unfamiliar systems and procedures, we reviewed our existing management-by-objectives (MBO) system and used it for setting objectives and implementing strategies. We did this to ensure that the TP activities were not merely temporary but became an integral, permanent part of the work itself. Through this process, top management's objectives are broken down in minute detail to the section, group and individual levels.

New-KPS

Origins of New-KPS

To reform our organisational culture, we reviewed our old MBO system over the 2-year period from 1986 through 1987, updating it to permit a more strategic approach to objective-setting and deployment. We called the resulting system the Kashima Production System (KPS). Although this system was not as all-embracing as the culture of comprehensive employee involvement that can be achieved through TQM, it did include a programme of continuous improvement (kaizen) activities on the plant floor.

However, although totally-participative kaizen activities are an excellent Japanese invention, they are not entirely without their drawbacks. For example:

1. They tend to be neither comprehensive nor strategic, and the activities of individual employees or teams do not necessarily produce significant results for the company as a whole. The activities also sometimes leave people feeling overworked and put upon.

2. They do not always lead to technical and structural reform.

As a result of extensive discussions, mainly among the plant's top managers, we decided to base the future management of the Kashima Plant on the sentiments expressed by the slogans given below, and to replace the production system we had been developing so far (KPS) with a new one (New-KPS).

From "campaign" to "strategy"

From "partial" to "total"

From "improvement" to "reform"

From "work + α" to "work itself"

Basic Concept

In developing our new management approach, we had to clarify our vision (our idea of what the Kashima Plant should be like in the future), our image of how this should be achieved, and our objectives. As mentioned earlier, Kaneka Corporation has formulated a long-term business plan to guide it into the 21st century. In addition to specific business goals, this plan (called "EX-21") incorporates the following corporate philosophy and business vision:

Corporate Philosophy

To create real value and contribute to the world through harmonious relationships between people and technology.

Business Vision

To meet the needs of world industrial markets by providing highly-reliable products and services based on superior technology.

Our company's operations plans, production engineering plans and R & D plans have all been drawn up on the basis of this corporate philosophy and business vision. New-KPS is our long-term concept for the Kashima Plant. It was formulated with the idea of envisioning a "model plant for the 21st century" and making steady progress towards attaining this dream while conforming to the above plans. Figure 7.2 illustrates the basic concept behind New-KPS.

New-KPS embodies the following three key ideas:

1. We want to expand the Kashima Plant, raise its profile in the Kantō market (Eastern Japan) and increase its share of this market, while simultaneously sharpening our employees' commercial awareness.
2. We want to minimise the losses associated with the shift to high-variety production and respond to the diversification of our customers' needs by introducing high-variety, small-lot production systems and reforming our view of the production process.
3. We want to ensure that we all taste success together by seeing to it that every individual's efforts lead directly to significant overall results.

These desires form the basic concept of New-KPS, and are encapsulated in the slogan "Make the Kashima Plant Bigger, Newer and Stronger".

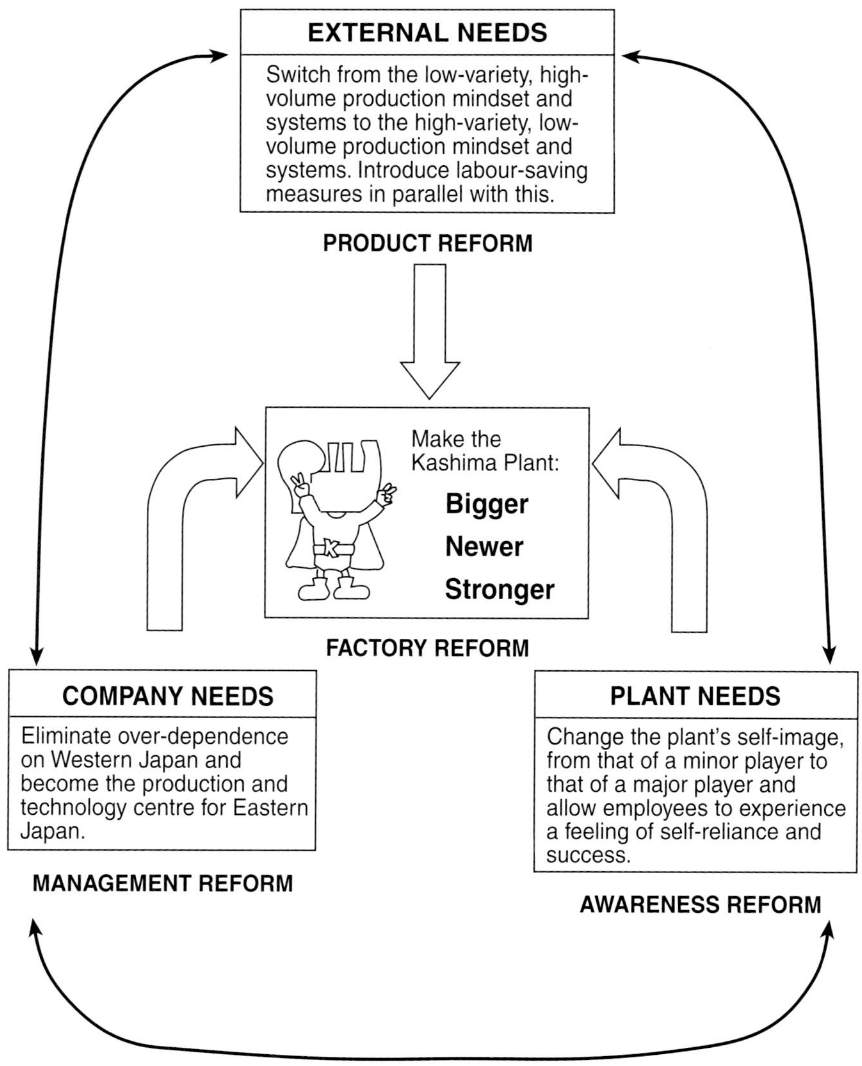

Figure 7.2 Basic Concepts of New-KPS

Objective Deployment

New-KPS is in three main sections, each corresponding to one part of the above slogan. These three sections are:

Section 1: Increase the scale of our operations
Section 2: Reform our production systems
Section 3: Revitalise our organisation

Section 2, "Reform our production systems", is made up of the following three plans (see Figure 7.3):

The K Plan: develop production systems able to cope with a diversity of products.

The P Plan: introduce computer-controlled high-variety, small-lot production systems.

The A Plan: create an agreeable working environment.

The Kashima Plant received its TP Prize for its development and implementation of the K Plan.

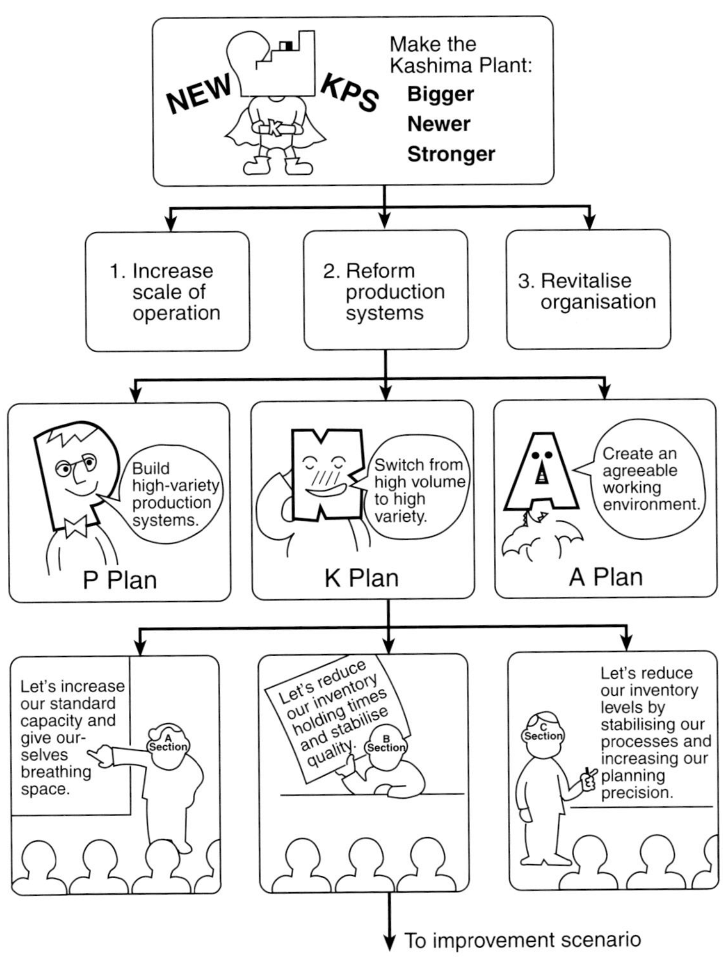

Figure 7.3 Structure of New-KPS

The ultimate objective of New-KPS was to create a totally automated, computer-integrated plant while making it a pleasant place in which to work. As the first step in this, we established three overall objectives, corresponding respectively to the K Plan, the P Plan and the A Plan.

The overall objective for the K Plan was to reform the production system into one able to handle a diversity of products. Two specific targets were set for this, based on the precondition that each section had to increase the number of product grades it produced by a certain multiple. These two specific objectives were (1) to achieve an availability of at least 95%, and (2) to reduce product inventories by specified amounts (each process line had its own target for this).

Based on the overall objectives, each section discussed what its key points were in terms of productivity (P), quality (Q), cost (C) and delivery (D), and established section objectives in each of these areas (see Figure 7.4).

Significance of High-Variety Production

The fabrication and assembly industries have long been familiar with the need to establish high-variety, small-lot production systems in order to cope with the diversification of their customers' demands, but it is still a relatively new issue for process industries. We resolved to reform our production system into one able to handle a wider variety of products because we realised that our ability to cater to the increasingly diverse applications and processing methods used by our customers (plastic products manufacturers) is an important element of our competitiveness.

In general terms, the chemical industry has the following two characteristics:

1. Product differentiation is difficult because products are usually developed for general use rather than specific purposes.

2. The equipment itself is also more suited to low-variety, high-volume production for the following reasons:

    A larger plant yields better economies of scale.
    Chemical engineering is based on an assumption of the steady state.
    Control systems are not good at coping with unsteady conditions.

Moreover, any moves towards introducing high-variety production encounter problems such as the following:

1. More frequent product changeovers result in lower productivity, greater amounts of defective product and increased workloads.

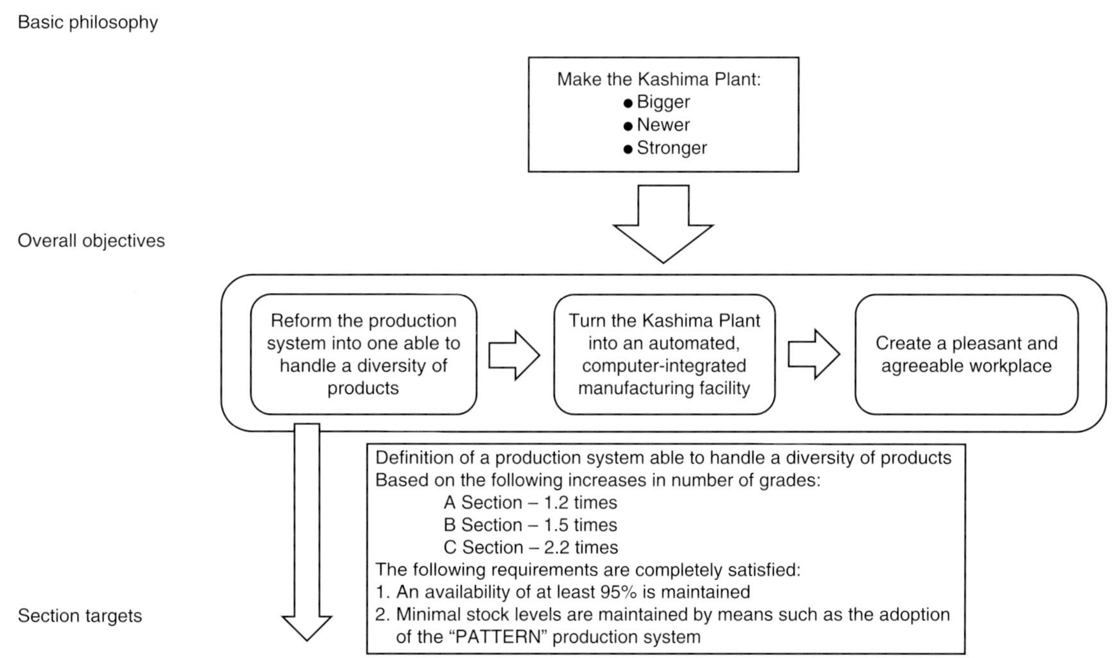

Section	Target	Q	C	D	P
A Section	Production capacity: + xx tonnes	Increase number of soft grades Improve extrudability	Increase plant investment efficiency	Reduce lead times	Increase availability Increase production capacity
B Section	Inventory holding time xx days → yy days	Achieve uniform foaming characteristics (reduce variation)	Reduce inventory interest rates Reduce internal distribution costs	Reduce lead times	Increase availability Increase production capacity
C Section	Halve inventory levels	Free up space for new operations	Reduce product storage costs Reduce inventory interest rates	Reduce lead times	Increase availability Increase production capacity

Figure 7.4 Overall objectives

2. Greater product variety creates managerial difficulties such as increased inventories and more complex production control arrangements.

Various strategies are available for overcoming these problems, such as increasing the number of process lines, installing automated systems, running continuous improvement programmes and so on. However, introducing these individually can lead to problems such as increased costs and technical constraints. Ultimately, we require the kind of management that can move a plant efficiently towards its goal of high-variety, small-lot production by adroitly marshalling all the plant's technical capabilities. This is why we became interested in TP Management.

Kashima Plant's TP Management System

TP Management System

The Kashima Plant's TP Management system is implemented in the following three phases:

1. Topics are identified by the MAP technique.
2. The topics thus identified are organised systematically by drawing up an improvement scenario.
3. Strategies are selected and implemented by means of the plant's existing MBO system.

As mentioned previously, before 1987 we had been using KPS (our old production system) to deploy our objectives, mainly by means of MBO and kaizen activities, but the kaizen campaign had reached the limits of its effectiveness, and more and more people were making the following types of comments:

"We have no clear idea of where we are heading, so we feel no sense of achievement."

"We feel pressurised and put upon".

"We have to do too many different things at once".

With New-KPS, we tried to achieve the following:

Structure our objectives, paint a clear picture of where we want to go (i.e. draw up an improvement scenario), and display section, group and individual objectives as part of a single integrated system of objectives for the plant as a whole.

Prioritise the issues based on a comprehensive review of all processes.

To achieve the above, develop a shared awareness and commitment by having top management set clear overall objectives and involving everyone in identifying the issues to be addressed.

Through this, we hoped to reach our objectives more rapidly and effectively, eliminate feelings of coercion and oppression, and create a setup that would give everyone a collective sense of achievement. Specifically, we decided to incorporate the MAP technique and the systematisation of topics by the improvement scenario method into our TP Management system (see Figure 7.5).

Features of TP Management System

The principal feature of our TP Management system is the way in which it is organically and solidly constructed around three main classes of axis: "system" axes forming the basic framework, "input" axes chanelling the driving force, and "output" axes along which the results emerge (see Figure 7.6).

The three input axes

The first of the three input axes is "top-down vision". This consists of the Kashima Plant's New-KPS reform plan based on Kaneka Corporation's long-term business plan (EX-21). It consists of our factory policy (our overall objective), which paints a clear picture of the kind of plant we want to turn ourselves into in ten years' time in order to survive into the 21st century, plus the steps we must take to get there, together with section managers' policies (guidelines for identifying the topics to be tackled and achieving the intermediate objectives).

The second input axis consists of a "reiteration loop", a system for converting the objectives into specific annual, semi-annual and monthly strategies and checking and following up the progress of implementation of these strategies at corresponding intervals.

The third input axis is "total employee involvement", an approach designed to harness the knowledge and ideas of everyone from experienced employees to new entrants, based on the fundamental requirement of total participation by all personnel in identifying the tasks to be tackled.

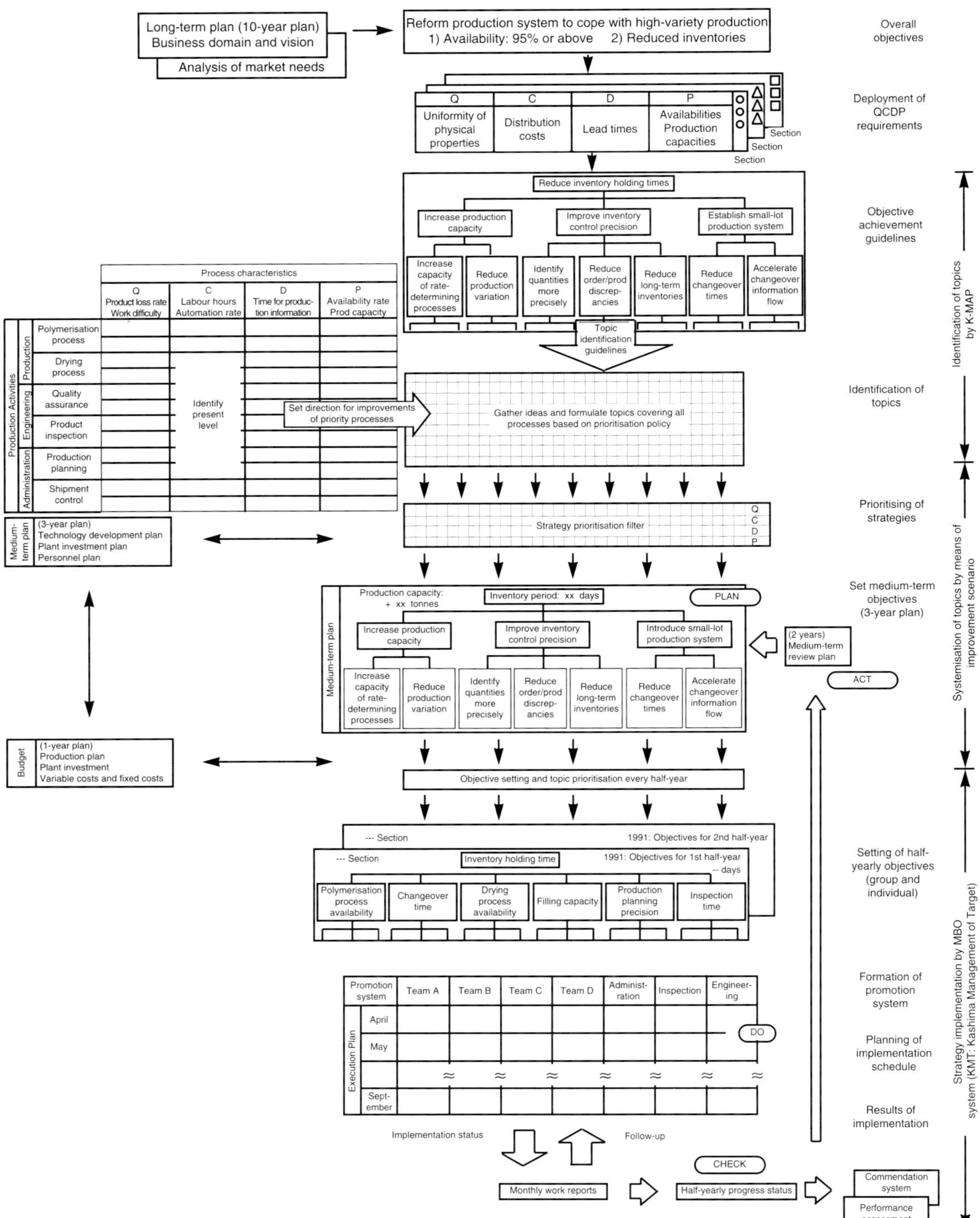

Figure 7.5 Kashima Plant's TP Management System

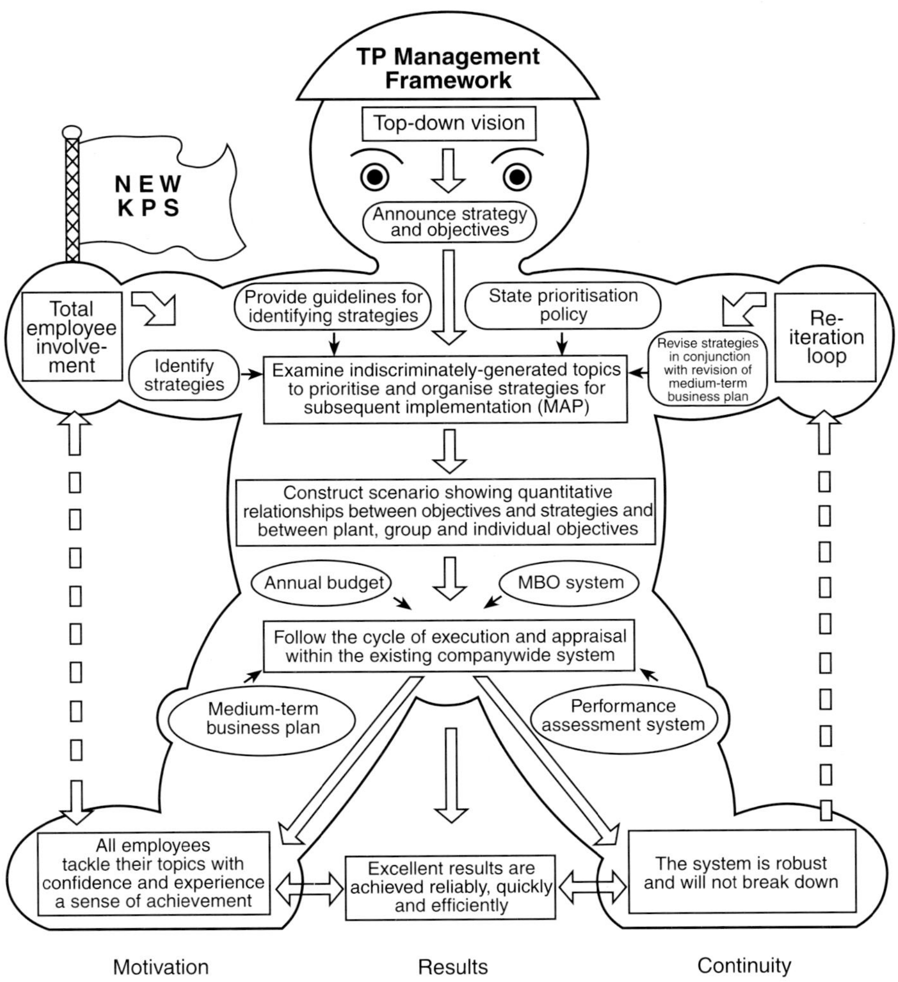

Figure 7.6 TP Management Framework

The three system axes

The three system axes consist of the MAP technique, the improvement scenario method, and the existing MBO system. The MAP technique and the improvement scenario method will be described in more detail later, since they are central features of the Kashima Plant's TP Management system.

The three output axes

The major outputs of this TP Management system can be summarised into the following three categories:

Motivation:	All employees tackle their topics with confidence and experience a sense of achievement.
Results:	Excellent results are achieved reliably, quickly and efficiently.
Continuity:	The system is robust and will not break down.

The MAP Technique

The MAP technique was proposed by the Engineering Institute of Japan as an effective method of improving operational efficiency with the participation of all employees. Kaneka Corporation has had considerable experience with this technique, using it for energy-saving, suggestion schemes, and administrative reform. We were able to combine it smoothly with our TP Management system because we were already familiar with its application.

The MAP technique was originally devised as an effective method of carrying out bottom-up type improvement activities in which individual processes identify and solve their own particular problems. However, when using it as part of our TP Management system at the Kashima Plant, we decided to start by setting top-management objectives and drawing up a provisional scenario for achieving those objectives, and then proceeding to communicate these comprehensively to our employees, carefully explaining the reasoning behind them. On top of this, we wanted to involve all employees in identifying the specific topics that had to be addressed in order to achieve the overall objectives, while giving them guidelines as to how to identify those topics.

In short, our aim was to utilise the MAP technique to build up a picture of how we were going to achieve our objectives efficiently, precisely and comprehensively through a skilful combination of the top-down and bottom-up approaches. To distinguish this approach from the conventional application of the MAP technique, we renamed it K-MAP.

Structure of MAP

The K-MAP system we used in our TP campaign was structured as shown in Figure 7.7 (although the actual diagrams we used had their vertical and horizontal axes reversed). This diagram is identical to the topic identification section of Figure 7.5.

The vertical plane of the diagram is a schematic depiction of a provisional scenario for achieving the plant's overall objectives and section objectives based on the New-KPS concept. It also shows guidelines for identifying the specific tasks to be accomplished in order to achieve those objectives. In other words, it is the "top-down" plane. We call this section of the diagram our "system of objectives"; Figure 7.8 gives a specific example.

On the horizontal plane, P, Q, C and D process characteristics are selected for all processes including engineering and administration and are ranked on a 5-step scale ranging from "world-class" at the top to "unsatisfactory" at the bottom. This allows everyone to see exactly where the plant's strengths and weaknesses lie. In other words, this is the "situation appraisal" plane. Figure 7.9 gives some specific examples of process characteristics. Based on these guidelines for identifying the tasks, everybody participates in the process of pooling ideas and formulating topics to tackle for all processes.

Photograph 7.1 is a photograph of the MAP diagram actually produced at the plant. This diagram covered an area of nearly 20 square feet. 400-500 topics were identified, their potential benefits and degrees of difficulty were assessed, and all the topics were entered into a computerised database that is continually updated to show progress.

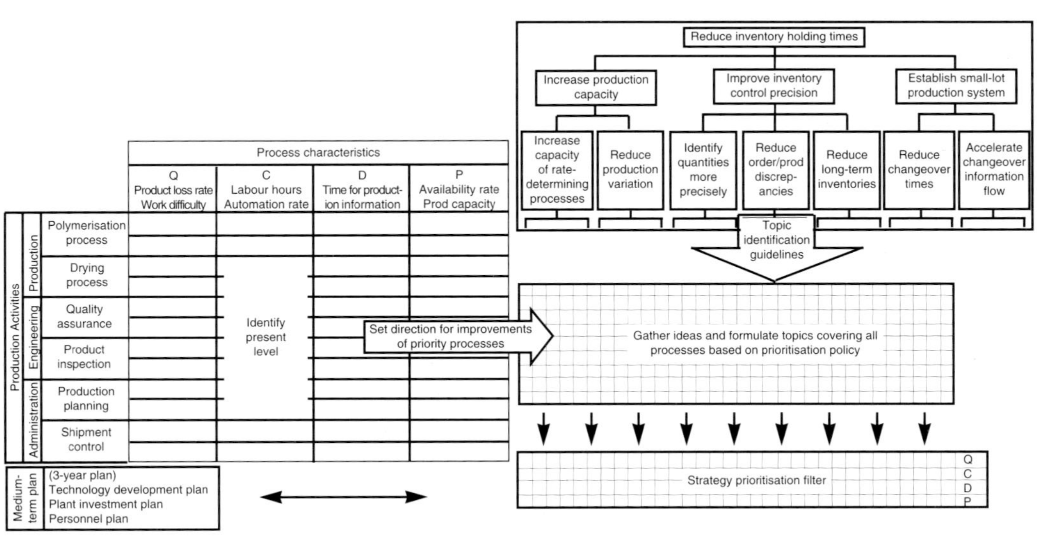

Figure 7.7 K-MAP System

Major	Intermediate	Detailed
Establish small-lot production system	Reduce changeover times	Reduce purging times
		Reduce cleanout times
		Reduce startup times
	Accelerate changeover information flow	Avoid duplication of changeovers
		Reduce inspection times
Improve inventory control precision	Identify quantities more precisely	Identify production volumes more accurately
		Reduce production variation
	Reduce long-term inventories	Reduce order quantities
		Increase precision of long-term inventory information
Increase production capacity	Increase capacity of rate-determining processes	Increase polymerisation productivity
		Eliminate rate-determining processes
		Forestall problems
	Reduce product variation	Reduce variation
		Reduce safety stocks

Figure 7.8 System of Objectives

Approach					Guidelines for identifying topics	
Establish small-lot production system	Reduce changeover times	Reduce purging times	Eliminate quality constraints	1	Can purging be speeded up by ensuring that no residues are left in tanks?	1
				2	Can purging be speeded up by matching contamination tolerances more accurately to specific product grades?	
				3	Can purging be speeded up by changing the temperatures to prevent deterioration of residues?	
				4	Can purging be speeded up by revising the permissible residue moisture contents?	
			Eliminate equipment constraints	1	Can waiting times be reduced by increasing the discharge rates?	2
				2	Can discharge rates be increased by altering the number or capacities of storage tanks?	
				3	Can purging be speeded up by modifying the areas and vibration rate of the xxx unit?	
				4	Can purging be speeded up by altering switch layouts or operating panel locations?	
			Eliminate operating constraints	1	Can purging be speeded up by improving the automatic cleaning procedure?	3
				2	Can waiting times be reduced by changing the sequence and manning of purging operations?	
				3	Can purging be speeded up by changing the treatment conditions to correspond more exactly to slurry densities and quantities?	
				4	Can purging be speeded up by revising the start times and manning schedules for filling operations?	
		Reduce cleanout times	Review cleaning standards	1	Can cleanout times be reduced by establishing clear assessment criteria for storage tank residues?	
				2	Can cleanout times be reduced by establishing clear-cut cleaning standards for parts of equipment where residues easily collect?	
				3	Can cleanout times be reduced by establishing clear-cut standards for pressures and volumes of compressed air and cleaning water?	
				4	Can unnecessary cleaning be eliminated by revising the production sequence for products that require little cleaning between changeovers?	
				1	Can cleaning operations be simplified by redesigning equipment in which residues easily collect?	

Figure 7.8 (continued) MAP Checklist

- Select process characteristics from standpoint of system of objectives
- Evaluate process characteristics on five-step scale and fill in with appropriate colour

Process characteristic		Definition	Blue	Green	Yellow	Pink	Red
P	Availability	Overall production efficiency (%)	--	--	--	--	--
	Production capacity	Individual process capacities (tonnes/month)	--	--	--	--	--
	------	------------	--	--	--	--	--
Q	Product loss rate	Monthly proportion of defective product (%)	--	--	--	--	--
	Work difficulty	Degree of requirement for skilled workers (labour-hours/month)	--	--			--
			--	--	--	--	--
C	Automation rate	Work automation rate (%)	--	--	--	--	--
	------	------------	--	--	--	--	--
D	Changeover time	Time per changeover (h/changeover)	--	--	--	--	--
	Time required to obtain production information	Time required to obtain results data (h/result)	--	--	--	--	--
	------	------ -------	--	--	--	--	--

Minor ← Severity of problem → Major

Figure 7.9 Process Characteristics

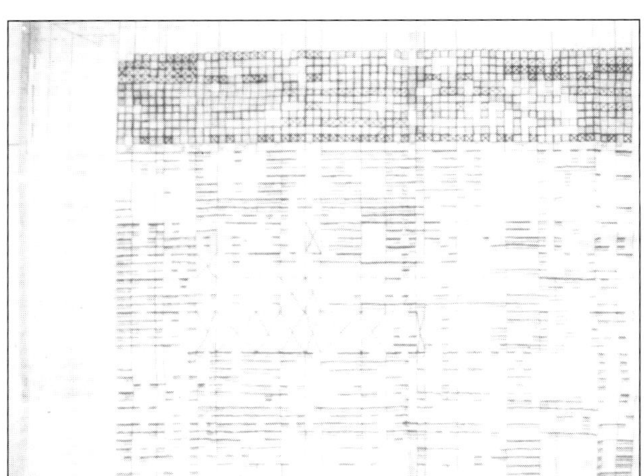

Photograph 7.1 MAP Chart

Construction of Improvement Scenario

It would not be sensible to try to implement all the tasks identified by the MAP technique indiscriminately. Top management therefore considers the current objectives and the strengths and weaknesses of the various processes and specifies the direction of improvement for each of the major processes. The resulting "prioritisation policy" acts as a filter for selecting the topics to be implemented.

The topics elicited on the basis of the prioritisation policy are assigned in accordance with the first provisional improvement scenario; their logical connections to the objectives are then checked, and any necessary calculations are performed. If it is found that certain topics will not lead to the achievement of the objectives, new ones are sought. This is the stage at which the top-down objectives are integrated with the bottom-up strategies. Figure 7.10 depicts this process.

The improvement scenario developed in this way is to be turned into reality over a 1.5-year or 2-year period, and it is incorporated into the company's medium-term business plan. A new improvement scenario is drawn up every half-year at the strategy implementation stage in order to fit in with the six-monthly management cycle used in the MBO system. In this way, we move on to the next step every six months while checking how much progress has been made over the previous six-month period.

The improvement scenario for each six-month period is displayed in the plant's control room as shown in Photograph 7.2 to enable anyone to see at a glance who is tackling what topic, and how success with one's own particular task relates to the achievement of the section and group objectives.

These scenarios were unexpectedly effective in raising people's awareness of the relevant issues. This is because they display the state of progress and show immediately how each individual's tasks relate to the overall task of his or her section and to other individual's tasks. They can also be adapted to suit the characteristics of particular workplaces.

PDCA by Existing System

Each medium-term improvement scenario is coordinated with the R & D plan, equipment plan, personnel plan and budget and incorporated into the medium-term business plan. As noted above, new scenarios are drawn up every six months and fresh group objectives and topics are established. Each group breaks down its objectives to the level of individual employees, and each employee prepares a monthly implementation plan. Employees report their achievements at monthly progress meetings, where they have an opportunity to receive advice from their supervisors. Progress towards achievement of the targets is reflected in six-monthly performance

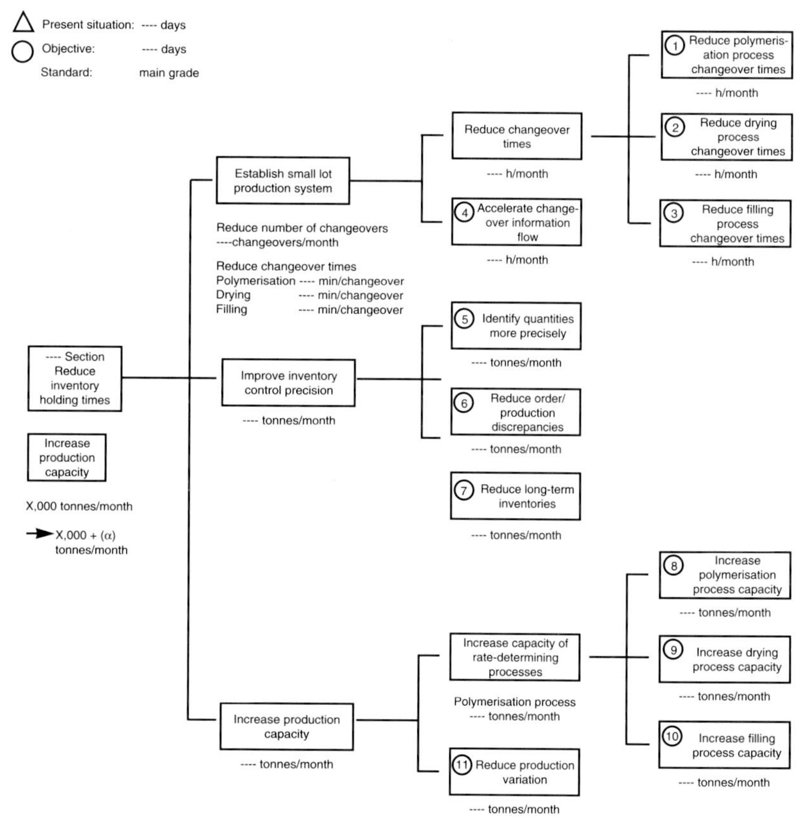

(1) Reduce polymerisation process changeover times

Topic No.	Contribution
A-01-03-02	
A-03-03-16	
B-02-03-10	12.2
B-06-03-20	0.9
B-06-03-21	4.1
B-06-03-22	4.1
B-07-03-17	
B-08-03-29	
TOTAL	

(2) Reduce drying process changeover times

Topic No.	Contribution
A-01-04-05	0.5
A-01-04-06	0.4
A-01-04-07	6.0
A-03-04-17	0.2
A-05-04-22	1.6
A-05-04-23	
A-06-04-27	4.0
A-07-04-29	1.9
A-07-04-35	0.5
A-08-04-39	
A-10-04-57	0.5
A-13-04-62	0.6
B-08-04-41	
B-08-04-42	0.1
B-08-04-43	0.3
TOTAL	

(3) Reduce filling process changeover times

Topic No.	Contribution
A-01-05-01	0.8
A-06-05-08	1.9
A-11-06-11	
A-13-06-14	0.1
B-02-06-02	
B-01-06-05	
B-05-05-06	0.3
B-05-05-55	0.8
TOTAL	

(4) Accelerate changeover information flow

Topic No.	Contribution
C-10-01-05	5.7
A-12-06-02	4.4
A-12-06-03	
A-12-06-04	15.3
A-1--08-11	1.9
TOTAL	

(5) Identify quantities more precisely

Topic No.	Contribution
B-15-02-03	
A-16-05-02	
B-15-05-01	0.5
A-16-07-13	
B-14-07-01	
B-01-08-01	5.0
TOTAL	

(6) Reduce order/production discrepancies

Topic No.	Contribution
B-20-01-07	5.0
A-17-01-06	0.8
B-20-08-01	1.1
C-17-08-02	5.8
TOTAL	

(7) Reduce long-term inventories

Topic No.	Contribution
A-25-05-18	1.3
B-22-05-19	0.7
A-22-06-18	2.7
B-21-08-05	12.5
C-21-08-06	3.8
TOTAL	

(8) Increase polymerisation process capacity

Topic No.	Contribution
A-26-03-02	
A-26-03-03	5.9
A-26-03-04	3.5
A-27-03-07	0.6
A-29-03-13	7.8
A-33-03-19	
A-33-03-21	1.3
B-27-03-06	8.4
B-28-03-09	26.7
B-28-03-12	12.4
B-30-03-15	1.7
B-30-03-16	7.9
B-31-03-18	11.2
B-31-03-17	10.5
TOTAL	

(9) Increase drying process capacity

Topic No.	Contribution
A-27-04-11	4.4
A-29-04-13	
A-30-04-17	14.8
A-31-04-19	8.3
A-34-04-25	4.1
A-34-04-26	2.4
B-26-04-04	4.9
B-26-04-05	
B-30-04-16	6.9
B-34-04-24	1.8
TOTAL	

(10) Increase filling process capacity

Topic No.	Contribution
B-30-06-05	25.0
B-31-05-07	47.5
B-35-05-11	5.0
B-35-05-12	20.0
B-35-05-13	10.0
TOTAL	

(11) Reduce production variation

Topic No.	Contribution
A-41-02-00	0.7
A-30-05-20	2.0
A-41-05-05	
A-37-08-21	10.9
A-41-08-19	0.5
A-41-08-22	5.0
B-38-08-12	4.0
B-38-08-14	12.5
TOTAL	

Figure 7.10 Medium-Term Improvement Scenario

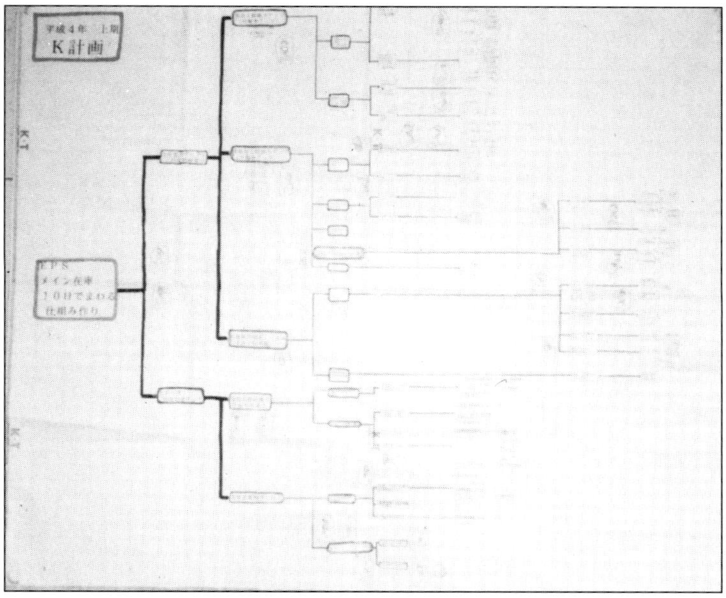

Photograph 7.2 6-Monthly Improvement Scenario

assessments, and are also used in revising the current scenario when the medium-term business plan is reviewed at the end of each financial year.

We thus use our existing system to follow the PDCA (plan-do-check-act) cycle in this way, in order to ensure that the strategies for achieving the overall objectives are faithfully implemented. Figure 7.11, the bottom half of the TP Management diagram given in Figure 7.5, shows this process in action.

Results

Since introducing TP Management, we have increased our equipment availability, which directly affects our standard production capacity, by approximately 15 per cent (see Figure 7.12). Taking into account the fact that the number of product changeovers has increased by a factor of 1.4 during this period, this means that the availability has actually increased by nearly 20 per cent. An increase in capacity commensurate with this increase in availability has also been achieved. This capacity increase is equivalent to a standardised equipment investment amounting to over £12.5 million. Even though some money was spent on improvements, the net figure represents a considerable saving on capacity expansion expenditure.

The results achieved by C Section show that the original target of halving inventory levels was achieved, while the increased production capacity was also accompanied by the planned increases in labour productivity, changeover time reduction, and reduction in amount of defective product.

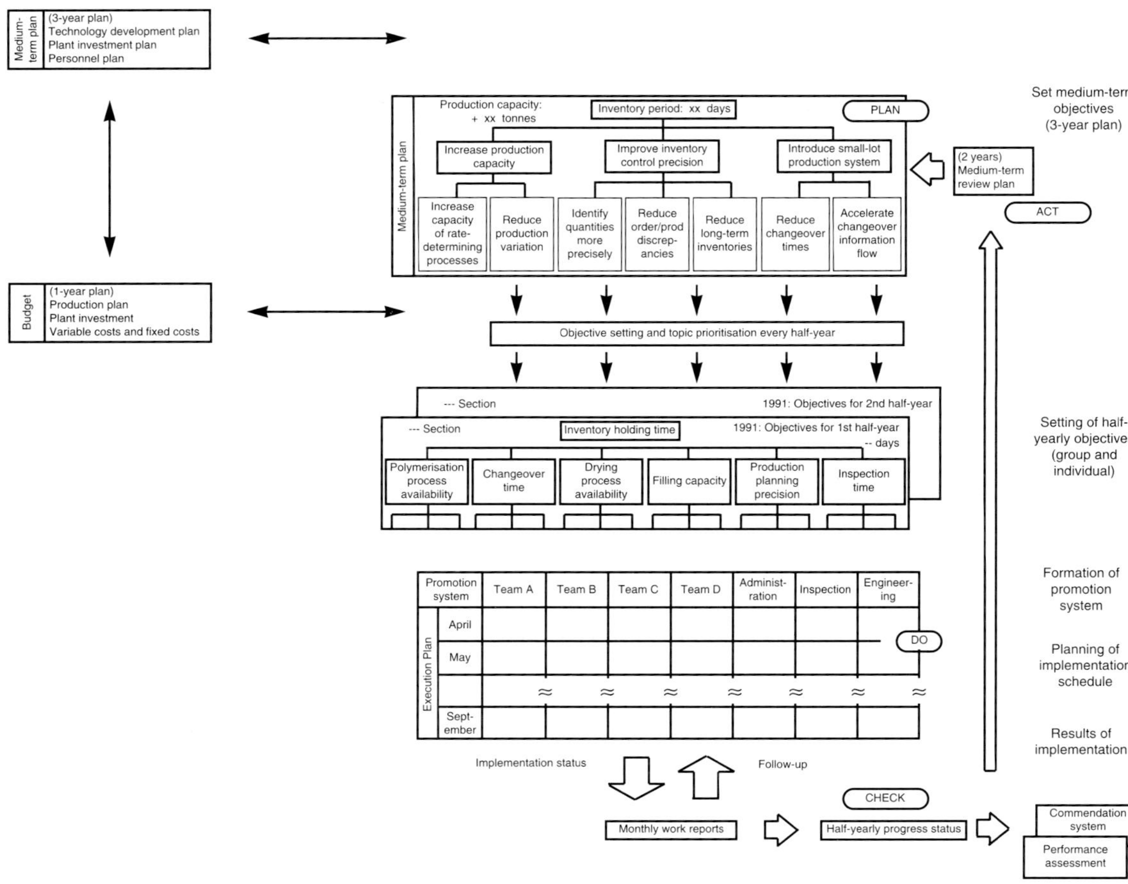

Figure 7.11 Detail of TP Management System

In addition to these tangible results, we were also extremely concerned with the extent to which the activities would increase the organisation's vitality. Figure 7.13 summarises the results of a questionnaire completed by all the members of our production sections. It shows that the activities produced good results both at the section and individual levels.

Taken together, these results indicate that we more or less achieved the aims of our original plan – to create a system that would allow us to experience a collective sense of achievement.

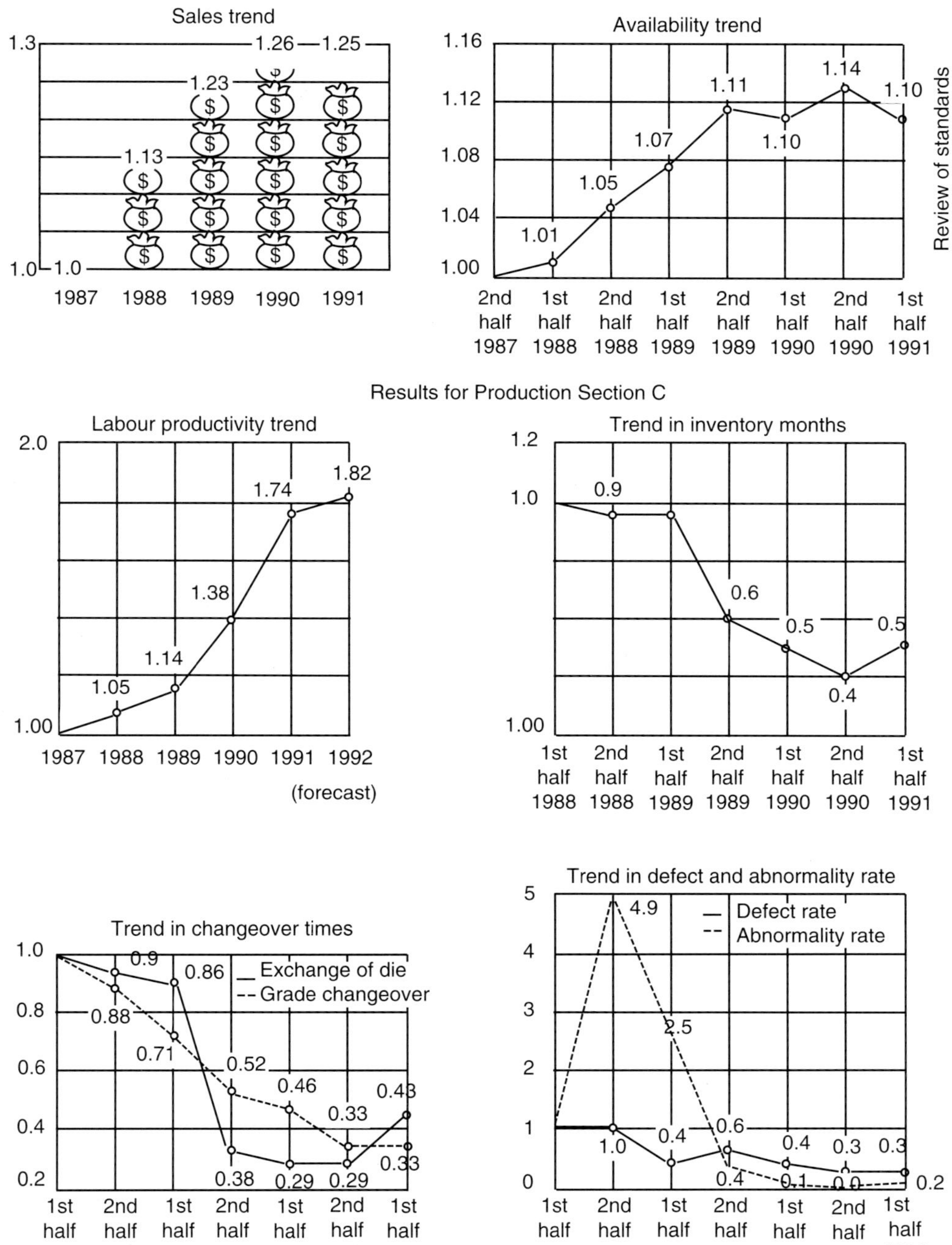

Figure 7.12 Overall Plant Results

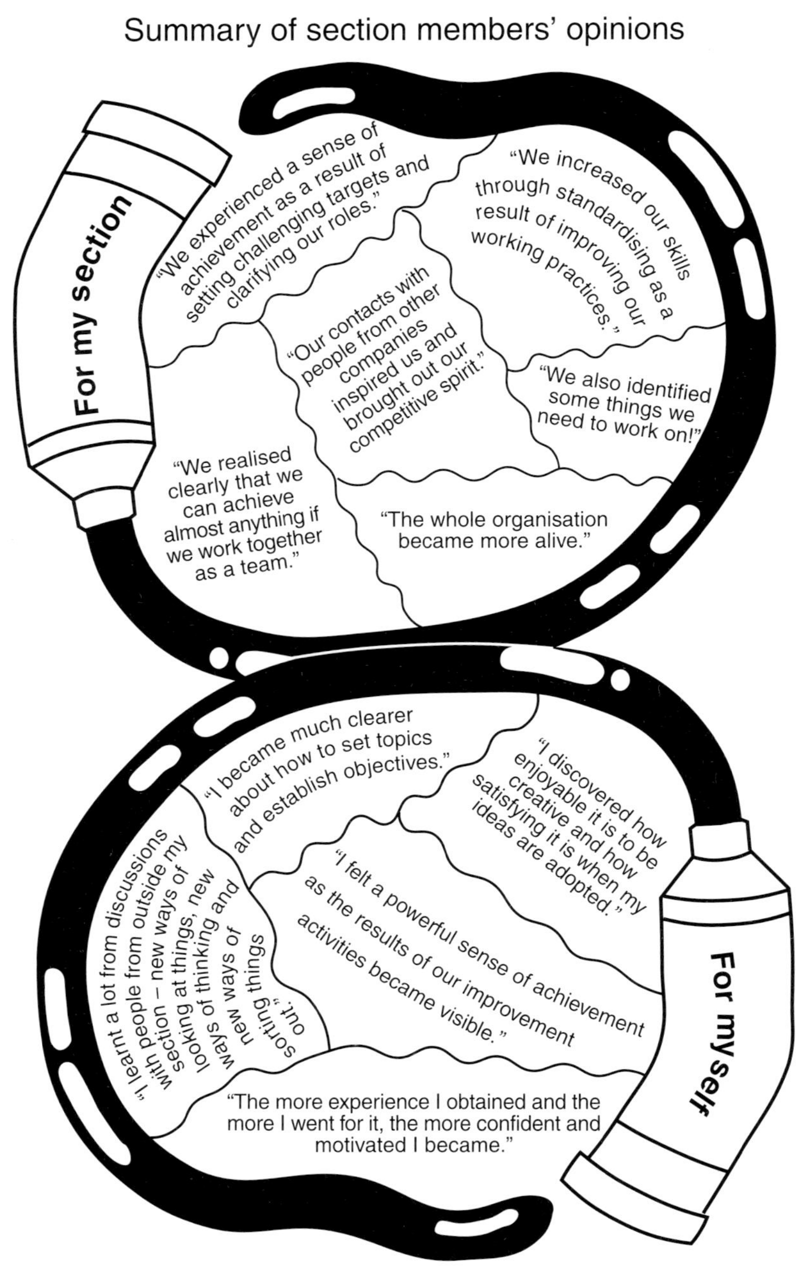

Figure 7.13 Review of Flexible Production System Campaign Activities

1. Combine TP Management with customer-focused product strategy
2. Introduce automated, computer-integrated manufacturing systems
3. Paint a clearer picture of our final destination
4. Develop fresh responses to environmental protection and recycling issues

Figure 7.14 Future Tasks

Future Development

We see our main task for the future as deepening and internalising our customer-focused approach by analysing customer needs even more thoroughly when setting our objectives, and then incorporating the results into our product strategy. We also aim to introduce comprehensive factory automation and computer-integrated manufacturing systems as the next step after the introduction of the New-KPS system (see Figure 7.14).

We believe that, in order to achieve this, we must paint an even clearer picture of our final destination, and we are now actively engaged in this process.

8
Snow Brand Milk Products, Atsugi Plant

Creating a Highly Flexible Production System and an Excellent Working Environment

Akira Takahashi, General Manager, Production Department,
Kanto Regional Division (formerly General Manager, Atsugi Plant)
Takashi Kaneko, Manager, Fluid Milk Technical Section ,
Fluid Milk & Ice-Cream Production Department
Snow Brand Milk Products Co., Ltd.

Introduction

Company Profile

Snow Brand Milk Products Co., Ltd. started life in 1925, adopting its present name in 1950. The company, which will celebrate its 70th anniversary in 1995, has the following vital statistics:

Capital: ¥27,800 million (March 1993)

Sales: ¥542,300 million (FY 1992)

Ordinary profit: ¥15,200 million (FY 1992)

Number of employees: 7,779 (end of March 1993)

Business operations: Manufacture and marketing of milk, milk products, ice cream, soft drinks, desserts, frozen foods, alcoholic drinks, pharmaceuticals, baby foods and other products.

Profile of Atsugi Plant

The Atsugi Plant, located in the centre of Kanagawa Prefecture to the south-west of Tokyo, came on-stream in 1967 as Snow Brand's main facility for the manufacture of milk products (milk, yoghurt and desserts). The plant's principal products are refrigerated items such as milk and yoghurt, and long-life goods such as long-life milk, soft ice-cream mix, and long-life cream for use in coffee. Yoghurt accounts for approximately 40% of the Atsugi Plant's total production, and it is the only Snow Brand plant to manufacture soft ice-cream mix and individual portions of long-life cream.

Besides being Snow Brand's distribution centre for the Tokyo metropolitan region, the Atsugi Plant accepts trainees from overseas and provides training for production technology personnel.

Size of plant (as of October 1992)

Number of items produced: 50 (in 103 formats)
Site area: 52,660 m^2
Factory footprint: 18,197 m^2
Number of employees: approx. 200
Number of supplier companies: 6 (approx. 250 employees)
Sales: ¥29,500 million (FY 1992)

Features of the Milk Products Business

Product Features

In recent years, products such as milk and yoghurt have achieved the status of "health foods" on the Japanese market. All food production in Japan is tightly regulated, but milk products are subject to particularly stringent quality and safety controls in the form of official ordinances specifying standards for their composition.

Milk products are ordered, manufactured and shipped on a daily basis, and are ideally delivered at specified times with zero in-plant inventory. For such products, freshness – as defined by date of manufacture – is an important selling point. Sales of these products fluctuate considerably according to the season, day of the week, weather, and other factors.

Features of the Distribution System

Changes in the dairy industry's distribution system have brought about corresponding changes in the marketing of its products. There has been a major shift away from dairy outlets and general retailers towards supermarkets, convenience stores and vending machines. In line with this trend, dairy chains have streamlined their distribution systems, setting up joint distribution centres, and goods are now despatched to these centres in larger quantities than before.

In addition to this, consumers' demands for better freshness in daily-delivery products have led to more stringent requirements regarding sell-by-dates and delivery times, and supermarkets and convenience stores are demanding more frequent deliveries.

Changes in Order-Processing Systems

In the past, orders from dairy outlets, supermarkets and convenience stores came in by telephone and fax. However, the need for greater accuracy and speed has resulted in a gradual shift towards on-line order-processing using mainframe computers (see Figure 8.1).

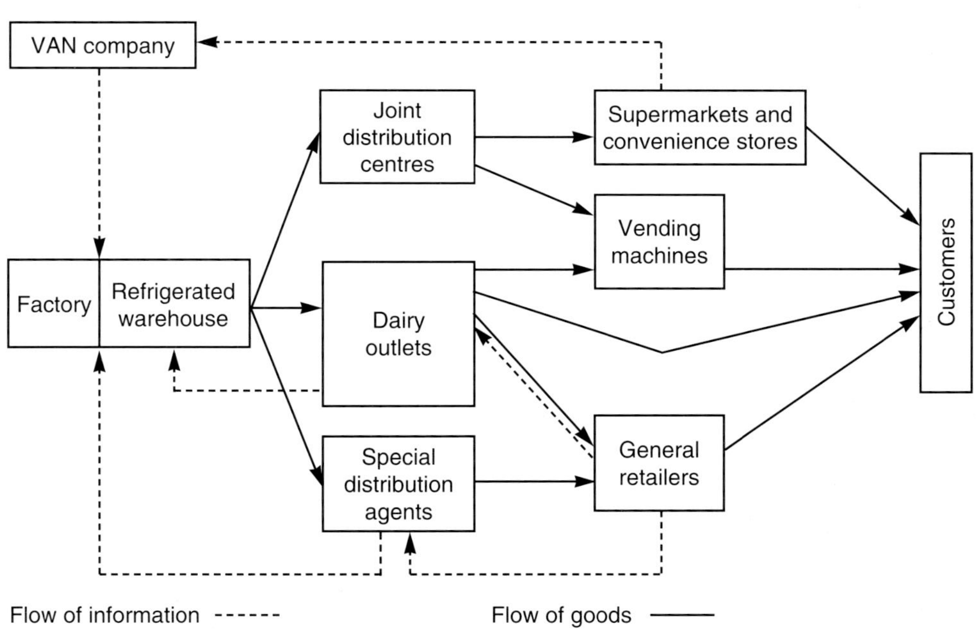

Figure 8.1 The Process Sequence: Order Processing → Manufacturing

Features of Our Production System

Snow Brand Milk Products produces to daily orders, with the projected production figures finalised daily. We have to meet delivery deadlines at multiple destinations,so we produce numerous batches of the same item at frequent intervals. To keep pace with fluctuating market demands, we manufacture a wide range of products in variable quantities. Our milk-products operation can therefore be summed up as "variable-type,variable-quantity production".

Note: Simple high-variety production leaves fairly long lead-times between order-processing and delivery. Variable-type, variable-quantity production is this plus the just-in-time concept – making the required products in exactly the right quantities at exactly the right times.

How TP Management was Introduced at Atsugi Plant

Some years ago, Snow Brand Milk Products began to apply industrial engineering methods to its production operations in order to raise their efficiency. To help our company accommodate market demands, we implemented various strategies at our factories, including (1) high-variety, small-lot production, and (2) improving the efficiency of our delivery systems. However, times moved on, and Japan saw major political and economic upheavals. Drastic changes took place on the market, in the distribution infrastructure, and in consumer needs, and we realised that we needed a radical new approach.

After reviewing the situation, the company came up with a medium-term management plan called "FRESH 70". One of the strategic tasks we set ourselves in production was to improve our plant management, and we resolved to introduce TP Management for this purpose. The Atsugi Plant, our leading milk-products factory in terms of both production volume and facilities, was selected as a "guinea pig" for the transformation process.

TP Management was introduced to the Atsugi Plant between 1989 and 1992. Figure 8.2 shows the progress of the campaign.

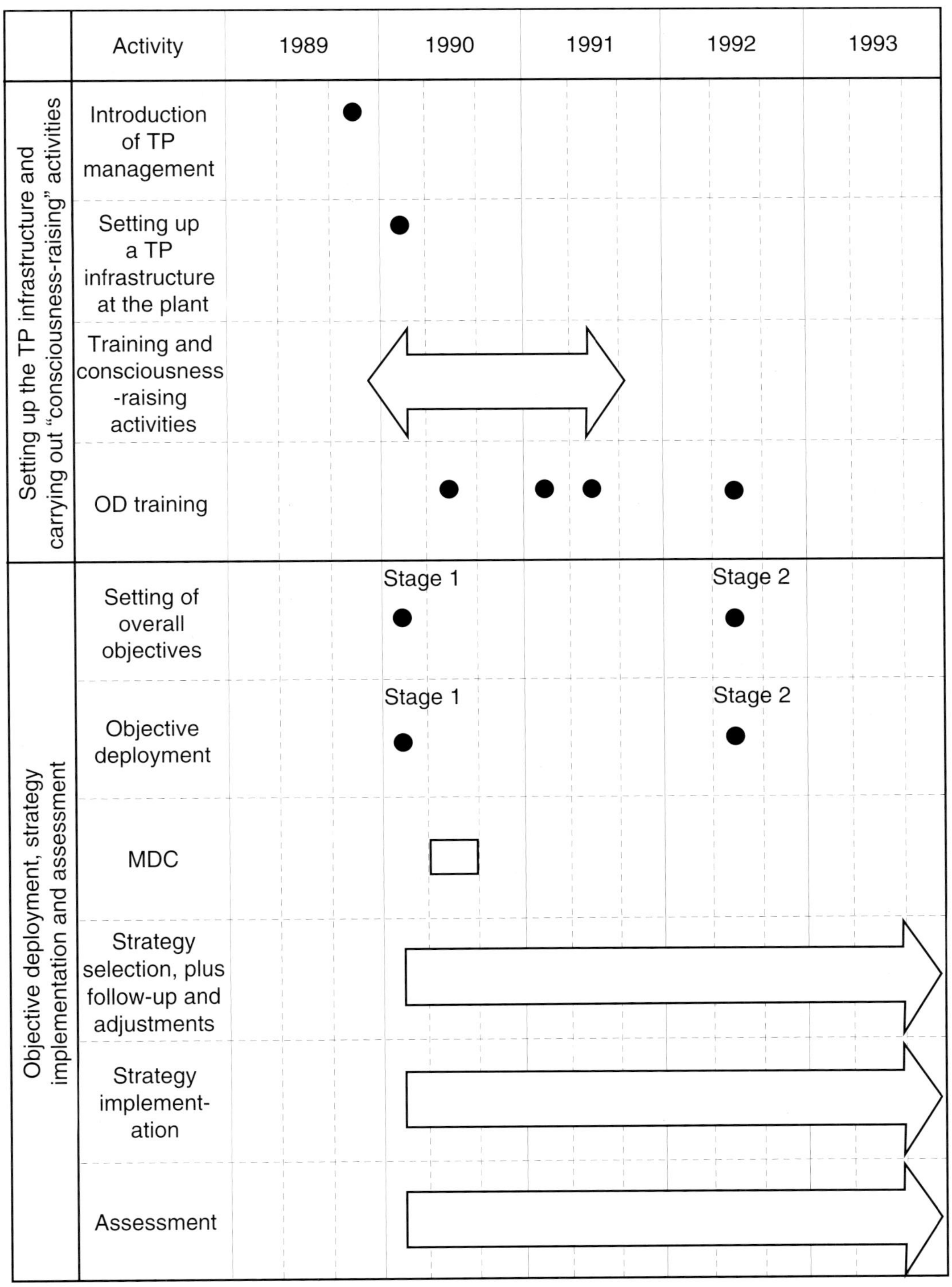

Figure 8.2 Progress of TP Management at Atsugi Plant

OD – Organisation Development
MDC – Method Design Concept

Our TP Management Philosophy

Introducing TP Management as the Guiding Principle in the Running of the Plant

We introduced TP Management as our basic philosophy behind the running of the Atsugi Plant. All the activities carried out at the plant are now based on the concept of a perpetual drive towards overall optimisation rather than piecemeal or individual optimisation.

Setting Overall Objectives in terms of Customer Satisfaction (CS) and Employee Satisfaction (ES)

Our deployment of TP Management was built around our vision of the future of the Atsugi Plant: a milk-products plant oriented towards Customer Satisfaction (CS) and underpinned by Employee Satisfaction (ES). We set ourselves the overall objective of "establishing a flexible production and delivery system able to accommodate the variable-type, variable-quantity production and frequent delivery requirements of a milk-products plant".

Figure 8.3 shows how our concepts of Customer Satisfaction and Employee Satisfaction were developed. CS, ES, and "customer" are defined below.

Customer Satisfaction (CS): What customers feel as a result of being supplied with highly attractive products and services which exceed their expectations.

Employee Satisfaction (ES): The physical and mental wellbeing which employees gain through their work; that which motivates employees and inspires them to display their full capabilities.

The relationship between ES and CS: Raising ES increases the enthusiasm and ability of employees, leading to greater CS through the resulting improvement in product and service quality.

"The customer": (1) Ordinary consumers (2) Retailers, supermarkets and convenience stores (3) School meal services, workplaces (hospitals, etc.) (4) Commercial users (including other food manufacturers).

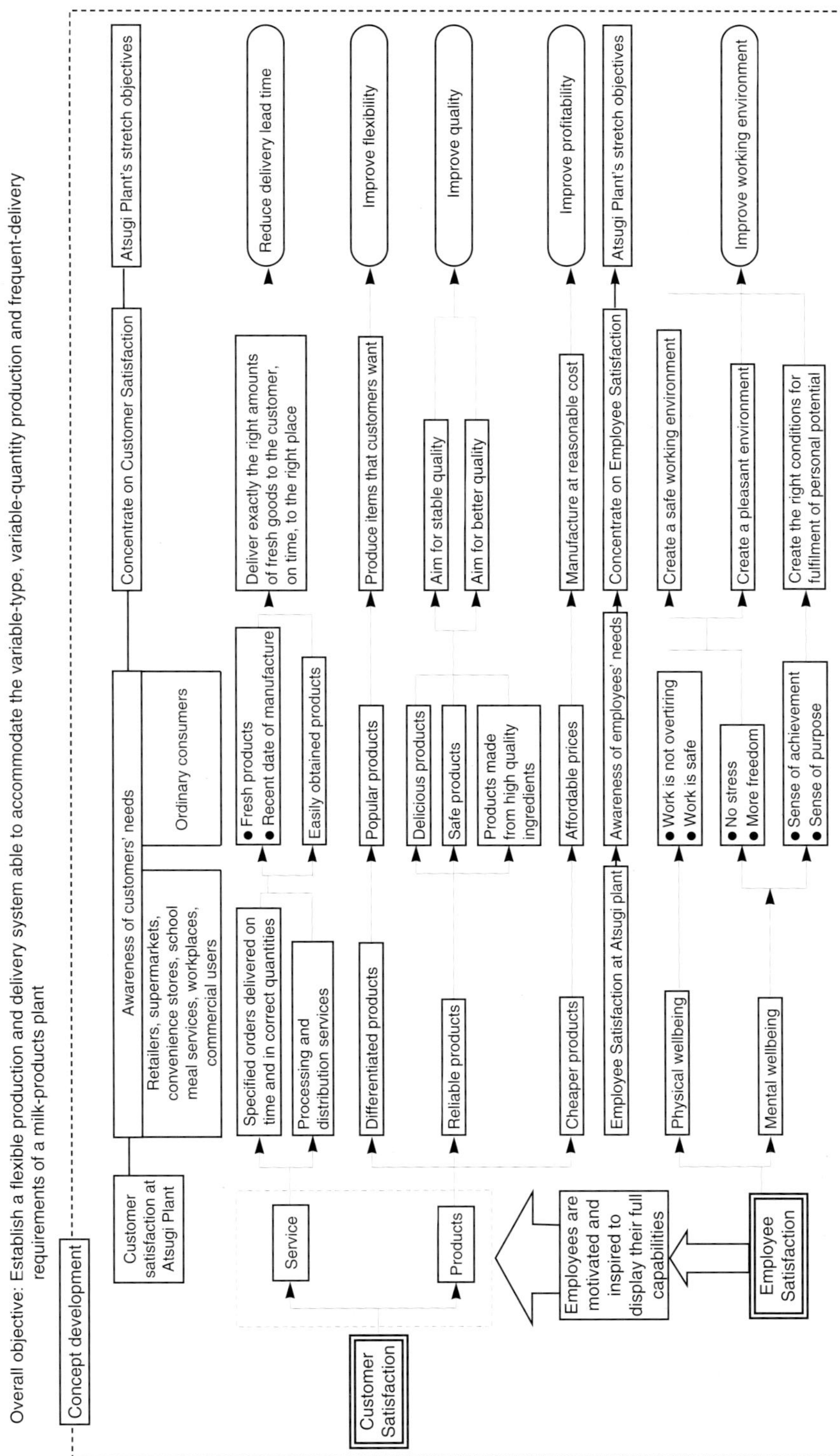

Figure 8.3 TP Management Concept Development at Atsugi Plant

Setting Stretch Objectives

From our analysis of CS and ES as illustrated in Figure 8.3, we worked out how the Atsugi Plant would have to change over the next five years in order to acquire the flexibility to cope with a fluctuating market. As a result, we arrived at the following five stretch objectives, also shown in the diagram:

1. *Reduce delivery lead time (D)* . Reduce the total time from finalising incoming orders to shipping the goods, in order to deliver the products to the customer more quickly for greater freshness.

2. *Improve flexibility (F).* Create a highly efficient production system in order to raise our ability to perform variable-type, variable-quantity production and keep pace with customer needs by accommodating a widely-varying product range.

3. *Improve quality (Q).* Provide reliable, delicious and safe products to improve the health and quality of life of our customers.

4. *Improve profitability; i.e. reduce costs (C).* Produce goods at low enough cost to ensure that the plant is profitable.

5. *Improve working environment (W).* Improve employees' quality of working life by creating an environment which allows them to work safely and fulfil their personal potential.

Targets for stretch objectives (for FY 1993)

1. Delivery lead-time reduction (D)
   Manufacturing: 14% down on 1989
   (relative to production volume)
   Shipping: 9% down on 1989
   (relative to production volume)
2. Flexibility (F)
   Increase by factor of 1.2 (relative to 1989)
3. Quality (Q)
   Double (relative to 1989)
4. Profitability; i.e. Cost (C)
   Reduce labour costs by 24% (relative to production volume)
5. Working environment (W)
   Improve by 10% (relative to 1991)

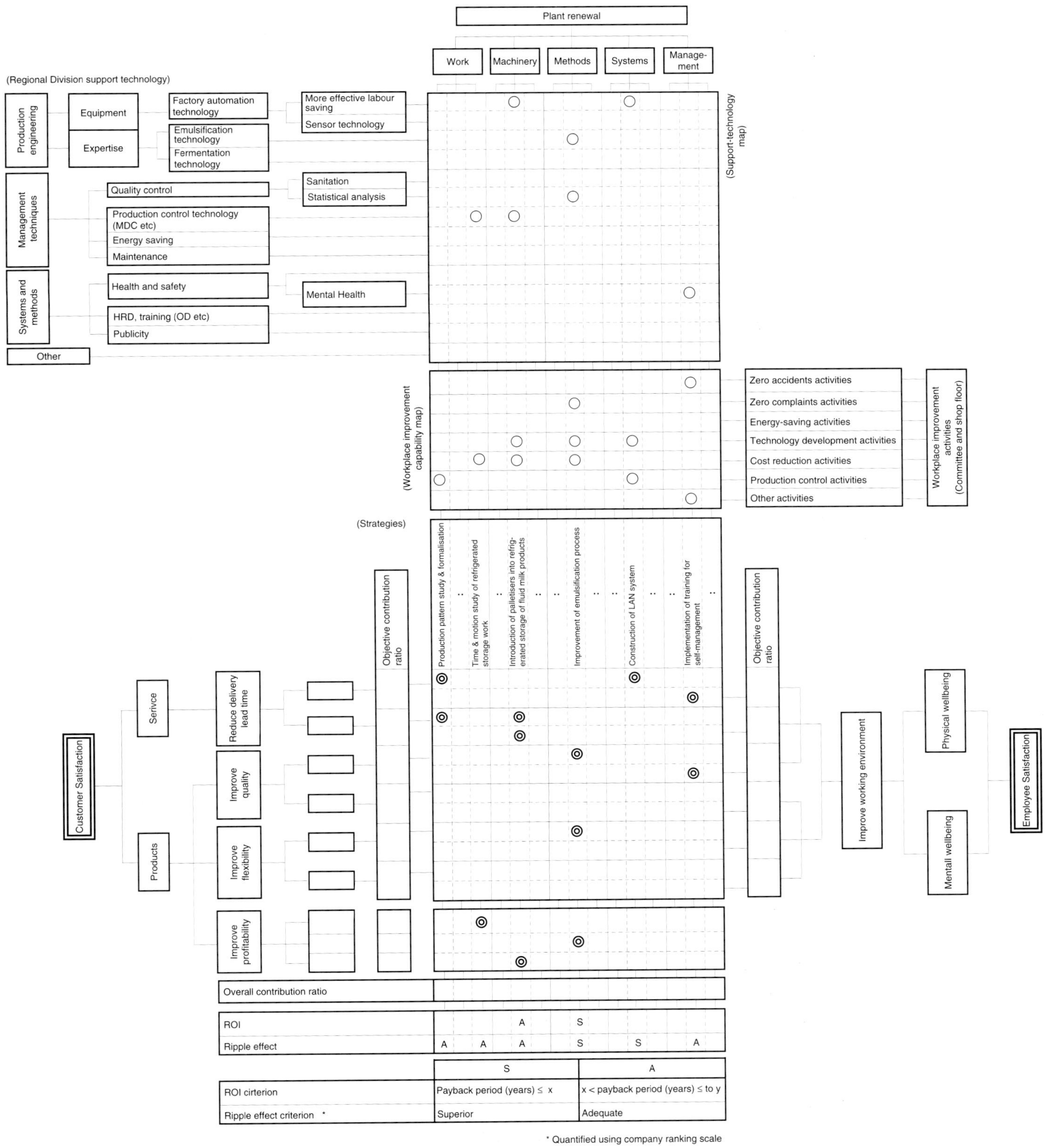

Figure 8.4 Overall TP Management System at Atsugi Plant

Overall TP Management System

Figure 8.4 shows the overall TP Management system at the Atsugi Plant, clearly demonstrating the relationship between the stretch objectives and the strategies used to attain them. The strategies were designed to bring about a gradual "renewal" of the plant (in terms of equipment, expertise, and management) through Head Office support technology and workplace improvement capabilities. The aim was to create a combination of an excellent working environment and a flexible manufacturing system.

Objective Deployment

Basic Principles of Objective Deployment

In order to attain the stretch objectives we had set ourselves, we deployed them in a number of distinct stages. In Stage I, we took a particular stretch objective, broke it down into one or two priority objectives, and established a target value for each of these. We then broke down the priority objectives in further stages, eventually reaching a set of individual objectives for each line. which we employed as indicators of total productivity.

We assigned different priorities to the stretch objectives, depending on the characteristics of the product group or line in question. As Figure 8.5 shows, priority was given to reducing delivery lead time for chilled products such as milk, while greatest emphasis was placed on improving flexibility and quality for long-life products. For yoghurt, the most important stretch objectives were improving flexibility, improving quality, improving profitability and improving the working environment.

A Practical Example of Objective Deployment

Figure 8.6 shows how the objective deployment process was carried out for lead-time reduction. The overall lead-time reduction targets were shared out among the various production lines, and a set of individual objectives and targets was established for each line. For example, the objective "reduce manufacturing lead time" in the case of Line A was divided up into a number of elements, such as "reduce product changeover time", "reduce time lost through problems", and "reduce setup time", with a numerical target for each.

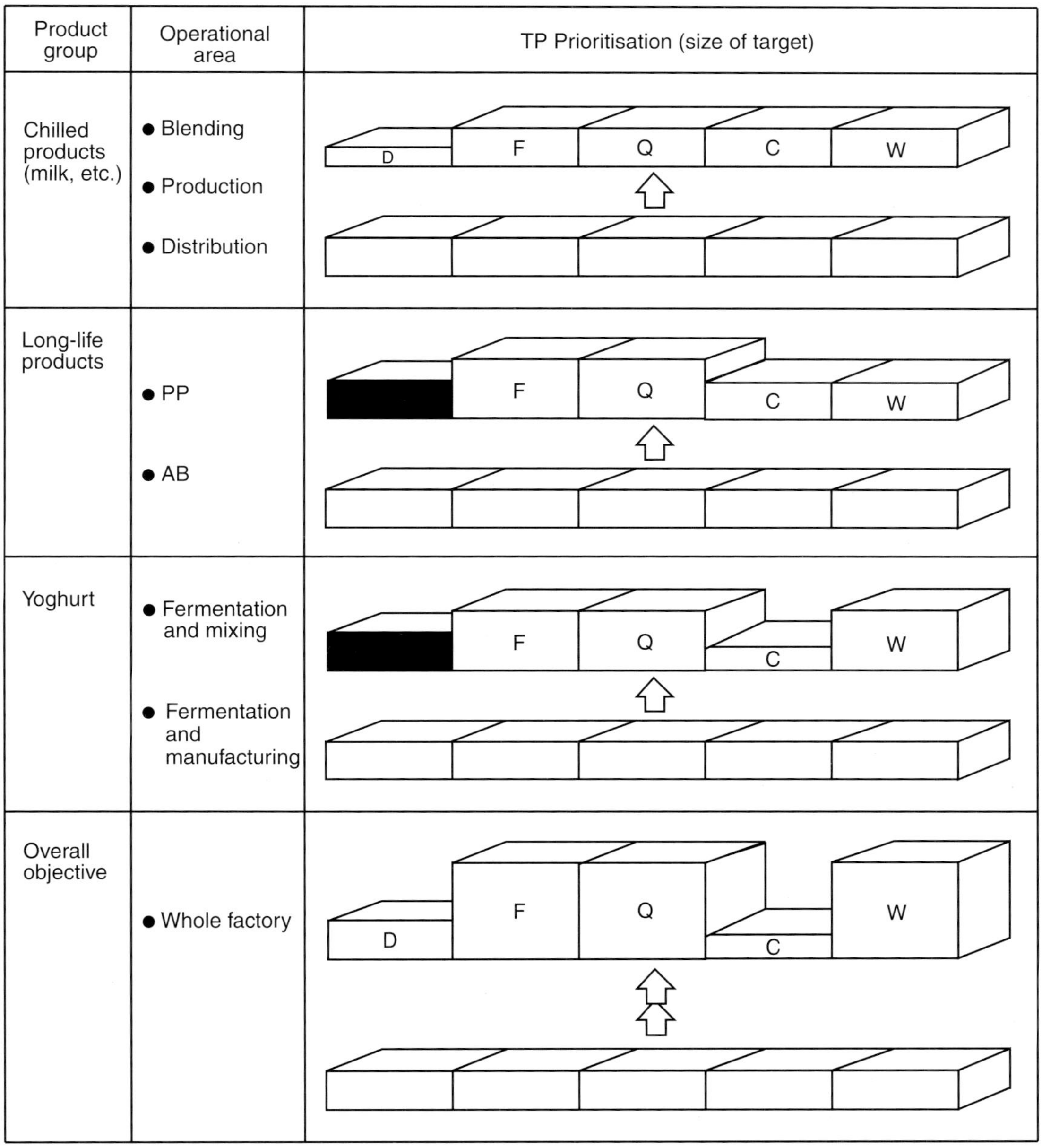

[Overall objective (total productivity)]

$$\text{Total productivity for Atsugi Plant} = \frac{F\uparrow \times Q\uparrow \times W\uparrow}{D\downarrow \times C\downarrow}$$

NOTE: In this diagram, the objective of improving profitability is represented as reducing costs (C)

Figure 8.5 Prioritisation of Stretch Objectives for Particular Product Groups and Lines

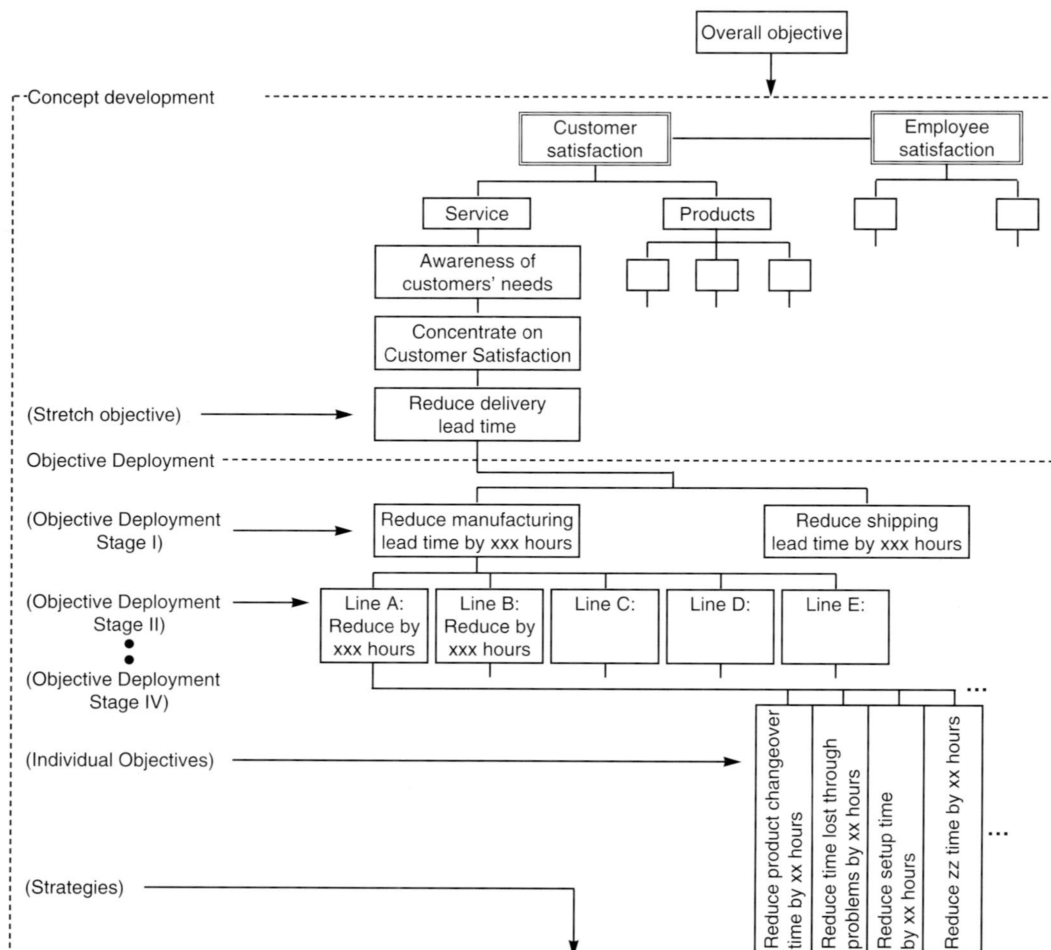

Workplace responsible			Progress	Strategy	Objective contribution ratio	xx%	xx%	xx%		Total %
Committee	Operational area	Other depts involved								
	Fluid milk products			A			xxx			xxx
	Fluid milk products	Regional division		B				xxx		xxx
	Fluid milk products			C		xxx				xxx
	Fluid milk products	Regional division		D				xxx		xxx
	Fluid milk products			E		xxx				xxx
"Fresh-Up"	Distribution	Kantō Regional division		F		xxx				xxx

Figure 8.6 Example of Objective Deployment: "Reduce Delivery Lead Time"

Strategy Selection

Reasoning Behind Strategy Selection

As Figure 8.4 (our overall TP deployment diagram) shows, we arrived at our strategies by deploying the stretch objectives and checking the results against an analysis of the Head Office support technologies and workplace improvement capabilities available. We then calculated the overall contribution ratio for each strategy (the percentage contribution it could be expected to make towards the achievement of the overall objective) and screened the strategies in order of their overall contribution ratios, based on their predicted return on investment (ROI). Finally, we selected particular strategies on the basis of their "ripple effect" (their beneficial side-effects).

For example, Figure 8.4 shows that the strategy of improving the emulsification process contributes to improving quality, flexibility and profitability, and that it combines the Head Office support technologies for emulsification and quality control with the workplace improvement activities of ZC (zero complaints), technology development and cost reduction. This strategy's ROI is high, and it also has an excellent ripple effect.

As Figure 8.7 shows, the overall contribution ratio for a particular strategy is the sum of the individual contribution ratios of that strategy to the stretch objectives. It is calculated in order to assess the effect of each strategy on the overall objectives, from the standpoint of overall optimisation.

Eliciting Strategies

Using the MDC (Method, Design, Concept) approach, we drew up a "desired scenario" for the Atsugi Plant's production and distribution systems, and designed a concrete plan to attain this vision. At the same time, we used OD (organisation development) training to create an atmosphere brimming with vitality throughout the plant and encourage the development of bottom-up strategies. We then elicited a wealth of possible strategies by combining the MDC analysis and OD training approaches while incorporating Head Office support technologies and workplace improvement capabilities (see Figure 8.8). The key point in our approach was the use of a Support Technology Map and a Workplace Improvement Map to create and operate a system for eliciting strategies efficiently and exhaustively.

The aims of our OD training were as follows:

- To raise our employees' "TP consciousness" to make it easier to implement TP activities.
- To give our employees a stronger sense of participation in TP activities.

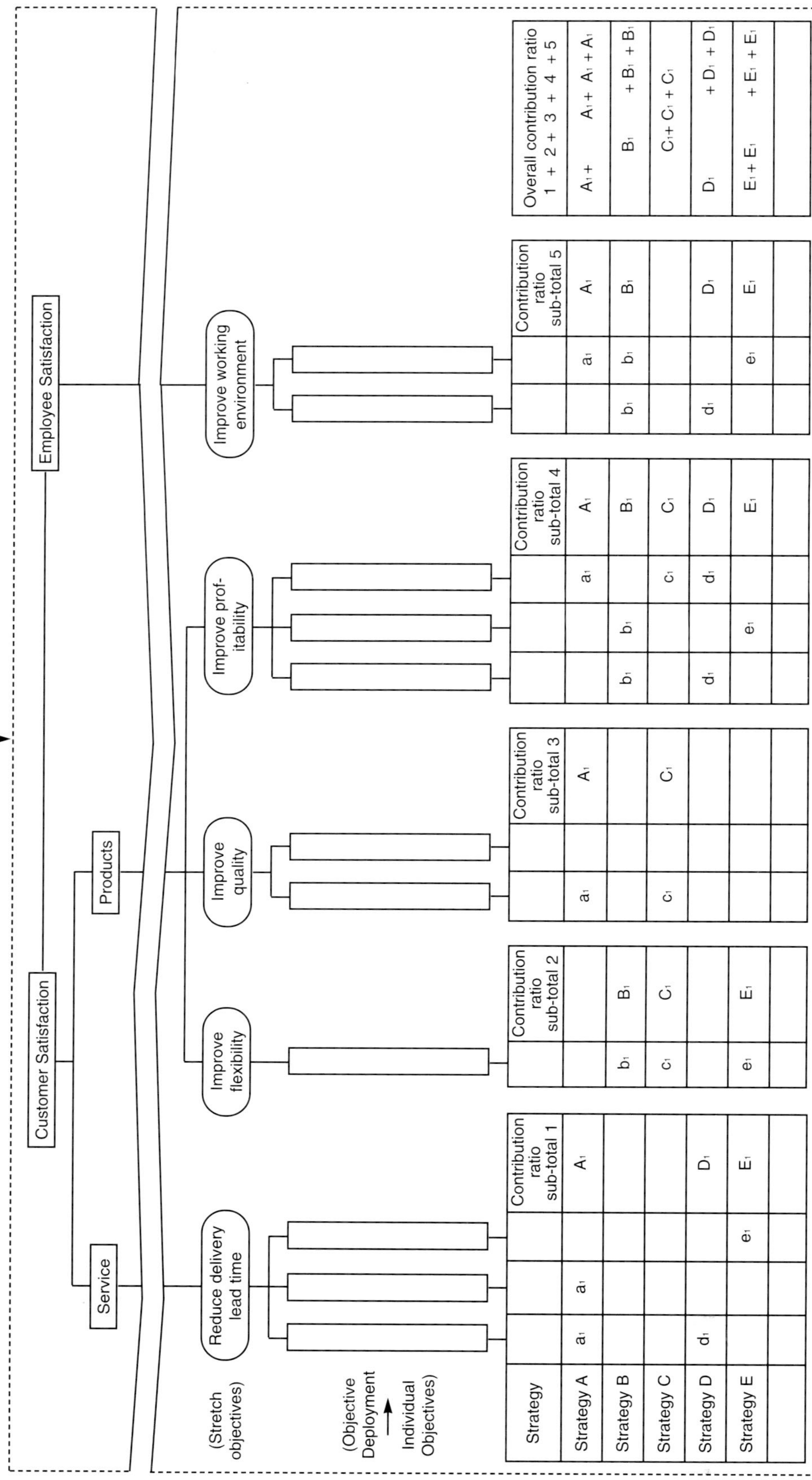

Figure 8.7 Calculation of Overall Contribution Ratios

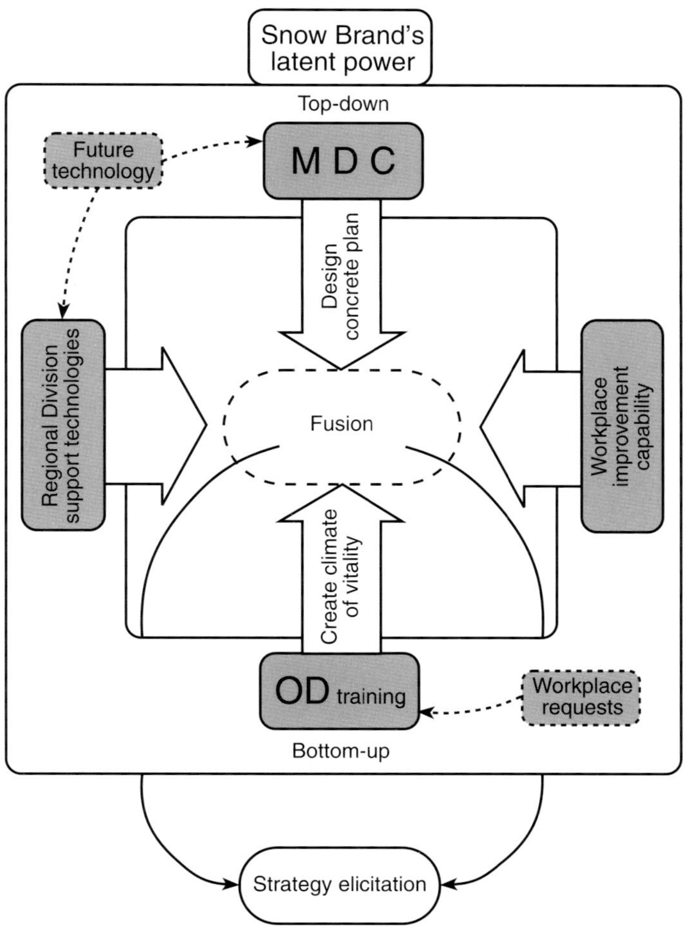

Figure 8.8 The Strategy Creation Process

TP Implementation System

Plant Operation Setup

In the course of introducing TP activities at the Atsugi Plant, we set up a system of TP committees to run our existing activities and created a brand-new organisation based around a TP Council (a plant operation council) in order to make our implementation setup transparent and efficient.

The TP Council is responsible for coordinating all TP activities. This applies to all stages, starting with the formulation of plant management policy based on our overall CS- and ES-based TP concept, continuing with the setting of overall objectives and

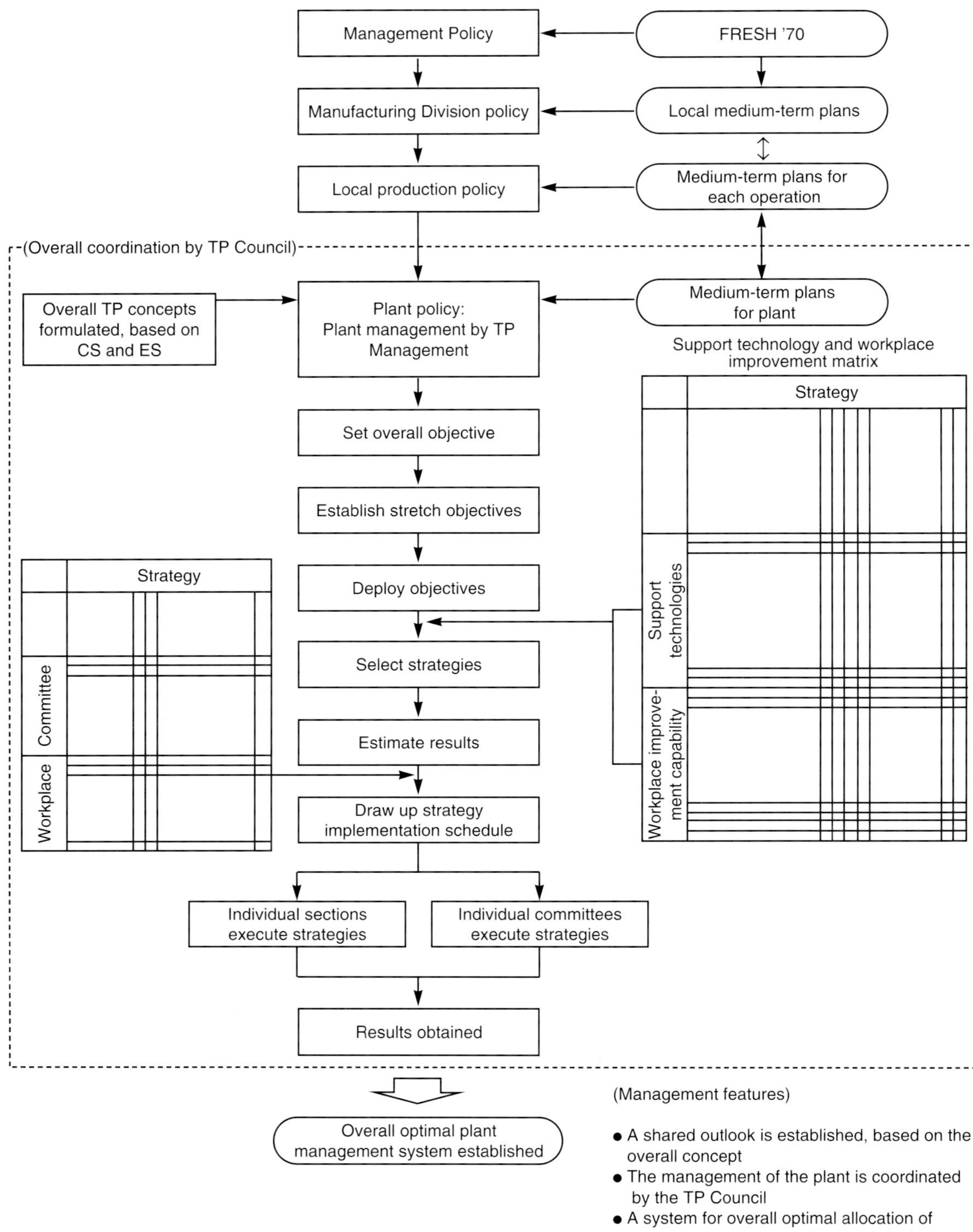

Figure 8.9 Plant Operation Setup

stretch objectives, objective deployment and strategy selection, estimation of results, and implementation (see Figure 8.9). We also established a TP Secretariat responsible for planning and administering TP activities, monitoring progress and reporting back to individual workplaces and TP committees.

Strategy Progress Control

As Figure 8.10 shows, visibility was the order of the day in controlling the progress of strategy implementation, and great care was taken to show plainly who was responsible for what. Progress was controlled by the TP Secretariat, which circulated progress reports after authorisation by the TP Council. Strategy progress charts were colour-coded with blue stickers to indicate completed strategies, yellow to mark those still in progress and red to mark those suspended or aborted.

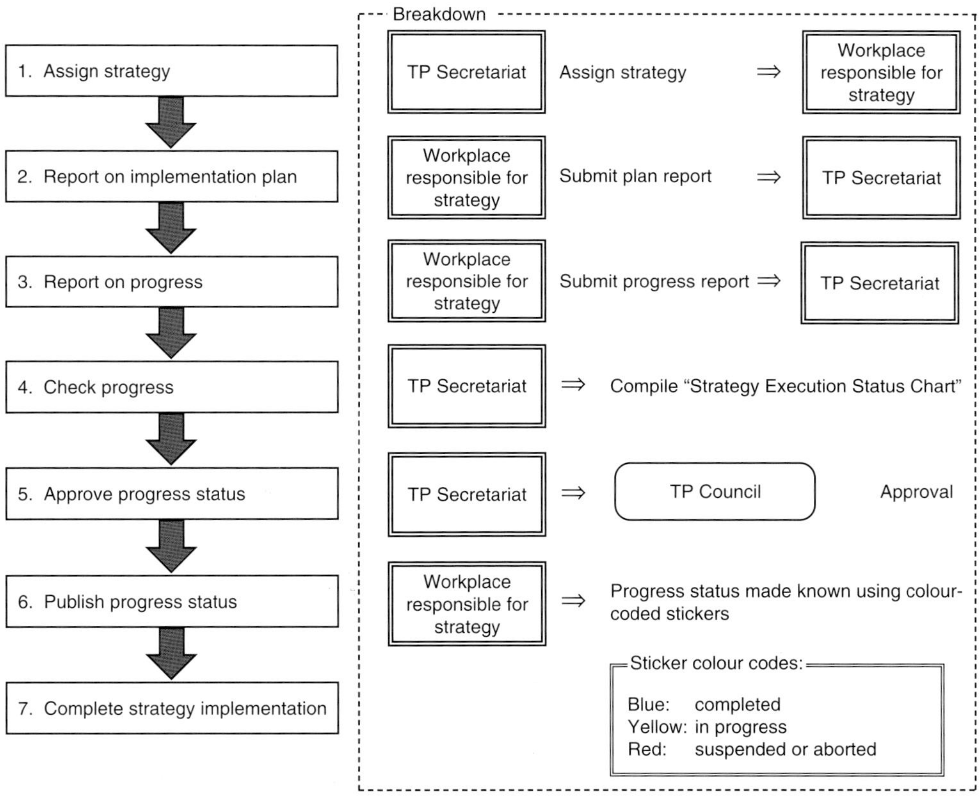

Figure 8.10 Progress Control Flowchart

A Specific Example of TP Activities

The purpose of improving the working environment was to create safe and pleasant working conditions and improve mental and physical health to enable employees to work comfortably at our plant. We took "overall health" as our indicator of mental and physical health, and we shall now look at the specific example of "physical wellbeing", one of the two components of this indicator.

Assessing Physical Wellbeing

Based on our criteria for assessing physical wellbeing, we worked out a numerical rating for "working conditions" and "working environment" for each component task, then calculated the number of improvement points needed to achieve the required level of physical wellbeing. As Figure 8.11 shows, we set a target of 70 points for each task, and calculated the actual points scored on the basis of our assessment criteria. For example, "skim milk powder dissolution" rated 7 points for conditions and 8 points for environment, so it scored 56 points (7 x 8) for physical wellbeing. To achieve the targeted level of physical wellbeing in this task, an improvement of 14 points was needed.

Many tasks were found to require improvement in terms of physical wellbeing. The target values were attained by introducing computer control for the process in question, as shown in Photograph 8.1, or by automating the process, as shown in Photograph 8.2.

Photograph 8.1 Controlling Processes by Computer

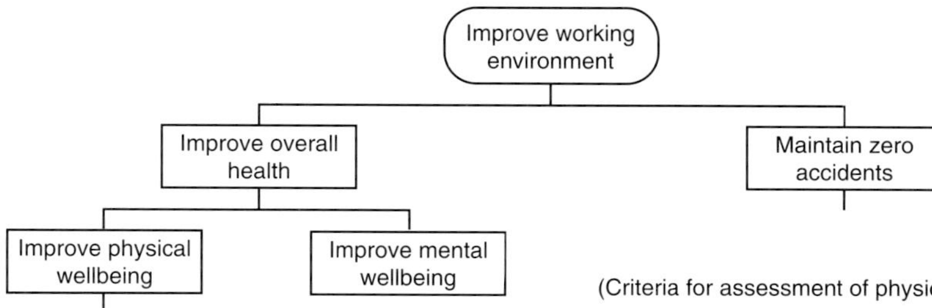

(Criteria for assessment of physical wellbeing)

	Score	1 Point	2 Points	3 Points
Working conditions	Monotonous work	None	up to 4 hours	4 hours or more
	Arduous work	None	up to 25 kg/cycle	25 kg/cycle or more
Working environment	Temperature	15 - 28°C	28 - 35°C	35°C or over
	Humidity	50% or under	50 - 65%	65% or over
	Danger level	Items of protective equipment: 0	Items of protective equipment: 2	Items of protective equipment: 3

Workplace responsible for strategy		Blending			Production		Packaging										
Component tasks		Skim milk powder dissolution	Handling of ingredients	Line control	Operating fillers	Product inspection	Operating sterilisers	Packaging products									
Target (number of points)		70	70	70	70	70	70	70									
Working conditions	Monotonous work	3	3	2	2	3	1	2									
	Arduous work	1	1	2	2	3	3	2									
Total points for working conditions		7	7	7	8	9	7	7									
Working conditions	Temperature	1	1	1	3	3	1	2	1	1	1	1	1	1	1	3	1
	Humidity	1	1	1	3	3	1	2	1	1	1	1	1	1	1	3	3
	Danger level	3	3	3	3	3	3	2	3	3	2	2	2	2	2	1	1
Total points for working environment		8	8	8	11	11	8	9	8	10	9	9	9	9	8	13	8
Points for physical wellbeing		56	56	56	88	99	56	63	64	70	45	45	45	56	64	90	56
Improvement required (points)		14	14	14	0	0	14	7	6	0	25	25	25	14	6	0	14
Contribution ratio (%)		5	5	5	0	0	5	2	2	0	9	9	9	5	2	0	5
Strategy		Develop bag-opening device	Enlarge materials storage space	Automate process			Provide air-conditioning	Automate process	Eliminate human labour		Automate process	Automate materials handling	Automate process	Modify line	Introduce packaging machine		Eliminate human labour

Figure 8.11 Assessment of Physical Wellbeing

Photograph 8.2 Process Automation

8 Results

Through the activities we have described, we achieved the following results over the three years from 1990 to 1992 (see Figure 8.12).

Lead time (manufacturing lead time):
    Reduced by 13%

Flexibility:
    Increased by a factor of 1.2

Quality:
    Increased by a factor of 1.4

Profitability (labour reduction):
    Increased by 22%

Working environment:
    Improved by 4% (over the two-year period from 1991 to 1992)

(Note that the Working Environment diagram shows only workplace morale, just one of the indicators of overall health.)

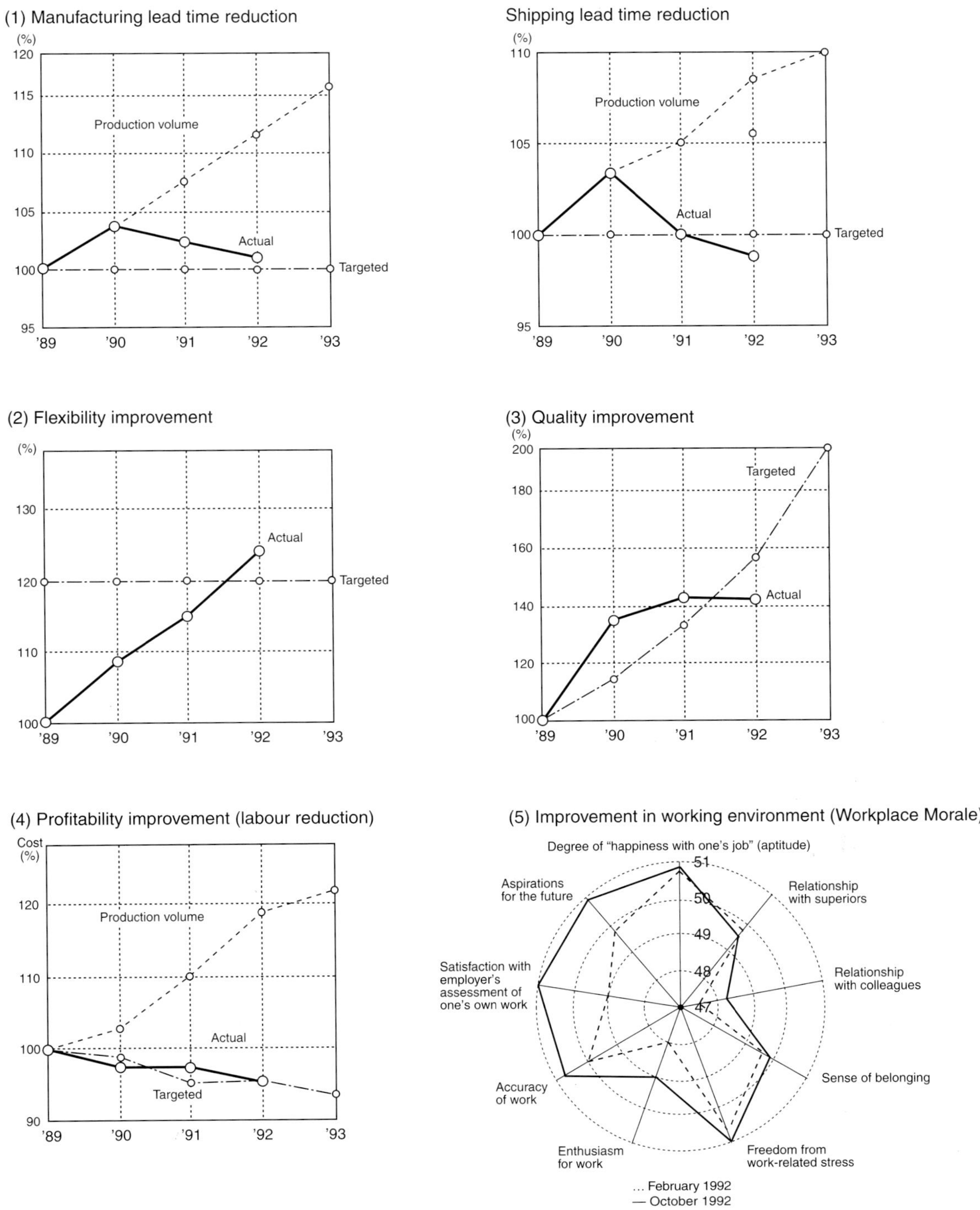

Figure 8.12 Results

We also achieved the following additional results:

1. We now have a much clearer idea of where we should be heading, and we can run the plant on a priority-orientated basis.

2. The relationship between objectives and strategies is clearly spelled out, so everyone knows their role and can predict the results of their work. This has improved our employees' motivation.

3. TP Council meetings have enabled us to manage our plant in a much more "holistic" way.

4. Our ES-related strategies have made the workplace more vibrant and created an atmosphere of willingness to tackle new challenges.

Future Developments

Future Development at Atsugi Plant

1. *Further Improve Customer Satisfaction (CS) and Employee Satisfaction (ES)*
   We must develop CS and ES even further, and use TP Management as the basic framework for additional improvements in product competitiveness and production capability, moving ever closer to our ultimate vision of how the Atsugi Plant should be.

2. *Incorporate Social Satisfaction (SS)*
   We must incorporate the concept of social satisfaction(serving society) into the company's mission and plant management setup, with the aim of gaining the respect of the local community.

3. *Formalise the Methods Used to Implement TP Management at the Plant*
   We must further systematise and formalise the methods used to deploy the stretch objectives for quality, delivery lead time, flexibility, profitability and working environment so as to make our TP Management system even easier to use in the future.

Future Development at Snow Brand Milk Products

We aim to extend TP Management to all our milk-products plants by the time the 70th anniversary of our foundation comes around in 1995. However, for the time being, we are concentrating on our plants in the Kanto and Kansai regions, and have already carried out detailed preparatory studies aimed at extending TP Management into these in the second half of 1993. If all goes well in our milk-products plants, we will consider extending it to other operations. In future, we intend to use TP Management to run all our production operations.

9
Nissan Diesel, Ageo Plant

Back-to-Basics TP Management Combining Higher Customer Satisfaction with an Improved Factory Constitution

Takeo Yamazoe, Director (formerly Ageo Plant Manager)
Jirō Minekawa, Deputy General Manager, Ageo Plant TP Promotion Office
Nissan Diesel Motor Company Ltd

Introduction to Nissan Diesel

Company Outline

Nissan Diesel Motor Company Ltd. was founded under the name Nihon Diesel in 1935. It is now an all-round heavy vehicle manufacturer supplying trucks and buses to countries over the globe. In 1992, it had 5,600 employees and achieved sales amounting to over £2,000 million, with a total production of 85,000 units (including those made for Nissan Motor Company Ltd. as well as those for sale to the domestic and export markets). The company has three main factories, at Ageo, Gunma and Kōnosu, all not far from Tokyo.

Principal Products

In addition to trucks ranging in size from the 2-tonne class to the 10-tonne class, Nissan Diesel also makes buses, mobile cranes, engines and co-generation systems.

Outline of Ageo Plant

The Ageo Plant, located in Saitama Prefecture, is Nissan Diesel's flagship factory, accounting for approximately 65% of both total workforce and total sales. The plant began operating in 1952 and now produces mainly heavy-duty and light-duty trucks and engines. It has a subsidiary plant at Han'yu City, also in Saitama Prefecture (see Figure 9.1).

Site area:	683,840 m^2 (including subsidiary plant)
Factory footprint:	274,700 m^2
Number of employees:	3,300

Table 9.1

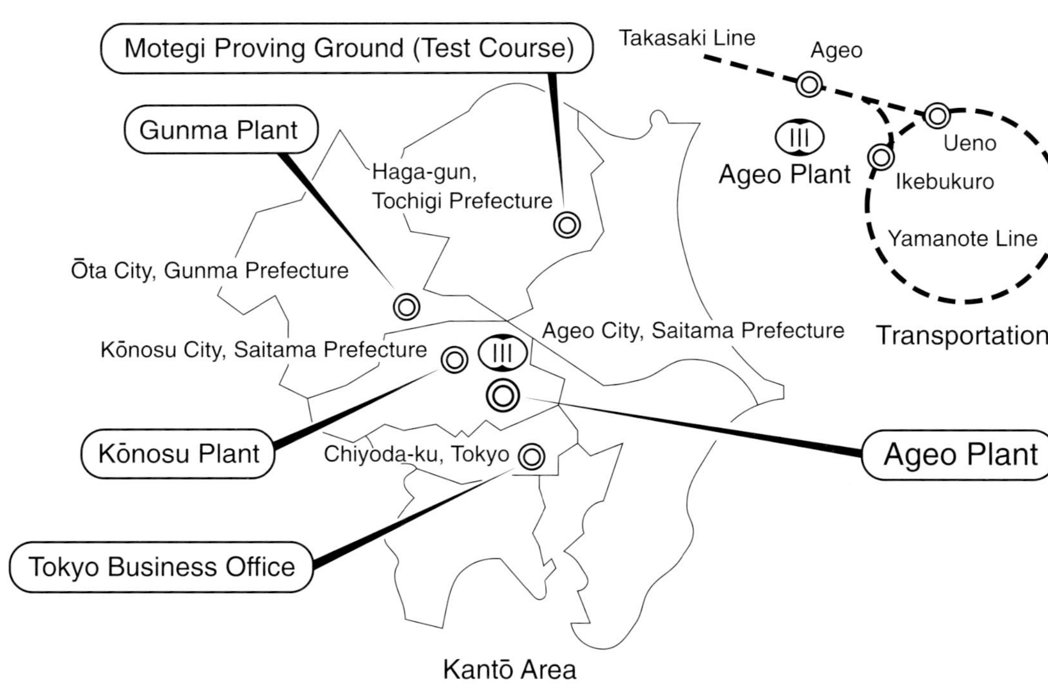

Figure 9.1 Location of Nissan Diesel Facilities

Corporate Philosophy and Factory Policy

Corporate Philosophy

Nissan Diesel's corporate philosophy is as follows: "We will contribute to the world by providing goods that delight our customers and suit the social environment". We have three fundamental medium-term management objectives for the next three years. The first of these is to improve our profitability, the basis of the Nissan Diesel Group's prosperity. The second is to develop new, environmentally-friendly, safe technologies. The third is to promote customer satisfaction (CS), on which everything else depends.

Factory Policy

Based on our corporate philosophy and fundamental management objectives, our factory policy is "To improve the quality of all our operations so as to become the top plant in our industry". To this end, we aim to achieve one-piece-flow production, the kind of production regime that any company intending to become an industry leader must achieve.

We have also established the following three activity guidelines based on CS considerations, specifying the basic attitudes we expect our employees to adopt in carrying out their manufacturing work:

1. Respond sensitively to the voice of the customer.
2. Pay strict attention to quality.
3. Be cost-conscious.

Background to Introduction of TP Management

History of Factory Reform Activities

Progress of Activities

Activity campaigns at Nissan Diesel generally last for three years, in synchronisation with the group's medium-term business plans. The campaign starting in 1987 was called the "AA 64" campaign (where 64 stands for Shōwa 64 (1989), the final year of the campaign according to the Japanese era dating system). The one after that (starting in 1990) was called the "AA 92" campaign. This year (1993) we are using our achievement in winning the TP Prize as the springboard for our next round of activities, the "AA 95" campaign. As noted below, we altered the meaning of the double A in the titles of the successive campaigns to communicate the necessity of continually upgrading to suit the changing times and changing environment.

AA 64 ('87-'89): Active Ageo (becoming active)
AA 92 ('90-'92): Advance Ageo (being active and moving forward)
AA 95 ('93-'95): Aggressive Ageo (taking on more challenging topics)

The AA 64 Campaign

To understand the objectives of the AA 92 campaign, it is necessary to know a little about its precursor, the AA 64 campaign. The recession in the commercial-vehicle industry, which had continued since 1982, had had a serious effect on both manufacturers and dealers. To try to extricate itself from this crisis, Nissan Diesel mobilised its entire resources to achieve the restructuring objectives of its '87-'89 medium-term business plan.

The Ageo Plant also joined in the AA 64 campaign, which aimed to completely reform the factory environment with the major emphasis on cutting costs. Fortunately, we were able to get everybody thoroughly involved in the activities, and consequently succeeded in achieving our principal objective, reducing total factory expenses.

The AA 64 campaign thus achieved excellent results, thanks partly to the general sense of crisis engendered by the bursting of Japan's asset-price-inflated "bubble economy" and the particularly severe recession affecting our industry. However, since we had concentrated on fairly easily achievable improvements, we were left with the following impressions:

1. Individual improvement objectives were not linked closely enough to the plant's overall objectives.
2. The activities were confined mainly to the shop floor, with insufficient backup from production engineering staff.
3. Too much stress was placed on achieving numerical targets, leaving some people feeling that they had been put under too much pressure.
4. The management cycle (the PDCA, or Plan-Do-Check-Act, cycle) had not been properly followed.

The AA 92 Campaign

As mentioned above, the AA 64 campaign produced excellent results, and the objectives of the '87-'89 medium-term business plan were achieved. Over the three-year period from 1990 to 1992, we introduced new heavy-duty, medium-duty and light-duty truck models, updating the styles of all three classes. Based on our achievements up to that point, we adopted a more proactive management stance in addressing the requirements of our '90-'92 medium-term business plan.

As already noted, one of the tasks remaining from the AA 64 campaign was to link individual sub-objectives more intimately to the plant's overall objectives. We made the decision to introduce TP Management at this stage, believing it to be the best system for achieving this linkage. In the first year of the AA 92 campaign, we laid the groundwork for the introduction of TP Management by making the necessary organisational preparations and arranging training sessions to familiarise people with TP Management concepts. Then, in 1991, we began using TP Management in the area of labour reduction.

Not only did we obtain unexpectedly good results from this initiative, we also discovered the wisdom of observing the following three precepts:

1. Clearly spell out the objectives.
2. Create systems for following the PDCA cycle.
3. Promote campaigns with the emphasis on activity.

With these lessons in mind, we commenced in 1992 to apply TP Management in earnest to the three areas of quality (Q), cost (C) and delivery (D).

Aims of TP Management

In introducing TP Management, we had the following three major aims:

1. To achieve all our overall objectives simultaneously.
2. To keep our programme of activities on the boil by operating a system of "activity management".
3. To unite our production-engineering expertise with our shop-floor improvement capabilities.

Let us examine these in turn. In our AA 92 campaign, we were ambitious enough to attempt two categories of overall objective; our "externally-focused" objectives (arising from our corporate philosophy of delighting our customers) and our "internally-focused" objectives (arising from our factory policy of becoming the top plant in our industry).

In setting our externally-focused objectives, we reflected on the fact that we had paid insufficient attention to the outside world in the past, and decided to start by highlighting our corporate philosophy. In this category, we decided to set parallel objectives in the three areas of Q, C and D.

Our factory policy of making ourselves the best plant in our industry could be described as an internally-focused objective. We clarified this as meaning "creating a factory constitution capable of achieving one-piece flow", and we resolved first to work out the necessary scenario for achieving this and then to turn this vision into reality.

As already mentioned, the first of our major TP Management aims was to achieve these externally-oriented and internally-oriented overall objectives simultaneously. In other words, we wanted to achieve customer satisfaction while at the same time strengthening our factory's constitution (the plant's entire production setup and internal environment).

The intention behind the second of our major TP Management aims, the operation of a system of "activity management", was to run the plant in such a way as to focus all its activities on improvement. By doing this, we hoped to give prominence to practical activity, invigorating the factory and thereby achieving better performance.

Our third major TP Management aim was, as noted earlier, to combine our manufacturing technology with the improvement activities taking place on the shop floor. Engineering staff and front-line employees had already been working together on improvements, but there had been little systematic division of responsibilities for achieving the objectives, and we realised this on reviewing the AA 64 campaign. We therefore tried to build closer collaboration between the two areas by creating a matrix-type organisation and getting everyone to participate in selecting the priority strategies.

The Ageo Plant's TP Campaign Symbol

To help get the Ageo Plant's TP campaign off the ground, we held a plantwide contest to find the best symbol to represent it. The design shown in Figure 9.2 was voted in, and it is now displayed at the main gate of the factory as well as on all our employees' badges and helmets.

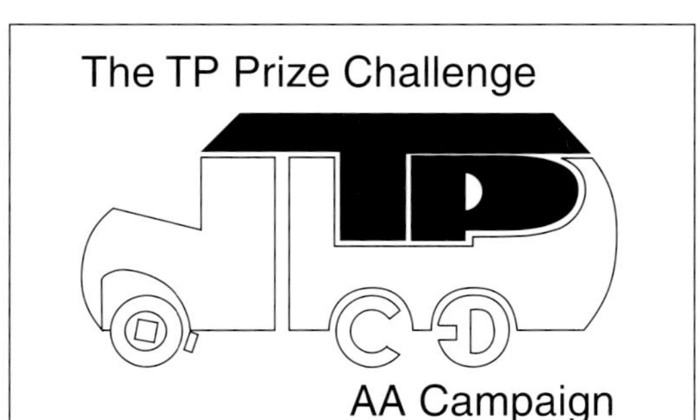

Figure 9.2 TP Campaign Symbol

Our Style of TP Management

System of TP Activities in AA 92 Campaign

Figure 9.3 shows the main features of our TP programme.

We set overall objectives which combine our externally-oriented goal of achieving greater customer satisfaction by providing them with products that delight them (on the left-hand side of the diagram) with our internally-oriented goal of improving the factory's constitution and becoming the best in our industry (on the right-hand side of the diagram).

We call our externally-oriented objectives "performance objectives", as they represent the final results we are hoping to achieve. They were devolved to the level of front-line supervisors, while "priority strategies" were worked out to show where the activities should be primarily directed.

Correspondingly, we call our internally-oriented objectives "constitution objectives", since they are aimed at strengthening the factory's internal environment and making it capable of one-piece-flow manufacturing. We analysed the conditions required for this into eight different elements, and prepared an evaluation manual for the quality element (we had already investigated quality in considerable depth). This exercise showed us exactly what we meant by a strong factory constitution and what priority strategies we should implement in order to achieve it.

The two main classes of priority strategies (those for achieving the performance objectives and those for achieving the constitution objectives) indicated the directions in which the respective activities should proceed, while our detailed breakdown of the numerical targets showed us how far the activities needed to be taken. In other words, the objectives were broken down into vectors showing both direction and quantity.

So far, this had been a top-down process. The bottom-up approach was then used to combine the two classes of priority strategy by having front-line supervisors decide on "specific strategies" for implementing them. We laid our plans for achieving our objectives by skilfully fusing the top-down and bottom-up approaches in this way. We called the activities undertaken for achieving the two types of objective "performance management" and "constitution management" respectively.

Next, we decided to boost the vitality of the activities by using a newly-introduced system of "activity management" to promote progress towards the overall objectives. This is a mechanism designed to stimulate, encourage and guide all activities in the direction of reaching the objectives. If achieving greater customer satisfaction by attaining the performance objectives is one wheel of the TP campaign and improving the factory's internal environment by attaining the constitution objectives is the other, activity management is the motor that supplies the driving-force.

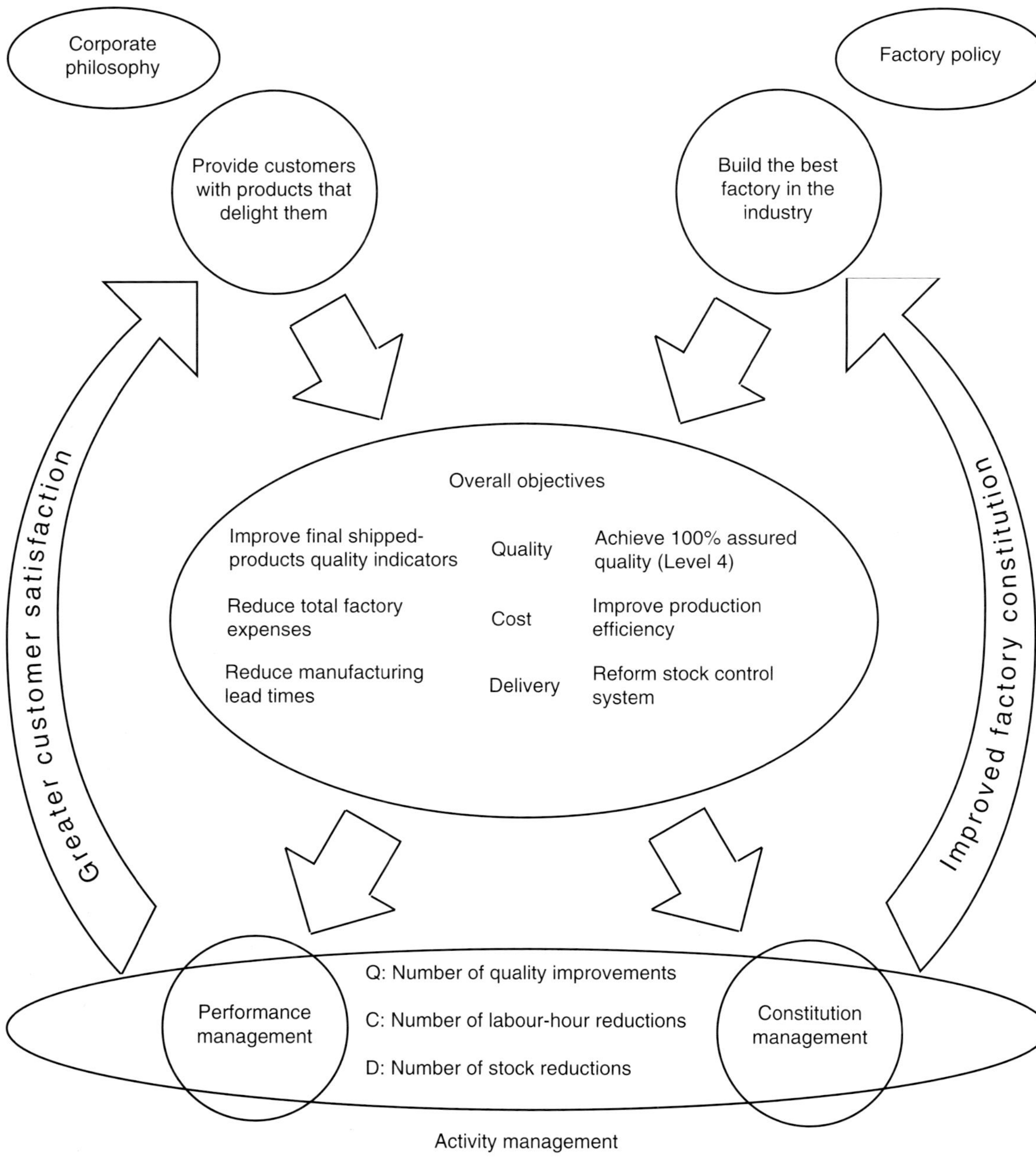

Figure 9.3 Features of TP Management at Ageo Plant

Setting Overall TP Objectives

As mentioned before, we set Q, C and D performance objectives based on our corporate philosophy of providing our customers with products that delight them. The objectives we settled on were as follows:

Quality: As our quality objective, we decided to improve the quality of our final shipped products by 25%.

Cost: For our cost objective, we decided to reduce our production costs in order to be able to offer cheaper products and at the same time reduce our total factory expenses in order to improve our group profitability (one of the objectives in the company's medium-term business plan). The Ageo Plant's share of Nissan Diesel's overall profitability improvement target was set at 5%.

Delivery: The Nissan Diesel Group is currently engaged in a groupwide campaign to improve its delivery performance. We settled on shortening manufacturing lead-times as the goal for our factory, using as our targets the figures allocated to us in the groupwide campaign – 8 days for heavy-duty trucks and 7 days for light-duty trucks. These targets represent a reduction of approximately one day compared with the lead times for the previous year.

Meanwhile, we decided on our constitution objectives for achieving one-piece-flow production. As noted earlier, we regarded the achievement of a manufacturing environment capable of one-piece-flow as being composed of eight principal elements. One of these concerned quality; we wanted each and every one of the products produced by our factory to be 100% reliable, so our basic ideal was to achieve 100% assured quality for every item leaving the plant. This was because we believe that this really is the fundamental issue in achieving customer satisfaction in any manufacturing operation.

We therefore drew up a set of quality assurance standards (called the "Green Files"), selecting eight control items for the "quality" element of the desired factory environment and defining five achievement levels for each of these items. Our aim was to reach Level 3 in all items by the end of FY 91 and Level 4 by the end of FY 92.

In addition to the performance and constitution objectives, we also devised activity management indicators. These consisted mainly of counts of the numbers of activities undertaken and were used for stimulating the activities and monitoring their vitality.

TP Promotion Organisation

To promote the TP campaign, we adopted the matrix-type organisation shown in Figure 9.4. It is headed by the AA 92 TP Promotion Council, under which are six committees (one for each line function) forming the vertical lines of the matrix, with three cross-functional teams forming the horizontal lines.

The three cross-functional teams were composed of members from the various functional committee. This facilitated the processes of aligning the activities in the required direction, sharing information, creating a common understanding of the problems faced, promoting lateral deployment (extending the activities horizontally to other areas), and achieving closer collaboration between functions.

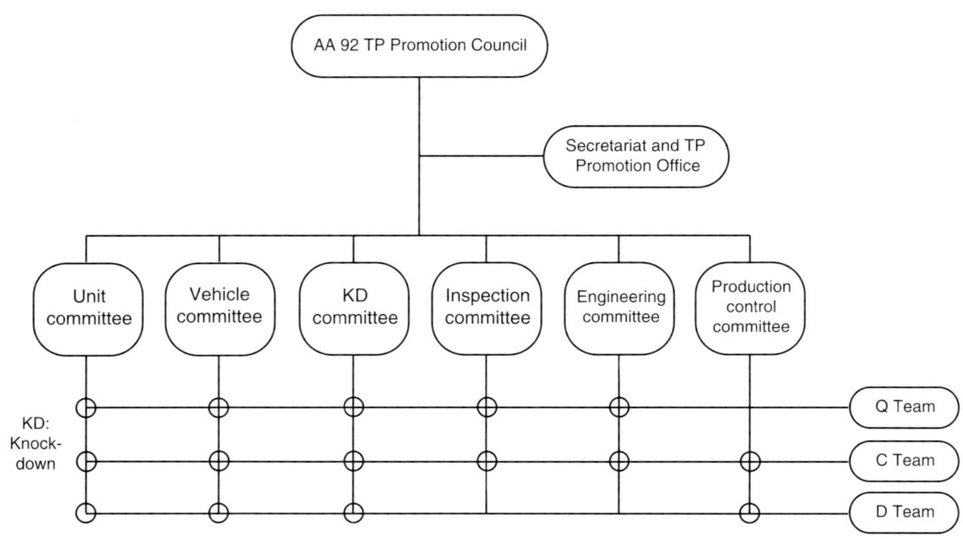

Figure 9.4 Activity Promotion System

Overview of TP Management System

Our TP Management system consists of five main subsystems, as shown by the five sections of Figure 9.5.

Section 1: This section shows the relationship between the customer satisfaction improvement objectives and the factory constitution improvement objectives. It indicates those activities designed to improve the factory constitution which naturally lead to greater customer satisfaction.

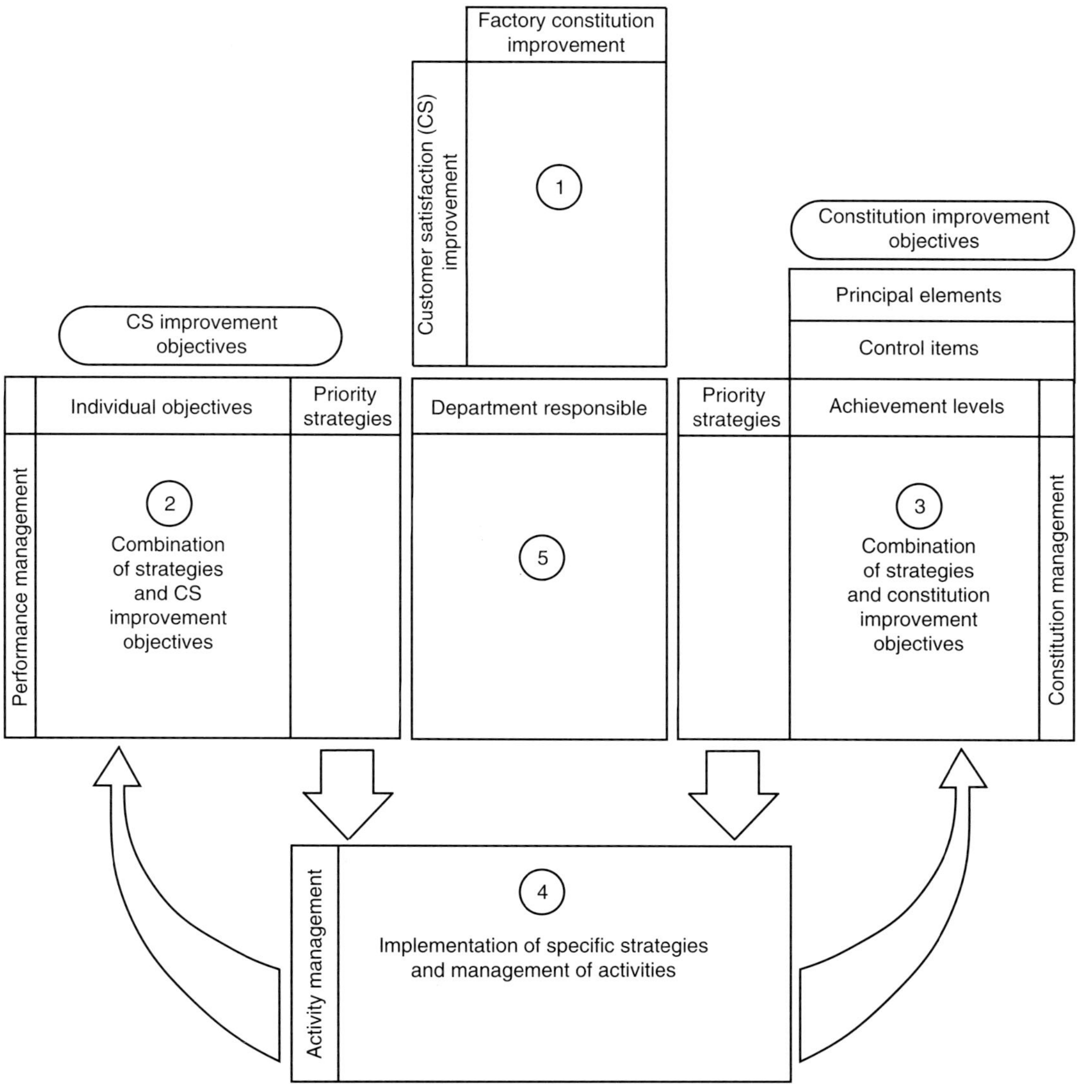

Figure 9.5 Overview of TP Management System

Section 2: In this section, the customer satisfaction improvement objectives verified in Section 1 are successively broken down from the factory level to the department, section and group levels, and the priority strategies necessary for achieving those objectives are established. As mentioned earlier, the system used for ensuring that the objectives are achieved is called "performance management".

Section 3: In this section, the constitution improvement objectives are broken down into principal elements, control items and achievement levels, which are then related to the priority strategies required for achieving the objectives. The process of managing these activities is called "constitution management".

Section 4: This is the "activity management" section of the diagram, used for monitoring and controlling the progress of the improvement activities. It is a chart of the specific strategies devised for implementing the customer satisfaction improvement and factory constitution improvement priority strategies.

Section 5: This section of the diagram shows which organisational unit is responsible for which priority strategies, both those for improving customer satisfaction and those for strengthening the factory constitution.

These five sections of the TP deployment diagram are now explained in more detail.

1. Section 1 (relation between customer satisfaction improvement objectives and factory constitution improvement objectives)

   We selected three main objectives as our overall customer satisfaction improvement objectives; improve final shipped-product quality indicators, reduce total factory expenses, and reduce manufacturing lead times.

   Similarly, we selected three main objectives as our overall factory constitution improvement objectives; achieve 100% assured quality, improve production efficiency, and reform the stock control system. These two categories of objective are related to each other in Section 1 of the TP deployment diagram.

2. Section 2 (performance management: see Figure 9.6)

   As already explained, overall performance objectives were established in the three areas of quality, cost and delivery. In quality, this meant improving the final/shipped-product quality indicators. In cost, it meant reducing total factory expenses in terms of five items (labour costs, materials costs, administrative costs,

Customer Satisfaction Improvement Objectives

Performance management		Factory objectives	Department objectives	Section objectives	Priority strategies
		Improve final shipped-product quality indicators XX points or less	No.1 Manufacturing Dept: --%	Machine Section: --% Engine Section: --%	. Prevent misassembly (wrong or missing parts) . Introduce Poka-Yoke (error-proofing) devices . Reduce chronic defects . Prevent secondary recurrences . .
			No.2 Manufacturing Dept: --%	Press Forming Section: --% Body Section: --%	
	Reduce total factory expenses	Labour costs: £---,000	No.1 Manufacturing Dept: £---,000	Machine Section: £---,000	. Abolish adjustments . Reduce number of attachments . Effect line-side improvements . Improve assembly tools . Improve bottleneck processes . Make labour-saving investments . . . .
			No.2 Manufacturing Dept: £---,000	Press Forming Section: £---,000	
		Materials costs: £---,000	No.1 Engineering Dept: £---,000	No.1 Engineering Section: £---,000	
			No.2 Engineering Dept: £---,000	No.2 Engineering Section: £---,000	
		Administrative costs: £---,000	No.1 Manufacturing Dept: £---,000	No.1 Works Section: £---,000	
			No.2 Manufacturing Dept: £---,000	No.2 Works Section: £---,000	
		Distribution costs: £---,000	Production Control Dept: £---,000	Control Section: £---,000	
			Knock-Down Dept: £---,000	Knock-Down Section: £---,000	
		Knock-down packaging costs: £---,000	Knock-Down Dept: £---,000	Knock-Down Section: £---,000	
		Reduce manufacturing lead times XX days or less	No.1 Manufacturing Dept: --- days	Machine Section --- days Machine Section --- days	. Improve packaging . Review production schedules . Reduce WIP
			No.2 Manufacturing Dept: --- days	Press Forming Section: --- days Body Section: --- days	

Figure 9.6 Performance Management

distribution costs and knock-down packaging costs). In delivery, it meant reducing the manufacturing lead time from initial machining in the factory to shipping of the completed vehicle, and various targets were set for this using number of days' work in progress (WIP) as the control characteristic.

The objectives were broken down successively from the factory level to the department, section and group levels (not shown in the diagram). Then, priority strategies required for attaining the objectives were established in their respective areas (quality, cost and delivery). In selecting these priority strategies, we encouraged the selection of specific improvement strategies suited to the characteristics of particular workplaces. As a result, priority strategies were set for each individual process.

3. Section 3 (constitution management: see Figure 9.7)

As explained, the Ageo Plant is pursuing a programme of activities for achieving one-piece-flow production, with the aim of becoming best-in-class. To achieve one-piece flow, it is necessary to arrive at a situation in which quality, productivity and inventory (both within and between processes) are at their ideal levels, the 6 Ss are thoroughly implemented, and the plant's processes can be operated by any of our trained workers – in other words, the ideal factory environment.

Note: We define the 6 Ss (industrial housekeeping) as the usual 5 Ss – seiri (sorting out), seiton (arranging efficiently), seisō (checking-through-cleaning), seiketsu (cleanliness and honesty), and shitsuke (self-discipline) – plus shitsukoku (doing all these painstakingly and perseveringly).

As mentioned earlier, we defined this kind of factory environment in terms of eight principal elements; quality (the ability to ship each and every product with complete assurance of quality), inventory (the ability to operate with the bare minimum of stocks on and off the factory floor), and the 6 Ss (the basis of all our activities), together with setup, equipment, process control, operations, and production technology. Each of these elements was then further subdivided into eight control items; for example, quality was broken down into maintenance of quality standards, maintenance of standardised assessment criteria, and so on.

Our constitution management activities have just begun to take shape; assessment criteria have been drawn up for the quality and 6-S control items, and supervisors in each workplace are performing self-assessments of their groups' activities in these areas. A five-level achievement scale has been established for these items;

Constitution improvement objectives

Principal element	Quality				Inventory				6 S's			Setup			Equipment			Process control				Operations			Production technology			
Control items	Maintenance of quality standards	Maintenance of standardised assessment criteria	Quality checking	▪	Stock level	Stocktaking precision	WIP	▪	Seiri (sorting out)	Seiton (arranging efficiently)	▪	Maintenance of setup standards	Setup planning precision	▪	Inspection	Cleaning	▪	Process levelling	Process sequencing	▪	▪	Work completion rate	Parts availability	▪	Equipment knowledge	Product knowledge	▪	▪
Priority strategies / Level	△ ●	△ ●																										
Prepare operation manuals	○	○																										
Check actual work against operation manuals	○																											
Establish conditions specified in operation manuals	○		○																									
Draw up process control charts	○	○																										
▪																												
Establish and maintain standard stock levels					○	○																						
Formulate rules for dealing with discrepancies					○		○																					
Establish frequent-delivery system					○																							
▪																												
Create permanent locations for work tools									○	○																		
Formulate inspection and replacement criteria										○																		
Standardise cleaning equipment									○																			

Figure 9.7 Constitution Management

current levels are indicated on the diagram by triangles and targeted levels by black circles. We plan to extend the programme gradually to the remaining elements.

Priority strategies are established for each of the principal elements and control items with the aim of raising the factory's level in that area. A circle in one of the cells of the matrix indicates that a relationship exists between the particular strategy and control item associated with that cell.

4. Section 4 (activity management: see Figure 9.8)

Our activity management system is designed for effective supervision and control of the actual improvement activities. One of the most important parts of this system is the progress control chart, which tracks the progress made in implementing specific priority strategies for achieving both the customer satisfaction improvement objectives and the factory constitution improvement objectives.

Improvement projects, classified under the headings of quality (quality improvement), cost (labour reduction) and delivery (lead-time reduction), are recorded on this chart in order to facilitate progress control in the workplace. The chart clearly shows who is responsible for each project, together with the project schedule, allowing monthly progress checks to be made. The chart also indicates where an improvement item affects more than one area (quality, cost or delivery), showing the number of improvements planned, together with the predicted benefits.

Activity management objectives were also established with the aim of keeping the activities on the boil and ensuring they made effective progress. The overall (factory-level) objectives were successively broken down to the department, section and group levels, and the management of the group-level activities (the heart of our improvement campaign) was kept simple by treating the number of improvements effected as the control characteristic.

5. Section 5 (department responsible)

This section of the TP deployment diagram shows which organisational unit is responsible for implementing which priority strategy for achieving both the customer satisfaction improvement objectives and the factory constitution improvement objectives.

Activity Management

Progress Control Chart for Specific Strategies																
	Improvement item	Quality improvement		Labour reduction					Lead-time reduction		Person responsible	'92 (1st half)				
		Number of improvements		min/machine		Number of machines	hours/month		Stock-reduction value			4	5	6	7	8
		Planned	Actual	Planned	Actual		Planned	Actual	Planned	Actual						
1	Improvement of gearbox installability			0.1		140	2.4				Mishima			○		
2	Oil usage reduction	1	1	5.0	5.0	640	10	10			Mishima		●			
3	Improvement of prop shaft installability			0.2		140	2.2	2.2			Mishima	●				

Activity Management Targets			
Target	Indicators		
	Departmental indicators	Section indicators	Group indicators
Number of quality improvements	No.1 Manufacturing Dept -- improvements	Machine Section -- improvements	-- Group -- improvements
	No.2 Manufacturing Dept -- improvements	Engine Section -- improvements	-- Group -- improvements
		Axle Section -- improvements	-- Group -- improvements
			-- Group -- improvements
Labour reduction rate (TP reduction rate)	No.1 Manufacturing Dept -TP reduction rate	Machine Section -- TP reduction rate	-- Group -- cases
	No.2 Manufacturing Dept -TP reduction rate	Engine Section -- TP reduction rate	-- Group -- cases
			-- Group -- cases
Stock-reduction value	No.1 Manufacturing Dept -Stock reduction rate	Machine Section -- cases	-- Group -- cases
	No.2 Manufacturing Dept -Stock reduction rate	Engine Section -- cases	-- Group -- cases
			-- Group -- cases

Figure 9.8 Activity Management

Objective Deployment (Figure 9.9)

As Figure 9.9 shows, the overall Q, C and D objectives were broken down successively from the factory level to the department, section and group levels. This process was carried out for a combination of the customer satisfaction improvement objectives, factory constitution improvement objectives, and activity management objectives.

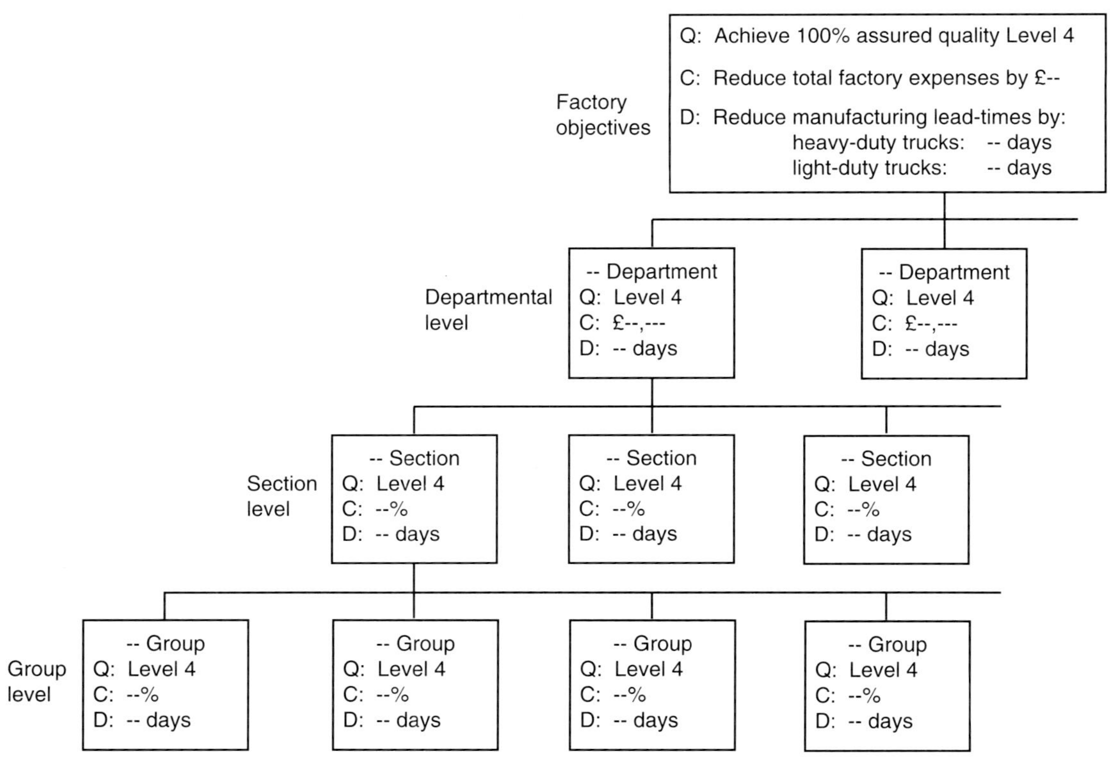

Figure 9.9 Breakdown of Objectives

Examples of Specific TP Management Activities

Activity Management System (Figure 9.10)

The system of activity management at our plant is designed to ensure that the efforts aimed at achieving the specific objectives worked out through the objective deployment process described above actually produce the desired results. It does this by following the PDCA cycle (see opposite), accurately assessing activity and achievement by means of "TP portfolio" diagrams.

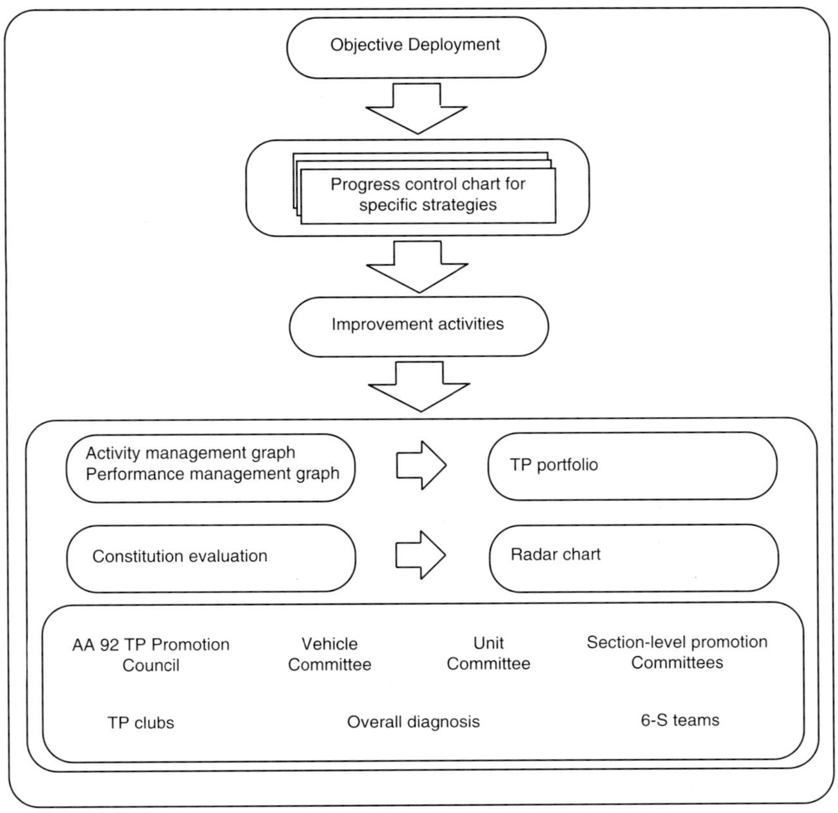

Figure 9.10 Overview of Activity Management

PDCA Cycle for Activity Management

P (Plan): Establish activity indicators
- Priority strategy selection tables
- Progress control charts for specific strategy items

D (Do): Implement strategy items
- 3-day focused improvements
- "100 beauty-spot" campaign

C (Check): Evaluate activities
- TP clubs
- TP portfolios
- Overall diagnoses

A (Act): Review and implement activity plan
- Review strategy tables
- Review system of activities

Activity Management and Performance Management

After receiving the table showing the breakdown of specific objectives, each workplace draws up a priority strategy selection table, and each team then prepares a specific-strategy progress control chart based on this and starts accumulating improvements.

We made a big effort to elicit the strategy items by the bottom-up approach, getting people to work out the desired scenario for their own processes and obtaining as many ideas as possible from the process workers themselves on the problems facing their processes and the issues needing to be addressed.

An activity management graph and a performance management graph are displayed in identical format, one beneath the other, on each team's display board, and the targets and actual results achieved are plotted on these monthly (see Figure 9.11).

We also use TP portfolio diagrams to assess the correlation between activity and performance in each of the three areas of Q, C and D and display how the results of the activities are actually reflected in achievement (see Figure 9.12). The significance of each quadrant of the diagram is as follows:

"TP Prize": The accumulated results of the improvement activities and the number of projects completed are better than scheduled, and performance is also better than planned. Find out what was done well and sow the seeds for the next round of improvements.

"Engine-racing": Improvements have been made, but they have not resulted in better performance. Use Why?-Why? analysis (a technique for probing the causes of a problem by repeatedly asking "Why?") to find the reasons for this, and identify more effective priority strategies.

"Bubble": Improvements are behind schedule, but unexpectedly good results have fortunately been achieved. However, this is due purely to good luck, and real improvements must be made before the bubble bursts.

"Doldrums": Activity is sluggish and results are poor. Unless something is done, there could be a financial crisis. Find a way out by getting back to the basics and reviewing everything from scratch.

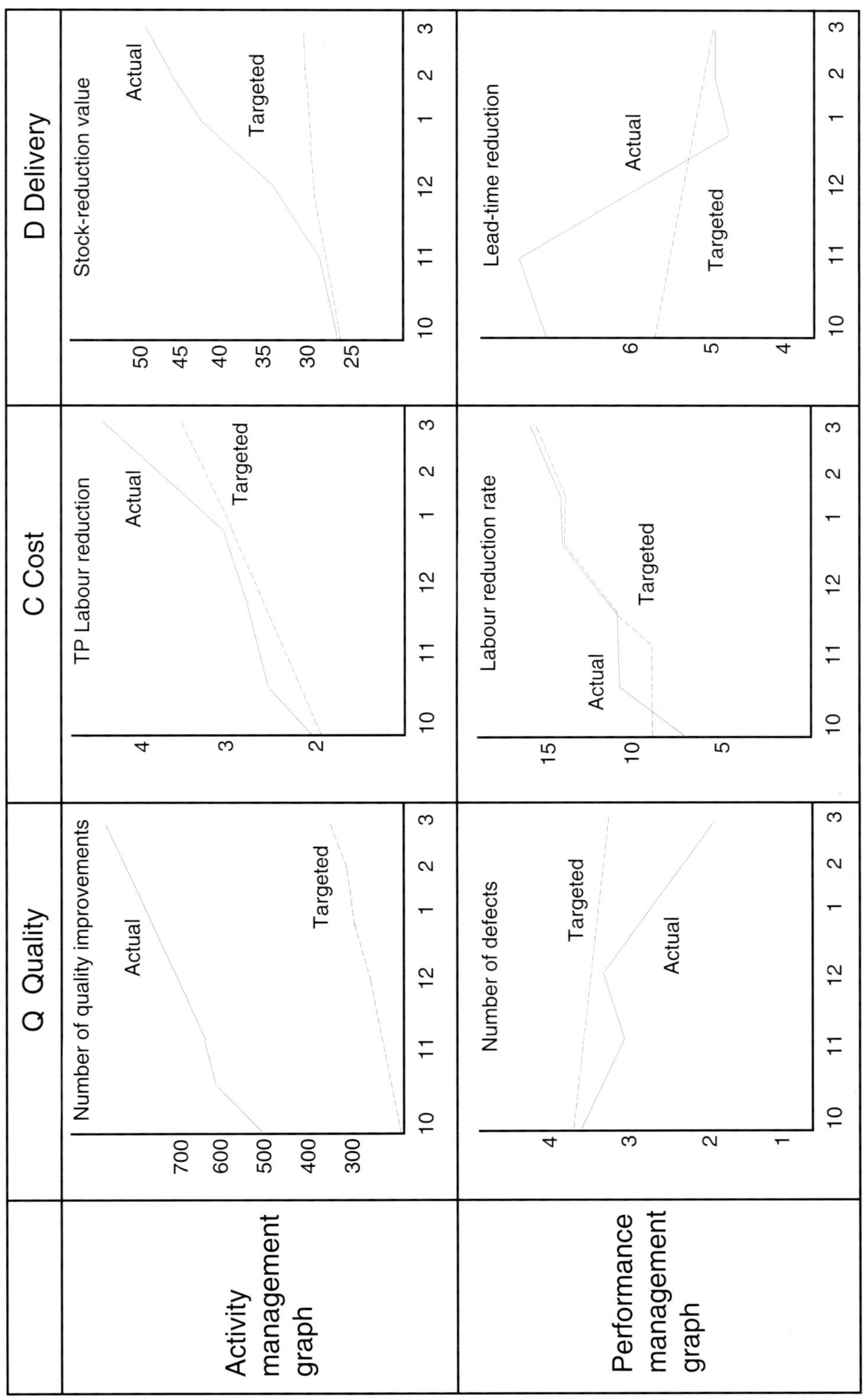

Figure 9.11 Activity Management and Performance Management

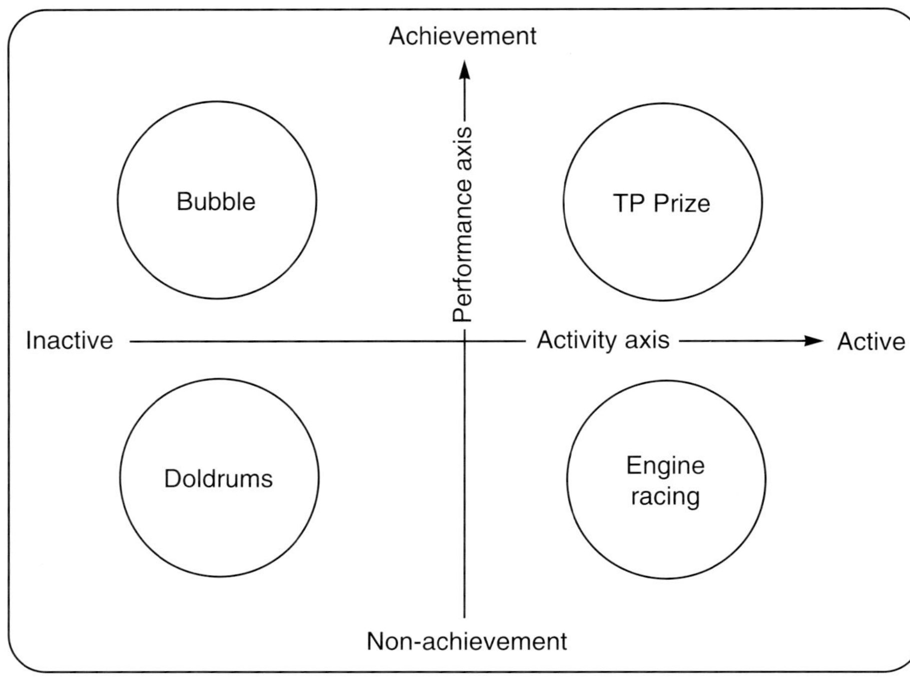

Figure 9.12 TP Portfolio

Constitution Improvement Activities

This section describes how we carried out our constitution improvement activities, using quality as an example (see Figures 9.13 and 9.14).

For the past three years, we at the Ageo Plant have been championing the cause of building a system to guarantee the quality of every final product. We have been setting up mechanisms to allow this to happen and have undertaken a programme of specific activities to this end. In carrying out these activities, quality teams were formed by representatives from each workplace and cross-functional initiatives were undertaken to devise a common set of criteria and measures for use throughout the plant.

Specifically, we rewrote the quality control regulations for each workplace and published them in the form of a set of quality assurance and production control standards known colloquially as the "Green Files" and "Yellow Files" respectively. As Figure 9.14 shows, the "quality" constitution element (achieving 100% assured quality) was split into two major categories (establish basic conditions and enhance preventative functions) that were then subdivided to yield eight control items (maintenance of quality standards, maintenance of standardised assessment criteria, etc.), and further subdivided to give a total of 44 sub-items. A five-step rating scale was established in order to enable the degree of attainment of each of the control items to be objectively evaluated. These are the "Green Files". On this five-step rating scale, Level 2 is defined as the usual level comparable with that of other companies, while Level 4 is defined as the situation in which the kind of quality that delights customers is continuously maintained and improved by periodically revising the standards and working practices.

To establish the assessment scales, each of the plant's processes (machining, press-forming, welding, painting, assembly and so forth) was examined, and the requirements for building quality into the product via the process were established. The checksheet method is used for the evaluation procedure; for example, the first control item (maintenance of quality standards) would be assessed by means of a detailed questionnaire, starting by asking whether or not a particular standard exists and then going on to enquire about what it includes and how it is used.

Together, the Green Files and the Yellow Files show what must be done in each process and what each process must be equipped with in order to achieve 100% assured quality. They have made it possible for anyone to judge the existing capabilities of a particular process in relation to this objective and understand why the particular improvement activities associated with that process are being undertaken.

In performing the evaluations, group and team leaders conduct self-diagnoses once every three months in conjunction with overall diagnoses by the plant's quality team. In

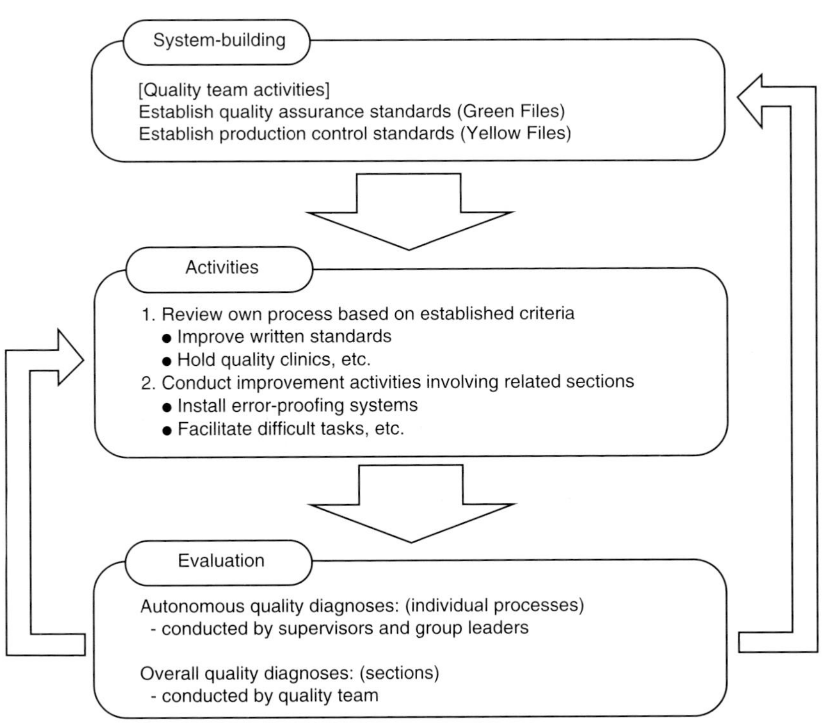

Figure 9.13 Overview of Constitution Improvement Activities

Items evaluated: 8 control items (44 sub-items)
Evaluation levels: 5

		1	2	3	4	5
Establish basic conditions	1. Maintenance of quality standards					
	2. Maintenance of standardised assessment criteria					
	3. Quality checking					
	4. Quality clinics					
Enhance preventative functions	5. Error-proofing activities					
	6. Improvement activities					
	7. Education and training					
	8. Information management					

Figure 9.14 Evaluation Items for 100% Assured Quality Constitution

the self-diagnoses, group and team leaders score themselves and identify the topics they need to tackle in the next round of activities. The purpose of the overall diagnoses is to eliminate variation among workplaces and allow managers to monitor the situation and support the activities. It was decided to display the results of these diagnoses in the form of quality radar charts. Using an octagonal radar chart (see Figure 9.17) highlights the weak points of each process, helping to show the direction in which the activities should be moving and speed up the improvement cycle.

Similar rating scales were set up for the constitution improvement activities. We have developed these for the 6 Ss as well as for quality and are achieving excellent results in both areas.

TP Promotion Organisation (Figure 9.15)

The organisation for promoting the TP activities consists of a pyramid-like structure of overlapping small groups. At the top is the AA 92 TP Promotion Council, chaired by our plant manager with a senior managing director in attendance. Under this are six departmental committees (unit committee, vehicle committee, and so on). The bottom layer consists of section-level promotion committees set up under each departmental committee. These committees meet once a month to discuss progress, identify future topics and work out how to proceed with the most promising improvement projects. We also allocated the responsibility for lateral deployment (extending the activities across all functions) and aligning all the plant's efforts in the same direction to cross-functional Q, C and D teams and "6-S teams" (teams responsible for creating attractive workplaces by promoting the 6 Ss throughout the factory).

The "TP Clubs" noted on the diagram are the plant manager's weekly visits to the activity boards of each group in order to obtain information from supervisors, assess the status of the activities, and give advice. These visits have proved extremely effective, providing an opportunity for the plant manager to exchange opinions with the front-line supervisors and weigh up the situation in the workplace, as well as motivating the supervisors and ensuring that everyone has a common understanding of the issues to be tackled.

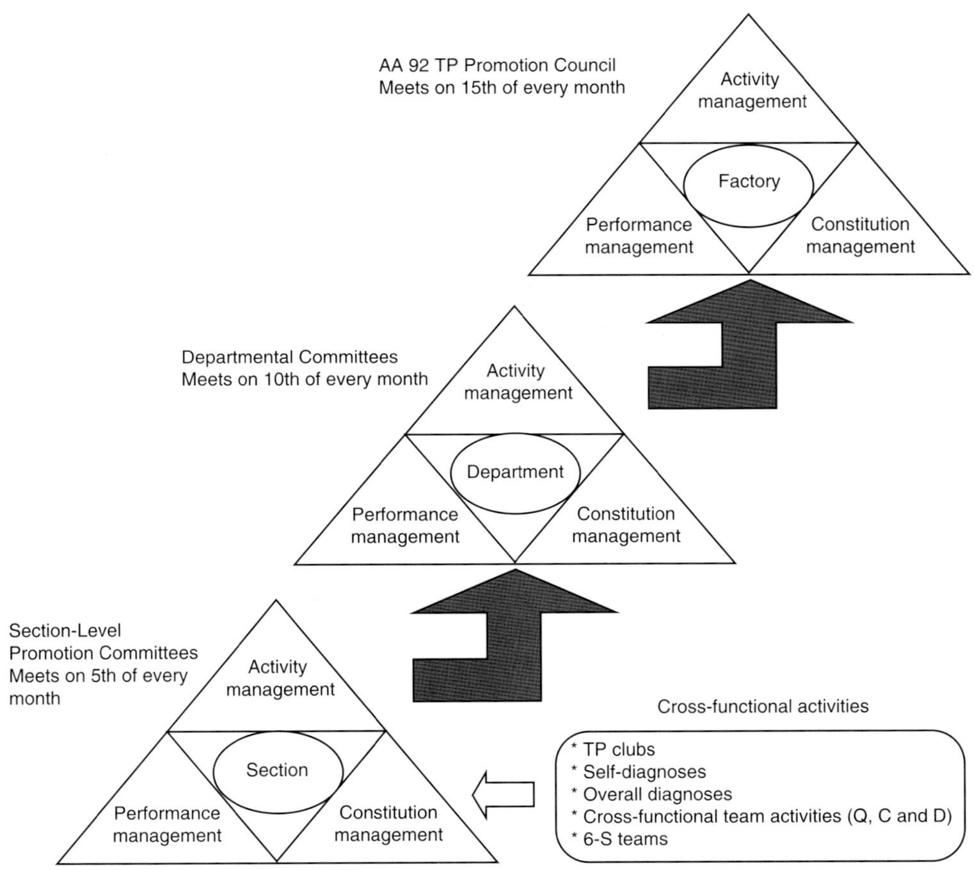

Figure 9.15 TP Promotion Organisation

Examples of Specific Improvement Activities

1. Three-day focused improvements

One of the pivotal and most effective improvement activities carried out is the "3-day focused improvement" programme, concentrating on topics such as cost reduction and quality improvement. In addition to achieving specific tangible results, a further aim of this programme is to "foster cross-functional improvement and develop improvement champions". The guidelines for the activities are as follows:

1. Promote cross-fertilisation between different trades.

   Generate fresh ideas by introducing different viewpoints through mixing people from different departments (assembly, machining and so on) in the same improvement team.

2. Encourage joint activities between neighbouring groups.

   Allow supervisors from neighbouring workplaces or similar trades within the same department to join each other's groups in order to pool ideas and take results and techniques back to their own areas.

3. Involve people from related workplaces in team activities.

   Include people from departments such as engineering, supply and works among the team members in order to make the activities as multi-faceted and dynamic as possible.

4. Initiate self-directed activities in the manufacturing department.

   When implementing improvements on their own processes, supervisors and team leaders themselves should take the initiative and improve the management of their workplaces by following the PDCA cycle, while developing themselves as engineers with a high level of improvement know-how.

5. Develop people's abilities through team selection.

   Form teams with the idea of nurturing young technicians and developing them into highly resourceful, effective employees.

In 1992, the following statistics were recorded for the 3-day focused improvement programme:

Number of improvement topics tackled: 427

Number of improvements effected: 5,316

Results achieved: 8,310 h/month labour reduction
(equivalent to approx. 50 employees)

2. New-line startup through TP Management

In January this year, we launched a new medium-duty truck, the Fine Condor. This is a good example of the use of TP Management in starting up a new line, as we employed it when setting up the cab-body welding and assembly lines for the new model.

Previously, the cabs for our heavy-duty and medium-duty trucks had been welded on separate lines. However, on introducing the new model, we decided to combine these two lines. There were many problems associated simply with connecting the new unified welding line to the separate final assembly lines for heavy-duty and medium-duty trucks, and we expected to encounter considerable difficulties with the project. We hoped that our TP techniques would help us to overcome these.

The following objectives were set for the manufacturing department's most critical task in initiating production of the new model – to achieve smooth startup and prompt stabilisation of production:

Raise the operating rates for the newly-installed automatic equipment.

Hold improvement clinics for all processes including sub-assembly processes.

Improve lineside areas through better parts supply and placement.

Ensure complete worker proficiency before startup, based on finalised process plans.

Guarantee the required quality precision.

Perform a preliminary trial at the targeted production cycle time of three minutes per cab body, including all of the above.

Specialist teams were set up to address each of these topics.

Learning from examples of problems encountered with starting up new lines in the past, we instituted a system of progress control as an advance countermeasure, but fresh problems cropped up every time a new item of equipment was introduced and tested. As a result of progressively refining the equipment by introducing over 600 improvements, we were able to achieve a 95% line operating rate before startup. We also attained our 98% operating rate target after the commencement of volume production in approximately 1/4 of the time that it had taken when we had previously introduced a similar full model change.

3. Creating Attractive Workplaces

As a final example of our TP Management activities, we shall describe the campaign to create "attractive workplaces".

Based on our belief that the bedrock for all our activities is the enlivenment of the workplace, we are promoting the 6 Ss as a plantwide activity. As described earlier, we have established 6-S evaluation criteria and have set up a system of quantitative assessment that allows us to say not just that a particular workplace has become clean and well-organised, but exactly how clean and how well-organised.

The new employees entering the company this spring were also soon able to play a part in the cleanup campaign based on these 6-S evaluation criteria. Everyone became involved in both activities and assessments, and the campaign was extremely effective in paving the way to success for the bottom-up approach. Also, as the campaign progressed and people began to see the results, they began to enjoy the activities more and more and experience a growing sense of achievement.

To enable people to see what improvements their colleagues had made and inspire them to higher levels of achievement, we introduced a programme of designating particularly noteworthy areas as "beauty spots". To qualify as a beauty spot, a workplace had to satisfy the following criteria:

Its improvement activities had to have a particular distinguishing feature (error-proofing, inventory reduction, equipment maintenance, etc.)

All the 6-S targets had to be met.

It had to be accident-free.

When a particular workplace regards itself as worthy of beauty-spot status, it puts in an application, and the plant manager and other managers conduct an on-site diagnosis. Successful workplaces receive a certificate and commemorative gifts.

To keep this programme alive, we came up with the idea of holding a "beauty spot stamp rally" to encourage employees to visit other workplaces and see what can be achieved. Each beauty spot designs its own symbol, and employees are given special books to stamp with these symbols as they tour the plant (see Figure 9.16).

The campaign started out with the initial aim of creating 100 of these beauty spots, and by last year this target had been exceeded by 34.

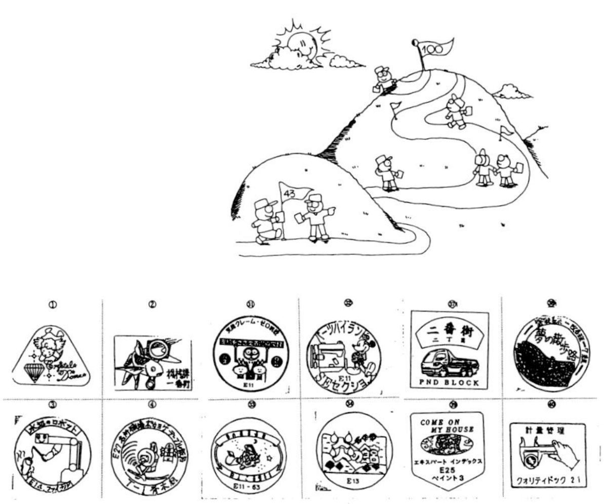

Figure 9.16 "Beauty Spot" stamp rally

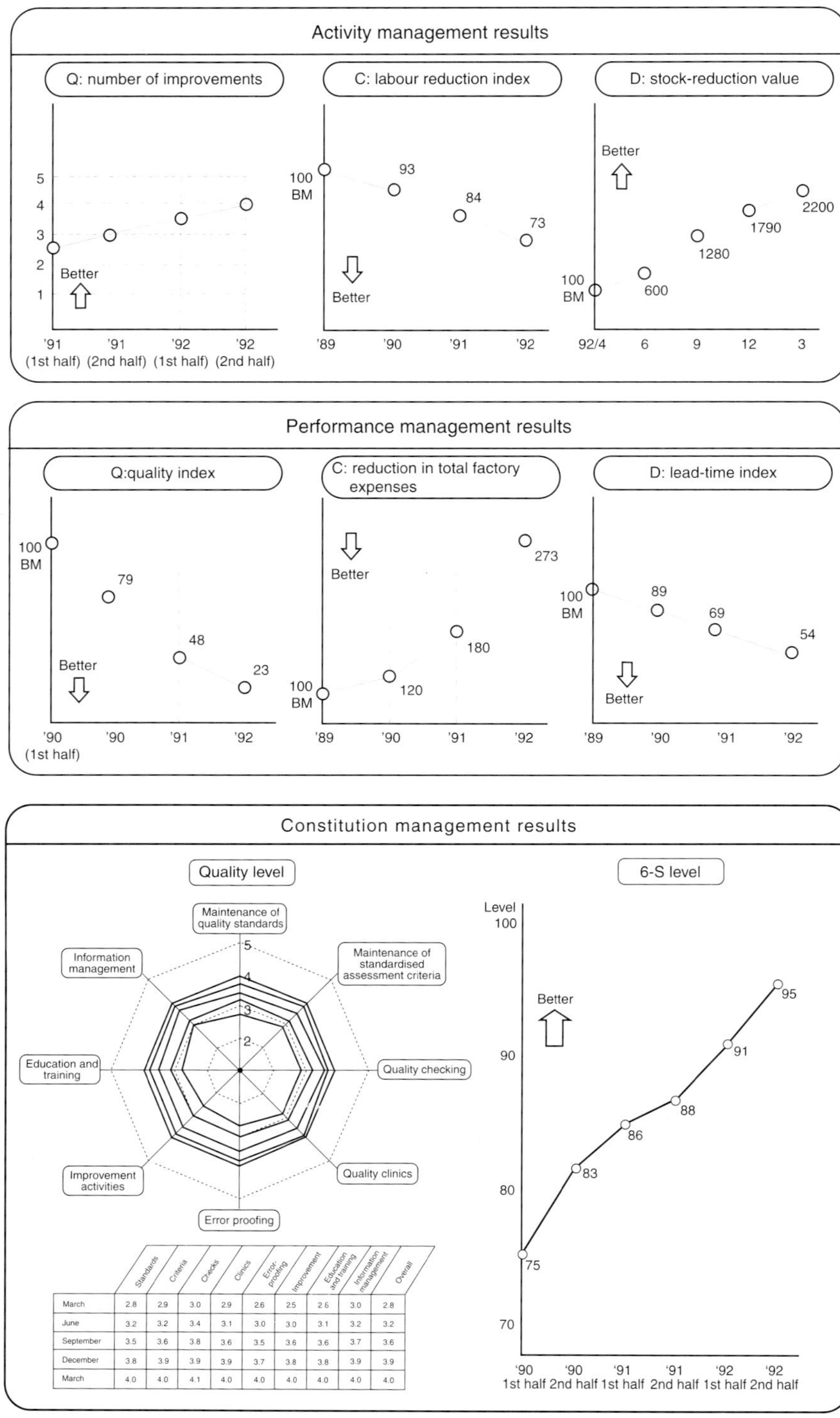

	Standards	Criteria	Checks	Clinics	Error-proofing	Improvement	Education and training	Information management	Overall
March	2.8	2.9	3.0	2.9	2.6	2.5	2.5	3.0	2.8
June	3.2	3.2	3.4	3.1	3.0	3.0	3.1	3.2	3.2
September	3.5	3.6	3.8	3.6	3.5	3.6	3.6	3.7	3.6
December	3.8	3.9	3.9	3.9	3.7	3.8	3.8	3.9	3.9
March	4.0	4.0	4.1	4.0	4.0	4.0	4.0	4.0	4.0

Figure 9.17 Results of Activities

Results of TP Activities

Figure 9.17 shows the results achieved through our activity management, performance management and constitution management programmes. As a result of the wide range of activities described in the previous sections, we are now enjoying the following benefits:

Firstly, we have achieved our targeted values for the performance indicators and activity indicators.

Secondly, thanks to our 100% assured quality drive, a system of constitution improvement activities relating to quality has been established and we have been able to achieve the targeted values for our assessment criteria in this area. At the same time, the elements of the constitution improvement activities have been identified and sorted out.

Thirdly, setting specific goals and proceeding steadily towards those goals has given everyone a sense of achievement and created a climate of delight in improvement. The shop floor takes the lead in the activities, and supervisors have begun to turn themselves into engineers, improving the management capabilities of the workplace. Production engineering expertise has combined with shop-floor improvement capabilities to establish a culture of back-to-basics improvement focused on tackling problems at their source.

Future Tasks

In addition to quality and the 6 Ss, we must also set up systems for the other six principal elements of constitution improvement (inventory, setup, equipment, process control, operations, and production technology).

We also wish to extend our TP activities beyond the shop floor, building a comprehensive TP Management system encompassing support departments, R & D and parts manufacturers. We do not have any specific ideas as to how to proceed with this at present, but we regard it as an important task for the future.

10
Mitsuba Electric Mfg Co., Ltd

Using TP Management to Raise Total Productivity

Hiroshi Ohta, Director
Ryoichi Kondo, TP Management Promotion Section,
Manufacturing Planning Department
Mitsuba Electric Mfg Co., Ltd

Company Profile

Overview

Mitsuba Electric Manufacturing Co., Ltd makes electrical equipment for automobiles at five sites in Japan (our Head Plant at Kiryū City, and our Akagi, Niisato, Onishi and Tone Plants). All are located in the famously beautiful Gunma Prefecture, north-west of Tokyo (see Figure 10.1).

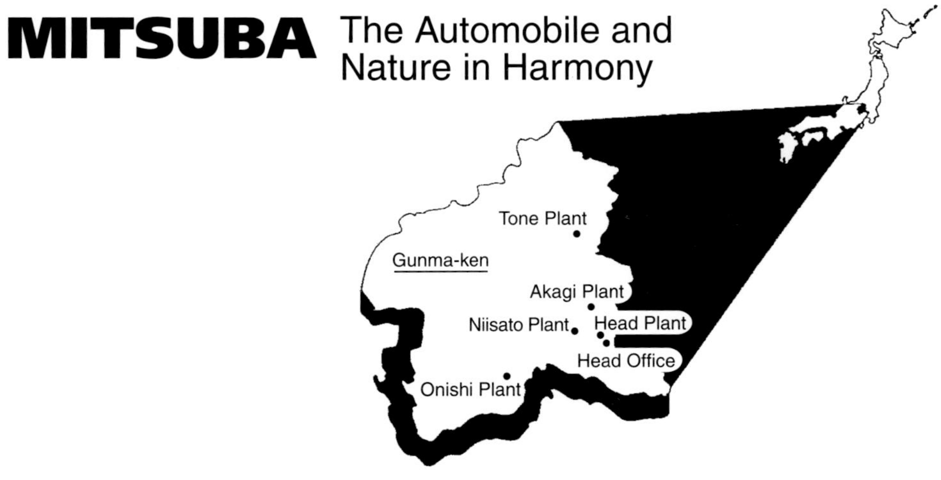

Figure 10.1 Company Overview

Founded in 1946, Mitsuba now (1993) has approximately £48 million in capital, with a workforce of 2,800 and annual sales of around £460 million. Our main products include windscreen wiper motors, starter motors, power relays, electric window motors, four-wheel steering motors, and controls of various types. As a manufacturer of comprehensive electrical systems for automobiles, we see our corporate role as helping to enhance vehicle performance, safety and comfort.

Management Vision and Plan

Mitsuba's "Management Vision 2001" business plan (see Figure 10.2) embodies our ambitions for the 21st century in terms of technology development, globalisation, and serving the local community. Our overall vision is broken down into three parts: an operational vision of turning Mitsuba into an international manufacturer of electrical system components, a management setup vision of turning Mitsuba into a more progressive, creative company, and a corporate culture vision of ensuring that human and corporate interests coexist in harmony. This manifesto makes it clear how we see our obligations to society.

Our Third Medium-Term Management Plan, shown in Figure 10.3, sets out the steps whereby our ultimate vision is to be achieved. The basic thrust of this plan is to expand our operations based on "market-in" (customer-focused) activities. This is subdivided

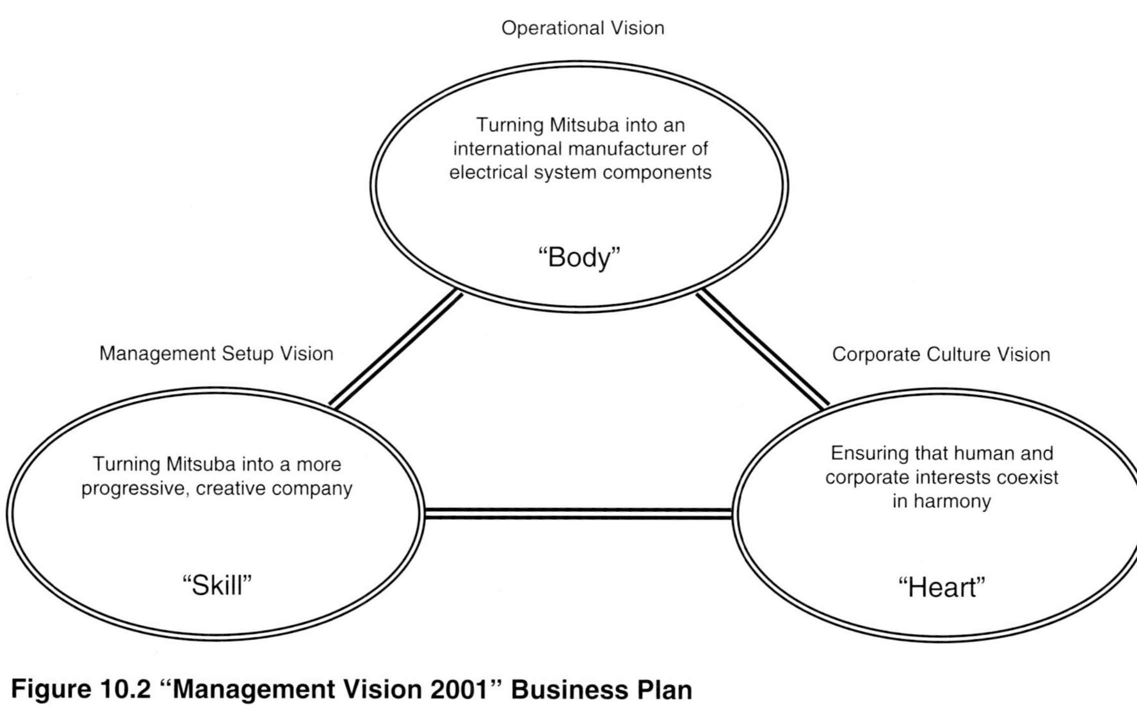

Figure 10.2 "Management Vision 2001" Business Plan

into three separate elements: "build a system driven by market-in activities", "establish the required management infrastructure" and "strengthen competitiveness throughout Mitsuba".

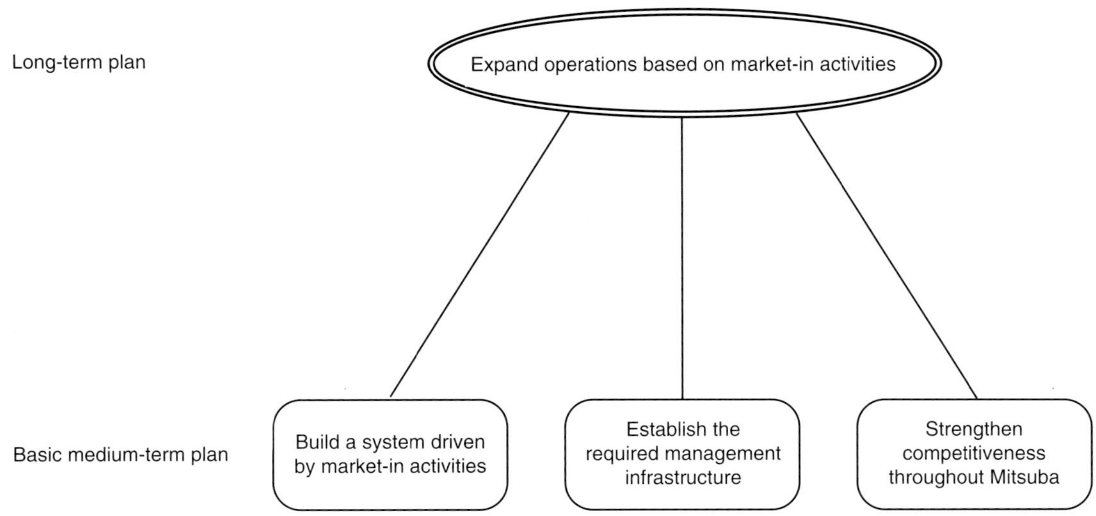

Figure 10.3 The Medium-Term Management Plan

TP Management Philosophy

We decided to introduce TP Management as a practical implementation of the management policy described above. Our desired management scenario is defined by our TP Management Philosophy (see Figure 10.4), which guides us in finding the most effective ways of deploying our management resources to cope with the many challenges posed by today's ever-changing business climate. The principal aim of our TP Management Philosophy is to set certain management objectives, and, by achieving those objectives, to revitalise the whole company. This aim can be broken down into the following three parts:

1. Deploy objectives for a wide range of management needs and policies, ultimately creating an organisational setup in which all employees participate in management.
2 Reform Mitsuba's corporate structure, increasing the company's ability to get things done through better internal cooperation.
3. Stimulate the company's development by enhancing its levels of CS (Customer Satisfaction), SS (Service to Society) and ES (Employee Satisfaction).

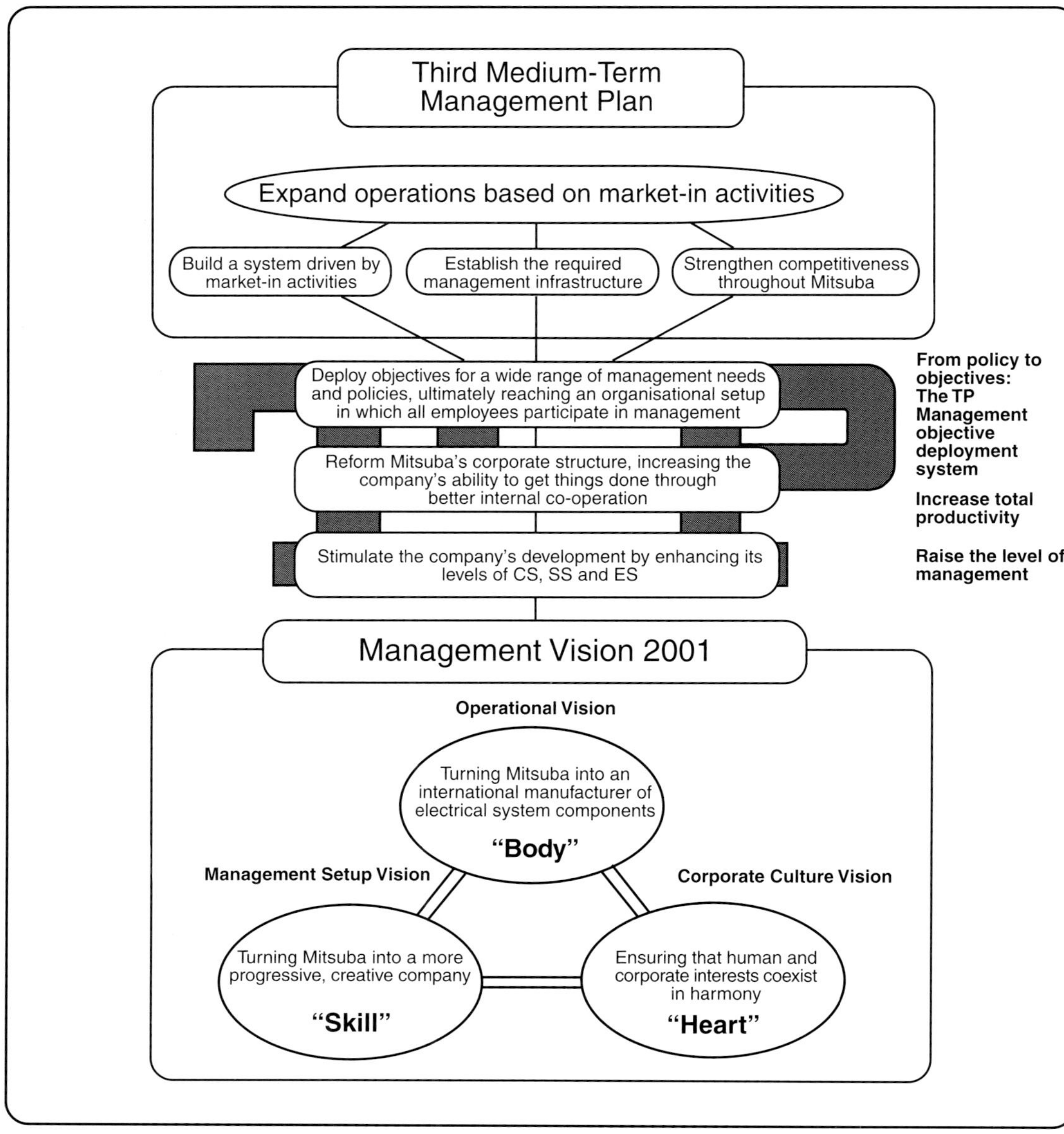

Figure 10.4 TP Management Philosophy

TP Management

MZMS Plan

Mitsuba began reforming itself in April 1977, under the aegis of the MZMS (Mitsuba Zooming Management System) Plan (see Figure 10.5). Feeling the urgent need for a leaner and fitter corporate structure when confronted by the unprecedented economic upheavals and management sea-changes following the first and second oil crises, we formulated the MZMS Plan in 1976, aiming to give our company's management a shot in the arm. For the ten years until 1986, we concentrated on reorganising our production systems, while from 1987 until 1989, we tried to improve the quality of our management. From 1990 until 1992, we focused on reducing development and production lead times and increasing productivity in our administrative and support departments.

After the Plaza Agreement, the yen grew stronger, and we used our hard-won know-how to good effect in moving some of our manufacturing operations overseas. The yen continued to rise in the following years, and the Japanese public became more environmentally aware and began to demand "greener" policies in industry. Our management goals had to accommodate both these trends.

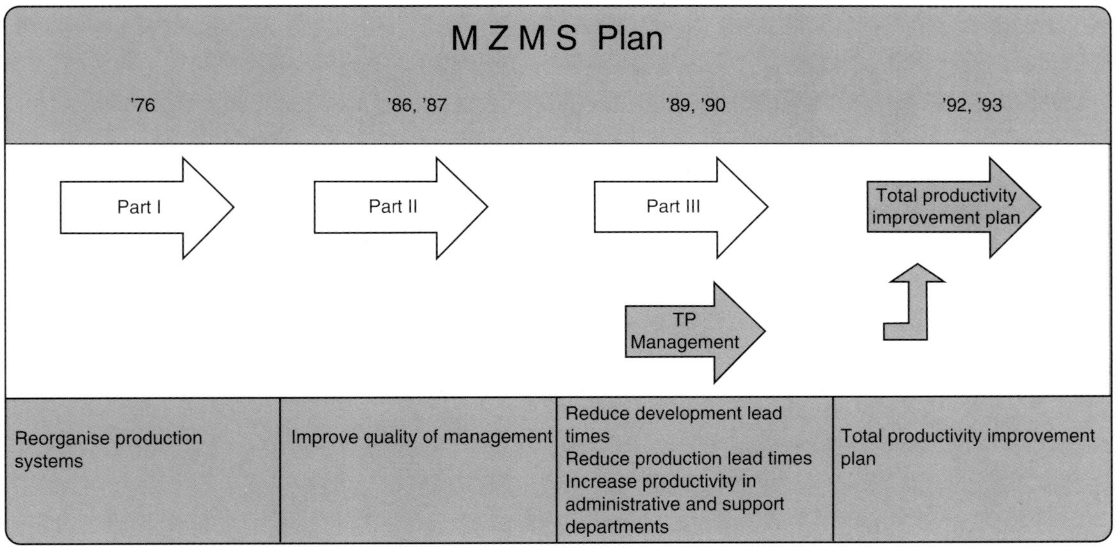

Figure 10.5 The Steps Leading Up to Constitutional Reform

The MZMS Plan was being executed on a companywide basis, but the relationships between our business objectives and results were not clear, and each department was acting independently. Consequently, some departments implemented the MZMS Plan more quickly than others, and there was little interdepartmental cooperation. Aware of these problems, we decided that we needed to raise productivity throughout the company. In TP Management terms, we needed "total productivity improvement".

Introducing TP Management

We began to investigate the possibility of introducing TP Management in 1990, and decided to introduce it in the 1991 financial year, starting with our manufacturing operations. This was also the point at which we formulated the TP Management Philosophy noted earlier. As already mentioned, one of the central tenets of this philosophy was to use TP Management's objective deployment process to create an organisational setup in which all employees participate in management. Another was to transcend departmental boundaries and raise our overall productivity by reforming the corporate structure to increase our ability to cooperate internally and get things done. The two main ideas behind this intention to remodel the corporate "constitution" (the entire internal environment and management setup) through TP Management were thus as follows:

1. Break down interdepartmental barriers.
2. Increase Mitsuba's ability to get things done.

Reforming the Corporate Constitution and Deploying TP Management

To ensure universal acceptance of our management objectives and create effective structures for departmental decision-making, assessment of contribution levels, and objective attainment, we knew that we had to break down interdepartmental barriers and increase our ability to get things done. To achieve these aims, we needed to be able to select strategies that would be "surefire winners" from the overall standpoint, we needed to be able to formulate reliable plans for achieving our objectives, and we needed to be able to effect improvements speedily and come up with alternative strategies whenever the original ones proved inadequate. We reformulated all these needs and aims in terms of the stages of TP Management deployment (see Figure 10.6), giving us a stable and robust foundation from which to pursue our program of constitutional reform with confidence and conviction. For us, deploying our management objectives through TP Management was synonymous with reforming our corporate constitution.

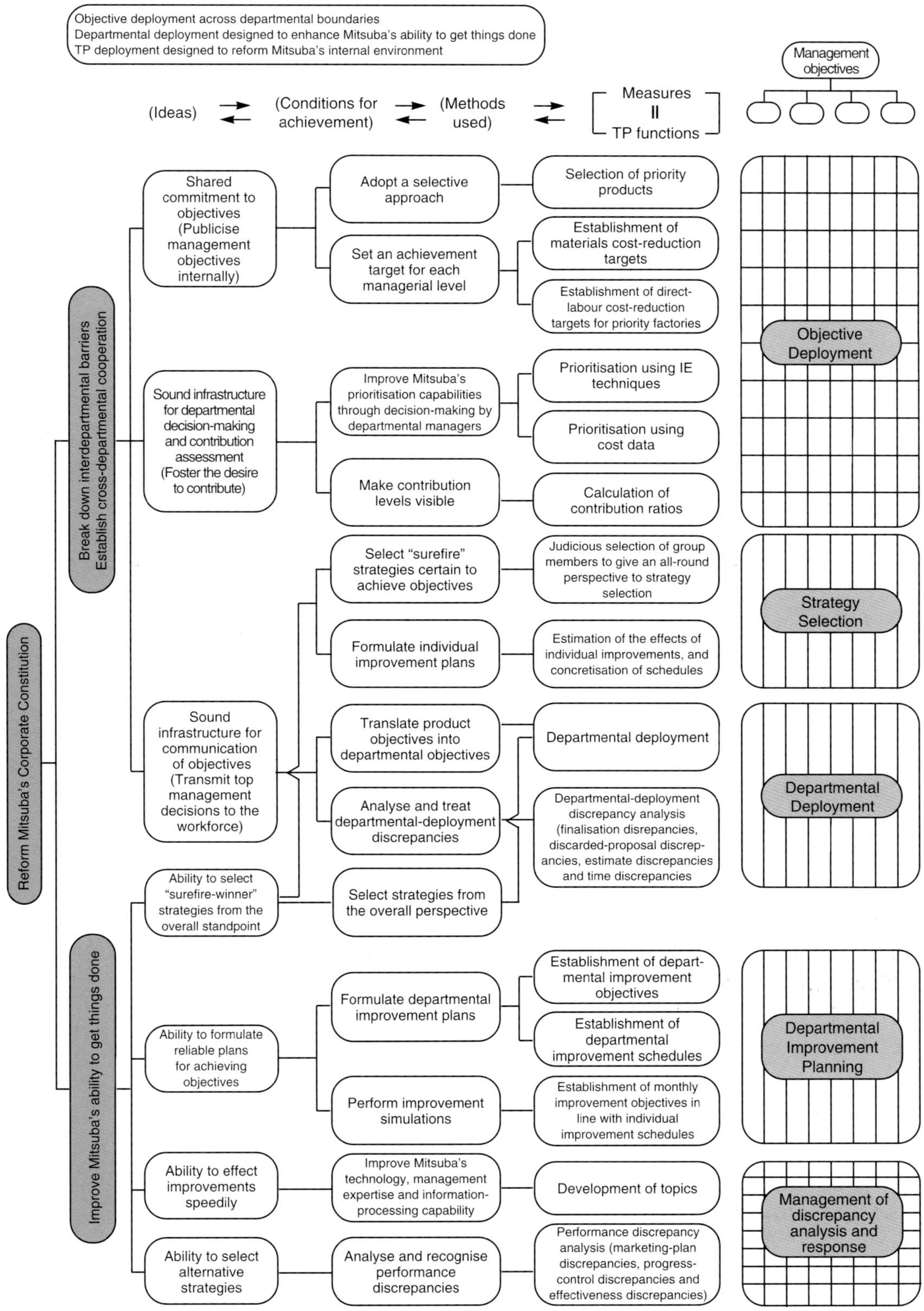

Figure 10.6 Corporate Constitutional Reform and TP Development

TP Management Deployment System

Figure 10.7 shows Mitsuba's TP Management deployment system. This system consists of a breakdown of our product lineup in terms of priority products, coordinated with a breakdown of two overall objectives (reducing costs and serving society) and two independent individual objectives (reducing development costs and reducing process defect losses).

Cost reduction is particularly important for a parts manufacturer, so the standard elements of the deployment of this objective (objective deployment and strategy selection) were augmented by a system of departmental deployment in conjunction with a computerised system called the Performance Control System. This is a centralised data-processing system that allows us to exercise integrated control of objectives and the progress of strategies, and track the results. This in turn enables us to monitor and deal with discrepancies between objectives and performance and coordinate the control activities carried out under the heading of cost-related improvement.

Setting and Deploying TP Objectives

As noted earlier, our TP objectives consisted of two overall objectives (cost reduction and service to society) and two independent individual objectives (reducing development costs and reducing process defect losses). However, certain products were given priority when deploying these objectives. How the priority products were selected is explained below.

Selection of Priority Products

Prioritising our product lineup meant determining the most important products for our company as a whole. At the same time, it meant setting our priorities in terms of what we needed to do in order to make our products more competitive. By breaking down all our TP objectives in terms of our priority products, we aimed to rationalise our activities, achieve our management objectives, and increase customer satisfaction by doing everything necessary to improve the competitiveness of our most important products. Products were prioritised as follows:

> We selected a range of possible priority products, based on an ABC analysis carried out on our predictions for sales to each of our main customers.
>
> In consultation with representatives from all our departments, we compared our products with those of our competitors in terms of cost, quality, performance and future prospects, and selected those products we considered to be the most important for the company as a whole.

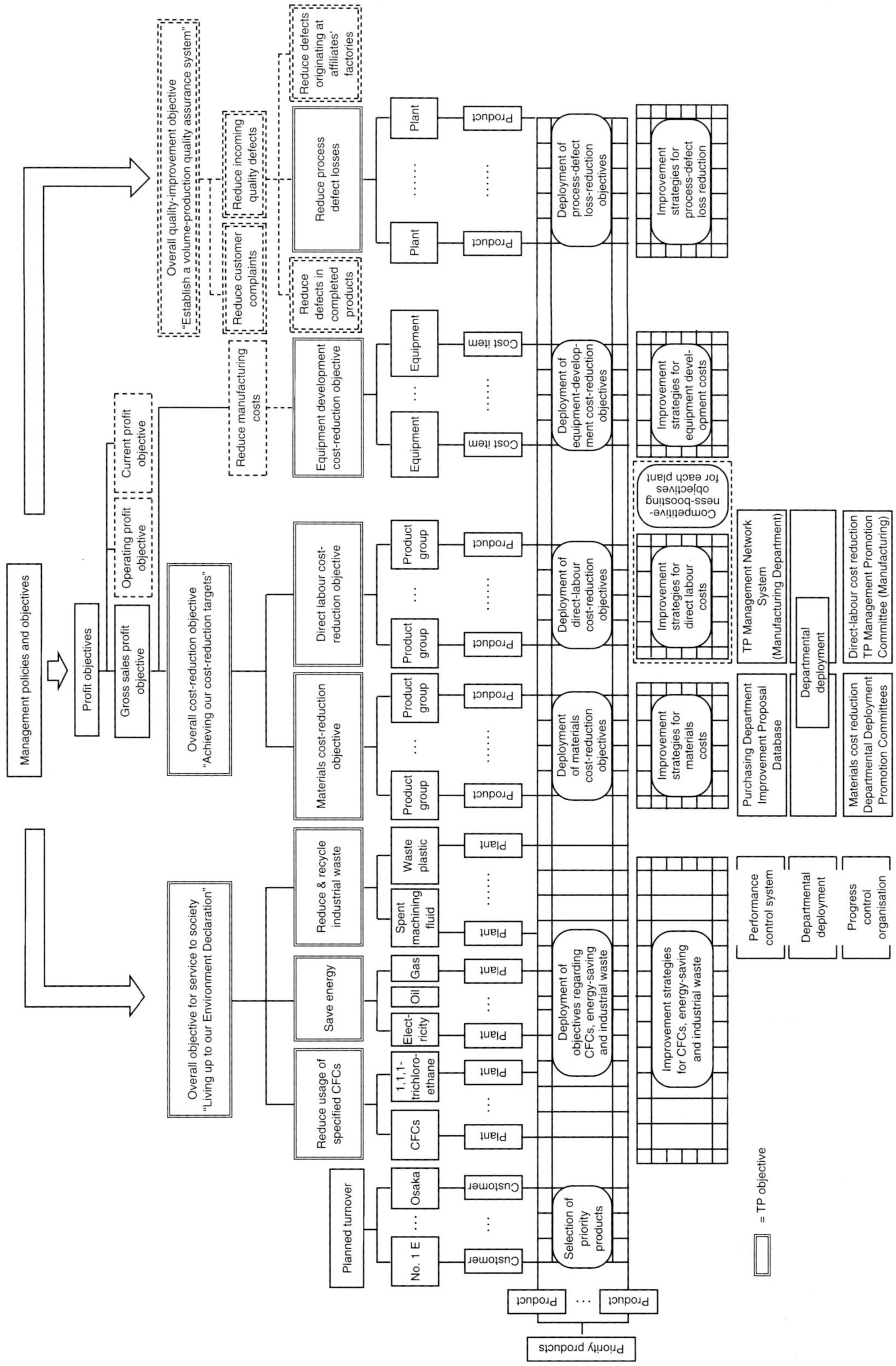

Figure 10.7 TP Management Deployment System

We decided what had to be done to further improve the competitiveness of each selected priority product, and set our priorities for the subsequent objective deployment process. These decisions were reflected in our selection of improvement strategies.

Prioritising our products in this manner enabled us to direct our productivity improvement activities in a focused, strategic way, on a companywide scale.

Setting and Deploying Our Overall Cost-Reduction Objective

When setting our overall cost-reduction objective, we bore in mind our TP Management Philosophy and ideas for corporate constitutional reform, noted earlier. We also clarified our ideas and expectations on cost-reduction activities as follows:

Our Ideas on Cost-Reduction Activities

All our employees were aware that, for a component manufacturer, reducing costs is just as important as improving quality.

Cost reduction was something we were working on even before we introduced TP Management. We therefore had a much surer grasp of the methods used and the roles of the various departments than in the case of our other TP activities.

We foresaw that cost-reduction activities would become increasingly important in the future.

Based on these attitudes, this is what we hoped to achieve by selecting and deploying cost reduction as an overall objective:

Position cost reduction in relation to our profit objective (one of our most important management objectives).

Translate our profit target into a valid, soundly-reasoned overall cost-reduction objective.

Obtain the active agreement and participation of all our employees in achieving that objective.

Effectively utilise the cost-reduction knowhow we had amassed over the years.

Establish an infrastructure for co-operation across departmental boundaries.

We were fully confident that our system for setting and deploying our overall cost-reduction objective would enable us to actualise our TP Management Philosophy and our ideas for corporate constitutional reform, as well as achieving our profit target through greater customer satisfaction. The actual setting and deployment of our overall cost-reduction objective (see Figure 10.8) was carried out as follows:

1. We calculated the discrepancy between our profit target based on our profit plan, and the profit estimated from a projected profit-and-loss account based on market orders.
2. We set our overall cost-reduction target, based on decisions made at top-management level.
3. To facilitate the objective deployment process, we subdivided the overall objective into two components: a materials cost-reduction objective and a direct-labour cost-reduction objective.

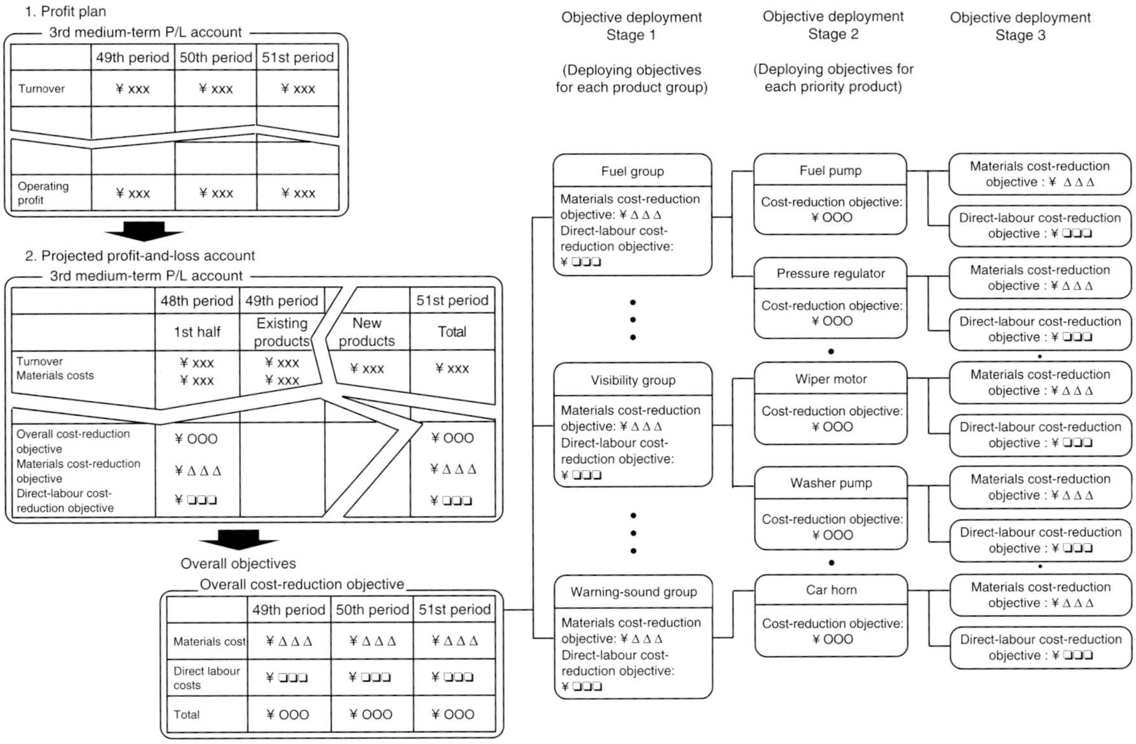

Figure 10.8 Setting Overall Cost-Reduction Objective and Breaking it Down by Priority Product

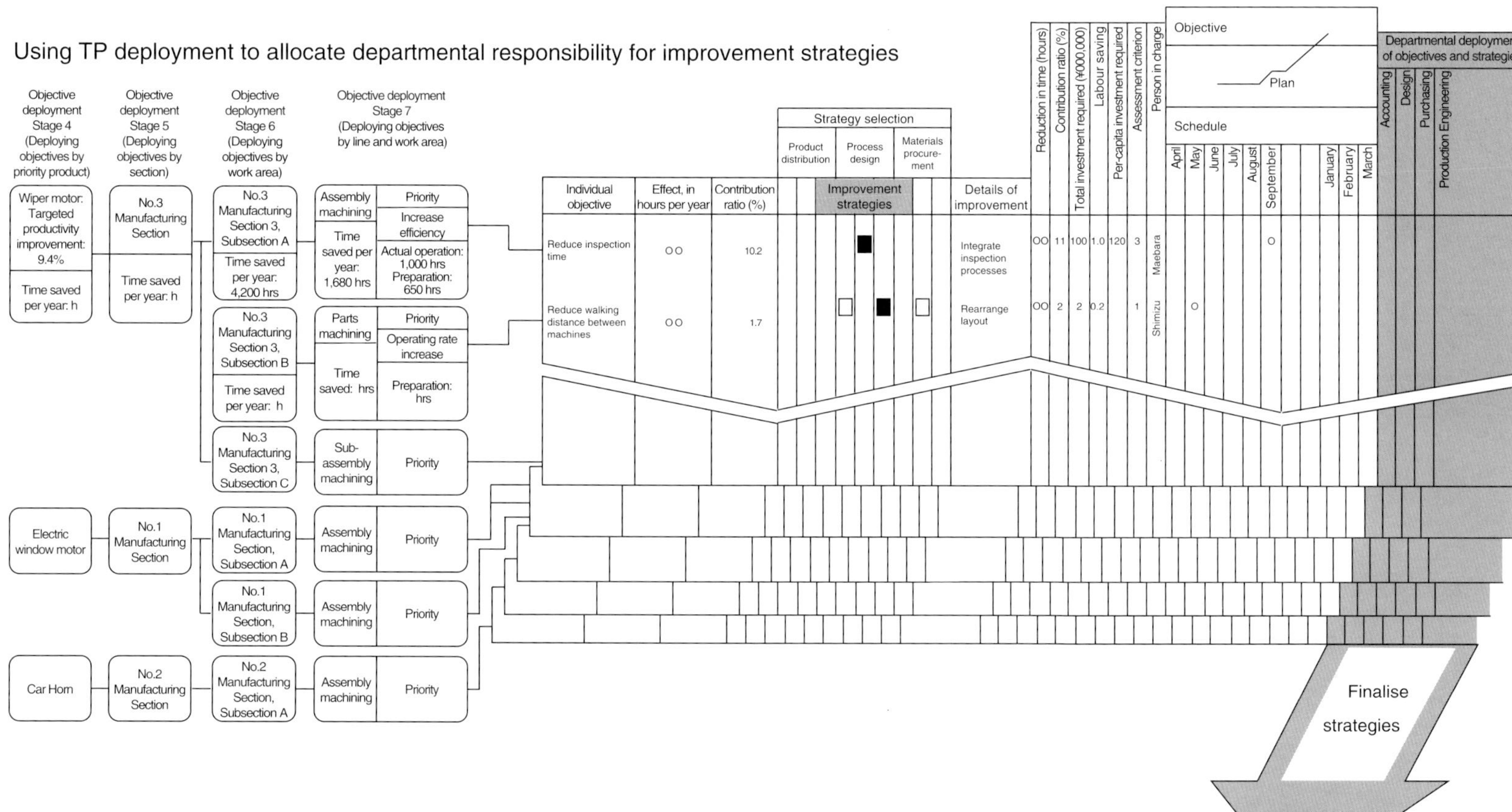

Figure 10.9 (above and below) Objective and Departmental Deployment by Priority Product, and Formulation of Departmental Cost-Reduction Proposals

Typical individual improvement proposal

Individual improvement proposal form

TP Management Individual Improvement Proposal Plant: OOO Section: 3 Subsection: A Surname: Maebara

Plant: OOO Assembly line: OO	Machine: OOO	Equipment code: OOOO-OOO-OO
Theme: Process integration	Improvement: Combine OO and ΔΔ inspection operations	Scheduled Implementation date: March 1, 1993
No. of machines/month:	Monthly saving: ¥150,000	
Labour-hours per item before improvement: OO minutes	Labour-hours per item after improvement: OO minutes	

	Outline Diagram	Explanation
Before improvement	OO inspection; ΔΔ inspection	OO and ΔΔ inspections are carried out by two people on two separate pieces of equipment
After improvement	OΔ inspection	Eliminate duplicated inspection items and reduce cycle time through equipment improvement

Department responsible for controlling improvement	Schedule	Other departments affected by improvement						
Details	April	May	June	July	August	Sept	Feb	March
Implementation schedule: 1. Hold discussions among departments involved		O						
2. Consider program			O					
3. Check quality aspect				O				
4. Perform tests and trials					O			

Comments by department controlling improvement:

Departmental deployment

Departmental cost-reduction proposal

Departmental deployment table for direct labour cost reduction

TP Management Promotion Plan

Departmental cost-reduction proposal form

Cost-reduction plan for OO Department

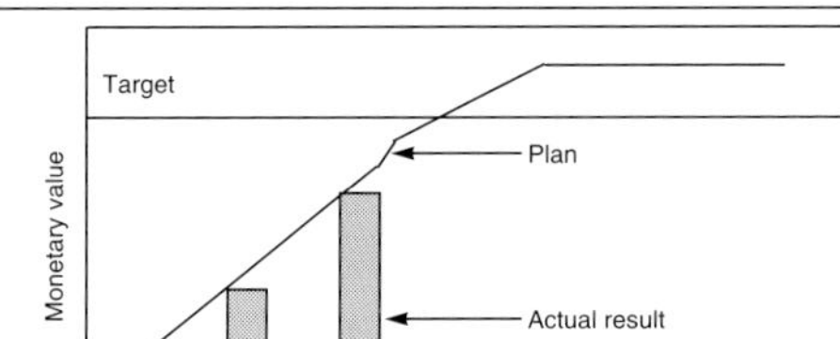

Priority product	No. produced	Time saved per item	Time saved: 120	Overall saving	Description of improvement	Department responsible		4	5	6	......	2	3
Wiper motor	OOO	OO	120	150	Integration of inspection processes	0.5	Planned		O 150	150	......		150
							Actual		● 120	140			
Total							Planned						
							Actual						

We then deployed these two objectives separately. Each was first broken down by product group (fuel, visibility and warning sound) and priority product (fuel pump, pressure regulator, etc.), after which an objective deployment table was drawn up for each priority product. Having deployed our objectives and selected our strategies, we finalised each improvement strategy by defining it on an individual improvement proposal form, feeding it into the departmental deployment system, and converting it into a departmental cost-reduction proposal (see Figure 10.9). In this way, we constructed a repeatable, rational, methodical system for converting product improvement objectives and policies into departmental improvement objectives.

In addition, to keep track of performance, we input the data from each improvement proposal form into a computer database and developed a system enabling us to plot and analyse the discrepancies between objective and performance for individual priority products and departments. The network system used to monitor and control the direct-labour cost-reduction objectives was named the TP Management Network System, while the corresponding system for the materials cost-reduction objectives was named the Purchasing Department Improvement Proposal Database. Together, these systems constituted the Performance Control System (see Figure 10.10).

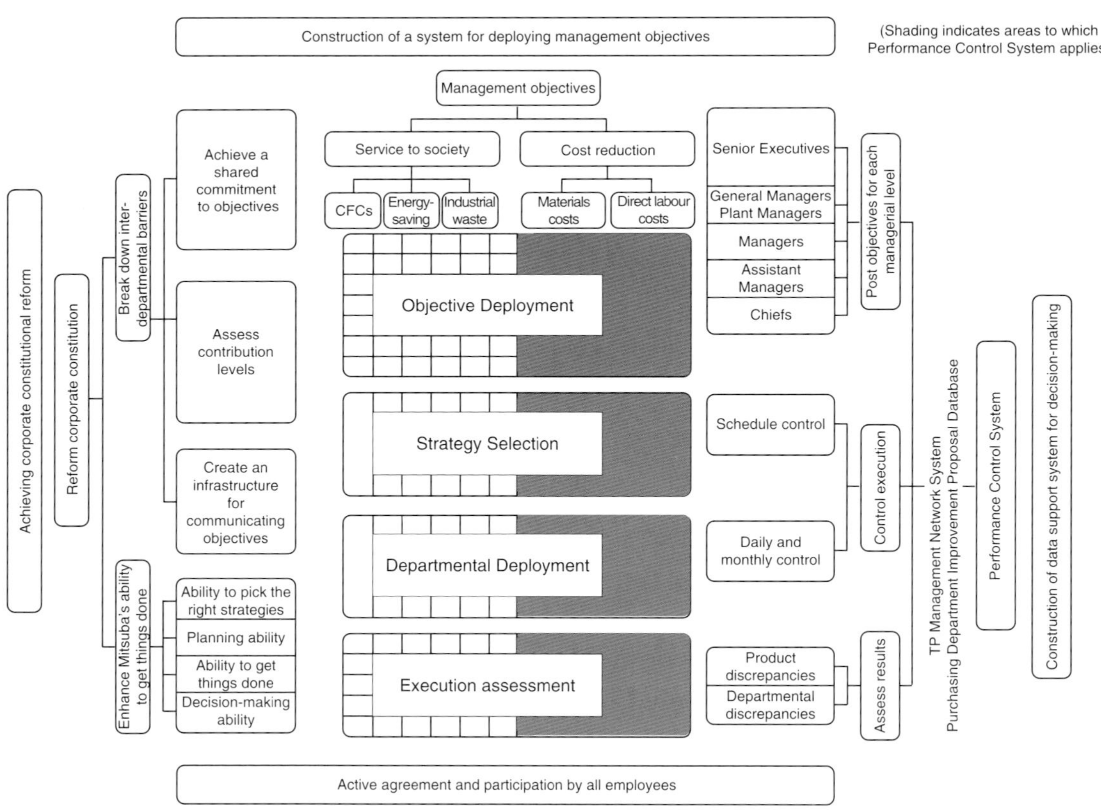

Figure 10.10 Performance Control System

Setting and Deploying Our Overall Objective for Serving Society

Our manufacturing facilities, as we said before, are all located in Gunma Prefecture. Somehow, these modern factories full of state-of-the-art equipment have to be integrated with the beautiful countryside surrounding them. We regard this as an essential management task, every bit as important as our business operation itself. In May 1993, we expressed our commitment to tackling environmental problems and publicly acknowledged our responsibility as a corporate citizen to the people with whom we share this planet, by issuing the Mitsuba Environmental Declaration. We introduced TP Management to help us put this Declaration into practice and achieve clear decision-making for ensuring our responsible corporate behaviour. We defined our overall objective for serving society as "living up to our Environmental Declaration" (see Figure 10.11) and broke it down into individual objectives for reducing our usage of specific CFCs, saving energy, and reducing our output of industrial waste. Having cascaded these down to each of our plants (see Figure 10.12), we drew up an objective deployment table for each plant.

1. Our approach to serving society

"We pledge to work towards the creation of a healthy and affluent society by actively developing technology to help economise on energy and materials and minimise environmental damage in all our corporate activities."

2. Our Environmental Declaration

1. We will make every effort to conserve resources in all our corporate activities, from development to production and marketing.
2. We will make every effort to reduce industrial waste and pollutants, and subject them to suitable processing.
3. We will make every effort to coexist harmoniously with the global environment, and maintain human health and safety.

Figure 10.11 Overall Objective of Serving Society

TP Management enabled us to implement our strategies for cost reduction and service to society and communicate our diverse management objectives to our entire workforce. It also allowed us to assess the contribution level of each strategy and create an infrastructure enabling us to manage our operations with the full participation of all employees.

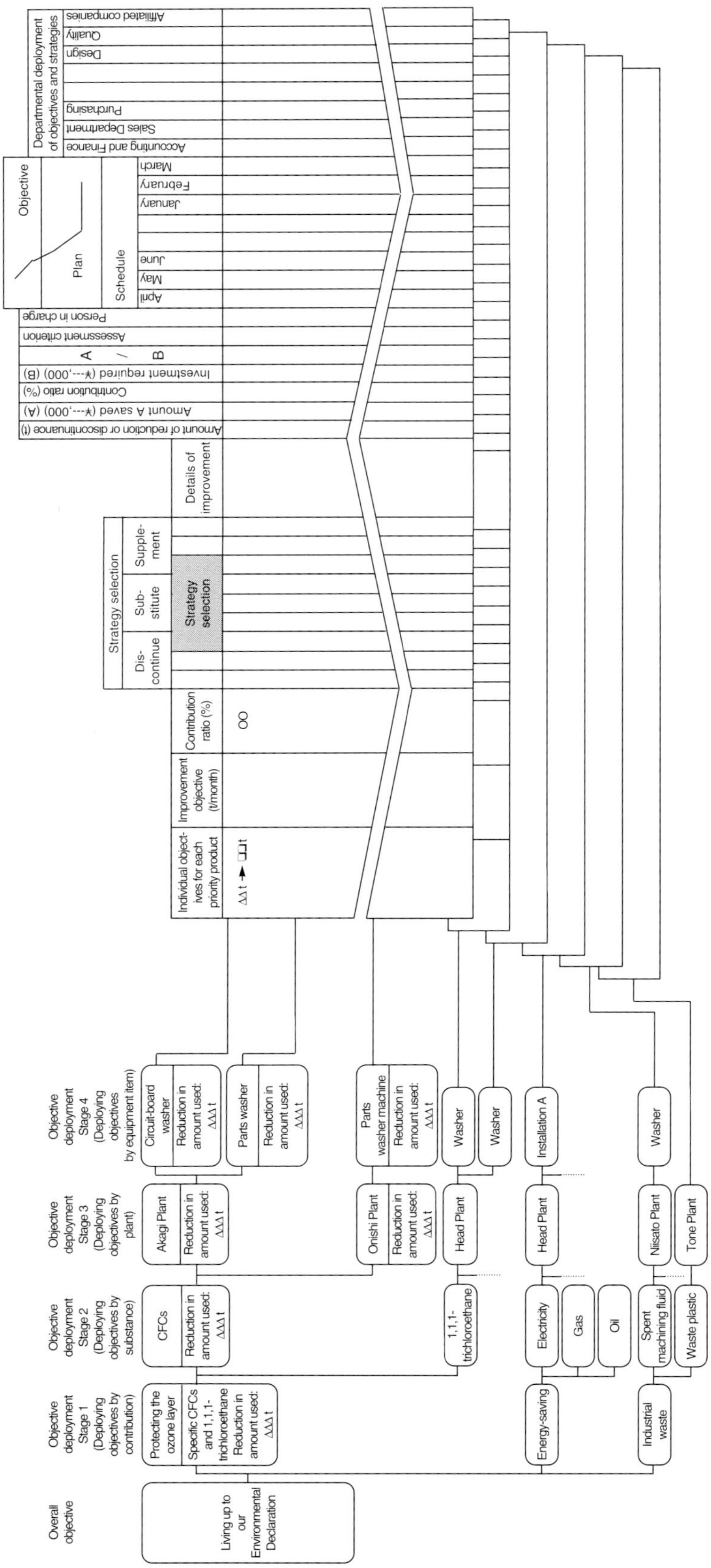

Figure 10.12 Overall Objective Deployment Chart for Service to Society

Setting and Deploying Objectives for Reducing Equipment Development Costs

At Mitsuba, we make most of our production equipment ourselves. Reasoning that cost-reduction activities of all kinds, including reducing equipment depreciation costs, are necessary in order to improve the price-competitiveness of our priority products, we decided to introduce TP in this area too. To this end, we drew up an objective deployment table for reducing equipment development costs, in which we set ourselves the target of achieving a 30% reduction (relative to Line No.1) in the cost of fabricating the equipment used in our automatic assembly lines (see Figure 10.13). The process of drawing up this table helped us to clarify our concepts, the constraints we faced, and our basic approach to cost reduction at every stage of the objective deployment process. It also concentrated our minds regarding the principles of our strategy selection, and the methods used to control costs and daily schedules at every stage from design to parts procurement and manufacturing.

Defining our ideal assembly line as "cheap to run, highly efficient and operator-friendly", we set our constraints in terms of improving equipment operating rates and operability in addition to achieving our cost-savings targets. We formulated our basic approach to cost reduction in the shape of the following selection of priorities for objective deployment:

Subject equipment to a radical "fat-trimming" exercise (elimination of waste), focusing on basic functions.

Use VE (value engineering) methods to assess functional value.

Downgrade any excessive requirements relating to versatility, durability, quality and so on.

When selecting strategies, we gave top priority to technology development, concentrating on providing expert backup and reducing parts costs. In controlling costs and daily schedules throughout the design, parts procurement and manufacturing stages, we compared actual performance very precisely with clearly-expressed planned figures for each installation and each cost item, and related each discrepancy to the action taken to deal with it.

Our schedule control system consisted of setting a manufacturing schedule for each installation, based on standardised manufacturing procedures. We again analysed discrepancies between objectives and performance, and established clear-cut methods for handling discrepancies (see Figure 10.14). In this way, focusing on priority products, we were able to achieve all-round cost reductions in the shape of reductions in equipment development costs and develop a system for monitoring and controlling the improvement process.

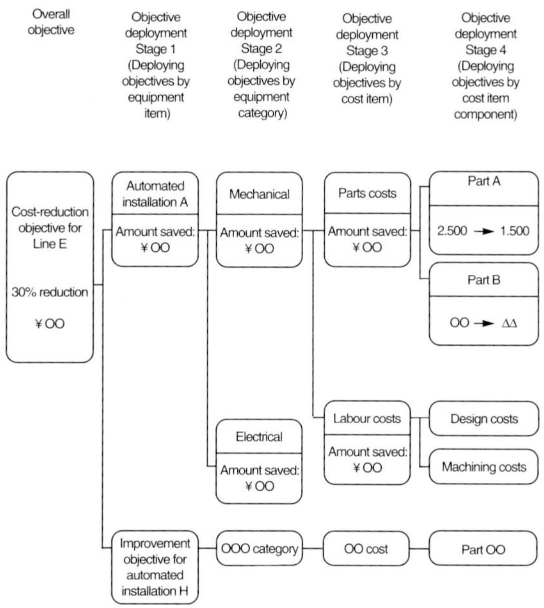

Reduction target	Contribution ratio %	Strategy selection: Fabrication	Strategy selection: Assembly	Strategy selection: Procurement	Details of improvement	Predicted reduction	Contribution ratio %	Actual reduction	Person in charge	Schedule: October	November								May	June
			Improvement strategies																	
▲¥1,000,000	OO				Integration of frames	▲1.500	O O	▲1.366	Kawakami		O		●							

Objective setting	Objective deployment	Strategy selection	From equipment design to parts procurement
Concept: "Lines that are cheap to run, highly efficient, and operator-friendly" Cheap to run: reduce fabrication cost by 30% Highly efficient: bring equipment operating rate up to 90% or higher	Basic approach to cost reduction: 1. Subject equipment to a radical "fat-trimming' exercise (elimination of waste), focusing on basic functions. 2. Use VE methods to assess functional value. 3. Downgrade excessive requirements relating to versatility, durability, quality, and so on.	Keynotes: 1. Technology development 2. Expert backup 3. Reduction of parts costs	● Fabrication cost-reduction activities Cost control Schedule control

Figure 10.13 Setting and Deploying Objectives for Reducing Equipment Development Costs

Cost control

		Press-fitting machine A		Washer B		•	• • •	Actual amount		Planned amount		Discrepancy	
Mechanical	Parts costs	4.802	▲ 49.7%	6.774	▲ 50.4%	•	• • •	OOO	▲ OO%	OOO	▲ OO%	OOO	▲ OO%
	Labour costs	6.451	Up 16.1%	2.621	▲ 3.4%	•	• • • •	OOO	▲ OO%	OOO	▲ OO%	OOO	▲ OO%
	Total	11.253	▲ 25.5%	9.395	▲ 42.6%	•	• • •	OOO	▲ OO%	OOO	▲ OO%	OOO	▲ OO%
Electrical	Parts costs												
	Labour costs												
	Total												
	Parts costs												
Discrepancy													

Schedule control

- Progress status ◎ Ahead of schedule ○ On schedule ▲ Behind schedule (but can still catch up) X Seriously behind schedule (action required)
- Fabrication process 17: Concept design completed 16: Assembly drawings completed 15: Time-chart completed 14: Parts drawings completed 13: —— 12: —— 11: —— 10: —— 9: —— 8: —— 7: —— 6: —— 5: —— 4: —— 3: —— 2: Production trial completed 1: Production quality checks completed 0: Volume production OK

Name of installation	Category	Person in charge	Progress status	October	November		May	Action status
Press-fitting Machine A	Mechanical Electrical	Kawakami Akusawa	○		⑰		② ① ⓪ ⓪	
Washer B		Yuasa Nishimura	X	⑰	16 15 ⑭		② ① ⓪ ⓪	
⋮	⋮	⋮	⋮	⋮	⋮	⋮	⋮	

Figure 10.14 Cost and Schedule Control

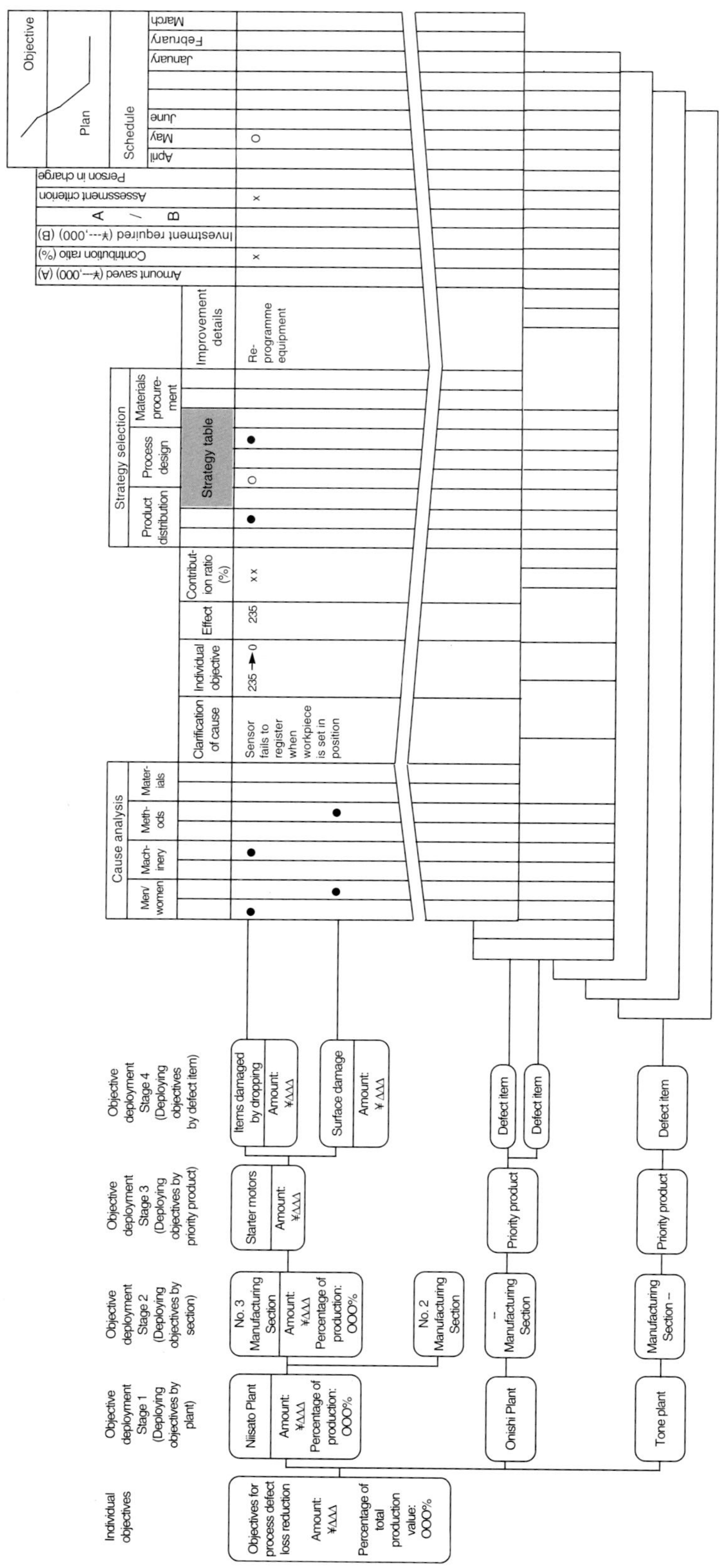

Figure 10.15 Setting and Deploying Objectives for Reducing Process Defect Losses

Setting and Deploying Objectives for Reducing Process Defect Losses

Aiming to improve customer satisfaction by reducing the number of quality defects in our shipped products, we introduced TP deployment into our process-defect loss-reduction activities. We set ourselves the objective of reducing process-defect losses by 70% relative to the figure for fiscal year 1991 (see Figure 10.15). The keynotes of our objective deployment process were as follows:

1. We deployed objectives for each priority product. Focusing on cost reduction and quality improvement, we used the priority products as the main axis of the objective deployment process.
2. After further breaking down the objective by type of defect, we analysed the cause of each defect and selected an appropriate improvement strategy.
3. In controlling the implementation stage, we first identified any discrepancy between the objective and the daily improvement schedule on the one hand, and actual achievement on the other. Then we worked out improvement strategies and machining technology improvements likely to bring success.

The introduction of TP Management allowed us to structure the entire improvement process of analysing the causes of defects, selecting appropriate strategies, identifying discrepancies between objectives and results, reanalysing the causes in order to correct the discrepancies, and finally working out the improvements needed in our machining technology.

TP Management Promotion Infrastructure

Figure 10.16 shows the infrastructure we used for promoting TP Management. Our TP Management system is a broad-ranging system of objective deployment centred on our management objectives, covering everything from development to manufacturing, and extending to our affiliates. We therefore established a TP Management Promotion Council headed by our Managing Director and staffed by directors responsible for Development, Quality, Purchasing, Production Engineering and Manufacturing. This council is in charge of three main subsidiary organisations, one dealing with cost reduction, one with service to society, and the other with promoting TP Management among our affiliates. The council and its sub-organisations are described in turn below.

TP Management Promotion Council

The membership of this council is as described above. Its aims and activities are as follows:

> Exercise management control by applying TP deployment with the aim of achieving certain management objectives.
>
> Discuss and finalise the setting of TP objectives, and consider and approve TP Management promotion plans, both on a financial-year basis.
>
> Analyse discrepancies between TP objectives and performance, and instruct the sub-organisations on how to handle them.

This council constitutes Mitsuba's machinery for decision making regarding our TP Management promotion plans.

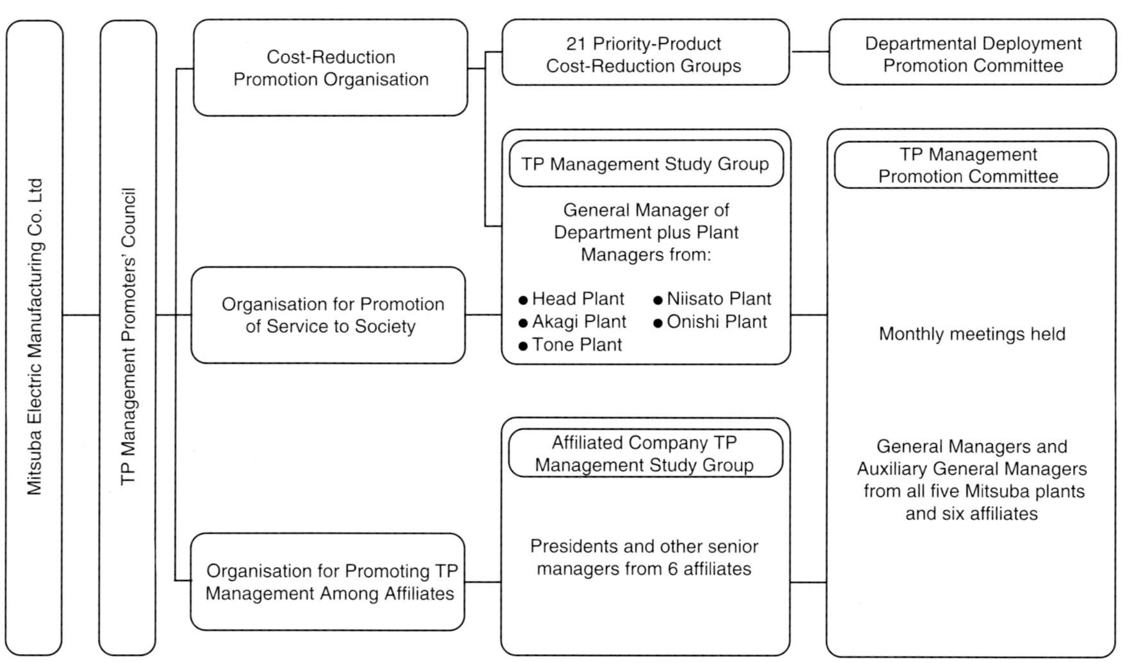

Figure 10.16 TP Management Promotion Infrastructure

Cost-Reduction Promotion Organisation

As mentioned earlier, we divided our cost-reduction objective into two components: materials cost reduction and direct-labour cost reduction. We set up a sub-organisation for each of these components.

1. The sub-organisation responsible for promoting reductions in materials costs has a two-layered structure, one layer consisting of 21 permanent Cost-Reduction Groups (one for each priority product), and the other consisting of a Departmental Deployment Promotion Committee.

   Each priority-product Cost-Reduction Group is made up of six or seven members from Sales, Design, Production Engineering, Purchasing, Quality and Manufacturing. These groups are responsible for drawing up objective deployment charts, selecting proposals for improvement strategies, recording strategies on individual improvement proposal forms, and selecting alternative strategies for handling discrepancies.

   Meanwhile, the Departmental Deployment Promotion Committee is made up of representatives from the relevant functional departments. This committee is responsible for formulating and controlling the execution of departmental cost-reduction plans based on individual improvement proposal forms compiled and assigned to the departments by the priority product Cost-Price Reduction Groups, managing the execution of the strategies involved, and handling discrepancies between objectives and performance.

2. The organisation for promoting reductions in direct labour costs consists of the TP Management Study Group and TP Management Promotion Committee.

   The TP Management Study Group is staffed by all the Plant Managers and the General Manager of the Production Engineering Department. It is responsible for matters such as selecting priority plants, establishing a TP Management system for direct-labour cost reduction, and ensuring that the best management expertise is diffused horizontally among the plants. Meanwhile, the TP Management Promotion Committee is staffed by General Managers and Auxiliary General Managers from each of the five Mitsuba plants and their six main affiliates. It is responsible for assessing each plant's level of success in achieving the objectives, analysing discrepancies, clarifying problems relating to the handling of discrepancies, and proposing and executing solutions.

The TP Management Study Group and the TP Management Promotion Committee are also responsible for promoting Mitsuba's service-to-society objectives, so the organisation for this aspect will not be further described here.

Organisation for Promoting TP Management Among Affiliated Companies

To promote TP Management among our affiliates, we set up an Affiliated Company TP Management Study Group composed of the Presidents and other senior managers from our six main affiliates. This group operates in concert with the aforementioned TP Management Promotion Committee as a progress control body. The Affiliated Company TP Management Study Group is responsible for setting the overall objectives for each affiliate, formulating financial-yearly TP Management promotion plans, and comparing notes on matters such as management systems using TP deployment.

Examples of Activities

This section describes some typical activities undertaken as part of the TP Management programme, focusing chiefly on the objective deployment system for direct-labour cost reduction. Working from the TP Management Deployment System shown in Figure 10.7, we shall now take four examples: "The Mitsuba Rules for Objective Deployment" (from the objective deployment stage), "Competitiveness-Boosting Objectives for Each Plant" (from the strategy selection stage), "The TP Management Network System" (from the execution control stage), and "Priority Control Through Sevenfold Discrepancy Analysis" (covering the stages from objective deployment to performance control).

The Mitsuba Rules for Objective Deployment

Since introducing TP Management, we have drawn up 70 to 80 objective deployment tables each financial year apart from the first. Since we had acquired a good deal of knowledge about objective deployment relating to each deployment system and plant during this process, we systematised it in the form of the "Mitsuba Rules for Objective Deployment" (see Figure 10.17). These rules represent a distillation of our success in setting and deploying clear objectives when compiling the objective deployment table for each priority product, selecting reliable strategies, and achieving credible results. We now use the Mitsuba Rules as guidelines for TP deployment in the workplace.

Similarly, we systematised our expertise concerning methods for deploying objectives in reducing process-defect losses and serving society. In this way, we managed to systematise all our knowhow for every management level, from the boardroom to the front line.

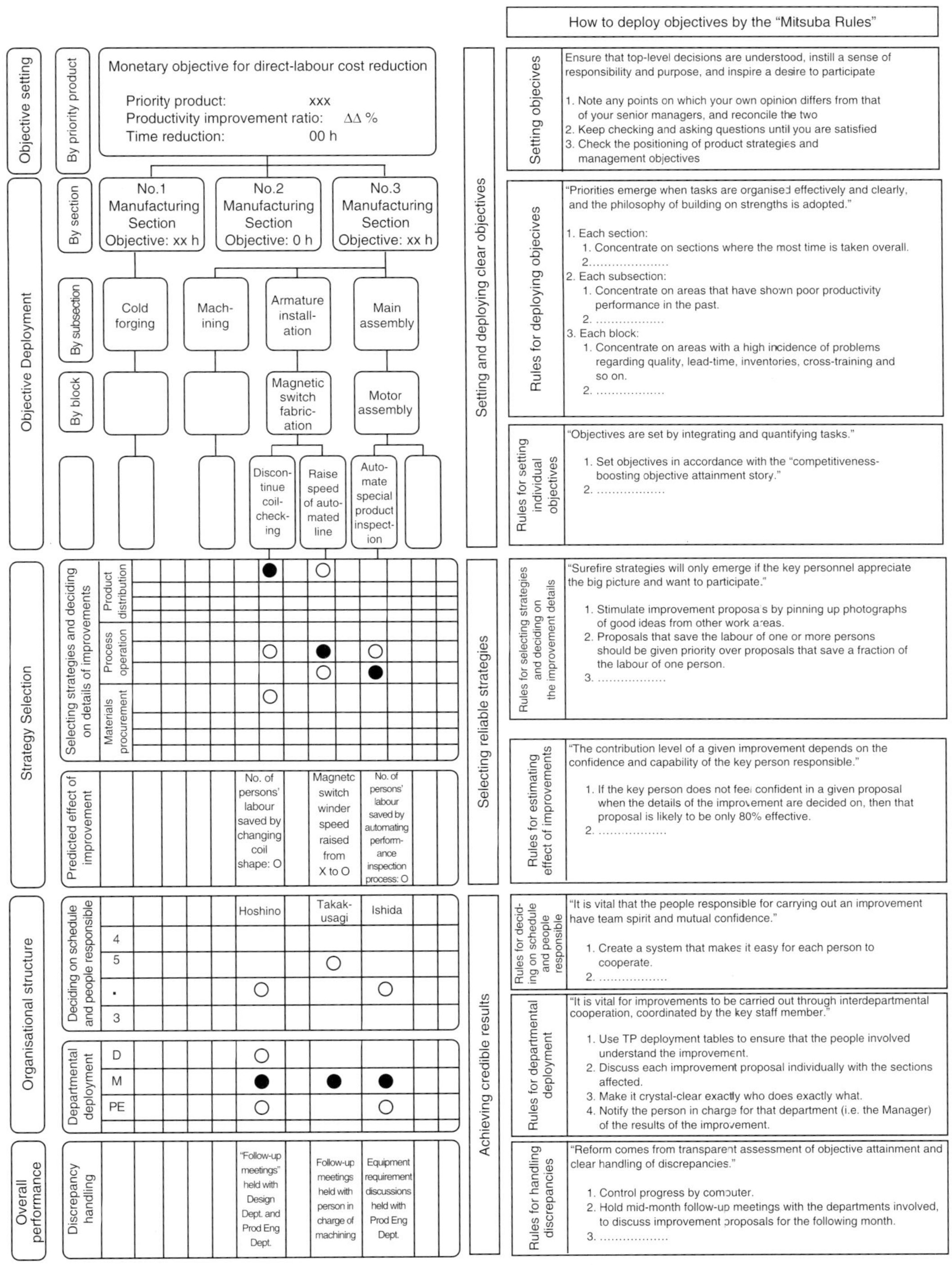

Key: D = Design
M = Manufacturing
PE = Production Engineering

Figure 10.17 Objective Deployment for Direct-Labour Cost Reduction According to "Mitsuba Rules"

Competitiveness-Boosting Objectives for each Plant

For three years after the introduction of TP Management, we kept a close check on our direct-labour cost reduction strategies. From the results, we found that the following trends were taking place at individual plants:

1. Different plants had different priorities in selecting their productivity improvement strategies. For example:

   The Head Plant was concentrating on strategies designed to raise productivity by improving the accuracy of parts processing.

   The Niisato Plant was concentrating on strategies for improving productivity by automating parts processing.

   The Akagi Plant was concentrating on strategies for increasing productivity by reducing the time spent on quality assurance.

   The Onishi Plant was concentrating on strategies for boosting productivity by making manual work more efficient.

   The Tone Plant was concentrating on strategies for raising productivity by bolstering its management systems.

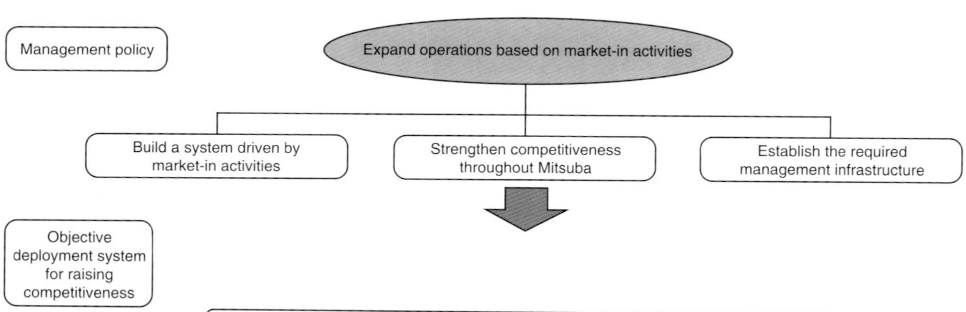

Product mix for each plant	Tasks involved in improving the competitiveness of priority products										
Plant \ Product group	Fuel	Visib-ility	Ventil-ation	Starter	Battery charging	Actuator	Control	Sensor	Relay	Warning sound	Competitiveness improvement objectives
Head Plant	○	○									Improve parts machining technology
Niisato Plant			○	○	○						Improve automation technology
Akagi Plant						○	○				Improve quality assurance technology
Onishi Plant								○	○	○	Improve cost-competitiveness
Tone Plant	○	○	○	○		○					Improve management productivity

Figure 10.18 Competitiveness-boosting Objectives for Each Plant

2. It emerged that these differences in approach were due to the following:

Differences in products and in the tasks involved in improving their competitiveness.

Differences in the volume and diversity of production.

Differences in the way in which Plant Managers prioritised the tasks concerned with raising productivity.

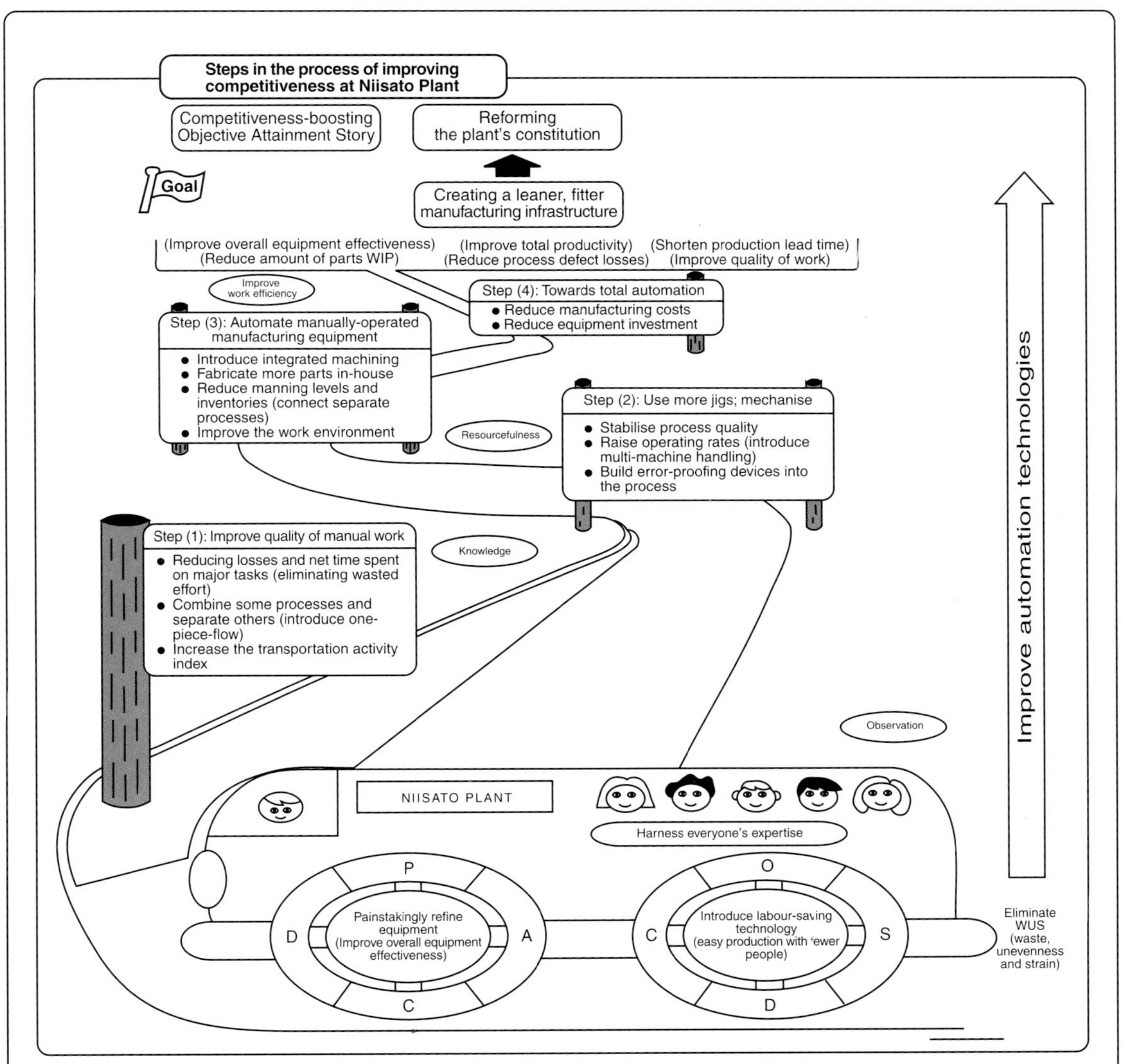

Figure 10.19 Competitiveness-boosting Objective Attainment Story (for Niisato Plant)

By systematising these features of our experience of TP deployment, according to the principle of "building on strengths" advocated in TP Management, we were able to formulate competitiveness-boosting objectives for each plant (see Figure 10.18). We then devised a "competitiveness-boosting objective-attainment story" for each plant, showing which competitiveness-boosting steps were to be given top priority in each case, and how the productivity-boosting activities were to be conducted so as to make the most of each plant's particular strengths (see Figure 10.19).

By linking our TP deployment of direct-labour cost-reduction objectives to our competitiveness-boosting objectives and top-priority competitiveness-boosting steps (see Figure 10.20), we aimed to do the following:

Enable our plants' General Managers to decide on their top-priority competitiveness-boosting steps for each financial year of TP deployment, and issue instructions accordingly.

Allow us to select improvement strategies in line with the top-priority competitiveness-boosting steps.

Ensure that our improvement strategies would enable us to simultaneously achieve our TP objectives and improve our competitiveness.

By managing the relationship between TP deployment and improving the competitiveness of each plant in this way, we achieved the following:

We created a productivity improvement management system that made it possible to raise productivity and improve competitiveness simultaneously.

By setting out the top-priority competitiveness-boosting steps in the form of a "competitiveness-boosting objective-attainment story", we were able to quantify the improvement in competitiveness achieved at each plant.

Most important of all, we were able to achieve universal agreement about our concept of raising productivity, i.e. that the most effective way of raising productivity is to let our General Managers build on their plants' own particular strengths.

This ultimately enabled us to create a "fully human" management system, by which we mean a system that combines the deployment of management objectives with doing whatever is necessary to raise the competitiveness of each product, and that sensibly incorporates the policies and ideas of the plants' General Managers.

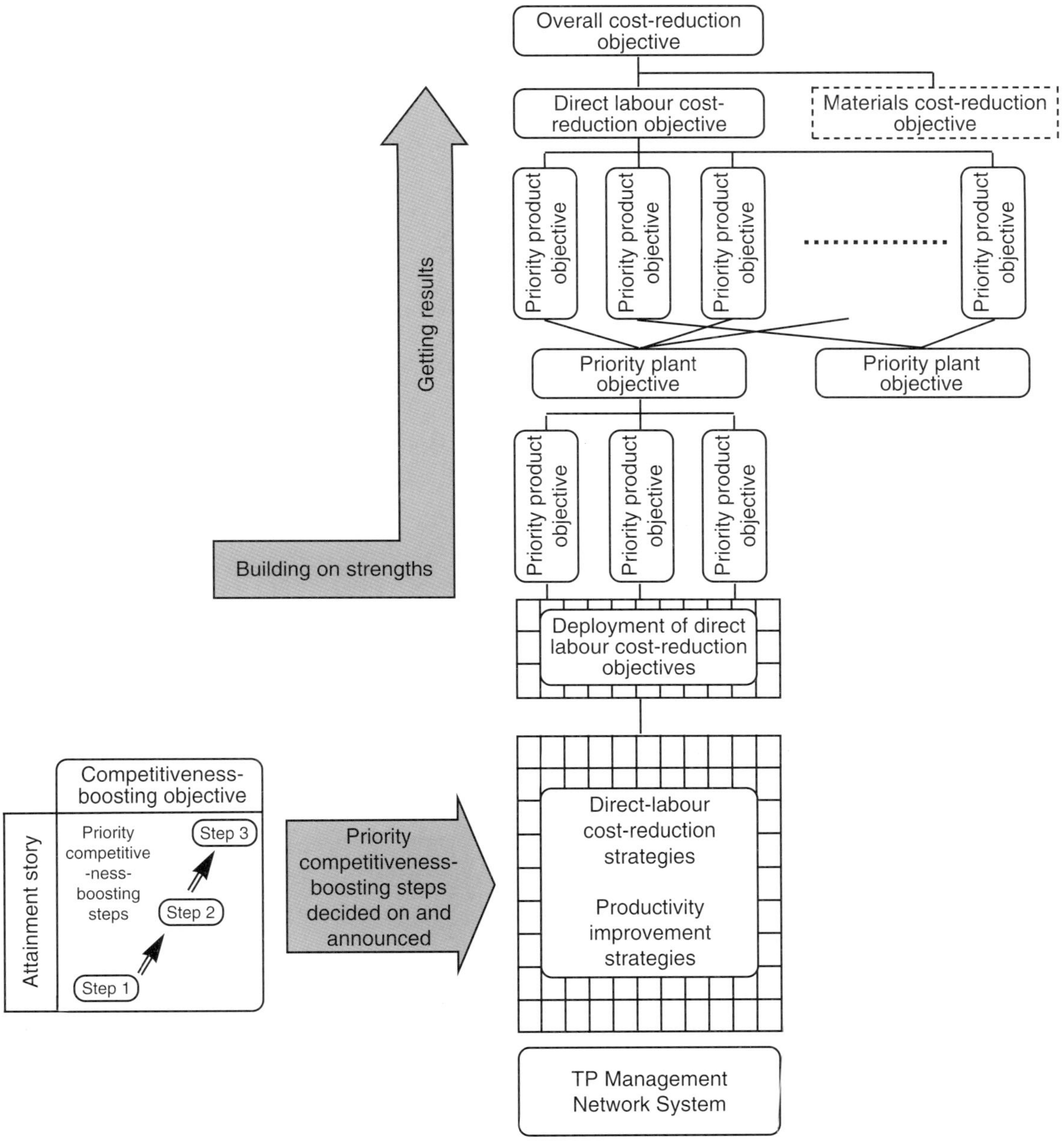

Figure 10.20 How TP Deployment Relates to Our Competitiveness Objectives and Priority Competitiveness-boosting Steps

TP Management Network System

The TP Management Network System, as noted earlier, is the system used to control our direct-labour cost-reduction objectives. Together with the Purchasing Department Improvement Proposal Database (which constitutes our control system for materials cost-reduction objectives), it forms our Performance Control System, which was developed for the following purposes:

1. To support the development of the management objective deployment system.
2. To revamp the decision-making system as a basis for the reform of the corporate constitution.

In other words, these objectives are premised on the inseparability of constitutional reform from information and decision-making. The Performance Control System focuses on the relationship between information and decision-making (see Figure 10.21).

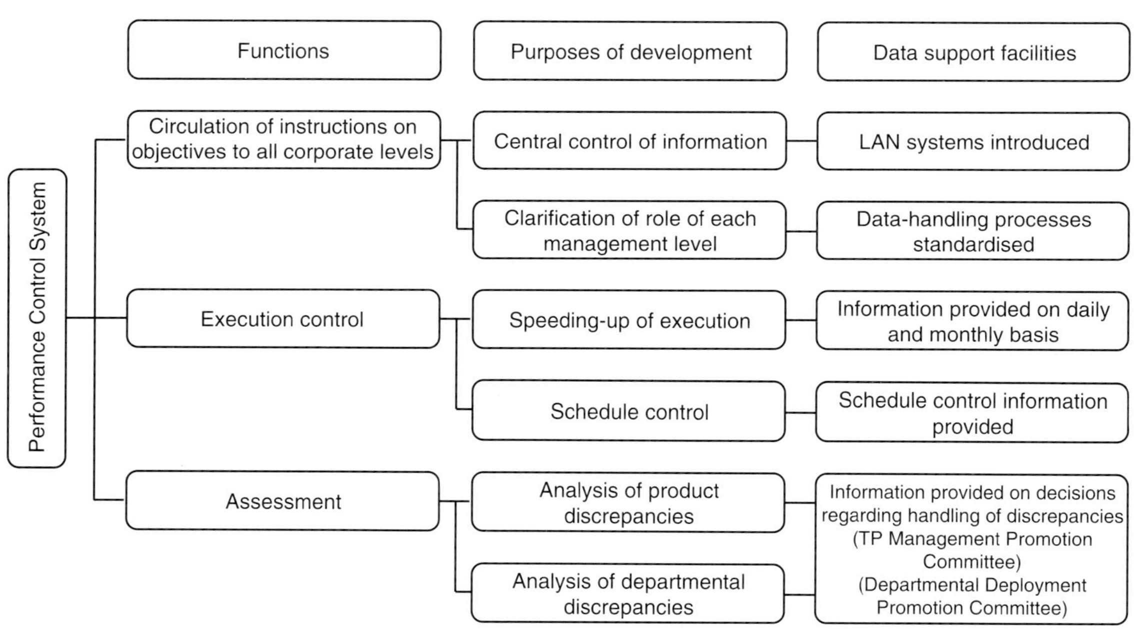

Figure 10.21 The Functions, Aims and Data Support Facilities of Our Performance Control System

The TP Management Network System was formed by linking together five separate LANs (Local Area Networks), one at each of our five plants (see Figure 10.22). The principal basic functions of the TP Management Network System are as follows:

1. Record the objectives for each priority product and each department.
2. Record data on individual improvement proposals.
3. Control the progress of improvement strategies.
4. Identify discrepancies between departmental objectives and results.
5. Identify discrepancies between objectives and results for individual priority products.

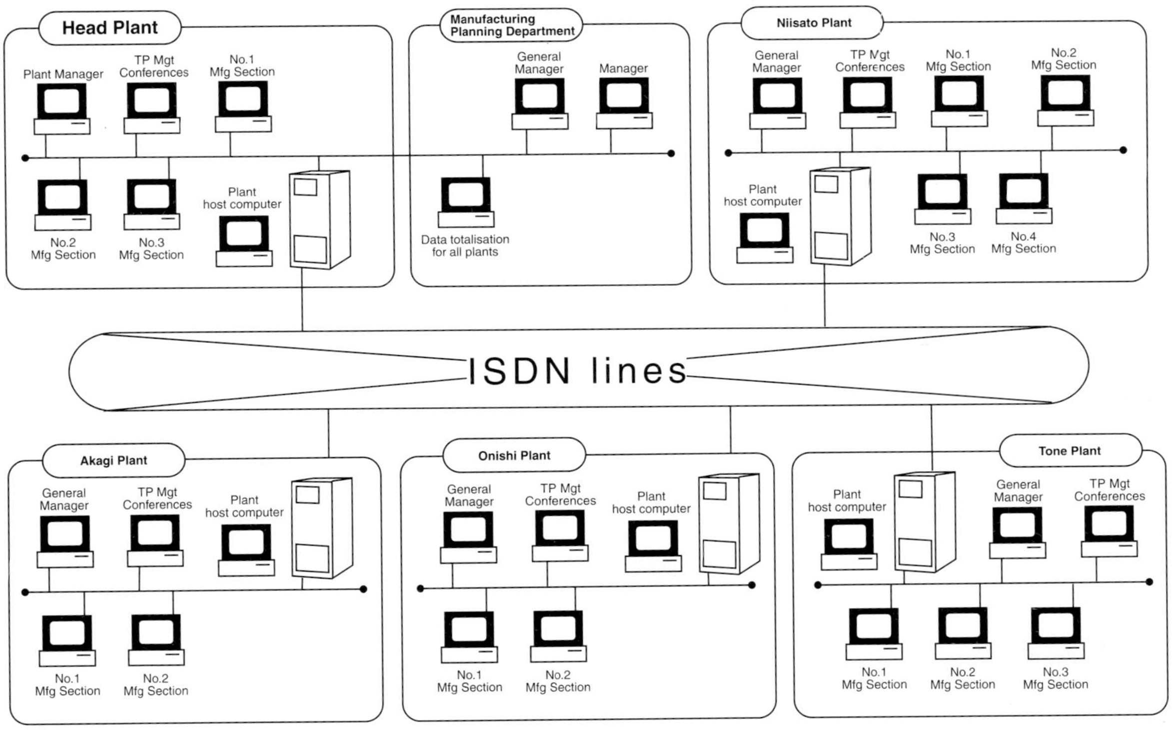

Figure 10.22 Schematic Diagram of TP Management Network System

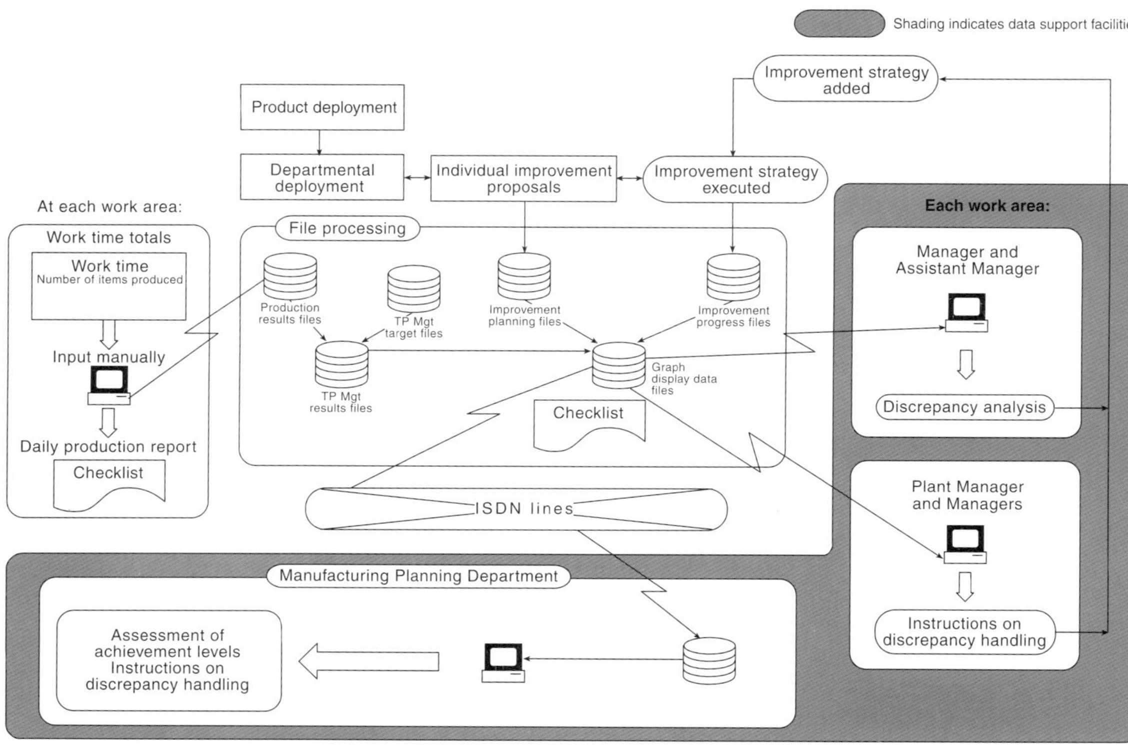

Figure 10.23 TP Deployment and the Flow of Information into the TP Management Network System

Figure 10.23 shows the flow of information that takes place after TP deployment, while Figure 10.24 shows some typical data support graphs. This data support system has enabled Mitsuba to use the TP Management Network System to make decisions about how to handle discrepancies. As shown in the discrepancy-handling decision-making procedure example in Figure 10.25, we have managed to reform our decision-making methods by radically rethinking our approach to data-handling. The procedure is as follows:

1. Monthly progress is monitored using a month-by-month reduction ratio graph.
2. Day-to-day trends are analysed using a day-to-day reduction ratio graph.
3. If a discrepancy is picked up, the schedule control table is used to clarify its origins and formulate instructions on handling it.

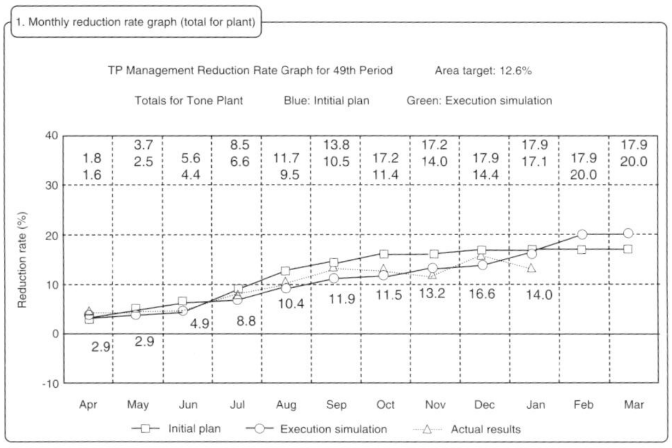

The "reduction rate" is the ratio of the time reduction relative to the standard number of labour hours

Initial plan : target line
Execution simulation : estimated effect of implementing current improvement
Actual result : actual results of improvement

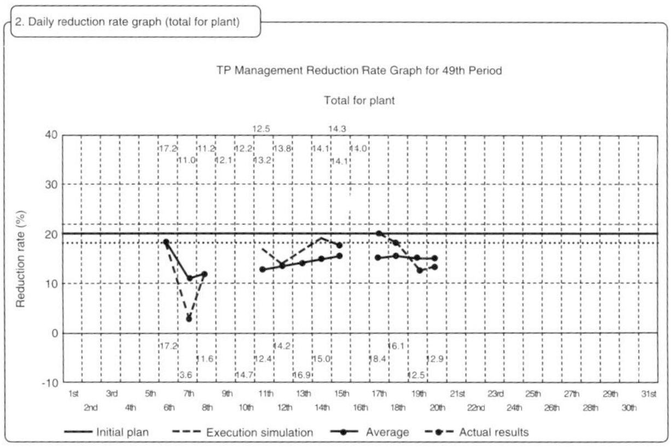

The "daily reduction rate" is the reduction rate per day

Initial plan : monthly target line
Execution simulation : estimated effect of executing current improvement in the current month
Average : Moving average of daily reduction rate
Actual result : actual results for daily reduction rate

3. Schedule Control Table (for each product)

	OO–4C	Initial target for reduction rate	Achievable reduction rate		Shortfall in hours	Initial target for reduction rate	Initial target for reduction in hrs	Achievable reduction rate	Achievable reduction in hrs	Shortfall in hrs
		12..6%	10.8%		-309	14.6%	634	10.5%	454	-179
Model	Improvement items for OO–4C	Time saved	Introduction scheduled for: (month)	Actual introduction	April May	June July	August September	October November	December January	February March
OO –4C	Automate shaft press-fitting process 1. P2–1	414	9	Abandoned						
	Automate shaft steel-ball hole-punching process 2. P2–1	443	9	Abandoned						
	Automate commutator press-fitting process 3. P2–1	885	9	Abandoned						
	Automate steel-ball hole-sealing process 4. P2–1	160	9	Abandoned						
	Condense process layout 5. P2–1	603	9	9			● Introduced on Sept 25			
	Improve length of winder feed chute 6. P2–1	00	6	6		● Introduced on June 7				
	Replace steel-ball hole-punch centre drill more often 7. P2–1	36	6	6		● Introduced on June 7				
	Change material of commutator cutter V-holder 8. P2–1	20	7	11			O - - - - ► ● Completed in July			

A "Schedule Control Table" is a control table showing the details, results and schedules for improvement strategies. It can be used to carry out "shortfall hours simulations" relating to the execution status of the strategies.

Figure 10.24 Typical Data Support Graphs

Data support system	Assessment	Decision

a) Monthly reduction rate graph
(Used to check past improvement speed and monthly progress)

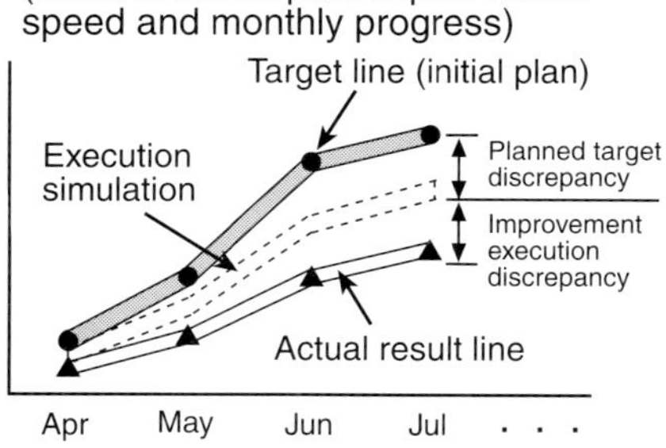

Verdict	Response
(Planned target discrepancy) ● Since the execution simulation line is lower than the target line (initial plan), the improvement strategy itself is inadequate.	● Supplement the improvement strategy. (Issue instructions for handling the discrepancy, referring to the product graph.)
(Improvement execution discrepancy) ● Since the performance line is lower than the execution simulation line, the improvement performance is inadequate.	● Check daily achievement status. (Check improvement progress status, using the daily reduction rate graph.)

b) Daily reduction rate graph
(Used for daily discrepancy handling)

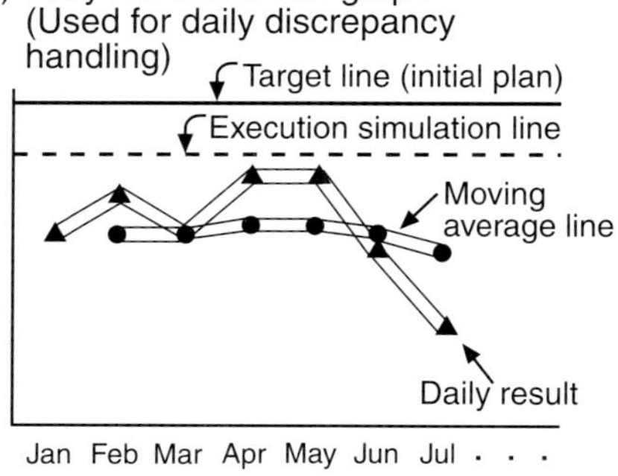

Verdict	Response
(Day-to-day fluctuations) ● Deviation detected (daily result is considerably below moving average).	● Identify causes and effects of deviation (working from product graphs, check with manager responsible.)
(Trend in moving average) ● Monthly target is unlikely to be achieved (trend of moving average is below execution	● Using the schedule control table for the product in question, check what needs to be done to expedite the individual improvement, and issue instructions accordingly.

c) Schedule Control Table (Used for controlling achievement of improvement strategies, and simulating their effect)

Product name	Target: OO hours		Shortfall: ΔΔ hours	
Improvement	Effect (hours)	Target (months)	Execution simulation (months)	Schedule
Improvement A	10	5	5	●
Improvement B	20	4	6	○→○
Improvement C	15	6	Abandoned	○
Improvement D	5	Added	7	○

Verdict	Response
(Improvement progress check) ● Improvement B is behind schedule.	● Confirm the reason for the delay and the measures needed to compensate for it. ● Issue instructions accordingly.
(Discrepancy handling) ● Because Improvement B is behind schedule, a time shortfall of ΔΔ hours has occurred.	● Circulate a proposal for a supplementary strategy to compensate for the shortfall.

Figure 10.25 Example of Procedure for Making Decisions Regarding Discrepancy Handling

Controlling Priorities through Sevenfold Discrepancy Analysis

The primary function of our TP Management Network System is to control the performance of each department and each priority product. To this end, we formulated a performance control table in which the performance of the company as a whole is assessed by means of a sevenfold discrepancy analysis. The direct-labour cost-reduction objective deployment system and the materials cost-reduction objective deployment system are both controlled on a monthly basis, using exactly the same approach and method (see Figure 10.26). This enables us to detect, and issue handling instructions for, discrepancies between objectives and improvement plans, and discrepancies between improvement plans and performance, occurring at all stages of objective deployment, throughout Mitsuba. In concrete terms, the sevenfold discrepancy analysis consists of the following:

> Four kinds of discrepancy can arise in the course of establishing improvement targets and departmental improvement objectives on the basis of improvement strategy selection after completion of the objective deployment process: finalisation discrepancies, discarded-proposal discrepancies, estimate discrepancies and time discrepancies. These four discrepancies are analysed under the heading "departmental deployment discrepancy analysis", which yields information on how to handle discrepancies at the planning stage.
>
> After departmental improvement objectives have been set, three more discrepancies can arise in departmental improvement results and cost-reduction results for each product: marketing-plan discrepancies, progress-control discrepancies and effectiveness discrepancies. These three discrepancies are analysed under the heading of "performance discrepancy analysis", which yields information on how to handle discrepancies at the execution stage.

By managing our priorities through this sevenfold discrepancy analysis, we have succeeded in creating an infrastructure that enables us to attain our objectives for the company as a whole and also helps us make the right decisions to correct faults in our strategies.

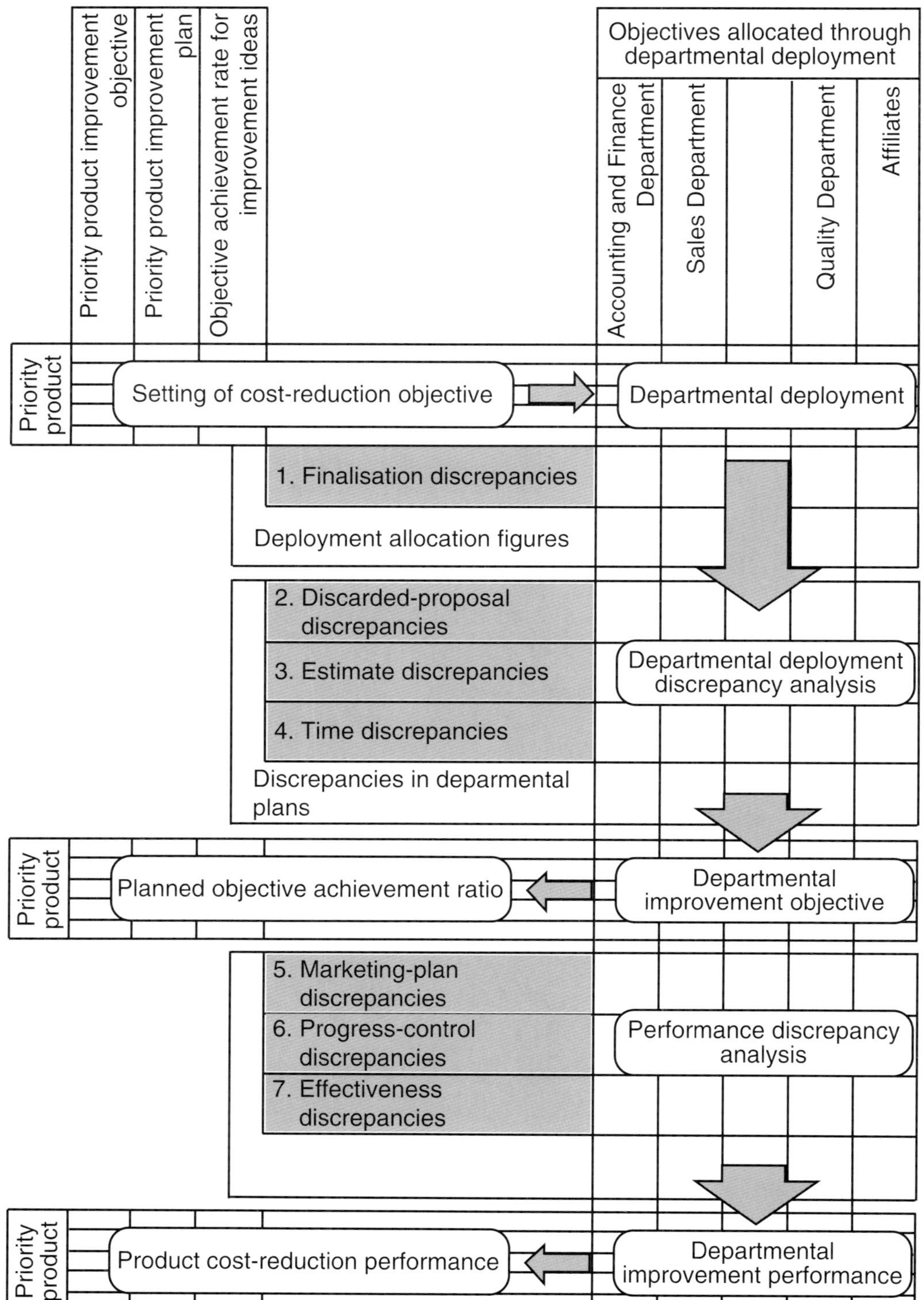

Figure 10.26a Controlling Priorities Through Sevenfold Discrepancy Analysis Covering All TP Management Stages from Objective Deployment to Performance Control

Definitions of discrepancies

Departmental deployment discrepancies	1. Finalisation discrepancy	A discrepancy in the figures for the effect of an improvement, incurred at the stage where the improvement is transposed from the Objective Deployment Table to an individual improvement proposal.
	2. Discarded-proposal discrepancy	A discrepancy in the figures for the effect of an improvement, arising when an individual improvement proposal deployed by a cost-reduction group to the department responsible for effecting the improvement is abandoned after review by the department. (In this case, the Departmental Deployment Promotion Committee holds a "strategy abandonment meeting" to decide and approve the action to be taken.)
	3. Estimate discrepancy	A discrepancy arising when the figures for the effect of an improvement given on an individual improvement proposal form are found to have been wrongly estimated, based on a study carried out by the department in charge of the improvement.
	4. Time discrepancy	A discrepancy in the figures for the effect of an improvement, arising when the improvement schedule on an individual improvement proposal form is changed when the departmental cost-reduction plan is formulated.
Performancet discrepancies	5. Marketing-plan discrepancy	A discrepancy in the figures for the effect of an improvement, arising from the discrepancy between the actual production figures and the standard production figures set on the basis of the sales plan given in the individual improvement proposal form.
	6. Progress-control discrepancy	A discrepancy in the figures for the effect of an improvement, arising from a delay relative to the improvement schedule in a departmental cost-reduction plan.
	7. Effectiveness discrepancy	A discrepancy between the actual figures for the effect of an improvement and the figures based on the departmental cost-reduction plan. Also includes discrepancies caused by abandoning the improvement at this stage.

Figure 10.26b Controlling Priorities Through Sevenfold Discrepancy Analysis Covering All TP Management Stages from Objective Deployment to Performance Control

Results of TP Campaign

As Figure 10.27 shows, measurable results for the two-year period from 1992 to 1993 were high across the board. This was a major factor in our improved business performance. The TP campaign also brought many intangible benefits, summarised as follows:

1. By managing our priorities for the company as a whole, we have succeeded in creating a deployment infrastructure that integrates the three major functions of production, marketing and engineering.

2. Through TP deployment, departmental deployment and other forms of deployment, we have developed an extremely reliable system for communicating our objectives to our entire workforce.
3. Departmental deployment has improved our organisational strength, helping us to view strategies from the overall standpoint and select ones that are certain to work.
4. Our improvement simulations have improved our ability to plan how to achieve our objectives.
5. Performance discrepancy analysis has made us better at handling discrepancies.
6. We have been able to improve information technology throughout Mitsuba.

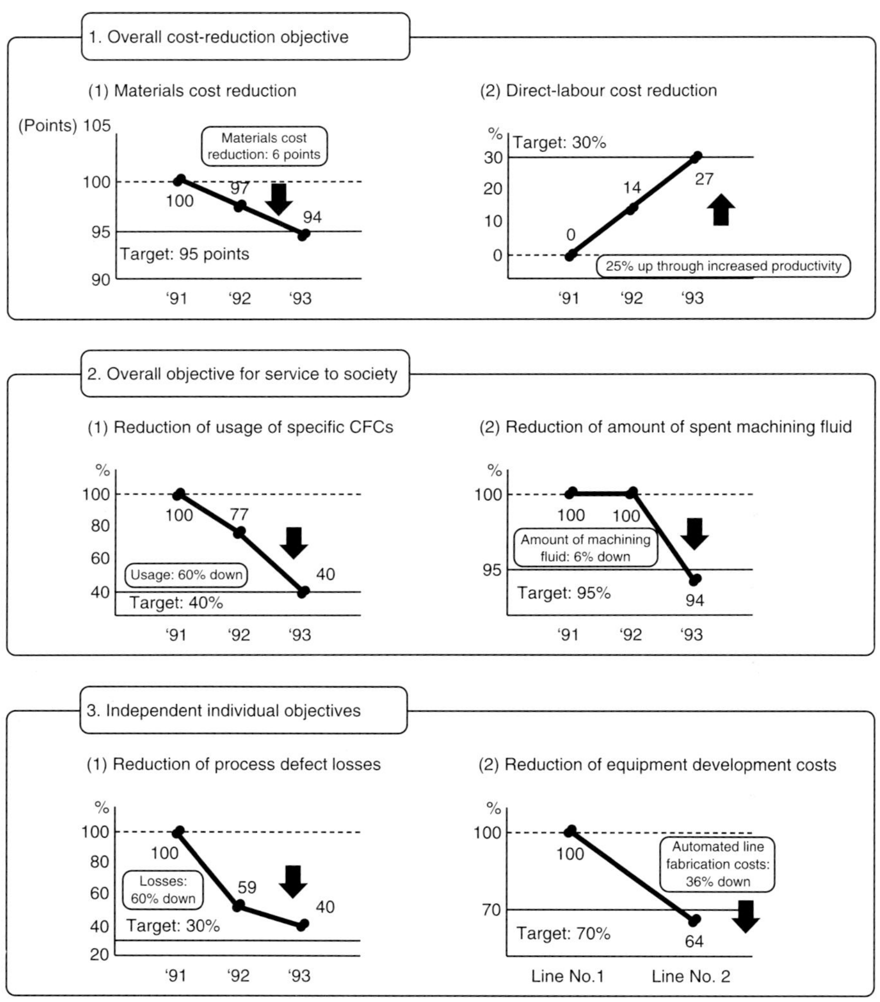

Figure 10.27 Results of the TP Promotion Plan

We have also managed to realise the visions of Mitsuba's TP Management Philosophy: namely, we have arrived at a situation in which all employees participate in management, and we have reformed our corporate structure to increase our ability to co-operate internally and get things done. A further significant benefit is that, by clarifying our management objectives, we have enabled our company to see exactly what needs to be done in order to achieve those objectives in terms of improving data-processing and other technologies, enhancing our management capabilities, and so on.

The Way Ahead

As a manufacturer of electrical parts for automobiles, we normally set our sales targets four years ahead. Our project for the future is to construct a medium-to-long-term objective deployment system that targets this point in time (see Figure 10.28). Here is an outline of the tasks this involves, in the form of an evolutionary sequence in line with our management policy:

1. Set operational strategies and marketing objectives, and create a medium-to-long-term objective deployment system, with the aim of expanding our operations based on market-in activities.
2. Use this system to deploy objectives based on the goals of "strengthening competitiveness throughout Mitsuba" and "building a system driven by market-in activities". By employing a product-by-product strategic marketing mix, set objectives for each product for each financial year.
3. Using the financial-yearly objective deployment system as a framework for the annual objectives for each product, deploy objectives, select strategies and control their execution in accordance with the product-by-product marketing mix. In Mitsuba's case, this means constructing a system for deploying our management objectives within the framework of the financial-yearly objective deployment system, and also setting up an infrastructure for the associated control activities.
4. The main task to be carried out within the financial-yearly objective deployment system is thus to establish effective deployment systems for an even wider range of management objectives, underpinning this by enhancing the data support system for decision-making and taking the process of constitutional reform even further.
5. We are aware that the success of all our efforts stands or falls by our ability to secure the active agreement and participation of our entire workforce: this is our most fundamental task.

In conclusion, we believe that the way ahead lies in taking TP Management right to the heart of our management strategy.

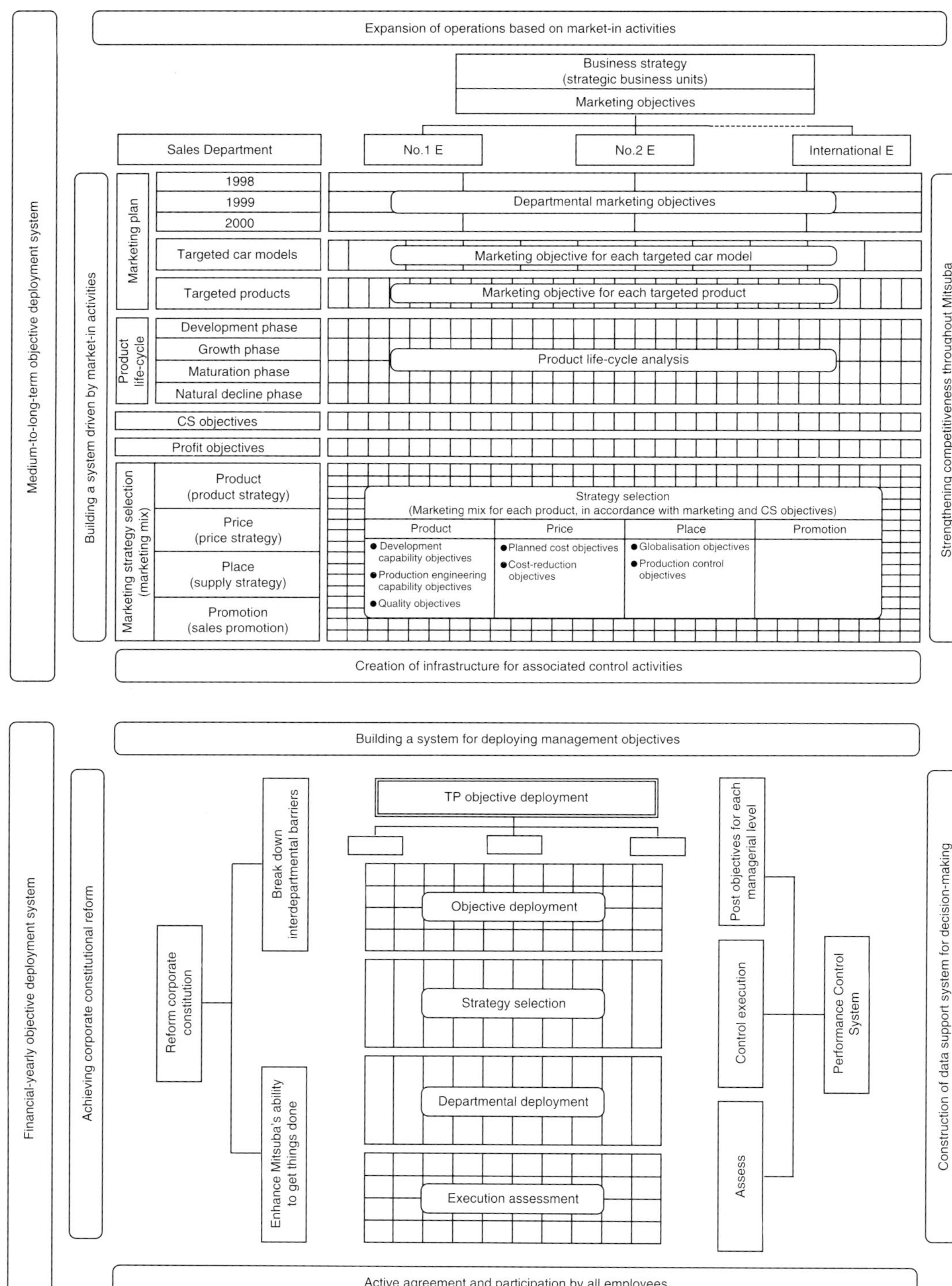

Figure 10.28 Construction of Medium-to-Long-Term Objective Deployment System

Appendix
The TP Prize

The TP Prize is awarded to companies and plants that have achieved outstanding results through superior management practices focused on improving overall productivity. The JMA first advocated TP Management in 1982 with the aim of highlighting the question as to how best to reform and improve industrial productivity. It established the TP Prize scheme in 1985, and has been energetically disseminating TP Management ever since.

To win a prize, a company or plant must adopt a strategic approach to setting its total productivity improvement objectives and selecting and implementing its priority strategies, and it must have achieved excellent results through scientifically operating and implementing its entire TP system. A further aim of establishing the TP Prize was to encourage and stimulate the widespread adoption of TP Management by industry

Since the second oil crisis, industry has concentrated on reducing its consumption of energy and other resources by developing innovative manufacturing technologies and automated systems. Companies have achieved excellent results through reducing costs by making individual improvements, mainly through quality circles and other small-group activities. However, although the introduction of equipment-focused reforms such as flexible manufacturing systems and computer-integrated manufacturing together with production control technology improvements such as JIT (just-in-time) has enabled manufacturers to cope with the increasing fragmentation and individualisation of market requirements, these initiatives have often been obstructed by the barriers that exist within conventional vertically-divided organisations.

In the 1980s, corporate operating structures themselves underwent a major transformation. What was required was a total productivity way of thinking that could dissolve interdepartmental and inter-organisational barriers. The changes that have taken place in total productivity activities as a result of introducing and disseminating TP Management throughout industry are exactly those reforms that manufacturing industry needed.

Up until the 1990s, companies introducing TP Management systematically deployed their overall objectives and accurately monitored their existing situations. As a result of this process, employees developed confidence in the activities they were required to undertake. The TP Management practiced during this period was a kind of total productivity revolution that changed entire workforces into groups of people with a sense of purpose and responsibility. It was an approach to total productivity improvement that was both exhaustive in its detail and highly transparent.

By 1993, more and more companies had developed TP programmes that enable them to respond swiftly and accurately to changes in the business environment and control their manufacturing operations comprehensively and flexibly. They had also established robust production systems that remain unperturbed by environmental changes, and were continuing to evolve their activities with an eye to the future. In other words, the approach to total productivity improvement had become more flexible and innovative.

The following pages list the TP Prizewinners from 1985 to 1995. We have given the title of each company's application to indicate the variety of TP application and the development of TP over these eleven years.

Inaugural Prize (1985)

Toshiba Corporation (Mie Plant) – "A Minimum-Stock Production System Able to Respond Rapidly to Change."

NEC Corporation (Shizuoka Plant) – "A Manufacturing Setup Able to Cope Effectively with Products in Six Different Fields through Top-Down Direction and Management by Objectives."

Canon, Inc. (Fukushima Plant) – "Utilising the Full Capabilities of Every Individual from Top Managers to Front-Line Workers."

Second Prize (1986)

Toyota Auto Body Co., Ltd (Production Division) – "Building in Flexibility and Close Attention to the Basics."

Matsushita Electric Industrial Co., Ltd (Washing-Machine Division) – "A Management and Implementation System Designed to Ensure Unerring Achievement of Objectives."

Hitachi, Ltd (Tokai Plant) – "Source Design and Routine Practical Action for Achieving High Productivity."

Third Prize (1987)

Mitsubishi Electric Corporation (Inazawa Plant) – "Customer-Focused Action Extending from Development through to Installation and Maintenance."

Nippon Sheet Glass Co., Ltd (Production Division) – "Companywide Evolution of Productivity Reform Activities in Pursuit of the Desired Scenario."

Fourth Prize (1988)

Lion Corporation (Manufacturing Division) – "Achieving World-Class Levels in Priority Areas and Disseminating Results Laterally through Focused Application of Technical Resources."

Nissan Motor Co., Ltd (Oppama Plant) – "Unified Deployment of Cost and Delivery Centered on Quality, together with QR Management."

Nissan Motor Co., Ltd (Zama Plant) – "Improving Managerial Capabilities of Line and Staff and Raising Productivity by means of 'Household Accounts'."

Hitachi, Ltd (Mito Plant) – "Answering Customers' Needs and Reforming the Factory by Enlarging the Menu of Standards and Promoting High Quality, Low Cost and Speedy Delivery."

Hitachi, Ltd (Kanagawa Plant) – "Integrating Technology and Management to Achieve Ultra-High Performance of Large Computers."

Fifth Prize (1989)

NEC Corporation (Ōtsuki Plant) – "Reforming Q, C and D by Boosting People's Vitality and Applying Knowledge Systems to All Areas."

Canon, Inc. (Chemical Products Plant) – "Establishing an Objective Deployment and Strategy Selection System that Utilises Every Opportunity for Profit Creation"

Hitachi Metals, Ltd (Kuwana Plant) – "Extending Our TP Pilot Plan for Process Integration from Our Sub-Plant to Our Main Plant."

Sixth Prize (1990)

NEC Corporation (Toyama Plant) – "Companywide Deployment of Accurate, Speedy TP Daily Management through Construction of Detailed Decision-Making Support System."

Sanden Corporation (Yattajima Plant) – "TP Management for Increased Product Competitiveness and Lower Prices in the Adverse Environment of a Strong Yen."

Seventh Prize (1991)

TDK Corporation (Mikumagawa Plant) – "Increasing Total Productivity and Reducing Costs through an Ideal Management by Objectives System."

Nissan Shatai Co., Ltd (Shōnan Plant) – "Detailed TP Deployment of Multiple Objectives (Customer Satisfaction, Production-Line Reform, and Labour Reduction)."

Toshiba Corporation (Ōme Works) – "Slashing Development, Production and Marketing Lead Times through CIM-Based TP Management."

Sekisui Chemical Co., Ltd (Kansai Heim Plant) – "Setting up a TP Management System in a Short Space of Time, Allowing Stocks to be Halved and New-Product Startup to be Accomplished Rapidly without Sacrificing Quality, while Doubling Scheduled Production Capacity."

Higashi Nihon Sekisui Co., Ltd – "Creating a Flow-Type Factory by Means of a Mixed-Model Manufacturing System."

Eighth Prize (1992)

Hitachi, Ltd (Data Storage and Retrieval Systems Division) – "An Integrated Stratification, Development and Lead-Time Management System for Developing World-Beating Technologies and Products."

Kaneka Corporation (Kashima Plant) – "Totally-Participative TP Management Integrating Technical and Managerial Capabilities Required for Achieving Objectives."

Hitachi Cable, Ltd (Hidaka Plant) – "Creating an Excellent Factory through TP Deployment with Customer Satisfaction and Employee Satisfaction as Overall Objectives."

Yamagata Casio Co., Ltd – "TP Management for Successful Corporate Reform through Integration of Managerial and Technical Capabilities."

Ninth Prize (1993)

Nissan Shatai Co., Ltd (Kyoto Plant) – "Creating a Cheerful, Healthy and Vigorous Factory."

Snow Brand Milk Products Co., Ltd (Atsugi Plant) – "Creating a Highly Flexible Production System and an Excellent Working Environment"

Nissan Diesel Motor Co., Ltd (Ageo Plant) – "Back-to-Basics TP Management Combining Higher Customer Satisfaction with an Improved Factory Constitution."

Tenth Prize (1994)

Mitsuba Electric Mfg Co., Ltd – "Using TP Management to Raise Total Productivity."

Kirin Brewery Co., Ltd (Yokohama Brewery) – "Deploying TP Management to Create a Multifunctional Brewery for the 21st Century."

Kansai Sekisui Kyōeikai – "Employing TP Management to Raise the Level of Management and Build an Integrated System of Co-operation with 20 Suppliers."

Tōa (Nitta Plant) – "Using TP Management to Achieve Integrated Manufacturing for Processes and Site."

NEC Corporation (Fukushima Plant) – "Absorbing Large Production Fluctuations by Dismantling Barriers between Direct and Indirect Departments."

Winner of Special Prize for TP Management Promotion Inaugural Prize (1994)

Nissan Shatai Co., Ltd (Shōnan Plant)

Eleventh Prize (1995)

Sumitomo Wiring Systems, Ltd – "Across-the-Board Reform of Business Results through Linking 8 Company Operating Sites and 10 Suppliers (a total of 30 plants) by a Single System Giving Comprehensive Coverage and Originality."

Ricoh Co., Ltd (Imaging System Business Group) – "Complete Reconstruction of the Operating Structure, Based on the Concept of Supplying the Market with Attractive, Highly Satisfactory, Optimally Timed Products"

TDK Corporation (Shizuoka Plant) – "Reform Based on a Comprehensive Overview of the Desired Scenario, by Means of an Objective Deployment System Centred on a System for Managing Ideal Objectives."

Samsung Electro-Mechanics Co., Ltd – "Establishing and Integrating the Threefold Objective of Boosting Production Capacity to Satisfy Customers, Creating an Information Infrastructure, and Achieving Employee Satisfaction."

Special Prize for TP Management Promotion

Hitachi Cable, Ltd, Hidaka Plant (1992 TP Prizewinner)

The Development of TP

The table overleaf outlines the development of TP during the period 1982 to 1994 and shows graphically how major groups have introduced TP practices into their plants over this period.

In Europe, the first TP seminars were held by Mr Nakamura and Productivity Europe in 1993, with presentations in the UK, Paris and Frankfurt. A number of companies are now implementing pilot projects in the UK, and the first US pilot project was launched in August 1995.

OVERVIEW OF THE SPREAD OF TP MANAGEMENT (MAJOR COMPANIES AND MAIN EVENTS ONLY)

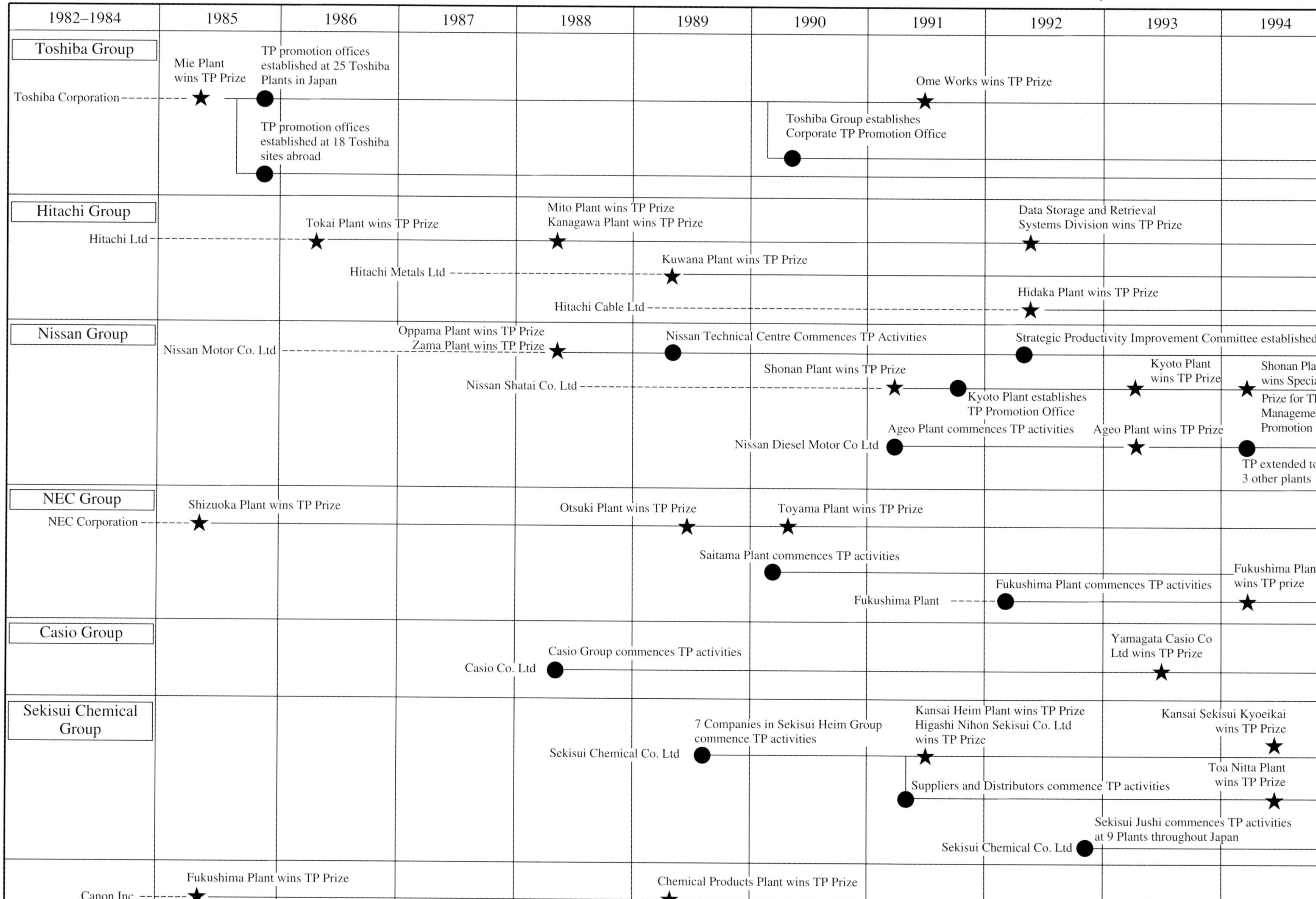

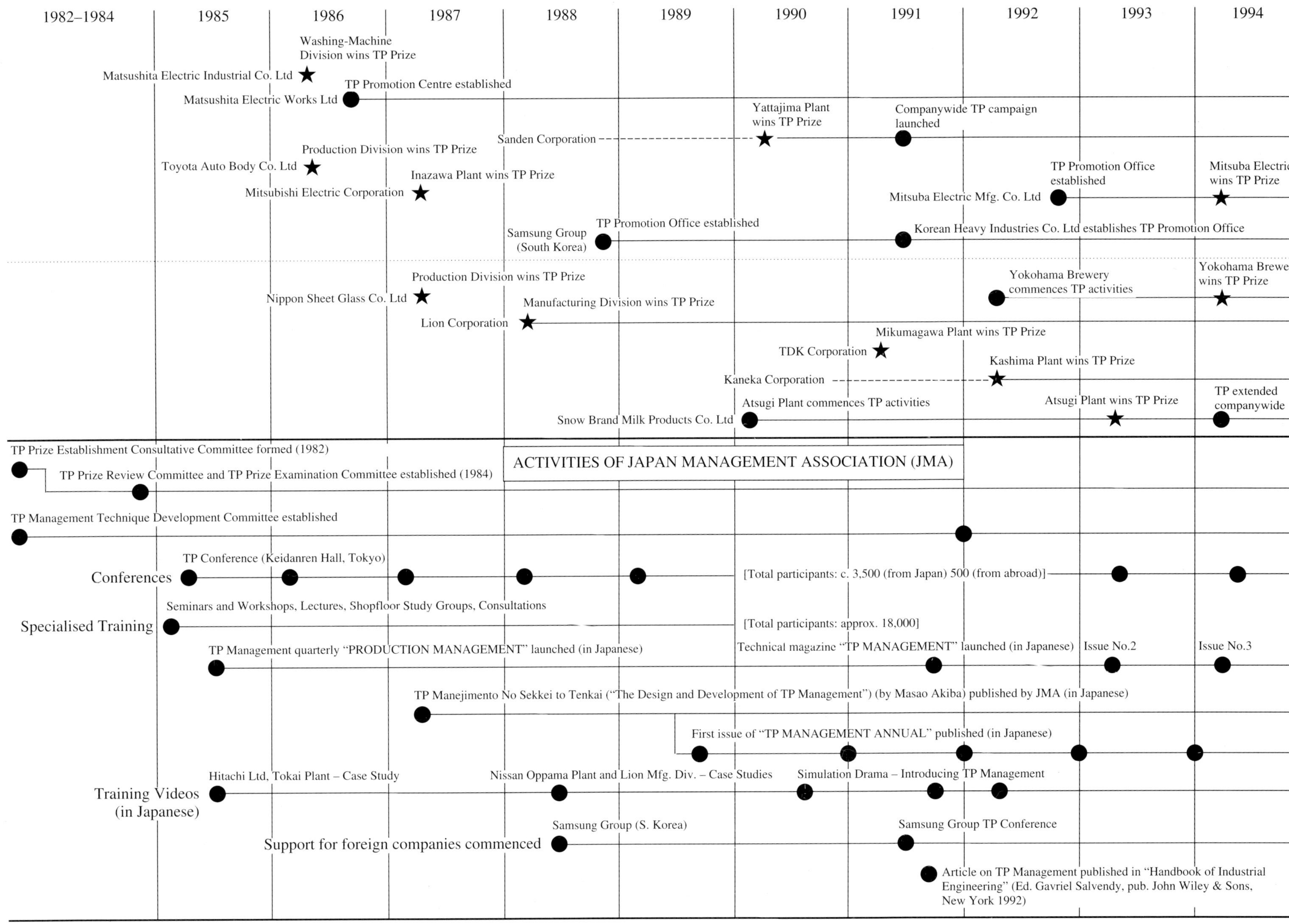
1982–1984
1985
1986
1987
1988
1989
1990
1991
1992
1993
1994
Washing-Machine Division wins TP Prize
Matsushita Electric Industrial Co. Ltd
TP Promotion Centre established
Matsushita Electric Works Ltd
Yattajima Plant wins TP Prize
Companywide TP campaign launched
Sanden Corporation
Production Division wins TP Prize
Toyota Auto Body Co. Ltd
Inazawa Plant wins TP Prize
Mitsubishi Electric Corporation
TP Promotion Office established
Mitsuba Electric wins TP Prize
Mitsuba Electric Mfg. Co. Ltd
TP Promotion Office established
Samsung Group (South Korea)
Korean Heavy Industries Co. Ltd establishes TP Promotion Office
Production Division wins TP Prize
Nippon Sheet Glass Co. Ltd
Manufacturing Division wins TP Prize
Lion Corporation
Yokohama Brewery commences TP activities
Yokohama Brewery wins TP Prize
Mikumagawa Plant wins TP Prize
TDK Corporation
Kashima Plant wins TP Prize
Kaneka Corporation
Atsugi Plant commences TP activities
Atsugi Plant wins TP Prize
TP extended companywide
Snow Brand Milk Products Co. Ltd
ACTIVITIES OF JAPAN MANAGEMENT ASSOCIATION (JMA)
TP Prize Establishment Consultative Committee formed (1982)
TP Prize Review Committee and TP Prize Examination Committee established (1984)
TP Management Technique Development Committee established
Conferences
TP Conference (Keidanren Hall, Tokyo)
[Total participants: c. 3,500 (from Japan) 500 (from abroad)]
Specialised Training
Seminars and Workshops, Lectures, Shopfloor Study Groups, Consultations
[Total participants: approx. 18,000]
TP Management quarterly "PRODUCTION MANAGEMENT" launched (in Japanese)
Technical magazine "TP MANAGEMENT" launched (in Japanese)
Issue No.2
Issue No.3
TP Manejimento No Sekkei to Tenkai ("The Design and Development of TP Management") (by Masao Akiba) published by JMA (in Japanese)
First issue of "TP MANAGEMENT ANNUAL" published (in Japanese)
Training Videos (in Japanese)
Hitachi Ltd, Tokai Plant – Case Study
Nissan Oppama Plant and Lion Mfg. Div. – Case Studies
Simulation Drama – Introducing TP Management
Support for foreign companies commenced
Samsung Group (S. Korea)
Samsung Group TP Conference
Article on TP Management published in "Handbook of Industrial Engineering" (Ed. Gavriel Salvendy, pub. John Wiley & Sons, New York 1992)